God's
Best
Secrets

Books by Andrew Murray
Abide in Christ
God's Best Secrets

God's Best Secrets

An Inspirational Daily Devotional

Andrew Murray

Newly Revised and Indexed for Today's Readers

kregel
CLASSICS

Grand Rapids, MI 49501

God's Best Secrets by Andrew Murray. Newly revised and indexed for today's readers.

Copyright © 1993 by Kregel Publications.

Published in 1993 by Kregel Classics, an imprint of Kregel Publications, P.O. Box 2607, Grand Rapids, MI 49501. Kregel Classics provides trusted, time-proven publications for Christian life and ministry. Your comments and suggestions are valued.

Cover Photograph: POSITIVE IMAGES,
                  Patricia Sgrignoli
Cover and Book Design: Alan G. Hartman
Editorial Review: Helen Bell

Library of Congress Cataloging-in-Publication Data
Murray, Andrew, 1828-1917.
    God's best secrets: an inspirational daily devotional /
Andrew Murray.
        p.   cm.
    Originally published: Los Angeles: Biola book, 1923.
    Includes Indexes
    1. Devotional calendars. I. Title.
BV4811.M82   1994   242'.2—dc20   93-39325
                                          CIP

ISBN 0-8254-3277-4 (paperback)

        2 3 4 5 Printing / Year 97

Contents

Publisher's Foreword

In evangelical circles today there is a reawakening to the work of the Holy Spirit which in past times has been downplayed, fearing either a vague, undefined mysticism or a wild, unharnassed emotionalism. Believers are also awakening to the realization that we have substituted disciplined times of Bible study and prayer (complete with our lists and our schedules) for the inner spirit's cry of "Abba, Father." We have forgotten to take delight in God Himself and to enjoy (in a humble, worshiping sense) our Heavenly Father's delight in us.

God's Best Secrets by Andrew Murray once again brings a new generation to its knees in adoration, praise, and pure enjoyment of our Heavenly Father, the Lord Jesus, and the Holy Spirit who indwells the believer and provides the strength and power for worship. Born in South Africa in 1828 and educated in Scotland, Murray returned to South Africa to minister in revival meetings, social and educational mission work, and devotional writing. He introduced the Keswick Movement to South Africa and from 1889 until his death in 1917 was considered the father of South African Keswick.

The Keswick Movement originated in the English Lake District and grew out of the Moody-Sankey revival of 1875. The movement emphasized prayer (especially invoking the Holy Spirit to indwell believers individually and corporately), reverent Bible study, missionary work, practical holiness, and the unity of believers. With its followers generally coming from the Reformed tradition, the movement stressed victorious living through total surrender to the Holy Spirit as the counterbalance to the sinful human nature (in contrast to the Wesleyan-Arminian emphasis on eradicationism).

The influence of the Keswick Movement is clearly seen in *God's Best Secrets*. Murray writes that a vast difference exists between the outpouring of the Holy Spirit at Pentecost and the work of the Reformation in regard to the doctrine of faith. "Most Christians strive, by holding fast their faith in justification, to stir and strengthen themselves for a life of gratitude and obedience. But they fail sadly because they do not know, do not in full faith yield themselves to Christ, to maintain His life in them. They have learned from Abraham the first lesson, to believe in God who justifies the ungodly. But they have not gone on to the second great lesson, to believe in God who quickeneth the dead and daily renews that life through Christ who lives in them and in whose life alone there is strength and fullness of blessing" (p. 122).

"There is so little insight into the deep truth that the world and the flesh that loves the world is enmity against God. Hence it comes that many Christians seek and pray for years for conformity to the image of Jesus and yet fail so entirely. They do not know, they do not seek with the whole heart to know, what it is to die to self and the world" (p. 191).

Murray also emphasizes the role of prayer as the means by which blessing is received, but with a corresponding emphasis upon holiness and sanctification that is missing in much of the contemporary practice of faith and prayer.

> Why then does the blessing so often tarry? In creating man with a free will and making him a partner in the rule of the earth, God limited Himself. He made Himself dependent on what man would do. Man by his prayer would hold the measure of what God could do in blessing (p. 71). If you only want the Spirit to help you to be a little better and to pray a little more, you will not get very far. But when you once understand that He has the name of Holy Spirit in order definitely to impart God's holiness and will sanctify you wholly, then you will begin to realize that the Holy Spirit dwells in your heart.
>
> And what will be the result? You will feel that He must have you wholly. He must rule and control the whole day. My whole life and conversation must be in the Spirit. My prayer, my faith, my fellowship with the Father, and all my work in God's service must be completely under His sway. As the Spirit of holiness, He is the Spirit of my sanctification (p. 310).

Murray's tone is always kind, helpful, and devotional in the best sense of the word—*God's Best Secrets* is an encouragement to exercise devotion in the Christian life, not merely fill a few moments with warm thoughts. Although he recommends a half an hour a day in the morning to enjoy the presence of the Heavenly Father through His Son, Jesus Christ, and in the power of the Holy Spirit, Murray encourages the reader to begin with ten minutes a day or possibly fifteen. He gives suggestions for one's prayers and then teaches the reader to listen for the voice of the Heavenly Father through his Word. He challenges the reader not only to guard one's little seed of faith but to plant it! The power of heaven is at the believer's disposal. The grace and power of God is waiting for one's bidding.

This new edition by Kregel Publications preserves the beauty and depth of Murray's original writing while at the same time updating archaic words and phrases. In those cases where a concluding prayer was lacking, material from that day's devotional has been incorporated into the prayer.

As Murray teaches us to pray to the Father for a lost world and to love one another as the Father loves us, he also reminds us "of the sin of restraining prayer, of the sloth and unbelief and selfishness that is the cause of it" (p. 51). For a new generation of readers faced with a technologically-based, violent, and confused world, Kregel Publications is pleased to offer a new edition of Andrew Murray's classic, *God's Best Secrets*—a timeless call to the Source of all power, blessing, and meaning in life.

HELEN BELL, KREGEL PUBLICATIONS

8

Introduction

The more I think of and pray about the state of religion in this country and all over the world, the deeper my conviction becomes that the low state of the spiritual life of Christians is due to the fact that they do not realize that the aim and object of conversion is to bring the soul, even here on earth, *to a daily fellowship with the Father in heaven.* When once this truth has been accepted, the believer will perceive how indispensable it is to the spiritual life of a Christian to take time each day with God's Word and, in prayer, to wait upon God for His presence and His love to be revealed.

But how can Christians be taught this lesson and live in obedience to it? The first thing is that they must be convinced of the great need of daily fellowship with God. They must be brought under the impression that it is not enough at conversion to accept forgiveness of sins or even to surrender themselves to God. That is only a beginning. The young believer must understand that he has no power of his own to maintain his spiritual life. No, he needs each day to receive new grace from heaven through communion with the Lord Jesus. This cannot be obtained by a hasty prayer or a superficial reading of a few verses from God's Word. He must take time quietly and deliberately to come into God's presence, to feel his weakness and his need, to wait upon God through His Holy Spirit, and to renew the heavenly light and life in his heart. Then he may rightly expect to be kept by the power of Christ throughout the day and all its temptations.

It has been my aim in writing this book to help Christians to see the absolute necessity of communion with the Lord Jesus. Without this the joy and power of God's Holy Spirit in daily life cannot be experienced. Many of God's children long for a better life but do not realize the need of giving God time day by day in their inner chamber for His Spirit to renew and sanctify their lives.

Meditate on this thought: *The feeble state of my spiritual life is mainly due to the lack of time day by day in fellowship with God.* New life will dawn in many a soul as a result of time spent in prayer alone with God.

To any reader who has found a blessing in reading this book—I pray you, share the blessing with others. If you have accepted the message that the Lord Jesus will from day to day grant you His presence and love—pass it on to others. However weak and unworthy you feel, your faith will be strengthened as you help others to realize the need of fellowship with Jesus daily.

As we think of the need of our country and church, as we think of souls around us, as we think of the extension of God's Kingdom, we ask you, O Christians, to help us find volunteers who, as true soldiers of the Cross, will persevere continually in prayer till God pour out His blessing upon us—

Your Servant in the love of Christ and in prayer,
ANDREW MURRAY

From Day to Day

"The inner man is renewed from day to day" (2 Cor. 4:16).

There is one lesson that all young Christians should learn, namely this— *the absolute necessity of fellowship with Jesus each day.* This lesson is not always taught at the beginning of the Christian life nor is it always understood by the young convert. He should realize that the grace he has received of the forgiveness of sins, of acceptance as God's child, of joy in the Holy Spirit can only be preserved by the daily renewal in fellowship with Jesus Christ Himself.

Many Christians backslide because this truth is not clearly taught. They are unable to stand against the temptations of the world or of their old nature. They strive to do their best to fight against sin and to serve God, but they have no strength. They have never really grasped the secret: *The Lord Jesus will every day* from heaven continue His work in me. But on one condition—*the soul must give Him time each day* to impart His love and His grace. Time alone with the Lord Jesus each day is the indispensable condition of growth and power.

Read Matthew 11:25–30. Listen to Christ's word: "Come unto Me, and I will give you rest. Learn of Me, and ye shall find rest unto your souls." The Lord will teach us just how meek and humble He is. Bow before Him, tell Him that you long for Him and His love, and He will let His love rest on you. This is a thought not only for young Christians but for all who love the Lord, and this book would gladly help those who desire to live this life of fellowship with Christ. We will try to put the message as clearly, as lovingly, as urgently as possible.

Blessed Father, for Christ's sake and in order to please Him, for my own sake and to enable me to enjoy this blessed experience each day, I will learn the lesson, to **spend time each day**—*without exception—* **in fellowship with Thee.** *So will my soul be renewed from day to day.* **Amen.**

Fellowship with God

"He that loveth Me shall be loved of my Father. I will love Him"
(John 14:21).

The Three Persons in the Godhead are the Father, the Son, and the Holy Spirit. Each one knows Himself as different from the others. God desires to reveal Himself as a Person. Each one of us is an individual, knowing himself as distinct from others and standing in certain relations to others. God will reveal Himself to us as a Person, and it is our holy calling to enter into fellowship with Him.

God greatly desires this fellowship with man. But sin has come between man and his God. Even in the Christian who thinks he knows God, there is often great ignorance and even indifference to this personal relationship of love to God.

People believe that at conversion their sins are forgiven, that God accepts them so that they may go to heaven, and that they should try to do God's will. But the idea is strange to them that even as a father and his child on earth have pleasure in fellowship, *so they may and must each day have this blessed fellowship with God.*

God gave Christ His Son *to bring us to Himself.* But this is only possible when we live in close fellowship with Jesus Christ. Our relationship to Christ rests on His deep, tender love to us. We are not able of ourselves to render Him this love. But the Holy Spirit will do the work in us. For this we need to separate ourselves each day from the world and turn in faith to the Lord Jesus, that He may shed abroad His love in our hearts, *so that we may be filled with a great love to Him.*

Dear soul, meditate quietly on this thought. Read the words of Christ in John 14:21, "He that loveth Me shall be loved of my Father. I will love Him." Take time to believe in this personal fellowship. Tell Him of your love.

Blessed Father, Thou hast loved me dearly; most earnestly do I desire to love Thee above all. Amen.

Jesus

"Thou shalt call His Name Jesus, for He shall save
His people from their sins" (Matt. 1:21).

As the Lord Jesus was a person, He had His own individual name. His mother, His disciples, all His friends called Him by this name—Jesus. But they probably thought little of what that name meant. And how little do the majority of Christians know what a treasure is contained in that name—Jesus—*"He shall save His people from their sins."*

Many think of His death on the cross, they think of His work in heaven as Intercessor, but do they, or do we, realize that He is a living Person in heaven who thinks of us each day and longs to reveal Himself? And He desires us each day to bring Him our love and adoration.

Christians pray to Christ to save them from their sins, but they know very little how the blessed work is done. The living Christ reveals Himself to us, and through the power of His love, the love of sin is expelled. It is *through personal fellowship* with Him that Jesus saves us from our sins. I must come as an individual, with my heart and all the sin that is in it, to Jesus as an Almighty personal Savior in whom God's holiness dwells. And as He and I commune together in the expression of mutual love and desire by the work of His Holy Spirit in my heart, His love will expel and conquer all the sin.

O Christian, learn the blessedness of each day in fellowship with Jesus. Finding the secret of happiness and holiness, your heart will long for the hour of prayer as the best hour of the day. As you learn to go apart with Him alone each day, you will experience His presence with you, enabling you all through the day to love Him, to serve Him, and to walk in His ways.

Blessed Father, through this unbroken fellowship with Thee, let me learn the secret of the power of a truly godly life. Amen.

The Inner Chamber

*"When thou prayest enter into thine
inner chamber" (Matt. 6:6, R.V.).*

Have you ever thought what a wonderful privilege it is that everyone each day and each hour of the day has the liberty of asking God to meet him in the inner chamber and to hear what He has to say? We should imagine that every Christian uses such a privilege gladly and faithfully.

"When thou prayest," says Jesus, "enter into thine inner chamber, and having shut thy door, pray to thy Father which is in secret." That means two things. Shut the world out, withdraw from all worldly thoughts and occupations, and shut yourself in alone with God to pray to Him in secret. Let this be your chief object in prayer, *to realize the presence of your heavenly Father*. Let your watchword be: Alone with God.

This is only the beginning. I must take time to realize His presence with me and pray to my Father who seeth in secret, in the full assurance that He knows how I long for His help and guidance and will incline His ear to me.

Then follows the great promise: "Thy Father which seeth in secret shall reward thee openly." My Father will see to it that my prayer is not in vain. All through the occupations of a busy day, the answer to my prayer will be granted. *Prayer in secret will be followed by the secret working of God in my heart.*

As the Lord Jesus has given us the promise of His presence and shows us the way to the inner chamber, He will assuredly be with us to teach us to pray. It is through Him that we have access to the Father. Be childlike and trustful in your fellowship with Christ. *Prayer in fellowship* with Jesus cannot be in vain.

Blessed Father, I confess each sin, I bring to Thee my every need. I offer my prayer to Thee in the name of Christ. Amen.

Faith

"Only believe" (Mark 5:36).

We have here a lesson of the greatest importance, namely this, that when alone in the inner chamber, we must send up our petitions trusting implicitly in the love of God and in the power of the Lord Jesus. Take time to ask yourself the question: Is my heart full of a great and steadfast faith in God's love? If this is not the case, do not begin to pray at once. Faith does not come of itself. Consider quietly how impossible it is for God to lie. He is ready with infinite love to give you a blessing. Take some text of Scripture in which God's power and faithfulness and love are revealed. Appropriate the words, and say: "Yes, Lord, I will pray in firm faith in Thee and in Thy great love."

It is a mistake to limit the word "faith" to the forgiveness of sins and to our acceptance as children of God. Faith includes far more. We must have *faith in all that God is willing to do for us.* We must have faith each day according to our special needs. God is infinitely great and powerful; Christ has so much grace for each new day that our faith must reach out afresh each day according to the need of the day.

When you enter into the inner chamber, even before you begin to pray, ask yourself: "Do I really believe that *God is here with me, and that the Lord Jesus will help me to pray,* and I may expect to spend a blessed time in communion with my God?"

Jesus often taught His disciples how indispensable faith was to true prayer. He will teach us this lesson too. Remain in fellowship with Him. Christ says to you and to me as to Martha: "Said I not unto thee that if thou wouldst believe, thou shouldst see the glory of God."

Blessed Lord Jesus, strengthen my faith in Thy Almighty power. Amen.

The Word of God

"Man shall not live by bread alone, but by every word that proceedeth out of the mouth of God" (Matt. 4:4).

The illustration that our Lord uses, in which the Word of God is compared to our daily bread, is most instructive.

Bread is indispensable to life. We all understand this. However strong a person may be, if he takes no nourishment, he will grow weaker, and life will become extinct. Even so with the Word of God. It contains a heavenly principle and works powerfully in them that believe.

Bread must be eaten. I may know all about bread. I may have bread and may give it to others. I may have bread in my house and on my table in great abundance, but that will not help me; if through illness I am unable to eat it, I shall die. And so a mere knowledge of God's Word and even the preaching of it to others will not avail me. It is not enough to think about it, I must feed on God's Word and take it into my heart and life. In love and obedience I must appropriate the words of God and let them take full possession of my heart. Then they will indeed be words of life.

Bread must be eaten daily. And the same is true of God's Word. The Psalmist says: "Blessed is the man whose delight is in the law of the Lord; and *in His law doth he meditate day and night"* and, "O how I love Thy law; it is my meditation *all the day."* To secure a strong and powerful spiritual life, God's Word every day is indispensable.

When on earth the Lord Jesus learned, loved, and obeyed the word of the Father. And if you seek fellowship with Him, you will find Him in His Word. Christ will teach you to commune with the Father through the Word, even as was His custom.

Lord Jesus, teach me, like Thee, to live solely for the glory of God and the fulfillment of Thy Word. Amen.

How to Read God's Word

"Blessed is the man whose delight is in the law of the Lord, and in His law doth he meditate day and night" (Ps. 1:1–2).

Here are some simple rules for Bible reading.

Read God's Word with great reverence. Meditate a moment in silence on the thought that the words come from God Himself. Bow in deep reverence. Be silent unto God. Let Him reveal His Word in your heart.

Read with careful attention. If you read the words carelessly, thinking that you can grasp their meaning with your human understanding, you will use the words superficially and not enter into their depths. When someone tries to explain anything wonderful or beautiful to us, we give our entire attention to try to understand what is said. How much higher and deeper are God's thoughts than our thoughts. "As the heaven is higher than the earth, so are My thoughts higher than your thoughts." We need to give our undivided attention to understand even the superficial meaning of the words. How much harder to grasp the spiritual meaning!

Read with the expectation of the guidance of God's Spirit. It is God's Spirit alone that can make the Word a living power in our hearts and lives. Read Psalm 119. Notice how earnestly David prays that God will teach him and open his eyes and give him understanding and incline his heart to God's ways. As you read, remember that God's Word and God's Spirit are inseparable.

Read with the firm purpose of keeping the Word day and night in your heart and in your life. The whole heart and the whole life must come under the influence of the Word. David said: "O how I love Thy law, it is my meditation all the day." And so in the midst of his daily work, the believer can cherish God's Word in his heart and meditate on it. Read Psalm 119 again, until you accept God's Word with all your heart.

Dear Father, teach me to understand Thy Word and carry out Its precepts in my life. Amen.

The Word and Prayer

"Quicken Me, O Lord, according to Thy Word" (Ps. 119:107).

Prayer and the Word of God are inseparable and should always go together in the quiet time of the inner chamber. *In His Word God speaks to me; in prayer I speak to God.* If there is to be true fellowship, God and I must both take part. If I simply pray, without using God's Word, I am apt to use my own words and thoughts. What really gives prayer its power is that I take God's thoughts from His Word and present them before Him. Then I am enabled to pray according to God's Word. How indispensable God's Word is for all true prayer

When I pray, I must seek to know God aright. It is through the Word that the Holy Spirit gives me right thoughts of Him. The Word will also teach me how wretched and sinful I am. It reveals to me all the wonders that God will do for me and the strength He will give me to do His will. The Word teaches me how to pray—with strong desire, with a firm faith, and with constant perseverance. The Word teaches me not only what I am, but what I may become through God's grace. And above all, it reminds me each day that Christ is the great Intercessor and allows me to pray in His Name.

O Christian, learn this great lesson, *to renew your strength each day in God's Word, and so pray according to His will.*

Then we turn to the other side—Prayer. We need prayer when we read God's Word—prayer to be taught of God to understand His Word, prayer that through the Holy Spirit I may rightly know and use God's Word—prayer that I may see in the Word that Christ is all in all and will be all in me.

Dear Father, it is in the blessed inner chamber, that I may approach Thee in Christ through the Word and prayer. There I offer myself to Thee and Thy service and am strengthened by the Holy Spirit, so that Thy love may be shed abroad in my heart and I may daily walk in that love. Amen.

Obedience

"Obey My voice . . . and I will be your God" (Jer. 11:4).

God gave this command to Israel when He gave them the law. But Israel had no power to keep the law. So God gave them a "new covenant" to enable His people to live a life of obedience. We read (Jer. 31:33), "I will write My law in their hearts" (Jer. 32:40), "I will put My fear in their heart, that they shall not depart from Me." (Ezek. 36:27), "I will cause you to walk in My statutes." These wonderful promises gave the assurance that obedience would be their delight.

Let us listen to what the Lord Jesus says about obedience (John 14:21–23). "He that keepeth My commandments, he it is that loveth Me; and he that loveth Me shall be loved of My Father, and I will love him, and We will make our abode with him." And in John 15:10, "If ye keep My commandments, ye shall abide in My love." These words are an inexhaustible treasure. Faith can firmly *trust Christ to enable us to live such a life of love and of obedience.*

No father can train his children unless they are obedient. No teacher can teach a child who continues to disobey him. No general can lead his soldiers to victory without prompt obedience. Pray God to imprint this lesson on your heart: *the life of faith is a life of obedience.* As Christ lived in obedience to the Father, so we too need obedience for a life in the love of God.

Alas, the thought is too common: "I cannot be obedient, it is quite impossible." Yes, impossible to you, but not to God. He has promised *"to cause you to walk in His statutes."* Pray and meditate on these words, and the Holy Spirit will enlighten your eyes so that you will have power to do God's will.

Dear Father, let my fellowship with Thee and with the Lord Jesus Christ have as its one aim and object—a life of quiet, determined, unquestioning obedience. Amen.

Confession of Sin

"If we confess our sins, He is faithful and just to forgive us our sins, and to cleanse us from all unrighteousness" (1 John 1:9).

Too often the confession of sin is superficial, and often it is quite neglected. Few Christians realize how necessary it is to be in earnest about the matter or feel that an honest confession of sin gives power to live the life of victory over sin. *In fellowship with the Lord Jesus we need to confess with a sincere heart every sin that may be a hindrance in our Christian lives.*

Listen to what David says, "I acknowledged my sin unto Thee; I said, I will confess my transgression, and Thou forgavest the iniquity of my sin. Thou art my hiding-place; Thou shalt compass me about with songs of deliverance" (Ps. 32:5–7). David speaks of a time when he was unwilling to confess his sin. "When I kept silence, Thy hand was heavy upon me." *But when he had confessed his sin, a wonderful change came.*

Confession means not only that I confess my sin with shame but that I hand it over to God, trusting Him to take it away. Such a confession implies that I am wholly unable to get rid of my guilt, but by an act of faith I reckon on God to deliver me. This deliverance means, in the first place, that I know my sins are forgiven, and secondly, that Christ undertakes to cleanse me from the sin and keep me from its power.

O Christian, if you are seeking to have fellowship with Jesus, do not fear to confess *each sin* in the confident assurance that there is deliverance. Let there be a mutual understanding between the Lord Jesus and yourself that you will confess each sin and obtain forgiveness. Then you will know your Lord as Jesus who saves His people from their sin.

Dear Father, I believe that there is great power in the confession of sin, for the burden of sin is borne by our Lord and Savior. Amen.

The First Love

*"I have somewhat against thee, because thou
hast left thy first love" (Rev. 2:4).*

In Revelation 2:2–3, eight signs are mentioned showing the zeal and activity of the Church at Ephesus. But there was one bad sign, and the Lord said: "Except thou repent, I will come unto thee, and will remove thy candlestick out of his place." And what was this sign? *"Thou hast left thy first love."*

We find the same lack in the Church of the present day. There is zeal for the truth, there is continuous and persevering labor, but that which the Lord values most is wanting, *the tender, fervent love to Himself.*

This is a thought of great significance—a church or a community or a Christian may be an example in every good work, and yet—*the tender love to the Lord Jesus in the inner chamber is missing.*

There is no personal daily fellowship with Christ, and all the manifold activities with which people satisfy themselves are as nought in the eyes of the Master Himself.

Dear brother and sister, this book speaks of the fellowship of love with Christ in the inner chamber. Everything depends on this. Christ came from heaven to love us with the love wherewith the Father loved Him. He suffered and died to win our hearts for this love. *His love can be satisfied with nothing less than a deep, personal love on our part.*

Christ considers this of the first importance. Let us do so too. Many ministers and missionaries and Christian workers confess with shame that in spite of all their zeal in the Lord's work, their prayer life is defective because they have left their first love. I pray you, write this down on a piece of paper and remember it continually—*The love of Jesus must be all*—in the inner chamber, in all my work, in my daily life.

Lord Jesus, I pray that Thou wilt be my all, in the inner chamber, in all my work, in my daily life. Amen.

The Holy Spirit

*"He shall glorify Me; for He shall receive of Mine,
and show it unto you" (John 16:14).*

Our Lord, in the last night that He was with His disciples, promised to send the Holy Spirit as a Comforter. Although His bodily presence was removed, they would realize His presence in them and with them in a wonderful way. The Holy Spirit as God would so reveal Christ in their hearts that they would experience His presence with them continually. The Spirit would glorify Christ and would reveal the glorified Christ in heavenly love and power.

How little do Christians understand and believe and experience this glorious truth. We would fail in our duty as ministers if, in a little book like this or in our preaching, we encouraged Christians to love the Lord Jesus without at the same time warning them that it is not a duty they can perform in their own strength. No, that is impossible; it is God, the Holy Spirit alone, who will shed abroad His love in our hearts and teach us to love Him fervently. *Through the Holy Spirit we may experience the love and abiding presence of the Lord Jesus all the day.*

But let us remember that the Spirit as God must have entire possession of us, He claims our whole heart and life. He will strengthen us with might in the inner man, so that we have fellowship with Christ and keep His commandments and abide in His love.

When once we have grasped this truth, we will begin to feel our deep dependence on the Holy Spirit and pray the Father to send Him in power into our hearts. The Spirit will teach us to love the Word, to meditate on it, and to keep it. He will reveal the love of Christ to us, that we may love Him with a pure heart fervently.

Dear Lord Jesus, help us begin to see that a life in the love of Christ in the midst of our daily life and distractions is a glorious possibility and a blessed reality. Amen.

Christ's Love to Us

"Even as the Father hath loved Me, I also have
loved you: abide ye in My love" (John 15:9, R.V.).

In communion between friends and relations everything depends on their love to each other. Of what value is abundance of riches if love is lacking between husband and wife or parents and children? And in our religion, of what value is all knowledge and zeal in God's work without the knowledge and experience of Christ's love? (See 1 Cor. 13:1–3.) O Christians, the one thing needful in the inner chamber is to know by experience *how much Christ loves you and to learn how you may abide and continue in that love.*

Think of what Christ says: "As the Father hath loved Me"—what a Divine, everlasting, wonderful love! "Even so have I loved you." It was the same love with which He had loved the Father and that He always bore in His heart which He now gave into the hearts of His disciples. He yearns that this everlasting love should rest upon us and work within us, that we may abide in it day by day. What a blessed life! Christ desires every disciple to live in the power of the self-same love of God that He Himself experienced. My brothers and sisters, do you realize that in your fellowship with Christ, in secret or in public, you are surrounded by and kept in this heavenly love? Let your desire reach out to this everlasting love. The Christ with whom you desire fellowship longs unspeakably to fill you with His love.

Read from time to time what God's Word says about the love of Christ. Meditate on the words, and let them sink into your heart. Sooner or later you will begin to realize: The greatest happiness of my life is that I am loved by the Lord Jesus. I may live in fellowship with Him all the day long.

Dear Lord Jesus, my heart continually says: Thy love to me is unspeakable, Thou wilt keep me abiding in Thy love. Amen.

Our Love to Christ

"Jesus Christ, whom not having seen, ye love: in whom, though now ye see Him not, yet believing, ye rejoice greatly with joy unspeakable and full of glory" (1 Peter 1:8 R.V.).

What a wonderful description of the Christian life! People who had never seen Christ yet truly loved Him and believed on Him, so that their hearts were filled with unspeakable joy. Such is the life of Christians who really love their Lord.

We have seen that the chief attribute of the Father and of the Son is love to each other and love to man. This love should be the chief characteristic of the true Christian. The love of God and of Christ is shed abroad in his heart and becomes a well of living water, flowing forth as love to the Lord Jesus.

This love is not merely a blessed feeling. It is an active principle. It takes pleasure in doing the will of the beloved Lord. It is joy to keep His commandments. The love of Christ to us was shown by His death on the cross; our love must be exhibited in unselfish, self-sacrificing lives. Oh that we understood this: *In the Christian life love to Christ is everything*!

Great love will beget great faith: faith in His love to us, faith in the powerful revelations of His love in our hearts, faith that He through His love will work all His good pleasure in us.

The wings of faith and love will lift us up to heaven, and we shall be filled with joy unspeakable. The joy of the Christian is an indispensable witness to the world of the power of Christ to change hearts and fill them with heavenly love and gladness.

O ye lovers of the Lord Jesus, take time daily in the inner chamber with Him anew to drink in His heavenly love. It will make you strong in faith, and your joy will be full.

Blessed Father, I pray that love, joy, and faith will be my life each day through the grace of our Lord Jesus. Amen.

Love to the Brethren

*"A new commandment I give unto you, that ye love
one another, even as I have loved you, that ye also
love one another" (John 13:34; 15:12).*

The Lord Jesus told His disciples that as the Father had loved Him, even so He loved them. And now, following His example, we must love one another with the same love. "By this shall all men know that ye are My disciples, if ye have love one to another" (John 13:35). He had prayed: "That they all may be one, as Thou, Father, art in Me, and I in Thee, that the world may believe that Thou hast sent Me" (John 17:21). If we exhibit the love that was in God toward Christ and in Christ to us, the world will be obliged to confess that our Christianity is genuine and from above.

This is what actually happened. The Greeks and Romans, Jews and heathen, hated each other. Among all the nations of the world there was hardly a thought of love for each other. The very idea of self-sacrifice was a strange one. When the heathen saw that Christians from different nations, under the powerful workings of the Holy Spirit, became one and loved one another even to the point of self-sacrifice in time of plague or illness—they were amazed and said: "Behold how these people love one another!"

Among professing Christians there is a certain oneness of belief and feeling of brotherhood, but Christ's heavenly love is often lacking, and we do not bear one another's burdens or love others heartily.

Pray that you may love your fellow-believers with the same love with which Christ loved you. If we abide in Christ's love and let that love fill our hearts, supernatural power will be given us to take all God's children unto our hearts in love.

Dear Father, as close as is the bond of love between the Father and the Son, between Christ and His followers, so close must the bond of love be between all God's children. Amen.

Love to Souls

*"Know that he which converteth a sinner from the error of his way,
shall save a soul from death" (James 5:20).*

What a wonderful thought—that I may save a soul from everlasting
death. How can this be? If I convert him from the error of his ways. This
is the calling not only of the minister, but of every Christian—to work for
the salvation of sinners.

When Christ and His love took possession of our hearts, He gave us
this love that we might bring others to Him. In this way Christ's Kingdom
was extended. Everyone who had the love of Christ in his heart was constrained to tell others. This was the case in the early Christian church. After the Day of Pentecost, people went out and told of the love of Christ,
which they had themselves experienced. Heathen writers have told us that
the rapid spread of Christianity in the first century was due to the fact that
each convert, being filled with the love of Christ, tried to bring the good
news to others.

What a change has come over the Church! Many Christians never try
to win others to Christ. Their love is so weak and faint that they have no
desire to help others. May the time soon come when Christians will feel
constrained to tell of the love of Christ. In a revival in Korea a few years
ago, the converts were filled with such a burning love to Christ that they
felt bound to tell others of His love. It was even taken as a test of membership that each one should have brought another to the Lord before being admitted to the church.

Let the reader examine himself and pray that in fellowship with Christ,
he may think not only of his own soul but, having received the gift of God's
love, he may pass it on to others. He will then know true happiness, the
joy of bringing souls to Christ.

---

*Dear Father, we pray earnestly to be so filled with Thy love that we
may wholeheartedly surrender ourselves to win others for Thee. Amen.*

The Spirit of Love

"The love of God is shed abroad in our hearts, by the Holy Spirit, which is given unto us" (Rom. 5:5).

"The fruit of the Spirit is love" (Gal. 5:22).

The thought sometimes arises as we consider Christ's love to us, our love to Christ, our love to one another or to souls around us: the demand is too great, it is unattainable, it is impossible for a Christian to live this life of love and to show it to one another and to needy souls. And because we deem it impossible and because of our unbelief and lack of faith in God's promises, we make little progress in this spirit of love.

We need continually to remind ourselves that it is not in our own strength or even by serious thought that we can attain to the love of Christ. We must realize the truth that the love of God is shed abroad in our hearts and will daily afresh be poured out by the Spirit of God. It is only as we are wholly surrendered to the leading of the Spirit that we will be able to live according to God's will. When the inner life of love is renewed from day to day, we shall feel compelled to work for souls.

Here is a prayer that you can offer: "I bow my knees unto the Father, that He would grant you, to be strengthened with might by His Spirit in the inner man, that Christ may dwell in your hearts by faith, that ye, *being rooted and grounded in love, may know the love of Christ which passeth knowledge.*" You may be rooted and grounded in this love and know the love that passeth knowledge—but on one condition—you must be *strengthened by the Spirit in the inner man, so that Christ may dwell in your heart.* Then you will indeed be rooted and grounded in love.

Christian, take this message from God's Word and let it influence your life. Unless you wait upon God daily on your knees for His Spirit to be revealed in your heart, you cannot live in this love. A life of prayer will make a life in the love of Christ, in the love of one another, and in love to souls, a blessed reality in your experience.

Blessed Father, we put our confidence each day in secret in the Holy Spirit—the Spirit of love which God gives to those who ask in faith. Amen.

Persevering Prayer

"Men ought always to pray, and not to faint" (Luke 18:1).

"Continue in prayer" (Rom. 12:12).

"Pray without ceasing" (1 Thess. 5:17).

One of the greatest drawbacks to the life of prayer is the fact that the answer does not come as speedily as we expect. We are discouraged by the thought: "Perhaps I do not pray aright," and so we do not persevere in prayer. This was a lesson that our Lord taught often and urgently. If we consider the matter we can see that there may be a reason for the delay, and the waiting may bring a blessing to our souls. Our desire must grow deeper and stronger, and we must ask with our whole heart. God puts us into the practicing school of persevering prayer that our weak faith may be strengthened. Do believe that there is a great blessing in the delayed answer to prayer.

Above all, God would draw us into closer fellowship with Himself. When our prayers are not answered, we learn to realize that the fellowship and nearness and love of God are more to us than the answers of our petitions, and we continue in prayer. What a blessing Jacob received through the delay in the answer to his prayer! He saw God face to face, and as a prince he had power with God and prevailed.

Christians, listen to this warning. Be not impatient or discouraged if the answer does not come. "Continue in prayer." "Pray without ceasing." You will find it an unspeakable blessing to do so. You will ask whether your prayer is really in accordance with the will of God and the Word of God. You will inquire if it is in the right spirit and in the Name of Christ. Keep on praying—you will learn that the delay in the answer to prayer is one of the most precious means of grace that God can bestow on you.

Our Father, help me to learn that those who have persevered often and long before Thee, in pleading Thy promises, are those who have had the greatest power in prayer. Amen.

The Prayer Meeting

"These all continued with one accord in prayer and supplication." "And they were all filled with the Holy Ghost" (Acts 1:14; 2:4). (See also Matt. 18:19–20.)

Great is the value of a genuine prayer meeting. There God's children meet together, not as in church to listen to one speaker, but to lift up their hearts unitedly to God. By this means Christians are drawn closer to each other. Those who are weak are strengthened and encouraged by the testimony of the older and more experienced members, and even young Christians have the opportunity of telling of the joy of the Lord.

The prayer meeting may become a great power for good in a congregation and a spiritual help to both minister and members. By means of intercession, God's blessing is poured out at home and abroad.

But there are also dangers to be considered. Many attend and are edified but never learn to pray themselves. Others go for the sake of social and religious fervor and have a form of godliness but do not know the hidden life of prayer. Unless there is *much and earnest prayer in the inner chamber*, attendance at a prayer meeting may be a mere form. There should be hearty love and fellowship between the members. It is well to ask: What constitutes a living prayer meeting?

The leaders should realize how great the influence of such a meeting may be, with its roots nourished by the life of prayer in the inner chamber. Prayer should include God's people and His church all over the world. And above all, as on the Day of Pentecost, there must be waiting on God for the filling with the Holy Spirit.

Dear reader, this book aims at helping you in your spiritual life. But remember, you do not live for yourself alone but are part of the Body of Christ. Your prayer must include in its intercession all Christians. As the roots of the tree hidden deep in the earth and the branches spread out to heaven are one, so the hidden prayer life is inseparably bound up with united prayer.

Dear Father, help me always to pray for all Christians. Amen.

Intercession

*"Praying at all seasons in the Spirit . . . in all perseverance
and supplication for all the saints" (Eph. 6:18).*

What an unspeakable blessing there is in intercession. That one should
pray down heavenly gifts on himself is a wonder of grace, but that he
should bring down blessings on others is indeed an inconceivable honor.
Will God indeed make the pouring out of blessing on others dependent on
our prayers? Yes, He makes us His remembrancers and fellow-workers. He
has taken us into partnership in His work; if we fail in doing our part, others will suffer and His work will suffer unspeakable loss.

God has appointed intercession as one of the means by which souls shall
be saved, and saints and ministers of the Gospel edified and built up in
the faith. Even the ends of the earth will receive life and blesssing through
our prayers. Should we not expect God's children to strive joyfully and
with all their powers, by means of intercession, to bring down blessing on
the world?

Christian, begin to use intercession as a means of grace for yourself and
for others. Pray for your neighbors. Pray for souls with the definite desire
that they may be won for Christ. Pray for your minister, for all ministers
and missionaries. Pray for your country and people, for rulers and subjects. Pray for all people. If you surrender yourself to the guidance of the
Holy Spirit and live a life wholly for God, you will realize that the time
spent in prayer is an offering well-pleasing to God, bringing blessing to
yourself and power into the lives of those for whom you pray.

Yes, "pray always with all prayer and supplication, watching thereunto
with all perseverance and supplication for all saints."

---

*Dear Father, help me to learn the lesson that intercession is the chief
means of winning souls and bringing glory to Thee. Amen.*

Prayer and Fasting

"And Jesus said unto them, 'Because of your unbelief. . . .
Howbeit this kind goeth not out but by prayer
and fasting'" (Matt. 17:20–21).

Our Lord here teaches us that a life of faith requires both prayer and fasting. That is, prayer grasps the power of heaven, fasting loosens the hold on earthly pleasure.

Jesus Himself fasted to get strength to resist the devil. He taught His disciples that even as with prayer and almsgiving, fasting should be in secret, and the Heavenly Father would reward openly. Abstinence from food, or temperance in taking it, helps to strengthen the soul for communion with God.

Let us learn this great lesson that abstinence, temperance, and self-denial in temporal things are a help to the spiritual life. After having partaken of a hearty meal, one does not feel much desire to pray. To willingly sacrifice our own pleasure or bodily enjoyment and to subdue the lust of the flesh and the lust of the eyes will help to set our minds more fully on heavenly things. The very exertion needed in overcoming the desires of the flesh will give us strength to take hold of God in prayer.

This great lesson is this. Our dullness in prayer comes from our fleshly desire of comfort and ease. "Those who are in Christ have crucified the flesh and its desires." Prayer is no easy work. It may easily become a mere form. For the real practice of prayer and taking hold of God and having communion with Him, it is necessary that all that can please the flesh must be sacrificed and given over to death.

Lord Jesus Christ, help us to deny ourselves daily in order to meet the Holy God and receive from Him heavenly blessings. Amen.

The Spirit of Prayer

"The Spirit maketh intercession for the saints" (Rom. 8:27).

"Prayer is not our work, but God's work, that He works within us by His almighty power." As we think of this, our attitude should be one of silent expectation that as we pray, the Holy Spirit may help our infirmities and pray within us with groanings that cannot be uttered.

What a thought! When I feel how defective my prayer is, when I have no strength of my own, I may bow in silence before God in the confidence that His Holy Spirit will teach me to pray. The Spirit is the Spirit of prayer. It is not my work but God's work in me. My very desire is a sign that God will hear me. When God would grant our requests, He first works the desire in our hearts, and the Spirit will perfect the work even in our weakness. We see this in the story of Jacob. The same One who wrestled with him and seemed to withhold the blessing was in reality strengthening him to continue and to prevail in prayer. What a wondrous thought! Prayer is the work of the Triune God: the Father who wakens the desire and will give all we need; the Son who through His intercession teaches us to pray in His Name; and the Holy Spirit who in secret will strengthen our feeble desires.

We have spoken of the Spirit of truth who will glorify Christ in us and of the Spirit of love who will shed this love abroad in our hearts. And now we have the Spirit of prayer through whom our life may be one of continual prayer. *Thank God. The Spirit has been given from heaven to dwell in our hearts and to teach us to pray.*

Christian, listen to the leading of the Spirit. Obey His voice in all things. He will make you a person of prayer. You will then realize the glory of your calling as intercessor.

Blessed Father, help us to ask great things of Thee for those around us, for the church, and for the whole heathen world. Amen.

Wholly for Christ

*"One died for all . . . that they which live should no
longer live unto themselves, but unto Him who for
their sakes died and rose again" (2 Cor. 5:14–15 R.V.).*

Here we have a threefold life described. First, the life of a Christian who lives according to his old nature: *he lives for himself alone.* The second, the life of a true Christian: *he lives wholly for Christ.* Thirdly, the life of Christ in heaven: *He lives wholly for us.*

Many a Christian needs to be convinced of the folly of living only for himself. At conversion he thinks more of his own salvation and less of the glory of God and the right that Christ who has redeemed us with His precious blood has upon him. Many Christians just live for themselves, content with doing a little for the Master. Happy the believer who realizes his high calling and the privilege and blessedness of consecrating His life entirely to God's service.

The great hindrance to such a life is the unbelief which says it is impossible. But when the truth takes hold of us: Christ in heaven lives wholly for me and will impart His life to me and will enable me to live wholly for Him, then we will be able to say joyfully: Dear Lord Jesus, from this moment let my prayer each day be—Wholly for Christ, Wholly for Christ.

Dear brothers and sisters, let nothing less be your earnest desire, your prayer, and your firm expectation: Christ has not only died for me but lives in heaven to keep and sanctify me, His purchased possession. Ponder this wonderful thought, that Christ will keep you as a member of His Body, to work and live for Him. Pray for grace to live wholly for God in seeking souls and in serving His people. Take time from day to day to be so united to Christ in the inner man that you can say with all your heart: I live wholly for Him who gave Himself wholly for me and now lives in heaven wholly for me.

---

*Dear Lord Jesus, give me the grace to live wholly for Thee in seeking
souls and in serving Thy people. Amen.*

The Cross of Christ

"I am crucified with Christ" (Gal. 2:20).

The cross of Christ is His greatest glory. Because He humbled Himself to the death of the cross, *therefore* God has highly exalted Him. The cross was the power that conquered Satan and sin.

The Christian shares with Christ in the cross. The crucified Christ lives in him through the Holy Spirit, and the spirit of the cross inspires him. He lives as one who has died with Christ. As he realizes the power of Christ's crucifixion, he lives as one who has died to the world and to sin, and the power becomes a reality in his life. It is as the crucified One that Christ lives in me.

Our Lord said to His disciples: "Take up your cross and follow me." Did they understand this? They had seen men carrying a cross and knew what it meant, a painful death on the cross. And so all His life Christ bore His cross—the death sentence that He should die for the world. And each Christian must bear his cross, acknowledging that he is worthy of death and believing that he is crucified with Christ and that the crucified One lives in him. "Our old man is crucified with Christ." "He that is Christ's hath crucified the flesh with all the lusts thereof." When we have accepted this life of the cross, we will be able to say with Paul: "Far be it from me to glory save in the cross of our Lord Jesus Christ."

This is a deep spiritual truth. Think and pray over it, and the Holy Spirit will teach you. Let the disposition of Christ on the cross, His humility, His sacrifice of all worldly honor, His Spirit of self-denial take possession of you. The power of His death will work in you, and you will become like Him in His death, and you will know Him and the power of His resurrection.

Heavenly Father, I desire to take time for Christ, through Thy Holy Spirit, to reveal Himself in my heart as the Crucified One. Amen.

The World

"Love not the world, neither the things that are
in the world. If any man love the world, the
love of the Father is not in him" (1 John 2:15).

John teaches us clearly what he means by the world. He says: "All that is in the world, the lust of the flesh, and the lust of the eyes, and the pride of life is not of the Father, but is of the world" (1 John 2:16).

The world is that disposition or power under which man has fallen through sin. And the god of this world, in order to deceive man, conceals himself under the form of what God has created. The world with its pleasures surrounds the Christian each day with temptations.

This was the case with Eve in the Garden of Eden. We find in Genesis 3 the three characteristics which John mentions: 1. The lust of the flesh— "The woman saw the tree that it was good for food." 2. The lust of the eyes—"It was pleasant to the eyes." 3. The pride of life—"A tree to be desired to make one wise." And the world still comes to us offering desirable food and much to please the fleshly appetites. And much that the eye desires, riches and beauty and luxury. And the pride of life, when a man imagines he knows and understands everything and prides himself on it.

Is our life in the world not full of danger with the allurements of the flesh—so much to occupy our eyes and our hearts, so much worldly wisdom and knowledge?

So John tells us: "Love not the world, for then the love of the Father is not in you." And our Lord calls us, as He called His disciples of old, to leave all and follow Him.

Christian, you live in a dangerous world. Cleave fast to the Lord Jesus. As He teaches you to shun the world and its attractions, your love will go out to Him in loyal-hearted service. But remember—There must be daily fellowship with Jesus. His love alone can expel the love of the world. Take time to be alone with your Lord.

Lord Jesus, I long for time alone with Thee. Thou art my Lord. Amen.

Put on Christ

*"As many of us as have been baptized with Christ,
have put on Christ" (Gal. 3:27).*

*"Put ye on the Lord Jesus Christ, and make not provision
for the flesh, to fulfill the lusts thereof" (Rom. 13:14).*

The word that is here translated "put on" is the same that is used in regard to putting on clothes. We have put on "the new man," and we have the new nature as a garment that is worn, by means of which all can see who we are. Paul says of the Christian when he has confessed Christ at baptism, that he has put on Christ. As a man may be recognized by the garment he wears, so the Christian is known as one who has put on Christ and exhibits Him in his whole life and character.

And again he says: "Put on the Lord Jesus." Not alone at conversion, but from day to day. As I put on my clothes each day and am seen in them, so the Christian must daily put on the Lord Jesus, so that he no longer lives after the flesh to fulfill its lusts but shows forth the image of his Lord and the new man formed in His likeness.

Put on Christ! This work must be done each day in the inner chamber. I must put on the Lord, the heavenly Jesus. But I need time to put on Christ. As my garments cover me and protect me from wind and sun, even so Christ Jesus will be my beauty, my defense, and my joy. As I commune with Him in prayer, He imparts Himself to me and strengthens me to walk as one who is in Him and bound to Him forever.

O soul, take time to meditate on this wonderful truth. Just as your clothing is a necessity as you go out into the world, let it be equally indispensable for you to put on Jesus Christ, to abide in Him and walk with Him all the day.

You feel that this cannot be done hastily and superficially. It takes time, quiet time in living fellowship with Jesus, to realize that you have put Him on. Take the time and the trouble. Your reward will be great.

Blessed Father, I long to put on Jesus Christ, to abide in Him and walk with Him all the day. Amen.

The Strength of the Christian

*"Finally, my brethren, be strong in the Lord, and
in the power of His might" (Eph. 6:10).*

The Apostle has reached the end of his Epistle and begins his last division with the words: "Finally, my brethren, be strong in the Lord."

The Christian needs strength. This we all know. The Christian has no strength of his own. This is also true. Where may strength be obtained? Notice the answer: "Be strong *in the Lord* and the power of His might."

Paul had spoken of this power in the earlier part of his Epistle (1:17–19). He had prayed God to give them the Spirit that they might know the exceeding greatness of His power according to the working of His mighty power which He wrought in Christ when He raised Him from the dead. This is the literal truth: *the exceeding greatness of His power*, which raised Christ from the dead, *works in every believer*. In me and in you, my reader. We hardly believe it, and still less do we experience it. That is why Paul prays, and we must pray with him, that God through His Spirit would teach us to believe in His almighty power. Pray with all your heart· Father, grant me the Spirit of wisdom, that I may experience this power in my life.

In chapter 3:16–17, Paul prays the Father to grant them, according to the riches of His glory, to be strengthened with might by His Spirit in the inner man, that Christ might dwell in their hearts. And then: "Now unto Him that is able to do exceedingly abundantly, above all we ask or think, *according to the power that worketh in us*, unto Him be glory."

Read over these two passages again and pray for God's Spirit to enlighten your eyes. Believe in the divine power working within you. Pray that the Holy Spirit may reveal it to you and appropriate the promise that God will manifest His Power in your heart, supplying all your needs.

Do you not begin to realize that time is needed, much time in communion with the Father and the Son, if you would experience the power of God within you?

Dear Father, I pray that Thy Holy Spirit will enlighten my eyes and that Thou wilt manifest Thy power in my heart. Amen.

The Whole Heart

"With my whole heart have I sought Thee" (Ps. 119:10).

Notice how often the Psalmist speaks here of the whole heart. "They that seek Him with the whole heart" (v. 2). "I shall observe Thy law with my whole heart" (v. 34). "I will keep Thy precepts with my whole heart" (v. 69). "I cried with my whole heart" (v. 145). In seeking God, in observing His law, in crying for His help—each time it is with the whole heart.

When we want to make anything a success in worldly affairs, we put our whole heart into it. And is this not much more necessary in the service of a holy God? Is He not worthy? Does not His great holiness and the natural aversion of our hearts from God demand it? The whole heart is needed in the service of God when we worship Him in secret.

And yet how little most Christians think of this. They do not remember how necessary it is—in prayer, in reading God's Word, in striving to do His will—to say continually: "With my *whole heart have I sought Thee.*" Yes, when we pray and when we try to understand God's word and to obey His commands, let us say: I desire to seek God, to serve Him, and to please Him with my whole heart.

"With my whole heart have I sought Thee." Dear reader, take this word into your heart. Think over it. Pray over it. Speak it out before God until you feel: I really mean what I say, and I have the assurance that God will hear my prayer. Say it each morning as you approach God in prayer: I seek Thee with my whole heart. You will by degrees feel the need of waiting in holy stillness upon God, that He may take possession of your whole heart, and you will learn to love Him with your whole heart and with all your strength.

Loving Father, I seek Thee with my whole heart. I wait in holy stillness upon Thee. I am learning to love Thee with my whole heart and strength. Amen.

In Christ

"Of God are ye in Christ Jesus" (1 Cor. 1:30).

The expression "in Christ" is often used in the Epistles. The Christian cannot read God's Word aright nor experience its full power in his life until he prayerfully and believingly accepts this truth: *I am in Christ Jesus.*

The Lord Jesus in the last night with His disciples used this word more than once. "In that day,"—when the Spirit had been poured out, "ye shall know that I am in the Father, and *ye in Me*." And then follows, "Abide *in Me*; he that abideth *in Me* beareth much fruit." "If ye abide in Me, ye shall ask what ye will, and it shall be done unto you." But the Christian cannot appropriate these promises unless he first prayerfully accepts the word: in Christ.

Paul expresses the same thought in Romans. "We are buried *with Christ*." "We are dead indeed unto sin, but alive unto God *through Jesus Christ* our Lord." "There is no condemnation to them which are *in Christ Jesus*." And in Ephesians: "God has blessed us with all spiritual blessings *in Christ*"; hath chosen us in Him; hath made us accepted *in the Beloved; in Him* we have redemption. And in Colossians: "*In Him* dwelleth all the fullness"; we are "perfect *in Christ Jesus*." "Walk ye *in Him*." "Ye are complete *in Him*."

Let our faith take hold of the words: "It is God that stablisheth us in Christ." "Of God I am in Christ Jesus." The Holy Spirit will make it our experience. Pray earnestly and follow the leading of the Spirit. The word will take root in your heart, and you will realize something of its heavenly power. But remember that abiding in Christ is a matter of the heart. It must be cultivated in a spirit of love. Only as we take time from day to day in fellowship with Christ will the abiding in Christ become a blessed reality, and the inner man will be renewed from day to day.

Lord Jesus, teach me to abide in Christ, renew me day to day. Amen.

Christ in Me

*"Know ye not . . . how that Jesus Christ
is in you?" (2 Cor. 13:5).*

The Apostle would have each Christian live in the full assurance: *Christ is in me.* What a difference it would make in our lives if we could take time every morning to be filled with the thought: Christ is in me. *As assuredly as I am Christ, Christ is also in me.*

In the last night Christ put it clearly to His disciples that the Spirit would teach them: "In that day ye shall know that I am in the Father, and ye in Me, and I *in you.*" First of all, *Ye in Me.* Through the power of God, all we who believe were crucified with Christ and raised again with Him. And as a result: *Christ is in us.* But this knowledge does not come easily. Through faith in God's Word, the Christian accepts it, and the Holy Spirit will lead us into all truth. Take time this very day to realize and appropriate this blessing in prayer.

How clearly Paul expresses the thought in the prayer of Ephesians 3:16: "That the Father would grant you according to the riches of His glory." Notice that it is not the ordinary gift of grace, but a special revelation of the riches of His love and power. That he grant you to be strengthened with might by His Spirit in the inner man, so that *Christ may dwell in your hearts by faith.* Have you grasped it? The Christian may really have the experience of being filled with the fullness of God.

Dear Christian, Paul said: "I bow my knees unto the Father." That is the only way to obtain the blessing. Take time in the inner chamber to realize: *Christ dwells in me.* Too little have I experienced this in the past, but I will cry to God and wait upon Him to perfect His work in me. Even in the midst of my daily work, I must look upon my heart as the dwelling place of the Son of God and say: "I am crucified with Christ, I live no more; *Christ liveth in me.*" Thus only will Christ's words, "Abide in Me, and I in you," become my daily experience.

---

*Dear Lord Jesus, I long for your words, "Abide in Me, and I in you,"
to become my daily experience. Amen.*

Christ Is All

"Christ is all and in all" (Col. 3:11).

In the eternal counsel of God, in the redemption on the cross, as King on the throne in heaven and on earth—*Christ is all*! In the salvation of sinners, in their justification and sanctification, in the upbuilding of Christ's Body, in the care for individuals, even the most sinful—this word avails, *Christ is all*. Every day and every hour, it affords comfort and strength to the child of God who accepts it in faith—*Christ is all*.

Have you perhaps thought in reading these pages that the full salvation here described is not meant for you? You feel too weak, too unworthy, too untrustworthy. My dear reader, do believe that if you will only accept the Lord Jesus in childlike faith, you have a leader and a guide who will supply all your need. Believe with your whole heart in the word of our Savior: "Lo, I am with you always," and you will experience His presence each day. However cold and dull your feelings may be, however sinful you are, meet the Lord Jesus in secret, and He will reveal Himself to you. Tell Him how wretched you are, and then trust Him to help and sustain you. Wait before Him until by faith you can rejoice in Him. Read this book over again, and read it with the thought: Christ is all. I have failed to remember this, but each day as I go to secret prayer, let this thought be with me: Christ is all. Let me take it as my motto—to teach me to pray, to strengthen my faith, to give me the assurance of His love and access to the Father, to make me strong for the work of the day: *Christ is all*. Yes, Christ, my Christ, is all I need. It will teach me to abide in His love. It will give me the assurance that He dwells in my heart, and I may know the love that passes knowledge. God be praised to all eternity: Christ, my Christ, is my all in all!

Blessed Father, give me the assurance that Christ dwells in my heart, and that I may know the love that passes knowledge. Christ is my all in all! Amen.

Intercession

"Pray one for another" (James 5:16).

What a mystery of glory there is in prayer! On the one hand, we see God, in His holiness and love and power, waiting, longing to bless man; and on the other, sinful man, a worm of the dust, bringing down from God by prayer the very life and love of heaven to dwell in his heart.

But how much greater the glory of intercession!—when a man makes bold to say to God what he desires for others and seeks to bring down on one soul, or it may be on hundreds and thousands, the power of the eternal life with all its blessings.

Intercession! Would one not say that this is the very holiest exercise of our boldness as God's children, the highest privilege and enjoyment connected with our communion with God—the power of being used by God as instruments for His great work of making us His habitation and showing forth His glory?

Would one not think that the Church would count this one of the chief means of grace and seek above everything to cultivate in God's children the power of an unceasing prayerfulness on behalf of the perishing world?

Would one not expect that believers, who have to some extent been brought into the secret, would feel what strength there is in unity and what assurance there is that God will certainly avenge His own elect who cry day and night to Him? It is when Christians cease from looking for help in external union and aim at all being bound together to the throne of God by an unceasing devotion to Jesus Christ and an unceasing continuance in supplication for the power of God's Spirit that the Church will put on her beautiful garments, and put on her strength too, and overcome the world.

Our gracious Father, hear our prayer and teach Thy Church and teach each of us what is the glory, what the blessing, and what the all-prevailing power of intercession. Give us, we pray Thee, the vision of what intercession means to Thee, as essential for carrying out Thy blessed purpose—what it means to ourselves as the exercise of our royal priesthood, and what it will mean to Thy Church and to those who are perishing in the bringing down of the Spirit in power—for Jesus' sake. Amen.

The Opening of the Eyes

"And Elisha prayed and said: Lord, open his eyes, that he may see. . . . And Elisha said, Lord, open the eyes of these men, that they may see" (2 Kings 6:17, 20).

How wonderfully the prayer of Elisha for his servant was answered! The young man saw the mountain full of chariots of fire and horsemen about Elisha. The heavenly host had been sent by God to protect His servant.

A second time Elisha prayed. The Syrian army had been smitten with blindness and so led into Samaria. There Elisha prayed for the opening of their eyes, and lo, they found themselves hopeless prisoners in the hand of the enemy.

We wish to use these prayers in the spiritual sphere. First of all, we wish to ask that our eyes may see the wonderful provision that God has made for His Church in the baptism with the Holy Spirit and with fire. All the powers of the heavenly world are at our disposal in the service of the heavenly Kingdom. How little the children of God live in the faith of that heavenly vision—the power of the Holy Spirit on them, with them, and in them for their own spiritual life and as their strength joyfully to witness for their Lord and His work!

But we shall find that we need that second prayer too, that God may open the eyes of those of His children who do not as yet see the power which the world and sin have upon His people. They are as yet unconscious of the feebleness that marks the Church, making it unable to do the work of winning souls for Christ and building up believers for a life of holiness and fruitfulness. Let us pray especially that God may open all eyes to see what the great and fundamental need of the Church is in intercession to bring down His blessing, that the power of the Spirit may be known unceasingly in its Divine efficacy and blessing.

Our Father, which art in heaven, Thou who art so unspeakably willing to give us the Holy Spirit in power, hear our humble prayer. Open our eyes, we pray Thee, that we may realize fully the low estate of Thy Church and people, and as fully what treasures of grace and power Thou art willing to bestow in answer to the fervent prayer of a united Church. Amen.

Man's Place in God's Plan

"The heaven, even the heavens, are the Lord's; but the earth hath
He given to the children of men" (Ps. 115:16).

God created heaven as a dwelling for Himself—perfect, glorious, and most holy. The earth He gave to man as his dwelling—everything very good, but only as a beginning with the need of being kept and cultivated. *The work God had done, man was to continue and perfect.* Think of the iron and the coal hidden away in the earth, of the steam hidden away in the water. It was left to man to discover and to use all this, as we see in the network of railways that span the world and the steamers that cover the ocean. God had created all to be thus used. He made the discovery and the use dependent on the wisdom and diligence of man. What the earth is today, with its cities and habitations, with its cornfields and orchards, it owes to man. The work God had begun and prepared was by man to be carried out in fulfillment of God's purpose. And so nature teaches us the wonderful partnership to which God calls man for the carrying out of the work of creation to its destined end.

This law holds equally good in the kingdom of grace. In this great redemption God has revealed the power of the heavenly life and the spiritual blessings of which heaven is full. *But He has entrusted to His people the work of making these blessings known and making men partakers of them.*

What diligence the children of this world show in seeking for the treasures that God has hid in the earth for their use! Shall not the children of God be equally faithful in seeking for the treasures hid in heaven, to bring them down in blessing on the world? It is by the unceasing intercession of God's people that His Kingdom will come and His will be done on earth as it is in heaven.

Ever blessed Lord, how wonderful is the place Thou hast given man in trusting him to continue the work Thou hast begun. We pray Thee, open our hearts for the great thought that, through the preaching of the Gospel and the work of intercession, Thy people are to work out Thy purpose. Lord, open our eyes—for Jesus' sake. Amen.

Intercession in the
Plan of Redemption

"O Thou that hears prayer, unto Thee shall all flesh come" (Ps. 65:2).

When God gave the world into the power of man, made in His own image, who should rule over it as a viceroy under Him, it was His plan that Adam should do nothing but with God and through God, and God Himself would do all His work in the world through Adam. Adam was in very deed to be the owner, master, and ruler of the earth. When sin entered the world, Adam's power was proved to be a terrible reality, for through him the earth with the whole race of man was brought under the curse of sin.

When God made the plan of redemption, His object was to restore man to the place from which he had fallen. God chose His servants of old who, through the power of intercession, could ask what they would, and it should be given them. When Christ became man, it was that, as man, both on earth and in heaven, He might intercede for man. And before He left the world, He imparted this right of intercession to His disciples in the seven-fold promise of the Farewell Discourse (John 15–17), that whatsoever they should ask, He would do for them. God's intense longing to bless seems in some sense to be graciously limited by His dependence on the intercession that rises from the earth. He seeks to rouse the spirit of intercession that He may be able to bestow His blessing on mankind. God regards intercession as the highest expression of His people's readiness to receive and to yield themselves wholly to the working of His almighty power.

Christians need to realize this as their true nobility and their only power with God—the right to claim and expect that God will hear prayer. It is only as God's children begin to see what intercession means in regard to God's Kingdom that they will realize how solemn their responsibility is.

Each individual believer will be led to see that God waits for him to take his part. He will feel in very truth that the highest, the most blessed, the mightiest of all human instrumentalities for the fulfillment of the petition, "as in heaven, so on earth," is the intercession that rises day and night, pleading with God for the power of Heaven to be sent down into the hearts of men. Oh that God might burn into our hearts this one thought.

Dear Father, burn into our hearts this one thought: Intercession in its omnipotent power is according to Thy will and is most certainly effectual! Amen.

God Seeks Intercessors

*"He saw that there was no man, and wondered
that there was no intercessor" (Isa. 59:16).*

From of old God had among His people intercessors to whose voice
He had listened and given deliverance. Here we read of a time of trouble
when He sought for an intercessor, but in vain. And He wondered! Think
of what that means—the amazement of God that there should be none who
loved the people enough or who had sufficient faith in His power to deliver, to intercede, on their behalf. If there had been an intercessor, He
would have given deliverance; without an intercessor, His judgments came
down (see Isa. 64:7; Ezek. 22:30–31).

Of what infinite importance is the place the intercessor holds in the
Kingdom of God! Is it not indeed a matter of wonder that God should give
men such power and yet that there are so few who know what it is to take
hold of His strength and pray down His blessing on the world?

Let us try to realize the position. When God had in His Son wrought
out the new creation and Christ had taken His place on the Throne, the
work of the extension of His Kingdom was given into the hands of men.
He ever liveth to pray; prayer is the highest exercise of His royal prerogative as Priest-King upon the throne. All that Christ was to do in heaven
was to be in fellowship with His people on earth. In His Divine condescension God has willed that the working of His Spirit shall follow the
prayer of His people. He waits for their intercession, showing the preparation of heart—where and how much of His Spirit they are ready to receive.

God rules the world and His Church through the prayers of His people.
"That God should have made the extension of His Kingdom to such a large
extent dependent on the faithfulness of His people in prayer is a stupendous mystery and yet an absolute certainty." God calls for intercessors; in
His grace He has made His work dependent on them; He waits for them.

---

*Our Father, open our eyes to see that Thou dost invite Thy children to
have a part in the extension of Thy Kingdom by their faithfulness in
prayer and intercession. Give us such an insight into the glory of this
holy calling that with our whole heart we may yield ourselves to its
blessed service. Amen.*

Christ as Intercessor

"He is able to save them to the uttermost that come unto God by Him, seeing He ever liveth to make intercession for them" (Heb. 7:25).

When God had said in Isaiah that He wondered that there was no intercessor, there followed the words: "Therefore His arm brought salvation unto Him. The Redeemer shall come to Zion" (Isa. 59:16, 20). God Himself would provide the true intercessor in Christ His Son, of whom it had already been said: "He bare the sin of many, and made intercession for the transgressors" (Isa. 53:12).

In His life on earth Christ began His work as Intercessor. Think of the high-priestly prayer on behalf of His disciples and of all who should through them believe in His Name. Think of His words to Peter, "I have prayed for thee, that thy faith fail not"—a proof of how intensely personal His intercession is. And on the Cross He spoke as intercessor: "Father, forgive them."

Now that He is seated at God's right hand, He continues, as our great High Priest, the work of intercession without ceasing. But with this difference, *that He gives His people power to take part in it.* Seven times in His farewell discourse He repeated the assurance that what they asked He would do.

The power of heaven was to be at their disposal. The grace and power of God waited for man's bidding. Through the leading of the Holy Spirit, they would know what the will of God was. They would learn in faith to pray in His Name. He would present their petition to the Father, and through His and their united intercession, the Church would be clothed with the power of the Spirit.

Blessed Redeemer, what wonderful grace that Thou callest us to share in Thy intercession! We pray Thee, arouse in Thy redeemed people a consciousness of the glory of this their calling and of all the rich blessing which Thy Church in its weakness can, through its intercession in Thy Name, bring down upon this earth. May Thy Holy Spirit work in Thy people a deep conviction of the sin of restraining prayer, of the sloth and unbelief and selfishness that is the cause of it, and of Thy loving desire to pour out the Spirit of prayer in answer to their petitions—for Thy name's sake. Amen.

47

The Intercessors God Seeks

"I have set watchmen upon Thy walls, O Jerusalem; they shall never hold their peace day nor night: ye that are the Lord's remembrancers, take ye no rest and give Him no rest" (Isa. 62:6–7).

Watchmen are ordinarily placed on the walls of a city to give notice to the rulers of coming danger. God appoints watchmen not only to warn men—often they will not hear—but also to summon Him to come to their aid whenever need or enemy may be threatening. The great mark of the intercessors is to be that they are not to hold their peace day or night, to take no rest, and to give God no rest until the deliverance comes. In faith they may count upon the assurance that God will answer their prayer.

It is of this that our Lord Jesus said: "Shall not God avenge His own elect, who cry to Him day and night?" From every land the voice is heard that the Church of Christ, under the influence of the power of the world and the earthly-mindedness it brings, is losing its influence over its members. There is but little proof of God's presence in the conversion of sinners or the holiness of His people. With the great majority of Christians there is an utter neglect of Christ's call to take a part in the extension of His Kingdom. The power of the Holy Spirit is but little experienced.

Amid all the discussions as to what can be done to interest young and old in the study of God's Word or to awaken love for the services of His house, one hears but little of the indispensable necessity of the power of the Holy Spirit in the ministry and the membership of the Church. One sees but little sign of the conviction and confession that it is owing to the lack of prayer that the workings of the Spirit are so feeble and that only by united fervent prayer a change can be brought about. If ever there was a time when God's elect should cry day and night to Him, it is now. Will you not, dear reader, offer yourself to God for this blessed work of intercession and learn to count it the highest privilege of your life to be a channel through whose prayers God's blessing can be brought down to earth?

Ever blessed Father, hear us, we pray Thee, and do Thou Thyself raise up intercessors such as Thou wouldst have. Give us, we beseech Thee, men and women to act as Thy remembrancers, taking no rest and giving Thee no rest until Thy Church again be a praise in the earth. Blessed Father, let Thy Spirit teach us how to pray. Amen.

The School of Intercession

*"Who in the days of His flesh, when He had offered up prayers
and supplications with strong crying and tears, . . . and
was heard in that He feared" (Heb. 5:7).*

Christ, as Head, is Intercessor in heaven; we, as the members of His
Body, are partners with Him on earth. Let no one imagine that it cost Christ
nothing to become an intercessor. He could not without this be our example. What do we read of Him? (Isaiah 53:10–12): "When Thou shalt make
His soul an offering for sin, He shall see His seed. . . . He shall see of the
travail of His soul. . . . I will divide Him a portion with the great, because
He hath poured out His soul unto death." Notice the thrice-repeated expression in regard to the pouring out of His soul.

The pouring out of the soul—that is the Divine meaning of intercession. Nothing less than this was needed if His sacrifice and prayer were to
have power with God. This giving of Himself over to live and die that He
might save the perishing was a revelation of the spirit that has power to
prevail with God.

If we as helpers and fellow-laborers with the Lord Jesus are to share
His power of intercession, there will need to be with us too *the travail of
soul that there was with Him, the giving up of our life and its pleasures
for the one supreme work of interceding for our fellowmen*. Intercession
must not be a passing interest; it must become an ever-growing object of
intense desire for which above everything we long and live. It is the life
of consecration and self-sacrifice that will indeed give power for intercession (Acts 15:26; 20:24; Phil. 2:17; Rev. 12:11).

The longer we study this blessed truth and think of what it means to
exercise this power for the glory of God and the salvation of men, the deeper will become our conviction that it is worth giving up everything to take
part with Christ in His work of intercession.

---

*Blessed Lord Jesus, be pleased to teach us how to unite with Thee in
calling upon God for the souls Thou hast bought. Let Thy love fill us
and all Thy saints that we may learn to plead for the power of Thy
Holy Spirit to be made known. Amen.*

The Name of Jesus: The Power of Intercession

*"Hitherto have ye asked nothing in My name. At that
day ye shall ask in My name; ask and ye shall receive,
that your joy may be full" (John 16:24, 26).*

During Christ's life upon earth, the disciples had known but little of the power of prayer. In Gethsemane, Peter and the others had utterly failed. They had no conception of what it was to ask in the name of Jesus and to receive. The Lord promised them that in that day which was coming they would be able to pray with such a power in His name that they might ask what they would, and it should be given to them.

"Hitherto nothing." "In that day ye shall ask in My name and shall receive." These two conditions are still found in the Church. With the great majority of Christians there is such a lack of knowledge of their oneness with Christ Jesus and of the Holy Spirit as the Spirit of prayer that they do not even attempt to claim the wonderful promises Christ here gives. But where God's children know what it is to abide in Christ and in vital union with Him and to yield to the Holy Spirit's teaching, they begin to learn that their intercession avails much and that God will give the power of His Spirit in answer to their prayer.

It is faith in the power of Jesus' name and in our right to use it that will give us the courage to follow on where God invites us to the holy office of intercessors. When our Lord Jesus in His farewell discourse gave His unlimited prayer promise, He sent the disciples out into the world with this consciousness: "He who sits upon the throne and who lives in my heart has promised that what I ask in His name I shall receive. *He will do it.*"

Oh, if Christians but knew what it is to yield themselves wholly and absolutely to Jesus Christ and His service, how their eyes would be opened to see that intense and unceasing prayerfulness is the essential mark of the healthy spiritual life and that the power of all-prevailing intercession will indeed be the portion of those who live only in and for their Lord!

---

*Blessed Savior, give us the grace of the Holy Spirit so to live in Thee
and with Thee and for Thee that we may boldly look to Thee for the
assurance that our prayers are heard. Amen.*

Prayer: The Work of the Spirit

*"God has sent forth the Spirit of His Son into your hearts, crying,
'Abba, Father'" (Gal. 4:6).*

We know what "Abba, Father" meant in the mouth of Christ in Gethsemane. It was the entire surrender of Himself to the very death that the holy will of God's love in redemption of sinners might be accomplished. In His prayer He was ready for any sacrifice, even to the yielding of His life. In that prayer we have revealed to us the heart of Him whose place is at the right hand of God, the wonderful power of intercession that He exercises there, and the power to pour down the Holy Spirit.

It is to breathe the very Spirit of His Son into our hearts that the Holy Spirit has been bestowed by the Father. Our Lord would have us yield ourselves as wholly to God as He did, to pray like Him that God's will of love should be done on earth at any cost. As God's love is revealed in His desire for the salvation of souls, so also the desire of Jesus was made plain when He gave Himself for them. And He now asks of His people that that same love should fill them too, so that they give themselves wholly to the work of intercession, and, at any cost, pray down God's love upon the perishing.

And lest anyone should think that this is too high and beyond our reach, *the Holy Spirit of Jesus is actually given into our hearts* that we may pray in His likeness, in His name, and in His power. It is the Christian who is wholly yielded to the leading of the Holy Spirit who will feel urged by the compulsion of a Divine love to the undivided surrender to a life of continual intercession, because he knows that it is God who is working in him.

Now we can understand how Christ could give such unlimited promises of answer to prayer to His disciples; they were first going to be filled with the Holy Spirit. Now we understand how God can give such a high place to intercession in the fulfillment of His purpose of redemption; it is the Holy Spirit who breathes God's own desire into us and enables us to intercede for souls.

Abba, Father! O grant that by Thy Holy Spirit there may be maintained in us the unceasing intercession of love for the souls for whom Christ died. Give, O give to Thy children the vision of the blessedness and the power which come to those who yield themselves to this high calling. Amen.

51

Jesus Christ: Our Example in Intercession

"He shall divide the spoil with the strong, because . . . He bare the sin of many and made intercession for the transgressors" (Isa. 53:12).

"He made intercession for the transgressors." What did that mean to Him? Think of what it cost Him to pray that prayer effectually. He had to pour out His soul as an offering for sin and to cry in Gethsemane: "Father, Thy holy will of love be done."

Think of what moved Him thus to sacrifice Himself to the very uttermost! It was His love to the Father—that His holiness might be manifest, and His love to souls—that they might be partakers of His holiness.

Think of the reward He won! As Conqueror of every enemy, He is seated at the right hand of God with the power of unlimited and assured intercession. And He would see His seed, a generation of those of the same mind with Himself, whom He could train to a share in His great work of intercession.

And what does this mean for us, when we indeed seek to pray for the transgressors? That we too yield ourselves wholly to the glory of the holiness and the love of the Father, that we too say: Thy will be done, cost what it may; that we too sacrifice ourselves, even to pouring out our soul unto death.

The Lord Jesus has in very deed taken us up into a partnership with Himself in carrying out the great work of intercession. He in heaven and we on earth must have one mind, one aim in life—that we should, from love to the Father and to the lost, consecrate our lives to intercession for God's blessing. The burning desire of Father and Son for the salvation of souls must be the burning desire of our heart too.

What an honor! What a blessedness! And what a power for us to do the work because He lives and by His Spirit pours forth His love into our hearts!

Everlasting God of love, open our eyes to the vision of the glory of Thy Son, as He ever liveth to pray. And open our eyes to the glory of that grace which enables us in His likeness also to live that we may pray for the transgressors. Father, for Jesus' sake. Amen.

God's Will and Ours

"Thy will be done" (Matt. 26:42).

It is the high prerogative of God that everything in heaven and earth is to be done according to His will and as the fulfillment of His desires. When He made man in His image it was, above all, that his desires were to be in perfect accord with the desires of God. This is the high honor of being in the likeness of God—that we are to feel and wish just as God. In human flesh man was to be the embodiment and fulfillment of God's desires.

When God created man with the power of willing and choosing what he should be, He limited Himself in the exercise of His will. And when man had fallen and yielded himself to the will of God's enemy, God in His infinite love set about the great work of winning man back to make the desires of God his own. As in God so in man, desire is the great moving power. And just as man had yielded himself to a life of desire after the things of the earth and the flesh, God had to redeem him and to educate him into a life of harmony with Himself. His one aim was that man's desire should be in perfect accord with His own.

The great step in this direction was when the Son of the Father came into this world to reproduce the Divine desires in His human nature and in His prayer to yield Himself up to the perfect fulfillment of all that God wished and willed. The Son, as Man, said in agony and blood, "Thy will be done," and made the surrender even to being forsaken of God, that the power that had deceived man might be conquered and deliverance procured. It was in the wonderful and complete harmony between the Father and the Son when the Son said, "Thy will of love be done," that the great redemption was accomplished.

And this is now the great work of appropriating that redemption that believers have to say, first of all for themselves and then in lives devoted to intercession for others: "Thy will be done in heaven as on earth." As we plead for the Church—its ministers and its missionaries, its strong Christians or its young converts—for the unsaved, whether nominally Christian or heathen, we have the privilege of knowing that we are *pleading for what God wills* and that through our prayers His will is to be done on earth as in heaven.

Our Heavenly Father, "Thy will be done in heaven as on earth." Amen.

The Blessedness of a Life of Intercession

"Ye that are the Lord's remembrancers, take ye no rest
and give Him no rest, till He make Jerusalem a
praise in the earth" (Isa. 62:6–7).

What an unspeakable grace to be allowed to deal with God in intercession for the supply of the need of others!

What a blessing, in close union with Christ, to take part in His great work as Intercessor and to mingle my prayers with His! What an honor to have power with God in heaven over souls and to obtain for them what they do not know or think!

What a privilege, as a steward of the grace of God, to bring to Him the state of the Church or of individual souls, of the ministers of the Word or His messengers away in heathendom, and plead on their behalf till He entrusts me with the answer!

What blessedness, in union with other children of God, to strive together in prayer until the victory is gained over difficulties here on earth or over the powers of darkness in high places!

It is indeed worth living for, to know that God will use me as an intercessor to receive and dispense here on earth His heavenly blessing and, above all, the power of His Holy Spirit.

This is in very deed the life of heaven, the life of the Lord Jesus Himself in His self-denying love, taking possession of me and urging me to yield myself wholly to bear the burden of souls before Him and to plead that they may live.

Too long have we thought of prayer simply as a means for the supplying of our need in life and service. May God help us to see what a place intercession takes in His Divine counsel and in His work for the Kingdom. And may our hearts indeed feel that there is no honor or blessedness on earth at all equal to the unspeakable privilege of waiting upon God and bringing down from heaven and of opening the way on earth for the blessing He delights to give!

O my Father, let Thy life indeed flow down to this earth and fill the hearts of Thy Children! As the Lord Jesus pours out His love in His unceasing intercession in heaven, let it even be thus with us also upon earth, a life of overflowing love and never ending intercession. Amen.

The Place of Prayer

"These all continued with one accord in
prayer and supplication" (Acts 1:14).

The last words which Christ spoke before He left the world give us the four great notes of His Church: "Wait for the promise of the Father." "Ye shall receive power after that the Holy Spirit is come upon you." "Ye shall be witnesses unto Me." "Both in Jerusalem and unto the uttermost parts of the earth."

United and unceasing prayer, the power of the Holy Spirit, living witnesses to the living Christ, from Jerusalem to the uttermost part of the earth—such are the marks of the true Gospel, of the true ministry, of the true Church of the New Testament.

A Church of united and unceasing prayerfulness, a ministry filled with the Holy Spirit, the members living witnesses to a living Christ with a message to every creature on earth—such was the Church that Christ founded and such the Church that went out to conquer the world.

When Christ has ascended to heaven, the disciples knew at once what their work was to be—continuing with one accord in prayer and supplication. They were to be bound together by the love and Spirit of Christ into one Body. It was this that gave them their wonderful power in heaven with God and upon earth with men.

Their own duty was to wait in united and unceasing prayer for the power of the Holy Spirit as the gift from on high for their witness to Christ to the ends of the earth. A praying Church, a Spirit-filled Church, a witnessing Church with all the world as its sphere and aim—such is the Church of Jesus Christ.

As long as it maintained this character, it had power to conquer. But alas, as it came under the influence of the world, how much it lost of its heavenly, supernatural beauty and strength! How unfaithful in prayer, how feeble the workings of the Spirit, how formal its witness to Christ, and how unfaithful to its worldwide mission!

Blessed Lord Jesus, have mercy upon Thy Church and give, we pray Thee, the Spirit of Prayer and supplication as of old, that Thy Church may prove what power from Thee rests upon her and her testimony for Thee, to win the world to Thy feet. Amen.

Paul as an Intercessor

"I bow my knees unto the Father, that He would grant you to be strengthened with might by His Spirit" (Eph. 3:14, 16).

We think of Paul as the great Missionary, the great Preacher, the great Writer, the great Apostle "in labors more abundant." We do not sufficiently think of him as the Intercessor who sought and obtained, by his supplication, the power that rested upon all his other activities and brought down the blessing that rested on the churches that he served.

We see above what he wrote to the Ephesians. Think of what he said in the first letter to the Thessalonians (3:10, 13): "Night and day praying exceedingly, that we might perfect that which is lacking in your faith, to the end He may stablish your hearts unblameable in holiness." To the Romans (1:9): "Without ceasing I make mention of you always in my prayers." To the Philippians (1:4): "Always in every prayer of mine for you all, making request with joy." And to the Colossians (1:9; 2:1): "We do not cease to pray for you. I would that ye knew what great conflict I have for you."

Day and night he cried to God in his intercession for them that the light and the power of the Holy Spirit might be in them; and as earnestly as he believed in the power of his intercession for them, did he also believe in the blessing that theirs would bring upon him. "I beseech you, that ye strive together with me in your prayers to God for me" (Rom. 15:30). "God will yet deliver us, ye also helping together by prayer for us" (2 Cor. 1:10–11). "Praying also for me, that I may open my mouth boldly" (Eph. 6:18–19; Col. 4:3; 2 Thess. 3:1). "This shall turn to my salvation through your prayer" (Phil. 1:19).

The whole relationship between pastor and people depends on the united continual prayerfulness. Their whole relationship to each other is a heavenly one, spiritual and Divine, and can only be maintained by unceasing prayer. It is when ministers and people waken up to the consciousness that the power and blessing of the Holy Spirit is waiting for their united and unceasing prayer that the Church will begin to know something of what Pentecostal Apostolic Christianity is.

Ever blessed Father, we do most humbly beseech Thee, restore again graciously to Thy Church the spirit of supplication and intercession—for Jesus' sake. Amen.

Intercession for Laborers

"The harvest truly is plenteous, but the laborers are few, pray ye therefore the Lord of the harvest, that He will send forth laborers into His harvest" (Matt. 9:37–38).

The disciples understood very little of what these words meant. Christ gave them as a seed-thought to be lodged in their hearts for later use. At Pentecost as they saw how many of the new converts were ready in the power of the Spirit to testify of Christ, they must have felt how the ten days of continuous united prayer had brought this blessing too as the fruit of the Spirit's power—laborers in the harvest.

Christ meant to teach us that however large the field may be and however few the laborers, prayer is the best, the sure, the only means for supplying the need.

What we need to understand is that it is not only in time of need that the prayer must be sent up, but that the whole work is to be carried on in the spirit of prayer so that the prayer for laborers shall be in perfect harmony with the whole of our life and effort.

In the China Inland Mission when the number of missionaries had gone up to 200, at a conference held in China they felt so deeply the need of more laborers for districts quite unprovided for. After much prayer, they felt at liberty to ask God to give them within a year 100 additional laborers and £10,000 to meet the expenses. They agreed to continue in prayer day by day throughout the year. At the end of the time the 100 suitable men and women had been found and also £11,000.

To meet the need of the world, its open fields and its waiting souls, the churches all complain of the lack of laborers and of funds. Does not Christ's voice call us to the united and unceasing prayer of the first disciples? God is faithful by the power of His Spirit to supply every need. Let the Church take the posture of united prayer and supplication. God hears prayer.

Blessed Lord Jesus, teach Thy Church what it means so to live and labor for Thee in the Spirit of unceasing prayerfulness that our faith may rise to the assurance that Thou wilt in very deed, in a way surpassing all expectation, meet the crying need of a dying world. Amen.

Intercession for Individual Souls

"Ye shall be gathered one by one, O ye children of Israel" (Isa. 27:12).

In our body every member has its appointed place. It is so too in society and in the Church. The work must always aim at the welfare and the highest perfection of the whole, through the cooperation of every individual member.

In the Church the thought is found too often that the salvation of souls is the work of the minister, whereas he generally only deals with the crowd but seldom reaches the individual. This is the cause of a twofold evil. The individual believer does not understand that it is necessary for him to testify to those close by—for the nourishment and the strengthening of one's own spiritual life and for the ingathering of souls. Unconverted souls suffer unspeakable loss because Christ is not personally brought to them by each believer they meet. The thought of intercession for those around us is all too seldom found. Its restoration to its right place in the Christian life—how much that would mean to the Church and its missions!

Oh, when will Christians learn the great truth that "what God in heaven desires to do *needs prayer on earth as its indispensable condition."* It is as we realize this that we shall see that intercession is the chief element in the conversion of souls. All our efforts are vain without the power of the Holy Spirit given in answer to prayer. It is when ministers and people unite in a covenant of prayer and testimony that the Church will flourish and that every believer will understand the part he has to take.

And what can we do to stir up the spirit of intercession? There is a twofold answer. Let every Christian, as he begins to get an insight into the need and the power of intercession, make a beginning in the exercise of it on behalf of single individuals. Pray for your children, for your relatives and friends, for all with whom God brings you into contact. If you feel that you have not the power to intercede, let the discovery humble you and drive you to the mercy-seat. God wants every redeemed child of His to intercede for the perishing. It is the vital breath of the normal Christian life—the proof that it is born from above.

Dear Father, we pray intensely and persistently that Thou wilt give the power of Thy Holy Spirit on us and Thy children around us, that the power of intercession may have the place that Thou wilt honor. Amen.

Intercession for Ministers

"And for me" (Eph. 6:19).

"Praying also for us" (Col. 4:3).

"Finally, brethren, pray for us" (2 Thess. 3:1).

These expressions of Paul suggest what the strength of his conviction must have been that the Christians had power with God and that their prayer would in very deed bring new strength to him in his work. He had such a sense of the actual unity of the Body of Christ, of the interdependence of each member—even the most honorable—on the life that flowed through the whole body, that he seeks to rouse Christians, both for their own sakes and for his sake and for the sake of the Kingdom of God, with his call: "Continue in prayer, and watch in the same with thanksgiving, withal praying also for us."

The Church depends upon the ministry to an extent that we very little realize. The place of the minister is so high, as the steward of the mysteries of God, as the ambassador for God to beseech men in Christ's name to be reconciled to Him, that unfaithfulness or inefficiency must bring a terrible blight on the Church that he serves. If Paul, after having preached for twenty years in the power of God, still needed the prayer of the Church, how much more does the ministry in our day need it?

The minister needs the prayer of his people. He has a right to it. He is in very truth dependent on it. *It is his task to train Christians for their work of intercession on behalf of the Church and the world.* He must begin with training them to pray for himself. He may have to begin still farther back and learn to pray more for himself and for them. Let all intercessors who are seeking to enter more deeply into their blessed work give a larger place to the ministry, whether of their own church or of other churches.

Let them plead with God for individuals and for special circles. Let them continue in prayer and watch therein, that ministers may be full of power, full of prayer, and full of the Holy Spirit. O brethren, pray for the ministry!

Our Father which art in heaven, we humbly pray Thee to arouse believers to a sense of their calling to pray for the ministers of the Gospel in the spirit of faith. Amen.

Prayer for All Saints

*"With all prayer and supplication praying at all seasons
in the Spirit, and watching thereunto in all perseverance
and supplication for all the saints" (Eph. 6:18 R.V.).*

Notice how Paul repeats the words in the intensity of his desire to reach the hearts of his readers. "With *all* prayer and supplication praying at *all* seasons, watching thereunto in *all* perseverance and *all* supplication." It is, "all prayer, all seasons, all perseverance, all supplication." The words claim thought, if they are to meet with the needed response.

Paul felt so deeply the unity of the Body of Christ, and he was so sure that that unity could only be realized in the exercise of love and prayer, that he pleaded with the believers at Ephesus unceasingly and fervently to pray for all saints, not only in their immediate circle, but in all the Church of Christ of whom they might hear. "Unity is strength." As we exercise this power of intercession with all perseverance, we shall be delivered from self with all its feeble prayers and lifted up to that enlargement of heart in which the love of Christ can flow freely and fully through us.

The great lack in true believers often is that in prayer they are occupied with themselves and with what God must do for them. Let us realize that we have here a call to all believers to give themselves without ceasing to the exercise of love and prayer. It is as we forget ourselves, in the faith that God will take charge of us, and yield ourselves to the great and blessed work of calling down the blessing of God on our brothers and sisters, that the whole Church will be fitted to do its work in making Christ known to every creature. This alone is the healthy and the blessed life of a child of God who is wholly yielded to Christ Jesus.

Blessed Father, we pray for Thy children and the Church around us, pray for all the work in which they are engaged, or ought to be, we pray at all seasons in the Spirit for all Thy saints. There is no blessedness greater than that of abiding communion with Thee. And there is no way that leads to the enjoyment of this more surely than the life of intercession for which these words of Paul appeal so pleadingly. Amen.

Missionary Intercession

*"When they had fasted and prayed, and laid their
hands on them, they sent them away" (Acts 13:3)*

How to multiply the number of Christians who will individually and collectively wield this force of intercession for the conversion and transformation of souls, *that is the supreme question of Foreign Missions*. Every other consideration and plan is secondary to that of wielding the forces of prayer.

That those who love this work and bear it upon their hearts will follow the Scriptural injunction to pray unceasingly for its triumph, we take for granted. To such, not only the Morning Watch and the hours of stated devotion, but all times and seasons will witness an attitude of intercession that refuses to let God go until He crowns His workers with victory.

Missions have their root in the love of Christ that was proved on the cross and now lives in our hearts. As men are so earnest in seeking to carry out God's plans for the natural world, so God's children should be at least as wholehearted in seeking to bring Christ's love to everyone. Intercession is the chief means appointed by God to bring the great redemption within the reach of all.

Pray for the missionaries, that the Christ-life may be clear and strong, that they may be people of prayer and filled with love in whom the power of the spiritual life is made manifest.

Pray for the native Christians, that they may know the glory of the mystery among the heathen, Christ in them the hope of glory.

Pray for the baptism classes and all the pupils in schools, that the teaching of God's Word may be in power. Pray especially for the native pastors and evangelists, that the Holy Spirit may fill them to be witnesses for Christ among their people.

Pray, above all, for the Church of Christ, that it may be lifted out of its indifference and that every believer may be brought to understand that the one object of his life is to help to make Christ King on the earth.

---

*Our gracious God, our eyes are unto Thee. Wilt Thou in mercy hear
our prayer and by the Holy Spirit reveal the presence and the power
of Christ in the work of Thy servants? Amen.*

The Grace of Intercession

"Continue in prayer, and watch in the same with thanksgiving, withal praying also for us" (Col. 4:2–3).

There is nothing that can bring us nearer to God and lead us deeper into His love than the work of intercession.

There is nothing that can give us a higher experience of the likeness of God than the power of pouring out our hearts into the bosom of God in prayer for those around us. There is nothing that can so closely link us to Jesus Christ, the great Intercessor, and give us the experience of His power and Spirit resting on us, as the yielding of our lives to the work of bringing the great redemption into the hearts and lives of others.

There is nothing in which we shall know more of the powerful working of the Holy Spirit than the prayer breathed by Him into our hearts, "Abba, Father," in all the fullness of meaning that it had for Christ in Gethsemane. There is nothing that can so help us to prove the power and the faithfulness of God to His Word as when we reach out in intercession to the multitudes, either in the Church of Christ or in the darkness of heathenism. As we pour out our souls as a living sacrifice before God with the one persistent plea that He shall in answer to our prayer open the windows of heaven and send down His abundant blessing, God will be glorified, our souls will reach their highest destiny, and God's Kingdom will come.

There is nothing that will so help us to understand and to experience the living unity of the Body of Christ and the irresistible power that it can exert as the daily and continued fellowship with God's children in the persistent plea that God will arise and have mercy upon Zion and make her a light and a life to those who are sitting in darkness. O my brothers and sisters, how little we realize what we are losing in not living in fervent intercession! What may we not gain for ourselves and for the world if we allow God's Spirit, as a Spirit of grace and of supplication, to master our whole being!

In heaven Christ lives to pray; His whole communion with His Father is prayer, an asking and receiving of the fullness of the Spirit for His people. God delights in nothing so much as in prayer. Shall we not learn to believe that the highest blessings of heaven will be unfolded to us as we pray more?

Blessed Father, pour down the Spirit of supplication and intercession on Thy people—for Jesus Christ's sake. Amen.

United Intercession

"There is one body, and one Spirit" (Eph. 4:4).

Our own bodies teach us how essential for their health and strength it is that every member should take its full share in seeking the welfare of the whole. It is even so in the Body of Christ. There are, alas, too many who look upon salvation only in connection with their own happiness. There are those, again, who know that they live not unto themselves and truly seek in prayer and work to bring others to share in their happiness; but they do not yet understand that in addition to their personal circle or Church, they have a calling to enlarge their hearts to take the whole Body of Christ Jesus into their love and their intercession.

Yet this is what the Spirit and the love of Christ will enable them to do. It is only when intercession *for the whole Church, by the whole Church* ascends to God's throne that the Spirit of unity and of power can have its full sway. The desire that has been awakened for closer union between the different branches of the Church of Christ is cause for thanksgiving. And yet the difficulties are so great and, in the case of different nationalities of the world, so apparently insuperable, that the thought of a united Church on earth appears beyond reach.

Let us bless God that there is a unity in Christ Jesus, deeper and stronger than any visible manifestation could make it; and that there is a way in which even now, midst all diversity of administrations, the unity can be practically exemplified and utilized as the means of an unthought-of accession of Divine strength and blessing in the work of the Kingdom. *It is in the cultivation and increase of the Spirit and in the exercise of intercession that the true unity can be realized.* As believers are taught what is the meaning of their calling as a royal priesthood, they are led to see that God is not confined in His love or promises to their limited spheres of labor, but invites them to enlarge their hearts and like Christ—we may say like Paul too—to pray for all who believe or can yet be brought to believe, that this earth and the Church of Christ in it will by intercession be bound to the throne of heaven as it has never yet been bound.

Dear Father, let us as Christians and ministers agree and bind ourselves together for this worldwide intercession. It will strengthen the confidence that prayer will be heard and that our prayers too will become indispensable for the coming of the Kingdom. Amen.

Unceasing Intercession

"Pray without ceasing" (1 Thess. 5:17).

How different is the standard of the average Christian with regard to a life in the service of God from that which Scripture gives us. In the former the chief thought is personal safety—grace to pardon our sin and to live such a life as may secure our entrance into heaven. How high above this is the Bible standard—a Christian's time and thought and love wholly yielded to the glorious God who has redeemed him and whom he now delights in serving, in whose fellowship is heaven begun.

To the former, the command, "Pray without ceasing," is simply a needless and impossible life of perfection. Who can do it? We can get to heaven without it. To the true believer, on the contrary, it holds out the promise of the highest happiness, of a life crowned by all the blessings that can be brought down on souls through his intercession. And as he perseveres, it becomes increasingly his highest aim upon earth, his highest joy, his highest experience of the wonderful fellowship with the holy God.

"Pray without ceasing." Let us take that word in a large faith, as a promise of what God's Spirit will work in us. How close and intimate our union and likeness to the Lord Jesus can be in His ever blessed intercession at the right hand of God. Let it become to us one of the chief elements of our heavenly calling, to be consciously the stewards and administrators of God's grace to the world around us. As we think of how Christ said, "I in them, and Thou in Me," let us believe that just as the Father worked in Him, so Christ *the interceding High Priest will work and pray in us.* As the faith of our high calling fills our hearts, we shall begin literally to feel that there is nothing on earth for one moment to be compared with the privilege of being God's priests, walking without intermission in His holy presence, bringing the burden of the souls around us to the footstool of His throne, and receiving at His hands the power and blessing to dispense to others.

Dear Lord Jesus, as we learn to "pray without ceasing," we will indeed fulfill the word of old, "Man created in the likeness and the image of God." Amen.

Intercession: The Link Between Heaven and Earth

"Thy will be done, as in heaven, so on earth" (Luke 11:2).

When God created heaven and earth, He meant heaven to be the Divine pattern to which earth was to be conformed; "as in heaven, so on earth," was to be the law of its existence.

The word calls us to think of what constitutes the glory of heaven. God is all in all there. Everything lives in Him and to His glory. And as we then think of what this earth has now become with all its sin and misery, with the great majority of the race without any knowledge of the true God and the remainder nominally Christians yet for the greater part utterly indifferent to His claims and estranged from His holiness and love, we feel what a revolution, what a miracle is needed if the word is to be fulfilled: "As in heaven, so on earth."

And how is this ever to come true? *Through the prayers of God's children. Our Lord teaches us to pray for it. Intercession is to be the great link between heaven and earth.* The intercession of the Son begun upon earth, continued in heaven, and carried on by His redeemed people upon earth, will bring about the mighty change: "As in heaven, so on earth." As Christ said, "I come to do Thy will, O God," until He prayed the great prayer in Gethsemane, "Thy will be done"; so His redeemed ones, who yield themselves fully to His mind and Spirit, make His prayer their own and unceasingly send up the cry, "Thy will be done, as in heaven, so on earth."

Every prayer of a parent for a child, of a believer for the saving of the lost, or for more grace to those who have been saved is part of the great unceasing cry going up day and night from this earth, "As in heaven, so on earth."

But it is when God's children not only learn to pray for their immediate circles and interests but enlarge their hearts to take in the whole Church and the whole world, that their united supplication will have power with God and hasten the day when it shall indeed be, "As in heaven so on earth"—the whole earth filled with the glory of God. Child of God, will you not yield yourself, like Christ, to live with this one prayer: "Father, Thy will be done on earth as in heaven"?

Our Father, which art in heaven, Hallowed be Thy Name, Thy Kingdom come, Thy will be done—as in heaven, so on earth. Amen.

The Fulfillment of God's Desires

"The Lord hath desired Zion for His habitation. Here will I dwell; for I have desired it" (Ps. 132:13–14).

Here you have the one great desire of God that moved Him in the work of redemption. His heart longed for man, to dwell with him and in him.

To Moses He said: "Let them make Me a sanctuary; that I may dwell among them." And just as Israel had to prepare the dwelling for God, even so His children are now called to yield themselves for God to dwell in them and to win others to become His habitation. As the desire of God toward us fills our hearts, it will waken within us the desire to gather others around us to become His dwelling too.

What an honor! What a high calling, to count my worldly business as entirely secondary and to find my life and my delight in winning souls in whom God may find His heart's delight! "Here will I dwell; for I have desired it."

And this is what I can above all do through intercession. I can pray to God for those around me, to give them His Holy Spirit. It is God's great plan that man himself shall build Him a habitation. It is in answer to the unceasing intercession of His children that God will give His power and blessing. As this great desire of God fills us, we shall give ourselves wholly to labor for its fulfillment.

Think of David, when he thought of God's desire to dwell in Israel, how he said: "I will not give sleep to my eyes, nor slumber to mine eyelids, until I find out a place for the Lord, an habitation for the mighty God of Jacob." And shall not we, to whom it has been revealed what that indwelling of God may be, give our lives for the fulfillment of His heart's desire?

Oh, let us begin as never before to pray for our children, for the souls around us, and for all the world. And we pray not only because we love them, but especially because God longs for them and gives us the honor of being the channels through whom His blessing is brought down. Children of God, awake to the realization of what it means that God is seeking to train you as intercessors through whom the great desire of His loving heart can be satisfied!

O God who hast said of human hearts, "Here will I dwell for I have desired it," teach us, we pray Thee, to pray day and night that the desire of Thy heart may be fulfilled. Amen.

The Fulfillment of Man's Desire

*"Delight thyself in the Lord; and He shall give
thee the desires of thine heart" (Ps. 37:4).*

God is love, an ever-flowing fountain out of which streams the unceasing desire to make His creatures the partakers of all the holiness and the blessedness there is in Himself. This desire for the salvation of souls is in very deed God's perfect will, His highest glory.

This loving desire of God, to get His place in the heart of men, He imparts to all His children who are willing to yield themselves wholly to Him. It is in this that the likeness and image of God consist—to have a heart in which His love takes complete possession and leads us to find spontaneously our highest joy in loving as He does.

It is thus that our text finds its fulfillment: "Delight thyself in the Lord," and in His life of love, "and He will give thee the desires of thine heart." Count upon it that the intercession of love, rising up to heaven, will be met with the fulfillment of the desire of our heart. We may be sure that, as we delight in what God delights in, such prayer is inspired by God and will have its answer. And our prayer becomes unceasingly, "Thy desires, O my Father, are mine. Thy holy will of love is my will too."

In fellowship with Him we gain courage and confidence that our prayers for the persons or the circles in which we are interested will be heard. As we reach out in yearning love, we shall get the power to take hold of the will of God to bless and to believe that God will work out His own blessed will in giving us the desire of our hearts, because the fulfillment of His desire has been the delight of our souls.

We then become, in the highest sense of the word, God's fellow-laborers. Our prayer becomes part of God's Divine work of reaching and saving the lost. And we learn to find our happiness in losing ourselves in the salvation of those around us.

Our Father, teach us that nothing less than delighting ourselves in Thee and in Thy desires toward men can inspire us to pray aright and give us the assurance of an answer. Amen.

My Great Desire

"One thing have I desired of the Lord, that will I seek after; that I may dwell in the house of the Lord all the days of my life, to behold the beauty of the Lord, and to inquire in His temple" (Ps. 27:4).

Here we have man's response to God's desire to dwell in us. When the desire of God toward us begins to rule the life and heart, our desire is fixed on one thing and that is to dwell in the house of the Lord all the days of our life, to behold the beauty of the Lord, to worship Him in the beauty of holiness. And then to inquire in His temple and to learn what it means that God has said: "I the Lord have spoken it, and will do it. And I will yet for this be inquired of by the house of Israel to do it for them."

The more we realize the desire of God's love to give His rest in the heart and the more our desire is thus quickened to dwell every day in His temple and behold His beauty, the more the Spirit of intercession will grow upon us to claim all that in His New Covenant God has promised. Whether we think of our Church and country, of our home and school, of our nearer or wider circle; whether we think of the saved and all their needs or the unsaved and their danger, the thought that God is indeed longing to find His home and His rest in the hearts of men, if He is only "inquired of," will rouse our whole being to strive for Zion's sake not to hold our peace. All the thoughts of our feebleness and unworthiness will be swallowed up in the wonderful assurance that He has said of human hearts: "This is my rest forever; here will I dwell; for I have desired it."

As our faith sees how high our calling is, how indispensable God has made fervent, intense, persistent prayer as the condition of His purpose being fulfilled, we shall be drawn to give up our life to a closer walk with God, to an unceasing waiting upon Him, and to a testimony to our brethren of what God will do in them and in us.

Is it not wonderful beyond all thought, this Divine partnership in which God commits the fulfillment of His desires to our keeping? Shame upon us that we have so little realized it!

Our Father in heaven, we beseech Thee, give, give in power, the Spirit of grace and supplication to Thy people—for Jesus' sake. Amen.

Intercession Day and Night

*"Shall not God avenge His own elect, which cry day and
night unto Him, though He bear long with them?" (Luke 18:7).*

When Nehemiah heard of the destruction of Jerusalem, he cried to God: "Hear the prayer of Thy servant which I pray before Thy face day and night." Of the watchman set on the walls of Jerusalem, God said: "Which shall never hold their peace day nor night." And Paul writes (1 Thess. 3:10, 13, R.V.): "Night and day praying exceedingly, to the end He may stablish your hearts unblameable in holiness before our God and Father."

Is such prayer night and day really needed and really possible? Most assuredly, when the heart is first so entirely possessed by the desire that it cannot rest until this is fulfilled. The life has so come under the power of the heavenly blessing that nothing can keep it from sacrificing all to obtain it.

When a child of God begins to get a real vision into the need of the Church and of the world, a vision of the Divine redemption which God has promised in the outpouring of His love into our hearts, a vision of the power of true intercession to bring down the heavenly blessing, a vision of the honor of being allowed as intercessors to take part in that work, it comes as a matter of course that he regards the work as the most heavenly thing upon earth—as intercessor to cry day and night to God for the revelation of His mighty power.

Let us learn from David who said: "The zeal of Thine house hath consumed me"; from Christ our Lord of whom these words were so intensely true, that there is nothing so much worth living for as this one thought—how to satisfy the heart of God in His longing for human fellowship and affection and how to win hearts to be His dwelling-place. And shall not we too give ourselves no rest until we have found a place for the Mighty One in our hearts and yielded ourselves to the great work of intercession for so many after whom the desires of God are going out.

God grant that our hearts may be so brought under the influence of these Divine truths that we may in very deed yield ourselves to make our devotion to Christ and our longing to satisfy the heart of God the chief object of our life.

---

*Lord Jesus, the great Intercessor, who findest in it all Thy glory,
breathe, we pray Thee, of Thine own Spirit into our hearts—for Thy
Name's sake. Amen.*

The High Priest and His Intercession

"We have such an High Priest, who is able to save them to the uttermost that come unto God by Him, seeing He ever liveth to make intercession for them" (Heb. 7:25–26; 8:1).

In Israel, what a difference there was between the high priest and the priests and Levites. The high priest alone had access to the Holiest of All. He bore on his forehead the golden crown, "Holiness to the Lord," and by his intercession on the great Day of Atonement bore the sins of the people. The priests brought the daily sacrifices and stood before the Lord and came out to bless the people. The difference between high priest and priest was great. But still greater was the unity; they formed one body with the high priest, sharing with him the power to appear before God to receive and dispense His blessing to His people.

It is even so with our great High Priest. He alone has power with God, in a never-ceasing intercession, to obtain from the Father what His people need. And yet, infinite though the distance is between Him and the royal priesthood that surround Him for His service, the unity and the fellowship into which His people have been taken up with Him is no less infinite than the apparent diversity. The blessing that He obtains from His Father for us, He holds for His people to receive from Him through their fervent supplication to be dispensed to the souls among whom He has placed them as His witnesses and representatives.

As long as Christians simply think of being saved and of a life which will make that salvation secure, they never can understand the mystery of the power of intercession to which they are called.

But when once they realize that salvation means a vital life union with Jesus Christ, an actual sharing of His life dwelling and working in us, and the consecration of our whole being to live and labor, to think and will and find our highest joy in living as a royal priesthood, the Church will put on her strength and prove, in communion with God and man, how truly the likeness and the power of Christ dwell in her.

Oh that God would open our hearts to know and prove what our royal priesthood is—what the real meaning is of our living and praying in the name of Jesus, that what we ask shall indeed be given us! O Lord Jesus, our Holy High Priest, breathe the spirit of Thine own holy priesthood into our hearts. Amen.

A Royal Priesthood

*"Call unto Me, and I will answer thee, and show thee great
and mighty things which thou knowest not" (Jer. 33:3).*

As you plead for the great mercies of the new covenant to be bestowed, take with you these thoughts:

(1) The infinite willingness of God to bless. His very nature is a pledge of it. He delights in mercy. He waits to be gracious. His promises and the experience of His saints assure us of it.

(2) Why then does the blessing so often tarry? In creating man with a free will and making him a partner in the rule of the earth, God limited Himself. He made Himself dependent on what man would do. Man by his prayer would hold the measure of what God could do in blessing.

(3) Think how God is hindered and disappointed when His children do not pray or pray but little. The low, feeble life of the Church, the lack of the power of the Holy Spirit for conversion and holiness is all owing to the lack of prayer. How different would be the state of the Church and of heathendom if God's people were to take no rest in calling upon Him!

(4) And yet God has blessed, just up to the measure of the faith and the zeal of His people. It is not for them to be content with this as a sign of His approval; but rather to say, if He has thus blessed our feeble efforts and prayers, what will He not do if we yield ourselves wholly to a life of intercession?

(5) What a call to penitence and confession that our lack of consecration has kept back God's blessing from the world! He was ready to save us, but we were not willing for the sacrifice of a whole-hearted devotion to Christ and His service.

Children of God, God counts upon you to take your place before His throne as intercessors. Awake, I pray you, to the consciousness of your holy calling as a royal priesthood. In this spirit take up the word with large expectations: "Call unto Me, and I will answer thee, and show thee great and mighty things which thou knowest not."

Let each one who has read thus far say whether he is not willing to make intercession the one chief object of his life? Is this asking too much? Is it too much to yield your life for this holy service of the royal priesthood to that blessed Lord who gave Himself for us?

---

*Blessed Father, we give ourselves to this blessed calling in the power
of Jesus Christ to make intercession for Thy Church and people and
for a dying world the one chief object of our lives. Amen.*

Intercession: A Divine Reality

*"And another angel came, . . . and there was given unto him much
incense, that he should offer it with the prayers of all saints upon
the golden altar which was before the throne" (Rev. 8:3).*

Are the thoughts to which this little book has given utterance not a sufficiently grave indictment of the subordinate place given to intercession
in the teaching and practice of the Church and with its ministers and members? Is it not in very deed of such supreme importance as to make it an
essential, altogether indispensable element in the true Christian life? To
those who take God's Word in its full meaning, there can be no doubt about
the answer.

Intercession is, by amazing grace, an essential element in God's redeeming purpose—so much so that without it the failure of its accomplishment
may lie at our door. Christ's intercession in heaven is essential to His carrying out of the work He began upon earth, but He calls for the intercession of the saints in the attainment of His object. Just think of what we
read: "All things are of God, who hath reconciled us to Himself by Jesus
Christ, and hath given to us the ministry of reconciliation." As the reconciliation was dependent on Christ's doing His part, so in the accomplishment of the work, He calls on the Church to do her part. We see how Paul
regarded intercession day and night as indispensable to the fulfillment of
the work that had been entrusted to him. It is but one aspect of that mighty
power of God which works in the heart of His believing people.

Intercession is indeed a Divine reality. Without it, the Church loses one
of its chief beauties, loses the joy and the power of the Spirit life for achiev-
ing great things for God. Without it, the command to preach the Gospel to
every creature can never be carried out. Without it, there is no power for
the Church to recover from her sickly, feeble life and conquer the world.
And in the life of the believer, minister, or member, there can be no entrance into the abundant life and joy of daily fellowship with God, except
as he takes his place among God's elect—the watchmen and remembrancers of God who cry to Him day and night.

Church of Christ, awake, awake! Listen to the call, "Pray without ceasing." Take no rest, and give God no rest. Let the answer be, even though
it be with a sigh from the depths of the heart, "For Zion's sake, will I not
hold my peace." God's spirit will reveal to us the power of a life of intercession as a Divine reality, an essential and indispensable element of the
great redemption and therefore also of the true Christian life.

Dear Father, help us to know and to fulfill our calling! Amen.

True Worship

"Worship God" (Rev. 22:9).

Those who have read the section on *The Secret of Intercession* have doubtless more than once asked: "What may be the reason that prayer and intercession are not a greater joy and delight? And is there any way in which we may become fitted to make fellowship with God our chief joy and as intercessors to bring down His power and blessing on those for whom we pray?"

There may be more than one answer to the question. But the chief answer is undoubtedly: *We know God too little*. In our prayer, His presence is not waited for as the chief thing on which our heart is set. And yet it should be so. We think mostly of ourselves, our need and weakness, our desire and prayer. But we forget that in every prayer *God must be First, must be All*. To seek Him, to find Him, to tarry in His presence, to be assured *that His Holy Presence rests upon us*, that He actually listens to what we say and is working in us—it is this alone that gives the inspiration that makes prayer as natural and easy to us as is the fellowship and conversation of a child with his father.

And how is one to attain to this nearness to God and fellowship with Him? The answer is simple: *We must give God time to make Himself known to us*. Believe with all your whole heart that just as you present yourself to God as a supplicant, *so God presents Himself to you as the Hearer of prayer*. But you cannot realize this except as you give Him time and quiet. It is not the multitude or the earnestness of your words in which prayer has its power, but in the living faith that *God Himself is taking you and your prayer into His loving heart*. He Himself will give the assurance that in His time your prayer will be heard.

Blessed Father, we begin this day with the word:

"Unto Thee, O Lord, do I lift up my soul." We bow before Thee in stillness, believing that Thou wilt look on us and will reveal Thy presence.

"My soul thirsteth for God, for the living God." Amen.

God Is a Spirit

*"God is a Spirit: and they that worship Him must
worship Him in spirit and in truth" (John 4:24).*

When God created man and breathed into him of His own spirit, man
became a living soul. The soul stood midway between the spirit and the
body and had either to yield to the spirit to be lifted up to God or to the
flesh and its lusts. In the Fall, man refused to listen to the spirit and became the slave of the body. The spirit in man became utterly darkened.

In regeneration it is this spirit that is quickened and born again from
above. In the regenerate life and in the fellowship with God, it is the spirit
of man that has ever to yield itself to the Spirit of God. The spirit is the
deepest, inward part of the human being. As we read in Psalm 2: "Thou
desirest truth in the *inward parts*, and in *the hidden part* Thou shalt make
me to know wisdom"; or in Jeremiah 31: "I will put My law in *their inward parts*." It is of this also that Isaiah says: "With my soul have I desired Thee in the night; yea, *with my spirit within me* will I seek Thee early."
The soul must sink down into the depths of the hidden spirit and call upon
that to stir itself to seek God.

God is a Spirit, most holy and most glorious. He gave us a spirit with
the one object of *holding fellowship with Himself*. Through sin that power
has been darkened and well-nigh quenched. There is no way for its restoration but by presenting the soul in stillness before God for the working
of His Holy Spirit in our spirit. Deeper than our thoughts and feelings, God
will in our inward part, in our spirits within us, teach us to worship Him
in spirit and in truth.

"The Father seeketh such to worship Him." He Himself by the Holy
Spirit will teach us this if we wait upon Him. In this quiet hour, be still
before God and yield yourself with the whole heart to believe in and to
receive the gentle working of His Spirit.

---

*My Father, As I pray, my very breath becomes my prayer to Thee, "My
soul, be thou silent unto God."*

*"With my soul have I desired Thee in the night, yea, with my spirit
within me I seek Thee early."*

"On Thee, O God, do I wait." Amen.

Intercession and Adoration

"Worship the Lord in the beauty of holiness" (Ps. 96:9).

The better we know God the more wonderful becomes our insight into the power of intercession. We begin to understand that it is the great means by which man can take part in the carrying out of God's purpose. God has entrusted the whole of His redemption in Christ to His people to make known and to communicate to others. In all this, intercession is the chief and essential element, because it is in it that His servants enter into the full fellowship with Christ and receive the power of the Spirit and of Heaven as their power for service.

It is easy to see why God had so ordered it. In very deed God desires to renew us after His image and likeness. And there is no other way to do this but by our making His desires our own, so that we breathe His disposition and in love sacrifice ourselves, so that we may become in a measure even like Christ, "ever living to make intercession." Such can be the life of the consecrated believer.

The clearer the insight into this great purpose of God, the more will the need be felt to enter very truly into God's Presence in the spirit of humble worship and holy adoration. The more we thus take time to abide in God's Presence, to enter fully into His mind and will, to get our whole soul possessed by the thought of His glorious purpose, the stronger will our faith become that God will Himself work out all the good pleasure of His will through our prayers. As the glory of God shines upon us, we shall become conscious of the depths of our helplessness and so rise up into the faith that believes that God will do above all that we can ask or think.

Intercession will lead to the feeling of the need of a deeper adoration. Adoration will give new power for intercession. A true intercession and a deeper adoration will ever be found to be inseparable.

The secret of true adoration can only be known by the soul that gives time to tarry in God's presence and that yields itself to God for Him to reveal Himself.

"Oh, come let us worship and bow down, let us kneel before the Lord our Maker; for He is our God."

"Give unto the Lord the glory due unto His name."

Dear Father, it is adoration of Thee that will indeed fit us for the great work of making Thy glory known. Amen.

The Desire for God

"With my soul have I desired Thee in the night" (Isa. 26:9).

What is the chief thing, the greatest and most glorious, that one can see or find upon earth? *Nothing less than God Himself.*

And what is the chief and the best and the most glorious thing that one needs every day and can do every day? Nothing less than to seek and to know and to love and to praise this glorious God. As glorious as God is, so is the glory which begins to work in the heart and life of those who give themselves to live for God.

My brothers and sisters, have you learned what is the first and the greatest thing you have to do every day? Nothing less and nothing greater than to seek this God, to meet Him, to worship Him, to live for Him and for His glory. It is a great step in advance in the life of Christians when they truly sees this and yields themselves *to consider fellowship with God every day as the chief end of life.*

Take time and ask whether this is not the truth, the highest wisdom and the one thing for which a Christian is above all to live—*to know God aright and to love Him wholeheartedly.* Do believe that it is not only in very deed true, but that God Himself is most desirous that you should live thus with Him and will in answer to prayer enable you to do so.

Begin today and take a word from God's Book to speak to Him in stillness of soul.

"O God—Thou art my God—early will I seek Thee—my soul thirsteth for Thee—my flesh longeth for Thee—my soul followeth hard after Thee" (Ps. 63:1, 8).

"I seek Thee with my whole heart" (see Ps. 119:2).

Repeat these words in deep reverence and childlike longing till their spirit and power enter your heart; and wait upon God till you begin to realize what the blessedness is of thus meeting with Him. As you persevere you will learn to expect that the fear and the presence of God can abide with you through all the day.

Father, my prayer is: "I waited patiently for the Lord; and He inclined unto me, and heard my cry" (Ps. 40:1). Amen.

Silent Adoration

*"My soul is silent unto God . . . . My soul, be thou silent unto
God; for my expectation is from Him" (Ps. 62:1, 5).*

When we in our littleness and God in His glory meet, we all understand that what God says has infinitely more worth than what we say. And
yet our prayer so often consists in the utterance *of our thoughts* of what
we need, that we give God no time to speak to us. Our prayers are often
so indefinite and vague. It is a great lesson to learn that to be silent unto
God is the secret of true adoration. Let us remember the promise, "In qui-
etness and confidence shall be your strength."

"My soul, wait thou only upon God; for my expectation is from Him."

"I will wait for the Lord; my soul doth wait, and in His word do I hope."

It is as the soul bows itself before Him to remember His greatness and
His holiness, His power and His love and seeks to give Him the honor and
the reverence and the worship that are His due, that the heart will be opened
to receive the Divine impression of the nearness of God and of the working of His power.

O Christian, do believe that such worship of God—in which you bow
low and ever lower in your nothingness and lift up your thoughts to realize God's presence as He gives Himself to you in Christ Jesus—is the sure
way to give Him the glory that is His due and will lead to the highest blessedness to be found in prayer.

Do not imagine that it is time lost. Do not turn from it, if at first it appears difficult or fruitless. Be assured that it brings you into the right relation to God. It opens the way to fellowship with Him. It leads to the blessed
assurance that He is looking on you in tender love and working in you
with a secret but Divine power. And as at length you become more accustomed to it, it will give you the sense of His presence abiding with you all
the day. It will make you strong to testify for God. Someone has said, "No
one is able to influence others for goodness and holiness, beyond the
amount that there is of God in him." Others will begin to feel that you have
been with God.

"The Lord is in His holy temple; be silent before Him, all the earth"
(Hab. 2:20).

"Be silent, O all flesh, before the Lord: for He is raised up out of His
holy habitation" (Zech. 2:13).

---

*Dear Father, my prayer is that I may learn to be silent before Thee.
Amen.*

The Light of God's Countenance

"God is light" (1 John 1:5).

"The Lord is my light" (Ps. 27:1).

Every morning the sun rises, and we walk in its light and perform our daily duties with gladness. Whether we think of it or not, the light of the sun shines on us all day.

Every morning the light of God shines upon His children. But in order to enjoy the light of God's countenance, the soul must turn to God and trust Him to let His light shine upon it.

When there is a shipwreck at midnight, with what longing the mariners look for the morning! How often the sigh goes up, When will the day break? Even so must Christians wait upon God and rest patiently until His light shines upon them.

"My soul waiteth for the Lord more than they that watch for the morning" (Ps. 130:6).

O my soul, begin each day with one of the prayers:

"Make Thy face to shine upon Thy servant" (Ps. 31:16).

"Lord, lift Thou up the light of Thy countenance upon us" (Ps. 4:6).

"Cause Thy face to shine, and we shall be saved" (Ps. 80:3, 7, 19).

Do not rest until you know that the light of His countenance and His blessing is resting on you. Then you will experience the truth of the word: *"They walk in the light of Thy countenance, in Thy name do they rejoice all the day"* (Ps. 89:15–16).

Children of God, do believe that it is the ardent longing of your Father that you should dwell and rejoice in His light all the day. Just as you need the light of the sun each hour, so the heavenly light, the light of the countenance of the Father is indispensable. As sure as it is that we receive and enjoy the light of the sun, so confidently may we count on it that God is longing to let His light shine on us.

Even when there are clouds, we still have the sun. So in the midst of difficulties, the light of God will rest upon you without ceasing. If you are sure that the sun has risen, you count upon the light all the day. *Make sure that the light of God shines upon you in the morning*, and you can count upon that light being with you all the day.

Rest not till you have said: *"There be many that say 'Who will show us any good?' Lord, lift Thou up the light of Thy countenance upon us.* Take time, take time, till that light shines in your heart.

Dear Father, help me to pray in the morning, "The Lord is my light and my salvation" (Ps. 27:1). Amen.

Faith in God

"Jesus said unto them: 'Have faith in God'" (Mark 11:22).

As the eye is the organ by which we see the light and rejoice in it, *so faith is the power by which we see the light of God and walk in it.*

We were made for God, in His likeness; our whole being formed after the Divine pattern. Just think of our wonderful power of thinking out all the thoughts of God hidden in nature. Think of the heart with its unlimited powers of self-sacrifice and love. We were made for God, to seek Him, to find Him, to grow up into His likeness and show forth His glory, in the fullest sense to be His dwelling. And faith is the eye which, turning away from the world and self, looks up to God and in His light sees light. To faith God reveals Himself.

How often we toil and try to waken thoughts and feelings concerning God which are but a faint shadow, and we forget "to gaze on the Incomparable Original."

Could we but realize it, in the depth of our soul God reveals Himself.

Without faith it is impossible to please God or to know Him. In our quiet time we have to pray to our Father which is in secret. There "*He hides us in the secret of His pavilion.*" And there, as we wait and worship before Him, He will in very deed, just as the light by its very nature reveals itself, let His light shine into our heart.

Let our one desire be to take time and be still before God, believing with an unbounded faith in His longing to make Himself known to us. Let us feed on God's Word to make us strong in faith. Let that faith have large thoughts of what God's glory is; of what His power is to reveal Himself to us; of what His longing love is to get complete possession of us.

"Abraham was strong in faith, giving glory to God; being fully persuaded that, what He had promised, He was able also to perform" (Rom. 4:20–21).

"I believe God, that it shall be even as it was told me" (Acts 27:25).

"Wait on the Lord: be of good courage, and He shall strengthen thine heart, wait, I say, on the Lord" (Ps. 17:14).

Dear Father, strengthen and exercise such faith in me that day by day in secret fellowship with Thee, the habit of my life becomes ever keeping the enjoyment of Thy presence and the experience of Thy saving power. Amen.

Alone with God

"And it came to pass, as He was alone praying" (Luke 9:18).

"He departed again into a mountain, Himself alone" (John 6:15).

We need God. God made us for Himself, to find our life and happiness in Himself alone.

We need to be alone with God. The Fall consisted in our being brought, through the lust of the flesh and the world, under the power of things visible and temporal. Our restoration is meant to bring us back to the Father's house, the Father's presence, the Father's love and fellowship. *Salvation means being brought to love and to delight in the presence of God.*

We need to be alone with God. Without this, God cannot have the opportunity to shine into our hearts, to transform our nature by His Divine working, to take possession and to fill us with the fullness of God.

We need to be alone with God, to yield to the presence and the power of His holiness, of His life, and of His love. Christ on earth needed it; He could not live the life of a Son here in the flesh without at times separating Himself entirely from His surroundings and being alone with God. How much more must this be indispensable to us!

When our Lord Jesus gave us the blessed command to enter our inner chamber, to shut the door, to pray to our Father in secret, all alone, He gave us the promise that the Father would hear such prayers and mightily answer them in our life before others.

Alone with God—that is the secret of true prayer; of true power in prayer; of real living, face-to-face fellowship with God; and of power for service. There is no true, deep conversion, no true, deep holiness, no clothing with the Holy Spirit and with power, no abiding peace or joy, *without being daily alone with God.* "There is no path to holiness, but in being *much and long alone with God."*

What an inestimable privilege is the institution of daily secret prayer to begin every morning. Let it be the one thing our hearts are set on, *seeking and finding and meeting God.*

Take time, O my soul, take time, to be alone with God. The time will come when you will be amazed at the thought that one could suggest that five minutes was enough.

O Heavenly Father, "Hearken unto the voice of my cry, my King and my God; for unto Thee will I pray" (Ps. 5:2).

"My voice shalt Thou hear in the morning, O Lord; in the morning will I direct my prayer unto Thee, and will look up" (Ps. 5:3). Amen.

Wholly for God

*"Whom have I in heaven but Thee? and there is none
upon earth that I desire beside Thee" (Ps. 73:25).*

Alone with God—this is a word of the deepest importance. May we seek grace from God to reach its depths. Then shall we learn that there is another word of equally deep significance—*Wholly for God.*

As we find that it is not easy to persevere in this being *"Alone with God,"* we begin to realize that it is because the other is lacking: we are not *"Wholly for God."* Because He is the Only God and He alone the Adorable One, God has a right to demand *that He should have us wholly for Himself.* Without this surrender He cannot make His power known. We read in the Old Testament that His servants, Abraham, Moses, Elijah, and David, gave themselves wholly and unreservedly to God so that He could work out His plans through them. It is only the fully surrendered heart that can fully trust God for all He has promised.

Nature teaches us that if anyone desires to do a great work, he must give wholly to it. This law is especially true of the love of a mother for her child. She gives herself wholly to the little one whom she loves. And shall we not think it reasonable that the great God of Love should have us wholly for Himself? And shall we not take the watchword, "Wholly for God," as the keynote for our devotions every morning as we rise? *As wholly as God gives Himself to us, so wholly He desires that we give ourselves to Him.*

Let us in the inner chamber meditate on these things alone with God and with earnest desire ask Him by His almighty power to work in us all that is pleasing in His sight.

Wholly for God! What a privilege. What wonderful grace to fit us for it. Wholly for God! What separation from people and work and all that might draw us away. Wholly for God! What ineffable blessedness as the soul learns what it means and what God gives with it.

"Thou shalt love the Lord thy God with all thine heart, and with all thy soul, and with all thy mind" (Deut. 6:5; Matt. 22:37).

"They sought Him with their whole desire, and He was found of them" (2 Chron. 15:15).

Dear Father, my prayer continually is, "With my whole heart have I sought Thee" (Ps. 119:10). Amen.

The Knowledge of God

"This is life eternal, that they might know Thee" (John 17:3).

The knowledge of God is absolutely necessary for the spiritual life. *It is life eternal.* Not the intellectual knowledge we receive from others or through our own power of thought, but the living, experimental knowledge *in which God makes Himself known to the soul.* Just as the rays of the sun on a cold winter's day warm the body, imparting its heat to us, *so the living God sheds the life-giving rays of His holiness and love into the heart that waits on Him.*

How is it we so seldom experience this life-giving power of the true knowledge of God? *Because we do not give God time enough to reveal Himself to us.* When we pray, we think we know well enough how to speak to God. And we forget that one of the very first things in prayer is to be silent before God, that He may reveal Himself. By His hidden but mighty power, God will manifest His presence, resting on us and working in us. To know God in the personal experience of His presence and love is life indeed.

You have heard of Brother Lawrence. He had a great longing to know God and for this purpose went into a monastery. His spiritual advisers gave him Prayer Books to use, but he put them aside. It helps little to pray, he said, *if I do not know the God to whom I pray.* And he believed that God would reveal Himself. He remained a long time in silent adoration in order to come under the full impression of the presence of this great and holy Being. He continued in this practice, until later he lived consciously and constantly in God's presence and experienced His blessed nearness and keeping power. As the sun rising each morning is the pledge of light through the day, so the quiet time waiting upon God, to yield ourselves for Him to shine on us, will be the pledge of His presence and His power resting with us all the day. See that you be sure that the sun has risen upon your soul.

Learn this great lesson that the sun each day proclaims: As the sun on a cold day shines on us and imparts its warmth, *believe that the living God will work in you with His love and His almighty power.* God will reveal Himself as life and light and joy and strength to the soul that waits upon Him.

"Lord, lift Thou up the light of Thy countenance upon us" (Ps. 4:6).
"Be still, and know that I am God" (Ps. 46:10).

Blessed Lord Jesus, reveal Thyself as life and light and joy and strength as I wait upon Thee. Amen.

God the Father

*"Baptizing in the name of the Father, and of the
Son, and of the Holy Spirit" (Matt. 28:19).*

It is well we should remember that the doctrine of the Holy Trinity has a deep devotional aspect. As we think of God, we remember the inconceivable distance that separates Him in His holiness from all sinners, and we bow in deep contrition and holy fear. As we think of Christ the Son, we remember the inconceivable nearness in which He came to be born of a woman, a daughter of Adam, and to die the accursed death and so to be inseparably joined to us to all eternity. And as we think of the Holy Spirit, we remember the inconceivable blessedness of God having His abode in us and making us His home and His temple through eternity.

When Christ taught us to say, "Our Father, which art in heaven," He immediately added, "Hallowed be Thy Name." As God is holy, so we are to be holy too. And there is no way of becoming holy but by counting that name most holy and drawing nigh to Him in prayer.

How often we speak that name without any sense of the unspeakable privilege of our relation to God. If we would just take time to come into contact with God and to worship Him in His Father love, how the inner chamber would become to us the gate of heaven.

Child of God, if you pray to your Father in secret, bow very low before Him and seek to adore His name as most holy. Remember that this is the highest blessedness of prayer.

"Pray to thy Father who is in secret; and thy Father who seeth in secret shall reward thee openly" (Matt. 6:6).

What an unspeakable privilege, to be alone with God in secret and say, "My Father." To have the assurance that He has indeed seen me in secret and will reward me openly, take time until you can say:

"I have seen God face to face, and my life is preserved" (Gen. 32:30).

Heavenly Father, I bow low before Thee. I adore Thy holy name. Amen.

God the Son

*"Grace to you and peace from God our Father
and the Lord Jesus Christ" (Rom. 1:7).*

It is remarkable that the Apostle Paul in each of his thirteen Epistles writes: "Grace to you, and peace, from God our Father, *and the Lord Jesus Christ*." He had such a deep sense of the inseparable oneness of the Father and the Son in the work of grace that in each opening benediction he refers to both.

This is a lesson for us of the utmost importance. There may be times in the Christian life when one thinks chiefly of God the Father and prays to Him. But later on we realize that it may cause spiritual loss if we do not grasp the truth that each day and each hour it is only through faith in Christ and *in living union with Him* that we can enjoy a full and abiding fellowship with God.

Remember what we read of the Lamb in the midst of the throne. John had seen One sitting on a throne. "And the four living creatures rest not day and night, saying, Holy, holy, holy, Lord God Almighty, which was, and is, and is to come" (Rev. 4:3, 8).

Later (Rev. 5:6) he sees "in the midst of the throne a Lamb as it had been slain." Of all the worshiping multitude, none could see God who did not first see Christ the Lamb of God. And none could see Christ without seeing the glory of God, the Father and Son inseparably One.

O Christian, if you would know and worship God aright, seek Him and worship Him *in Christ*. And if you seek Christ, seek Him and worship Him *in God*. Then you will understand what it is to have "your life *hid with Christ in God*," and you will experience that the fellowship and adoration of Christ is indispensable to the full knowledge of the love and holiness of God.

Be still, O soul, and speak these words in deepest reverence: "Grace and peace"—all I can desire—*"from God the Father and the Lord Jesus Christ."*

Take time to meditate and believe, to expect all from God the Father who sits upon the throne and from the Lord Jesus Christ, the Lamb in the midst of the throne. Then you will learn truly to worship God.

Dear Lord and Father, I give "Glory to Him that sitteth upon the throne, and to the Lamb" (Rev. 5:13). Amen.

God the Holy Spirit

"Through Him we both have access by one
Spirit unto the Father" (Eph. 2:18).

In our communion with God in the inner chamber, we must guard against the danger of seeking to know God and Christ in the power of the intellect or the emotions. *The Holy Spirit has been given for the express purpose that "by Him we may have access to the Father through the Son."* Let us beware lest our labor be in vain because we do not wait for the teaching of the Spirit.

Christ taught His disciples this truth in the last night. Speaking of the coming of the Comforter, He says: "In that day ye shall ask the Father in My name; ask, and ye shall receive, that your joy may be full." Hold fast the truth that the Holy Spirit was given with *the one great object of teaching us to pray.* He makes the fellowship with the Father and the Son a blessed reality. Be strong in the faith that He is working secretly in you. As you enter the inner chamber, give yourself wholly to His guidance as your Teacher in all your intercession and adoration.

When Christ said to the disciples on the evening of the resurrection day, "Receive ye the Holy Spirit," it was, for one thing, to strengthen and fit them for the ten days of prayer and their receiving the fullness of the Spirit. This suggests to us three things we ought to remember when we draw nigh to God in prayer:

First—We must pray in the confidence that the Holy Spirit dwells in us and yield ourselves, in stillness of soul, definitely to His leading. Take time for this.

Second—We must believe that the "greater works" of the Spirit for the enlightening and strengthening of the spiritual life—the fullness of the Spirit—will be given in answer to prayer.

Third—We must believe that through the Spirit, in unity with all God's children, we may ask and expect the mighty workings of that Spirit on His Church and people.

"He that believeth on Me, as the Scripture hath said, out of his belly shall flow rivers of living water" (John 7:38).

"Believest thou this?"

Dear Lord Jesus, may rivers of living water flow through me. Amen.

The Secret of the Lord

*"Enter into thy closet, and when thou hast shut thy door,
pray to thy Father which is in secret; and thy Father which
seeth in secret shall reward thee openly" (Matt. 6:6).*

Christ longed greatly that His disciples should know God as their Father and that they should have secret fellowship with Him. In His own life He found it not only indispensable but the highest happiness to meet the Father in secret. And He would have us realize that it is impossible to be true, wholehearted disciples *without daily communion with the Father in heaven* who waits for us in secret.

God is a God who hides Himself from the world and all that is of the world. God would draw us away from the world and from ourselves. He offers us, instead, the blessedness of close, intimate communion with Himself. Oh that God's children would understand this!

Believers in the Old Testament enjoyed this experience. *"Thou art my hiding-place." "He that dwelleth in the secret place of the most High shall abide under the shadow of the Almighty." "The secret of the Lord is with them that fear Him."*

How much more ought Christians in the New Covenant to value this secret communion with God. We read: "Ye are dead, and your life is *hid with Christ in God.*" If we really believe this, we shall have the joyful assurance that our life, hid with Christ in God in such Divine keeping, is safe and beyond the reach of every foe. We should day by day confidently seek the renewal of our spiritual life in prayer to our Father who is in secret.

Because we are dead with Christ, planted with Him in the likeness of His death and of His resurrection, we know that as the roots of a tree are hidden under the earth, so the roots of our daily life are hidden deep in God.

O soul, take time to realize:

"Thou shalt hide me in the secret of Thy presence" (Ps. 31:20).

"In the secret of His tabernacle shall He hide me" (Ps. 27:5).

Dear Father, impress on my heart as I pray, "I am alone with Thee and Thou art with me." Amen.

Half an Hour
Silence in Heaven

*"And there was silence in heaven about the space of half an
hour. And another angel came and stood at the altar; and
there was given unto him much incense that he should offer
it with the prayers of all saints upon the golden altar. And the
smoke of the incense, which came with the prayers of the
saints, ascended up before God" (Rev. 8:1, 3–4).*

There was silence in heaven about the space of half an hour—to bring
the prayers of the saints before God before the first angel sounded his trum-
pet. And so ten thousands of God's children have felt the absolute need of
silence and retirement from the things of earth for half an hour—to present
their prayers before God and in fellowship with Him be strengthened for
their daily work.

How often the complaint is heard that there is no time for prayer. And
often the confession is made that even if time could be found, one feels
unable to spend the time in real communion with God. No one needs ask
what it is that hinders growth in the spiritual life. *The secret of strength
can only be found in living communion with God.*

O my brothers and sisters, if you would only obey Christ when He says:
"When thou hast shut thy door, pray to thy Father which is in secret," and
have the courage to be alone with God for half an hour. Do not think: I
will not know how to spend the time. Just believe that if you begin and
are faithful and bow in silence before God, He will reveal Himself to you.

If you need help, read some passage of Scripture and let God's Word
speak to you. Then bow in deepest humility before God and wait on Him.
He will work within you. Read Psalm 61, 62, or 63 and speak the words
out before God. Then begin to pray. Intercede for your own household and
children, for the congregation, for the Church and minister, for schools and
missions. Keep on, though the time may seem long. God will reward you.
But above all, be sure you meet God.

Brothers and sisters, God longs to bless you. Is it not worth the trouble
to take half an hour alone with God? In heaven itself there was need for half
an hour's silence to present the prayers of the saints before God. If you persevere, you may find that the half-hour that seems the most difficult in the
whole day may at length become the most blessed in your whole life.

*Father, I believe the half an hour's silence before Thee each day is
the secret of living communion with you.
"My soul is silent unto God."
"My soul, be thou silent unto God; for my expectation is from Him"
(Ps. 62:1, 5). Amen.*

God's Greatness

"Thou art great, and doest wondrous things;
Thou art God alone" (Ps. 86:10).

When we commence an important work, we take time and give our attention to consider the greatness of the undertaking. Scientists, in studying nature, require years of labor to grasp the magnitude of, for instance, the sun and the heavenly bodies.

And is not our glorious God worthy that we should take time rightly to know and adore His greatness.

Yet how superficial is our knowledge of God's greatness. We do not allow ourselves time to bow before Him and so come under the deep impression of His incomprehensible majesty and glory.

Meditate on the following texts until you are filled with some sense of what a glorious Being God is.

"Great is the Lord, and greatly to be praised, and His greatness is unsearchable." "I will declare Thy greatness." "They shall abundantly utter the memory of Thy great goodness" (Ps. 145:3, 6–7).

Do not imagine that it is easy to grasp the meaning of these words. Take time for them to master the heart until you bow, it may be, in speechless adoration before God.

"Ah, Lord God, there is nothing too hard for Thee, the Great, the Mighty God, Great in counsel and Mighty in work" (Jer. 32:17–19).

And hear God's answer (v. 27): "Behold, I am the Lord, the God of all flesh; is there anything too hard for Me?"

The right comprehension of God's greatness will take time. But if we give God the honor that is His due and if our faith grows strong in the knowledge of what a great and powerful God we have, we shall be drawn to tarry in the inner chamber to bow in humble worship before this great and mighty God.

Blessed Father, in Thy abundant mercy Thou wilt teach us through the Holy Spirit to say:

"The Lord is a great God; Oh come, let us worship and bow down; let us kneel before the Lord our Maker" (Ps. 95:3, 6).

"The Lord is a great God, and a great King above all gods" (Ps. 95:3). Amen.

A Perfect Heart

*"For the eyes of the Lord run to and fro throughout
the whole earth, to show Himself strong in behalf of them
whose heart is perfect toward Him" (2 Chron. 16:9).*

In worldly matters we know how important it is that work should be done with the whole heart. In the spiritual region this rule still holds good inexorably. God has given the commandment: "Thou shalt love the Lord thy God *with all thine heart and with all thy might*" (Deut. 6:5). And in Jeremiah 29:13, "Ye shall seek Me, and find Me, when ye shall search for Me *with all your heart.*"

It is amazing that earnest Christians, who attend to their daily work with all their hearts, are so content to take things easy in the service of God. They do not realize that if anywhere, they should give themselves to God's service with all the power of their will.

In the words of our text we get an insight into the absolute necessity of seeking God with a perfect heart. *"The eyes of the Lord run to and fro throughout the whole earth, to show Himself strong* in behalf of them whose heart is perfect toward Him."

What an encouragement this should be to us to humbly wait upon God with an upright heart; we may be assured that His eye will be upon us and will show forth His mighty power in us and in our work.

O Christian, have you learned this lesson in your worship of God—to yield yourself each morning with your whole heart to do God's will? Pray each prayer with a perfect heart, in true whole-hearted devotion to Him; and then in faith expect the power of God to work in you and through you.

Dear Father, as I am silent before Thee, I realize that Thou art indeed working in secret in my heart.

"I wait for my God" (Ps. 69:3).

"In the secret of His tabernacle shall He hide me" (Ps. 27:5). Amen.

The Omnipotence of God

"I am the Almighty God" (Gen. 17:1).

When Abraham heard these words, he fell on his face; and God spoke to him and filled his heart with the faith in what God would do for him. O Christian, have you bowed in deep humility before God until you felt that you were in living contact with the Almighty, until your heart has been filled with the faith that the Almighty God is working in you and will perfect His work in you?

Read in the Psalms how the saints of old gloried in God and in His strength.

"I will love Thee, O Lord, my strength" (Ps. 18:1).

"God is the strength of my heart" (Ps. 73:26).

"The Lord is the strength of my life" (Ps. 27:1).

"Thou strengthenedst me with strength in my soul" (Ps. 138:3).

(See Ps. 18:32; 46:1; 59:17; 68:28, 35; 89:17.)

Take time to appropriate these words and to adore God as the Almighty One, your strength.

Christ taught us that salvation is the work of God and quite impossible to us. When the disciples asked, "Who then can be saved?" His answer was, "With men this is impossible, but with God all things are possible." If we firmly believe this, we shall have courage to believe that God is working in us all that is well-pleasing in His sight.

Think how Paul prays for the Ephesians that through the enlightening of the Spirit they might know "the exceeding greatness of His power to us-ward who believe, according to the working of His mighty power." And (Col. 1:11) "Strengthened with all might, according to His glorious power." When we fully believe that the mighty power of God is working without ceasing within us, we can joyfully say, "God is the strength of my life."

Do you wonder that many Christians complain of weakness and shortcomings? They do not understand that the Almighty God must work in them every hour of the day. That is the secret of the true life of faith.

Dear Heavenly Father, I will not rest until I can say, "I will love Thee, O Lord, my strength." Take complete possession of me, and I will be able to say with all God's people, "Thou art the glory of their strength." Amen.

The Fear of God

"Blessed is the man that feareth the Lord, that delighteth greatly in His commandments" (Ps. 112:1; 128:1, 4).

The fear of God—these words characterize the religion of the Old Testament and the foundation which it laid for the more abundant life of the New. "The gift of holy fear" is ever still the great desire of the child of God and an essential part of a life that is to make a real impression on the world around. It is one of the great promises of the new covenant in Jeremiah: "I will make an everlasting covenant with them; *and I will put, My fear in their hearts, that they shall not depart from Me."*

We find the perfect combination of the two in the Acts (9:31).

"The churches had peace, being edified, and walking in the fear of the Lord, and in the comfort of the Holy Spirit, were multiplied." And Paul more than once gives fear a high place in the Christian life. "Work out your own salvation with fear and trembling, for it is God that worketh in you." "Perfecting holiness in the fear of God" (2 Cor. 7:1).

It has often been said that the lack of the fear of God is one of the things in which our modern times cannot compare favorably with the times of the Puritans and the Covenanters. No wonder then that there is so much cause of complaint in regard to the reading of God's Word, of the worship of His House, and the absence of that spirit of continuous prayer which marked the early Church. We need texts like the one at the head of this reading expounded, and the young converts fully instructed in the need and the blessedness of a deep fear of God leading to an unceasing prayerfulness as one of the essential elements of the life of faith.

Let us in the inner chamber earnestly cultivate this grace. Let us hear the word coming out of the very heavens:

"Who shall not fear Thee, O Lord, and glorify Thy name? for Thou only art holy."

"Let us have grace whereby we may serve God acceptably with reverence and godly fear."

As we take the word, *"Blessed is the man that feareth the Lord,"* into our hearts and believe that here is one of the deepest secrets of blessedness, we shall seek in every approach to God, in His fear to worship toward His holy temple.

"Serve the Lord with fear, and rejoice with trembling."

Blessed Heavenly Father, in fear and trembling I worship toward Thy holy temple. Amen.

God Incomprehensible

*"Behold, God is great, and we know Him not. The
Almighty, we cannot find Him out: He is excellent
in power" (Job 36:26; 37:23).*

This attribute of God as a Spirit whose being and glory are entirely beyond our power of apprehension is one that we ponder all too little. And
yet in the spiritual life it is of the utmost importance to feel deeply that, as
the heavens are high above the earth, so God's thoughts and ways are infinitely exalted beyond all our thought.

With what deep humility and holy reverence it becomes us to look up
to God and then with childlike simplicity to yield ourselves to the teaching of His Holy Spirit.

*"Oh the depth of the riches both of the wisdom and knowledge of God!
How unsearchable are His judgments and His ways past finding out"* (Rom.
11:33).

Let our hearts respond, "O Lord, O God of gods, how wonderful art
Thou in all Thy thoughts, and Thy purposes how deep." The study of what
God is, ought ever to fill us with holy awe and the sacred longing to know
and honor Him aright.

Just think—

His Greatness .... Incomprehensible.

His Might .... Incomprehensible.

His Omnipresence . Incomprehensible.

His Wisdom .... Incomprehensible.

His Holiness .... Incomprehensible.

His Mercy .... Incomprehensible.

His Love .... Incomprehensible.

As we worship, let us cry out: What an inconceivable glory is in this
Great Being who is my God and Father! Confess with shame how little
you have sought to know Him aright or to wait upon Him to reveal Himself.

"Mine eyes are unto Thee, O God the Lord; in Thee is my trust" (Ps.
141:8).

"Be still, and know that I am God" (Ps. 46:10).

*Incomprehensible, All-Glorious God and Blessed Father, I thank Thee
that in a way passing all understand Thou art working in my heart
and life to give me in ever-growing measure the ability to know Thee
aright. Amen.*

The Holiness of God (O.T.)

"Be holy, for I am holy." "I am the Lord, that made you holy"
(Lev. 11:45; 19:2; 20:7–8; 21:8, 15, 23; 22:9, 16).

Nine times these words are repeated in Leviticus. Israel had to learn that as holiness is the highest and most glorious attribute of God, so it must be the marked characteristic of His people. He that would know God aright and meet Him in secret, must above all desire to be holy as He is holy. The Priests, who were to have access to God, had to be set apart for a life of holiness.

Even so also, the prophet who was to speak for Him (Isa. 6). Listen. "I saw the Lord sitting upon a throne, high and lifted up. And the seraphs cried one unto another: *'Holy holy, holy is the Lord of Hosts.'"* The voice of adoration; bow in deep reverence.

"Then said I: *'Woe is me, for I am undone; for mine eyes have seen the King, the Lord of Hosts.'"* The voice of a broken, contrite heart.

Then one of the seraphim touched his mouth with a live coal from off the altar, and said; *'Lo, thine iniquity is taken from thee, and thy sin is purged.'"* The voice of grace and full redemption.

Then follows the voice of God: *"Whom shall I send?"* And the willing answer is, *"Here am I, send me."* Pause with holy fear and ask God to reveal Himself as the Holy One.

"Thus saith the high and lofty One, that inhabiteth eternity, whose name is Holy: 'I dwell in the high and holy place, with him also that is of a contrite and humble spirit'" (Isa. 57:15).

Be still, and take time and worship God in His great glory and in that deep condescension in which He longs and offers to dwell with us and in us.

Child of God, if you would meet your Father in secret, bow low and worship Him in the glory of His holiness. Give Him time to make Himself known to you.

It is indeed an unspeakable grace to know God as the Holy One.

"Ye shall be holy: for I the Lord your God am holy."
"Holy, holy, holy is the Lord of Hosts."
"Worship the Lord in the beauty of holiness."

Dear Father, "Let the beauty of the Lord our God be upon us" (Ps. 90:17). Amen.

The Holiness of God (N.T.)

"Holy Father, keep through Thine own name those whom Thou hast given Me. Sanctify them. For their sakes I sanctify Myself, that they also might be sanctified through the truth" (John 17:11, 17, 19).

Christ ever liveth to pray this great prayer. Expect and appropriate God's answer.

Hear the words of St. Paul in 1 Thessalonians:

"Night and day praying exceedingly that the Lord may establish your hearts unblameable in holiness before God" (3:10–13).

"The very God of peace sanctify you wholly" (5:23).

"Who also will do it" (5:24).

Ponder deeply these words as you read them and use them as a prayer to God: "Blessed Lord, strengthen my heart to be unblameable in holiness. God Himself sanctify me wholly. God is faithful, who also will do it."

What a privilege to commune with God in secret, to speak these words in prayer, and then to wait upon Him until through the working of the Spirit, they live in our hearts, and we begin to know something of the holiness of God.

"Unto the church of God which is at Corinth, to them that are sanctified in Christ Jesus, called to be saints" (1 Cor. 1:2).

God's holiness has been revealed in the Old Testament. In the New, we find the holiness of God's people in Christ through the sanctification of the Spirit. Oh that we understood the blessedness of saying:

"Be ye holy, for I am holy."

"With you, O my children, as with Me, holiness should be the chief thing." For this purpose the Thrice Holy One has revealed Himself to us through the Son and the Holy Spirit. Let us use the word "holy"' with great reverence of God and then, with holy desire for ourselves. Worship the God who says:

"I am the Lord which hallow you."

Lord Jesus, as I bow before Thee in holy fear and strong desire and in the fullness of faith, I listen to the prayer promise:

"God Himself sanctify you wholly. Who also will do it." Amen.

Sin

*"The chief of sinners." "And the grace of our Lord
was exceeding abundant with faith and love
which is in Christ Jesus" (1 Thess. 1:14–15).*

Never forget for a moment, as you enter the secret chamber, that your whole relation to God depends on what you think of sin and of yourself as a redeemed sinner.

It is sin that makes God's holiness so awful. It is sin that makes God's holiness so glorious, because He has said: "Be ye holy. I am holy. I am the Lord which makes you holy" (Lev. 20:7–8).

It is sin that called forth the wonderful love of God in not sparing His Son. It was sin that nailed Jesus to the cross and revealed the depth and the power of the love with which He loved. Through all eternity in the glory of heaven, it is our being redeemed sinners that will tune our praise.

Never forget for a moment that it is sin that has led to the great transaction between you and Christ Jesus and that each day in your fellowship with God, His one aim is to deliver and keep you fully from its power and lift you up into His likeness and His infinite love.

It is the thought of sin that will keep you low at His feet and give the deep undertone to all your adoration.

It is the thought of sin, ever surrounding you and seeking to tempt you, that will give fervency to your prayer and urgency to the faith that hides itself in Christ.

It is the thought of sin that makes Christ so unspeakably precious, that keeps you every moment dependent on His grace and gives you the claim to be more than conqueror through Him that loved us.

It is the thought of sin that calls to us to thank God with the broken and contrite heart which God will not despise, that works in us that contrite and humble spirit in which He delights to dwell.

It is in the inner chamber in secret with the Father that sin can be conquered, the holiness of Christ can be imparted, and the Spirit of holiness take possession of our lives.

It is in the inner chamber that we shall learn to know and experience fully the Divine power of the precious words of promise.

**Thank you, Lord, for the promises: "The blood of Jesus Christ
cleanseth us from all sin." "He that abideth in Him sinneth not" (1
John 1:7; 3:6). Amen.**

The Mercy of God

"Oh, give thanks unto the Lord; for He is good:
for His mercy endureth forever" (Ps. 136:1).

This Psalm is wholly devoted to the praise of God's mercy. In each of the twenty-six verses we have the expression:

"His mercy endureth forever." The Psalmist was full of this glad thought. Our hearts too should be filled with the blessed assurance. The everlasting, unchangeable mercy of God is cause for unceasing praise and thanksgiving.

Let us read what is said about God's mercy in the well-known Psalm 103.

"Bless the Lord, O my soul: who crowneth thee with loving-kindness and tender mercies" (v. 4).

Of all God's other attributes, mercy is the crown. May it be a crown upon my head and in my life!

"The Lord is merciful and gracious, and plenteous in mercy" (v. 8). As wonderful as God's greatness is, so infinite is His mercy.

"As the heaven is high above the earth, so great is His mercy toward them that fear Him" (v. 11).

What a thought! *As high as the heaven is above the earth*, so immeasurably and inconceivably great is the mercy of God waiting to bestow His richest blessing.

"The mercy of the Lord is from everlasting to everlasting upon them that fear Him" (v. 17). Here again the Psalmist speaks of God's boundless lovingkindness and mercy.

O my soul, how frequently we have read these familiar words without the least thought of their immeasurable greatness! Be still and meditate until the heart responds in the words of Psalm 36:

"Thy mercy, O Lord, is in the heavens."

"How excellent is Thy loving-kindness, O God! therefore the children of men put their trust under the shadow of Thy wings."

"Oh, continue Thy loving-kindness unto them that know Thee."

Blessed Lord and Father, O my soul, I take time to thank Thee with great joy for the wonderful mercy with which Thou crownest my life.

"Thy loving-kindness is better than life." Amen

The Word of God

"The Word of God is quick and powerful" (Heb. 4:12).

For communion with God, His Word and Prayer are both indespensable; and in the inner chamber they should not be separated. In His Word, God speaks to me. In prayer, I speak to God.

The Word teaches me to know the God to whom I pray. It teaches me how He would have me pray. It gives me precious promises to encourage me in prayer. It often gives me wonderful answers to prayer.

The Word comes from God's heart and brings His thoughts and His love into my heart. And then the Word goes back from my heart into His great heart of love, and prayer is the means of fellowship between God's heart and mine.

The Word teaches me God's will—the will of His promises as to what He will do for me as food for my faith and also the will of His commands to which I surrender myself in loving obedience.

The more I pray, the more I feel my need of the Word and rejoice in it. The more I read God's Word, the more I have to pray about, and the more power I have in prayer. One great cause of prayerlessness is that we read God's Word too little or only superficially or in the light of human wisdom.

It is the Holy Spirit through whom the Word has been spoken who is also the Spirit of prayer. He will teach me how to receive the Word and how to approach God.

How blessed would the inner chamber be, what a power and an inspiration in our worship, if we only took God's Word as from Himself, turning it into prayer and definitely expecting an answer. It is the inner chamber, in the secret of God's presence that by the Holy Spirit God's Word will become our delight and our strength.

"God's Word in deepest reverence in our hearts and on our lips and in our lives will be a never-failing fountain of strength and blessing."

I believe that God's Word is indeed full of a quickening power that will make me strong, gladly to expect and receive great things from Thee. Above all, it will give me the daily blessed fellowship with Thee as the living God.

Heavenly Father, "Blessed is the man whose delight is in the law of the Lord; in His law doth he meditate day and night" (Ps. 1:2). Amen.

The Psalms

"How sweet are Thy words unto my taste! yea,
sweeter than honey to my mouth!" (Ps. 119:103).

This book seeks to help us to worship God. Of the sixty-six books in the Bible, the Book of Psalms is given us especially for this purpose. The other books are historical or doctrinal or practical. But the Psalms take us into the inner sanctuary of God's holy presence to enjoy the blessedness of fellowship with Him. It is a book of devotions inspired by the Holy Spirit.

Would you each morning truly meet God and worship Him in spirit and in truth, *then let your heart be filled with the Word of God in the Psalms.*

As you read the Psalms, underline the word "Lord" or "God," wherever it occurs, and also the pronouns referring to God, "I," "Thou," "He." This will help to connect the contents of the Psalm with God, who is the object of all prayer. When you have taken the trouble to mark the different names of God, you will find that more than one difficult Psalm will have light shed upon it. These underlined words will make God the central thought and lead you to a new worship of Him. Take them upon your lips and speak them out before Him. Your faith will anew be strengthened to realize how God is your strength and help in all circumstances of life.

The Psalms, as the Holy Spirit of old taught God's people to pray, will, by the power of that Spirit, teach us, too, ever to abide in God's presence.

Then take Psalm 119. Every time that the word "Lord" or "Thou" or "Thy" occurs, underline it. You will be surprised to find that each verse contains these words once or more than once. Meditate on the thought that the God who is found throughout the whole Psalm is the same God who gives us His law and will enable us to keep it.

The Psalm will soon become one of the most beloved, and you will find its prayers and its teaching concerning God's Word drawing you continually up to God in the blessed consciousness of His power and love.

Heavenly Father, "Oh, how love I Thy law! It is my meditation all the
day" (Ps. 119:97). Amen.

The Glory of God

"Unto Him be glory throughout all ages" (Eph. 3:21).

God Himself must reveal His glory to us; then alone are we able to know and glorify Him aright.

There is no more wonderful image in nature of the glory of God than we find in the starry heavens. The telescopes, which are continually made more powerful, have long proclaimed the wonders of God's universe. And by means of photography, new wonders of that glory have been revealed. A photographic plate fixed below the telescope will reveal millions of stars which could never have been seen by the eye through the best telescope. Man must step on one side and allow the glory of the heavens to reveal itself; and the stars, at first wholly invisible and at immense distances, will leave their image upon the plate.

What a lesson for the soul that longs to see the glory of God in His Word. Put aside your own efforts and thoughts. Let your heart be as a photographic plate that waits for God's glory to be revealed. The plate must be rightly prepared and clean; let your heart be prepared and purified by God's Spirit. *"Blessed are the pure in heart, for they shall see God."* The plate must be immovable; let your heart be still before God. The plate must be exposed sometimes for seven or eight hours to receive the full impression of the farthest stars; let your heart take time in silent waiting upon God, and He will reveal His glory.

If you keep silence before God and give Him time, He will put thoughts into your heart that may be of unspeakable blessing to yourself and others. He will create within you desires and dispositions that will indeed be as the rays of His glory shining in you.

Put this to the proof this morning. Offer your spirit to Him in deep humility and have faith that God will reveal Himself in His holy love. His glory will descend upon you. You will yourself feel the need of giving Him full time to do His blessed work.

"The Lord is in His holy temple; let all the earth keep silence before Him."

"My soul, wait thou only upon God; for my expectation is from Him."

"God hath shined in our hearts, to give the light of the knowledge of the glory of God in the face of Christ Jesus" (2 Cor. 4:6).

"Be still, and know that I am God."

Dearest Father, this morning I offer my spirit to Thee in deepest humility and have faith that Thou wilt reveal Thyself in Thy holy love and glory. Amen.

The Holy Trinity

"Elect according to the foreknowledge of God the Father,
through sanctification of the Spirit, unto obedience and
sprinkling of the blood of Jesus Christ" (1 Peter 1:2).

Here we have one of the texts in which the great truth of the blessed Trinity is seen to lie at the very root of our spiritual life. In this book we have spoken especially of the adoration of God the Father and the need of time, sufficient time each day, to worship Him in some of His glorious attributes. But we must remind ourselves that, for all our communion with God, the presence and the power of the Son and the Spirit are absolutely necessary.

What a field this opens for us in the inner chamber. We need time to realize how all our communion with the Father is conditioned by the active and personal presence and working of the Lord Jesus. It takes time to become fully conscious of what need I have of Him in every approach to God, what confidence I may have in the work that He is doing for me and in me, and what the holy and intimate love is in which I may count upon His presence and all-prevailing intercession. But oh to learn the lesson that it needs time and that that time will be most blessedly rewarded!

Even so too is it with the Divine and almighty power of the Holy Spirit working in the depth of my heart as the One who alone is able to reveal the Son within me. Through Him alone I have the power to know what and how to pray and, above all, how to plead the Name of Jesus and to receive the assurance that my prayer has been accepted.

Dear Christian reader, have you not felt more than once that it was as it were a mockery to speak of five minutes to be alone with God, to come under the impression of His glory? And now does not the thought of the true worship of God in Christ through the Holy Spirit make you feel more than ever that it needs time to enter into such holy alliance with God as shall keep the heart and mind all the day in His peace and presence? *It is in tarrying in the secret of God's presence that you receive grace to abide in Christ and all the day to be led by His Spirit.*

Just pause and think: "Elect according to the foreknowledge of God the Father, through sanctification of the Spirit, unto obedience and sprinkling of the blood of Jesus Christ!" What food for thought—and worship!

Father, my prayer is, "When Thou saidst, 'Seek ye My face,' my heart said unto Thee, 'Thy face, Lord, will I seek.'" Amen.

The Love of God

*"God is love; and he that dwelleth in love dwelleth
in God, and God in him" (1 John 4:16).*

The best and most wonderful word in heaven is Love. For God is Love.
And the best and most wonderful word in the inner chamber must be—
Love. For the God who meets us there is Love.

What is love? The deep desire to give itself for the beloved. Love finds
its joy in imparting all that it has to make the loved one happy. And the
heavenly Father, who offers to meet us in the inner chamber—let there be
no doubt of this in our minds—has no other object than to fill our hearts
with His love.

All the other attributes of God which have been mentioned find in this
their highest glory. The true and full blessing of the inner chamber is nothing less than a life in the abundant love of God.

Because of this, our first and chief thought in the inner chamber should
be faith in the love of God. Seek, as you set yourself to pray, to exercise
great and unbounded faith in the love of God.

Take time, O my soul, in silence to meditate on the wonderful revelation of God's love in Christ, until you are filled with the spirit of worship
and wonder and longing desire. Take time to believe the precious truth:
*"The love of God is shed abroad in our hearts by the Holy Spirit which is
given unto us."*

Let us remember with shame how little we have believed in, and sought
after, this love.

"Yea, I have loved thee with an everlasting love" (Jer. 31:3).

*"That ye, being rooted and grounded in love, may be able to compre-
hend with all saints what is the breadth, and length, and depth, and heighth;
and to know the love of Christ, which passeth knowledge" (Eph. 3:17–19).*

*"Behold what manner of love the Father hath bestowed upon us"
(1 John 2:1).*

---

*Dear Father, I am confident that my heavenly Father longs to manifest
His love to me. I am deeply convinced of the truth: He will and can do
it. Amen.*

Waiting upon God

"On Thee do I wait all the day" (Ps. 25:5).

Waiting upon God—in this expression we find one of the deepest truths of God's Word in regard to the attitude of the soul in its communion with God.

Waiting upon God. Just think—that He may reveal Himself in us; that He may teach us all His will; that He may do to us what He has promised; that in all things He may be the Infinite God.

It is the attitude of soul with which each day should begin. On awaking in the morning, in the inner chamber, in quiet meditation, in the expression in prayer of our ardent longings and desires, in the course of our daily work, in all our striving after obedience and holiness, in all our struggles against sin and self-will—in everything there should be a waiting upon God to receive what He will bestow, to see what He will do, to allow Him to be the Almighty God.

Meditate on these things, and they will help you truly to value the precious promises of God's Word.

"They that wait upon the Lord shall renew their strength; they shall mount up with wings as eagles." There we have the secret of heavenly power and joy.

"Wait on the Lord, be of good courage, and He shall strengthen thine heart; *wait, I say, on the Lord."*

"Rest in the Lord, and wait patiently for Him."

The deep root of all Scriptural theology is this: Absolute dependence on God. As we exercise this spirit, it will become more natural and blessedly possible to say:

"On thee do I wait all the day."

Dear Father, this is my prayer: "I wait for the Lord, my soul doth wait, and in His word do I hope" (Ps. 130:5).

"Rest in the Lord, and wait patiently for Him, and He shall give thee the desires of thine heart" (Ps. 37:4, 7). Amen.

The Praise of God

"Praise is comely for the upright" (Ps. 33:1).

Praise will ever be a part of Adoration. Adoration, when it has entered God's presence and had fellowship with Him, will ever lead to the praise of His name. Let praise be a part of the incense we bring before God in our quiet time.

It was when the children of Israel, at their birth as the people of God at the Red Sea, had been delivered from the power of Egypt, that in the song of Moses the joy of redemption burst forth in the song of praise:

"Who is like unto Thee, O Lord, among the gods? Who is like Thee, glorious in holiness, fearful in praises, doing wonders?"

In the Psalms we see what a large place praise ought to have in the spiritual life. There are more than sixty Psalms of praise, becoming more frequent as the Book draws to its close. See Ps. 95–101; 103–107; 111–118; 134–138; 144–150. The last five are Hallelujah psalms, with the word, *"Praise ye the Lord,"* as the beginning and the ending. And the very last repeats, *"praise Him,"* twice in every verse and ends, *"Let everything that hath breath praise the Lord."*

Let us take time to study this until our whole heart and life are one continual song of praise:

"I will bless the Lord at all times; His praise shall continually be in my mouth." "Every day will I bless Thee." "I will sing praises unto my God while I have my being."

With the coming of Christ into the world, there was a new outburst of praise in the song of the angels, the song of Mary, the song of Zechariah and the song of Simeon.

And then we find in the song of Moses and the Lamb (Rev. 15:3) the praise of God filling creation: *"Great and marvelous are Thy works, Lord God Almighty. Who shall not fear Thee, O Lord, and glorify Thy Name? for Thou only art holy";* ending (Rev. 19:1–6) with the fourfold *"Hallelujah, Amen!" "For the Lord our God, the Almighty, reigneth."*

Dear Father, in my inner chamber and my quiet time with Thee may I offer to Thee ever my heart filled with unceasing praise. Amen.

The Image of God

"And God said, 'Let us make man in our image,
after our likeness'" (Gen. 1:26).

Here we have the first thought of man—his origin and his destiny entirely Divine. God undertook the stupendous work of making a creature, who is not God, to be a perfect likeness of Him in His Divine glory. Man was to live in entire dependence on God and to receive directly and unceasingly from Himself the inflow of all that was holy and blessed in the Divine Being. God's glory, His holiness, and His love were to dwell in him and shine out through him.

When sin had done its terrible work and spoiled the image of God, the promise was given in Paradise of the seed of the woman in whom the Divine purpose would be fulfilled. "God's Son, the effulgence of His glory and the very image of His substance" (Heb. 1:3), was to become a Son of man in whom God's plan would be carried out, His image revealed in human form. The New Testament takes up the thought of Creation and speaks of those who are "foreordained to be conformed to the image of His Son"; of "the new man renewed after the image of Him that created him"; and gives the promise: "We know that when He shall be manifested, we shall be like Him; for we shall see Him as He is."

And, between the eternal purpose and its eternal realization, we have a wonderful promise in regard to the life here upon earth. *"We all, beholding the glory of the Lord, are changed into the same image, from glory to glory, as by the Spirit of the Lord"* (2 Cor. 3:18).

It was of this that Paul had said just before: "Shall not the ministration of the Spirit be glorious by reason of the glory that excelleth?" Let us take home the promise of the text as the possible and assured experience for daily life to everyone who gives Christ His place as the Glorified One. Let us keep the heart set upon the glory of that image of God in Christ in the assurance that the Spirit will change us into the same image day by day, from glory to glory. O my soul, take time to believe firmly and confidently that this promise will be made true in thy Christian life.

"Let that mind be in you, which was also in Christ Jesus." "I have given you an example, that ye should do as I have done to you."

"Lord, increase our faith."

Blessed Father who created me in Thy image, work out Thy purpose in changing me into the image of Christ Jesus by the power of Thy Holy Spirit. Amen.

The Obedience of Faith

"The Lord appeared to Abraham, and said unto him: 'I am
God Almighty: walk before Me, and be thou perfect. And
I will multiply thee exceedingly'" (Gen. 16:1–2).

In Abraham we see how God not only asks for faith and rewards faith, but also how He works faith by the gracious training that He gives. When God first called him, He at once gave the great promise, "In thee shall all the families of the earth be blessed" (Gen. 12:3). When he reached the land, God met him with the promise that the land should be his (Gen. 12:7). When Abraham returned from the battle against the kings, God again met him to renew the promise (Gen. 15:5). Before the birth of Isaac, in the words of our text, He sought to strengthen his faith (Gen. 17). And once more in the plains of Mamre, He spoke: "Is anything too hard for the Lord?" Step by step God led him until his faith was perfected for full obedience in the sacrifice of Isaac. As "by faith Abraham obeyed to go out," so by faith at the close of forty years he was able, without any promise, in fact in apparent conflict with all the promises, to obey God's will to the very uttermost.

Children of Abraham, children of God, the Father makes great demands on your faith. If you are to follow in Abraham's footsteps, you too are to forsake all to live in the land of spiritual promise with nothing but His word to depend upon, separated unto God. For this you will need a deep and clear insight that the God who is working in you is the Almighty who will work all His good pleasure. Do not think that it is a little thing and easy, to live the life of faith. It needs a life that seeks to abide in His presence all the day. Bow before God in humble worship until He speaks to you too: *"I am God Almighty: walk before Me, and be thou perfect.* And I will multiply thee exceedingly." When Abraham heard this, he "fell on his face: and God talked with him." There you have the secret birthplace of the power to trust God for everything that He promises.

So only can we go out like Abraham when we are called to a life of true consecration to God and of the obedience of faith to the very uttermost. Walk in the footsteps of Abraham. Hide deep in your heart the testimony of God's Word: *"He was strong in faith, giving glory to God; being fully persuaded, that what He had promised, He was able to perform."*

Blessed Father, teach me the power of faith and all Thou art willing to work "according to the exceeding greatness of His power in us who believe." Amen.

The Love of God

"Thou shalt love the Lord thy God with all thine heart, and with all thy soul, and with all thy might" (Deut. 6:5).

God taught Abraham what it was *to believe in God with all his heart*; he was strong in faith, giving glory to God. Moses taught Israel what the first and great commandment was: *to love God with all their heart*. This was the first commandment as the origin and fountain out of which the others naturally proceed. It has its ground in the relationship between God as the loving Creator and man made in His image as the object of that love. In the very nature of things it could never be otherwise; man finds his life, his destiny, and his happiness in nothing but just this one thing, *loving God with all the heart and all the strength*. Moses said: "The Lord has a delight in thy fathers, to love them" (Deut. 10:15); such a God was infinitely worthy of being loved. All our religion, all our faith in God and obedience to Him, our whole life is to be inspired by the one thought: *We are to love God with all our heart and all our strength.* Every day the child of God has as the first duty to live out this command.

How little Israel was able to obey the command we all knew well. But before Moses died, he was able, after speaking of the judgments God would bring upon His people for their sins, to make known the promise: *"The Lord thy God will circumcise thine heart"*—with a circumcision not made with hands, but the circumcision of Christ on the cross (Col. 2:11)—*"to love the Lord thy God with all thine heart, and with all thy soul"* (Deut. 30:6).

This blessed promise was the first indication of the New Covenant in which Jeremiah foretold of the law so written in the heart by the Holy Spirit, that they should no more depart from God but walk in His ways. But how little have Christians understood this; how easily they rest content with the thought that it is impossible.

Let us learn the double lesson. This perfect heart, loving God with all our might, is what God claims, is what God is infinitely worthy of, is what God—blessed be His Name!—*will Himself give and work in us*. Let our whole soul go out in faith to meet, to wait for, and to expect the fulfillment of the promise—to love God with the whole heart is what God Himself will work in us.

"The love of God is shed abroad in our hearts by the Holy Spirit given unto us."

Blessed Father, we thank Thee that the grace of loving God with all our hearts is most sure and blessed. Amen.

The Joyful Sound

"Blessed is the people that know the joyful sound: they walk, O Lord, in the light of Thy countenance. In Thy name do they rejoice all the day" (Ps. 89:15–16).

"Glad tidings of great joy," was what the angel calls the Gospel message. This is what is here spoken of as "the joyful sound." That blessedness consists in God's people walking in the light of God and rejoicing in His name all the day. Undisturbed fellowship, never-ending joy is their portion. Even in the Old Testament such was at times the experience of the saints. But there was no continuance; the Old Testament could not secure that. Only the New Testament can and does give it.

In every well-ordered family one finds the father delighting in his children and the children rejoicing in their father's presence. And this mark of a happy home on earth is what the Heavenly Father has promised and delights to work in His people—*walking in the light of His countenance and rejoicing in His Name all the day*. It has been promised; it has been made possible in Christ through the Holy Spirit filling the heart with the love of God. It is the heritage of all who are seeking indeed to love God with all their heart and with all their strength.

And yet how many there are of God's children who simply think it impossible and have even given up the hope, the desire for a life of rejoicing in God's presence all the day. And yet Christ promised it so definitely: "These things have I spoken unto you, that My joy may be in you, and that your joy may be fulfilled." "I will see you again, and your heart shall rejoice, and your joy no one taketh away from you."

Let us think of the Father's longing to have the perfect confidence and love of His children, of the children's need of the Father's presence every moment of the day for their happiness and strength. Let us think of the power of Christ by the Holy Spirit to maintain this life in us; and let us be content with nothing less than the blessedness of them that know the joyful sound: *"They walk in the light of Thy countenance, and rejoice in Thy Name all the day; for Thou art the glory of their strength!"*

The deeper we seek to enter into God's will for us, the stronger our faith will be that the Father can be content with nothing less than this, His child walking in the light of His countenance and rejoicing in His Name all the day; and the stronger will the assurance come that what the Father has meant for us will be wrought in us through Christ and the Holy Spirit.

Father, we hold fast the word—all the day, all the day. Amen.

The Thoughts of God

"As the heavens are higher than the earth, so are My thoughts higher than your thoughts" (Isa. 55:9).

In giving us His promises of what He will work in us, God reminds us that as high as the heavens are above the earth, so high His thoughts are above ours—altogether beyond our power of spiritual living apprehension. When He tells us that we are made in the image of God, that by grace we are actually renewed again into that image, and as we gaze upon God's glory in Christ, we are changed into the same image as by the Spirit of the Lord, this is indeed a thought higher than the heavens. When He tells Abraham of all the mighty work He was to do in him and in his seed and through him in all the nations of the earth, that again is a thought higher than the heavens—man's mind could not take it in. When God calls us to love Him with all our heart and promises to renew our hearts so that they shall love Him with all our strength, that again is a thought out of the very heights of heaven. And when the Father calls us to a life here on earth in the light of His face and rejoicing in His Name all the day, we have a gift out of the very depths of God's heart of love.

What deep reverence and humility and patience become us in waiting upon God by His Holy Spirit to impart to our hearts the life and the light that can make us feel at home with these thoughts dwelling in us. What need of daily, tender, abiding fellowship with God if we are in very deed to enter into His mind and to have His thoughts make their home in us. And what a faith especially is needed to believe that God will not only reveal the beauty and the glory of these thoughts, but will actually so mightily work in us that their Divine reality and blessing shall indeed fill our inmost being.

Just think of what Isaiah says, as quoted by Paul (1 Cor. 2:9): Things which eye saw not, and ear heard not, and which entered not into the heart of man, whatsoever things God prepared for them that love Him. But unto us God revealed them through the Spirit. When Christ promised His disciples that the Holy Spirit from the throne in heaven should dwell with them, He said that the Spirit would glorify Him, would fill us with the light and life of the heavenly world. It was that that would make Him and the purposes of God, higher than the heavens above the earth, their abiding experience.

Father in Heaven, I pray that every day the Holy Spirit will fill my heart with thoughts of Thee in all Thy heavenly power and glory. Amen.

The New Covenant
in Jeremiah 31

"I will make a new covenant with the house of Israel.
I will put My law in their inward parts, and in their
hearts will I write it" (Jer. 31:31, 33).

When God made the first covenant with Israel at Sinai, He said, "If ye will obey My voice indeed, and keep My covenant, then ye shall be a peculiar treasure unto Me from among all peoples" (Ex. 19:5). But Israel, alas, had not the power to obey. Their whole nature was carnal and sinful. In the covenant there was no provision for the grace that should make them obedient. The law only served to show them their sin.

In our text God promises to make a new covenant in which provision would be made to enable men to live a life of obedience. In this new covenant, the law was to be put in their inward parts and written in their heart, "not with ink, but *with the Spirit of the living God*," so that they could say to David: "I delight to do Thy will, O my God; yea, Thy law is within my heart." The law and delight in it would, through the Holy Spirit, take possession of the inner life with all its powers. Or, as we have it in Jer. 32:40, after God had said: "Is there anything too hard for Me?": *"I will make an everlasting covenant with them; and I will put My fear in their hearts, that they shall not depart from Me."*

In contrast with the Old Testament and its weakness which made it impossible to continue faithful, this promise ensures a continual, whole-hearted obedience as the mark of the believer who takes God at His Word and fully claims what the promise secures.

Learn the lesson that in the new covenant God's mighty power will be shown in the heart of everyone who believes the promise: *"They shall not depart from Me." "It shall be even so as it hath been spoken unto Me."* Bow in deep stillness before God and believe what He says. The measure of our experience of this power of God keeping us from departing from Him will ever be in harmony with the law: *"According to your faith be it unto you."*

We need to be at great pains to keep the contrast between the Old and the New Testament very clear. The Old had a wonderful measure of grace, but not enough for the continual abiding in the faith of obedience. That is the definite promise of the New Testament, the fruit of heart renewal and the power of the Holy Spirit leading the soul and revealing the fullness of grace to keep us "unblameable in holiness."

Lord Jesus Christ, keep us "unblameable in holiness." Amen.

The New Covenant in Ezekiel

*"I will sprinkle clean water upon you, and ye shall be clean;
from all your filthiness will I cleanse you. And I will put
My Spirit within you, and cause you to walk in My statutes,
and ye shall keep My judgment" (Ezek. 36:25–27).*

Here we have the same promise as in Jeremiah, the promise of such a heart cleansing from sin and such a gift of the Spirit in the new heart as would secure their walking in His statutes and keeping His judgments. Just as in Jeremiah God had said "I will put My law in their inward parts, and *put my fear in their hearts, that they shall not depart from Me,*" so here: *"I will cause you to walk in My Statutes, and ye shall keep My judgments."* In contrast with the old covenant in which there was no power to enable them to continue in God's law, the great mark of the new covenant would be a Divine power enabling them to walk in His Statutes and keep His judgments.

"Where sin abounded, grace did much more abound," working wholehearted allegiance and obedience. Why is this so little experienced? The answer is very simple: The promise is not believed, is not preached; its fulfillment is not expected. And yet how clearly we have it in a passage like Romans 8:1-4. There the man who had complained of the power "bringing him into captivity under the law of sin," thanks God that he is "now in Christ Jesus"; and that "the law of the Spirit of life in Christ Jesus has made him free from the law of sin and death," so that the requirement of the law is fulfilled in all who walk after the Spirit.

Once again, why are there so few who can give such testimony, and what is to be done to attain to it? Just one thing is needed—the faith in an omnipotent God who will by His wonderful power do what He has promised: *"I the Lord have spoken it, and will do it."* Oh, let us begin to believe that the promise will come true: "I will cleanse you from all your filthiness, and ye shall be clean; and will cause you to walk in My statutes, and ye shall keep them." Let us believe all that God here promises, and God will do it. To an extent beyond all power of thought, God has made His great and glorious promises dependent on our faith!

Dear Lord and Father, we know the promises will work that faith as we believe them. "According to your faith, be it unto you." Let us this very day put it to the proof we pray. Amen.

The New Covenant and Prayer

*"Call unto Me, and I will answer thee, and will shew thee great,
things, and difficult, which thou knowest not" (Jer. 33:3 R.V.).*

*"I the Lord have spoken it, and I will do it. For this
moreover will I be inquired of by the house of Israel,
to do it for them." (Ezek. 36:36–37).*

The fulfillment of the great promises of the new covenant is made dependent on prayer. In answer to the prayer of Jeremiah, God had said: "*I will put My fear in their hearts, that they shall not depart from Me.*" And to Ezekiel He had spoken: "*I will cause them to walk in My statutes, and ye shall keep My judgments.*" To us in our unbelief and our judging of the meaning of God's Word according to human thought and experience, there is no expectation of these promises being truly fulfilled. We do not believe that God means them to be literally true. We have not the faith in the mighty power of God that is waiting to make His promise true in our experience.

And God has said that without such faith, our experience will be but very partial and very limited. He has graciously pointed out the way in which such faith can be found. It is in the path of much prayer. "*Call unto Me, and I will answer thee, and show thee great things, and difficult, which thou knowest not.*" "*Moreover, I will be inquired of by the house of Israel to do it for them.*" It is when individual men and women turn to God with their whole heart to plead these promises that He will fulfill them. It is in the exercise of intense persevering prayer that faith will be strengthened to take hold of God and surrender itself to His omnipotent working. And then as one and another can testify of what God has done and will do, believers will help each other and take their place as the Church of the living God, pleading for and firmly expecting that His promises will be fulfilled in larger measure as a new enduement for the great work of preaching Christ in the fullness of His redemption to the perishing.

The state of the Church, the state of our ministers and members, our own state calls for unceasing prayer. We need to pray intensely and persistently that the need of the power of the Holy Spirit may be deeply felt and that a strong faith may be roused in the hearts of many to claim and to expect His mighty working. "*I the Lord have spoken it, and I will do it.*"

Heavenly Father, "I believe; Lord, help my unbelief." Amen.

The New Covenant in Hebrews

"For I will be merciful to their iniquities, and their sins will I remember no more" (Heb. 8:12).

Christ is called in this Epistle the Mediator of a better covenant enacted upon better promises (8:6). In Him the two parts of the covenant find their complete fulfillment. First of all, He came to atone for sin so that its power over man was destroyed and free access to God's presence and favor was secured. And with that came the fuller blessing, the new heart, freed from the power of sin, with God's Holy Spirit breathing into it the delight in God's law and the power to obey it.

These two parts of the covenant may never be separated. And yet, alas, how many there are who put their trust in Christ for the forgiveness of sin and yet never think of claiming the fullness of the promise—the new heart, cleansed from sin, with the Holy Spirit breathing in it such love and delight in God's law and such power to obey, that they have access to the full blessing of the new covenant, being God's people and knowing Him as their God.

Jesus Christ is "the Mediator of the new covenant," with the forgiveness of sin in the power of His blood and the law written in the heart in the power of His Spirit. Oh that we could understand that just as surely as the complete pardon of sin is assured, the complete fulfillment of the promises, "I will put my fear in their hearts, that *they shall not depart from Me*"; "I will cause you to walk in My statutes, *and ye shall keep them*," may be expected too.

But remember what God said to Abraham: "I am God Almighty . . . is anything too hard for the Lord?" He spoke that word to Jeremiah too in regard to the new covenant. It needs strong, whole-hearted desire for a life wholly given up to Him. It means to set aside all our preconceived opinions and in faith to believe in the mighty power of God. It means a surrender to Jesus Christ as the Mediator of the new covenant, a willingness to accept our place with Him, crucified to the world and to sin and to self; it means a readiness to follow Him at any cost. In one word, it means a simple, whole-hearted acceptance of Christ as Lord and Master, heart and life wholly His. God hath said it and will do it. *"I the Lord have spoken it, and I will perform it."*

Dear Lord Jesus, Thou art my Lord and Master, my heart and life are wholly Thine. Amen.

The Trial of Faith

"And Naaman's servants came near, and spake unto him, and said:
'My father, if the prophet had bid thee do some great thing, wouldst
thou not have done it? How much rather then, when he saith to
thee, Wash, and be clean'" (2 Kings 5:13).

In Naaman we have a striking Old Testament illustration of the place faith takes in God's dealing with us. It gives us a wonderful discovery of what faith really is. Think first of how intense the desire was for healing on Naaman's part. He would do anything, appeal to the King of Syria and the King of Israel; he would undertake a long journey and humble himself before the prophet who did not even deign to come out and see him. In this intensity of desire for blessing we have the root of a strong faith. And it is just this seeking for God and His blessing which is too much lacking in our religion.

The second mark of faith is that it has to give up all its preconceived opinion and to bow before the word of God. This was more than Naaman was willing to do, and he turned away in a rage. It was well for him that a wise and faithful servant gave him better advice. Faith is often held back by the thought how such a simple thing as to accept God's word can effect such a mighty revolution in the heart.

And then comes the third mark of faith. It submits implicitly to the word of God: "Wash, and be clean." At first all appears vain, but faith proves itself in obedience. It does it not once or twice, but seven times in the assurance that the mighty wonder will be wrought. It takes the simple word, "Wash, and be clean," and lo, it finds itself renewed as with the life of a little child, "clean, every whit." The mighty deed is done.

When God's word brings us to the promise: "*I will sprinkle clean water upon you, and ye shall be clean; from all your filthiness will I cleanse you.*" It is nothing but unbelief that holds us back. Let us believe that a simple, determined surrender of the whole will to God's promise will indeed bring the heart-cleansing we need. "There is a river, the streams whereof make glad the city of God." It flows from under the throne of God and the Lamb, through the channels of a thousand precious promises, and at each step the word is heard: "Wash, and be clean." Christ cleanses "by the washing of water with the Word." Every promise is a call: "Wash, and be clean; Wash, and be clean."

Lord Jesus, I hear Thee speak: "Ye are clean through the word that I have spoken unto you"—clean, every whit. I give Thee thanks. Amen.

Faith in Christ

"Ye believe in God, believe also in Me" (John 14:1).

In the Farewell Discourse (John 14–17), when Christ was about to leave His disciples, He taught them that they were to believe in Him with the same perfect confidence which they had reposed in God. "Ye believe in God, *believe also in Me*." "*Believe Me*, that I am in the Father." "*He that believeth on Me*, the works that I do shall he do also." Here on earth He had not been able to make Himself fully known to His disciples. But in heaven the fullness of God's power would be His; and He would, in and through His disciples, do greater things than He had ever done upon earth. This faith must fix itself first of all on the person of Christ in His union with the Father. They were to have the perfect confidence that all that God had done could now be done by Jesus too. The deity of Christ is the rock on which our faith depends. Christ as man, partaker of our nature, is in very deed true God. As the Divine power has worked in Christ even to the resurrection from the dead, so Christ can also, in His Divine omnipotence, work in us all that we need.

Dear Christians, do you not see of what deep importance it is that you take time to worship Jesus in His Divine Omnipotence as one with the Father? That will teach you to count on Him in His sufficiency to work in us all that we can desire. This faith must so possess us that every thought of Christ will be filled with the consciousness of His presence as an Almighty Redeemer, able to save and sanctify and empower us to the very uttermost.

Child of God, bow in deep humility before this blessed Lord Jesus and worship Him: my Lord and my God! Take time until you come under the full consciousness of an assured faith that as the Almighty God, Christ will work for you and in you and through you all that God desires and all that you can need. Let the Savior you have known and loved become as never before the *Mighty God*. Let Him be your confidence and your strength.

The Savior was about to leave the world. In His Farewell Charge on the last night He begins by telling them that everything would depend through their whole life on simply believing Him. By that they would even do greater things than He had ever done. And at the close of His address He repeats again: "Be of good cheer, I have overcome the world."

Dear Lord Jesus, Our one need is a direct, definite, unceasing faith in Thy mighty power working in us. Work in me today. Amen.

Christ's Life in Us

"Because I live, ye shall live also" (John 14:19).

There is a great difference in the teaching of the three first Evangelists and that of John. John was the bosom friend of Jesus. He could understand the Master better than the others and has recorded Christ's teaching of which they say nothing. This makes John 13-17 the inmost sanctuary of the New Testament. The others could speak of repentance and the pardon of sin as the first great gift of the New Testament. But of the new life which the new covenant was to bring, with the new heart in which the law had been put as a living power, they say little. It is, John records, what Christ taught about His very own life really becoming ours and our being united with Him just as He was with the Father. The other Evangelists speak of Christ as the Shepherd seeking and saving the lost. John speaks of Him as the Shepherd who so gives His life for the sheep, that His very life becomes theirs. "I came that they may have life, and may have it abundantly" (John 10:10. R.V.).

And so Christ says here, "I live, and ye shall live also." The disciples were to receive from Him not the life He then had, but the resurrection life in the power of its victory over death and of His exaltation to the right hand of God. He would from thenceforth ever dwell in them; a new, a heavenly, an eternal life—the life of Jesus Himself—should fill them. And this promise is to all who will accept it in faith.

Alas, how many there are who are content with the beginnings of the Christian life but never long to have it in its fullness, the more abundant life! They do not believe in it; they are not ready for the sacrifice implied in being wholly filled with the life of Jesus. Child of God, the message comes again to you: *"The things that are impossible with men are possible with God."* I pray you, do take time, and let Christ's wonderful promise take possession of your heart. Be content with nothing less than a full salvation, *Christ living in you, and you living in Christ.* Be assured that it is meant for everyone who will take time to listen to Christ's promises and will believe that the Almighty power of God will work in him the mighty wonder of His grace—Christ dwelling in the heart by faith.

Dear Lord Jesus, I know this message is for me as I take time to listen to Thy promises. Amen.

The Obedience of Love

"If ye keep My commandments, ye shall
abide in My love" (John 15:10).

The question is often asked: How can I come to abide in Christ always? To live wholly for Him? Such is my desire and fervent prayer. In our text the Lord gives the simple but far-reaching answer: "Keep My commandments." This is the only, the sure, the blessed way of abiding in Him. "If ye keep My commandments, ye shall abide in My love; even as I have kept My Father's commandments and abide in His love." Loving obedience is the way to the enjoyment of His love.

Notice how often the Lord speaks of this in the last night. *"If ye love Me, ye will keep* My commandments" (14:15). And then again twice over: "He that hath My commandments, *and keepeth them, he it is that loveth me*; and he that loveth Me shall be loved of My Father, and I will love him." "If a man love Me, *he will keep My words*; and My Father will love him, and we will come unto him, and make our abode with him." And so also three times in chapter 15, *"If My words abide* in you, ask whatsoever ye will, and it shall be done unto you." *"If ye keep My commandments*, ye shall abide in My love." "Ye are My friends, *if ye do the things which I command you*." Six times over the Lord connects the keeping of the commandments with loving Him and with the promise of the great blessing following on it, the indwelling of the Father and the Son in the heart. The love that keeps His commandments is the only way to abide in His love. In our whole relation to Christ, love is everything—Christ's love to us, our love to Him proved in our love to the brethren.

How little believers have accepted this teaching. How content many are with the thought that it is impossible. They do not believe that through the grace of God we can be kept from sin. They do not believe in the promise of the new covenant (Ezek. 36:27): "I will put My Spirit within you, *and cause you to walk in My statutes, and ye shall keep My judgments*." They have no conception how, to a heart fully surrendered and given over to Christ alone, He will make possible what otherwise appears beyond our reach: loving Him, keeping His commandments, abiding in His love.

The wonderful promise of the Holy Spirit as the power of Christ's life in them was the pledge that they would indeed love Him and keep His words. That was to be the great secret of abiding in Christ, of having the indwelling of Christ and of God, and of the Divine efficacy of their prayer to bring down God's blessing on all their work.

Dear Lord Jesus, in the gift of the Holy Spirit make possible what is beyond our reach, loving Thee, keeping Thy commandments, abiding in Thy love. We give Thee thanks. Amen.

The Promise of the Spirit

"If I go away, the Comforter will come unto you.
He shall glorify Me; for He shall take of Mine,
and shall declare it unto you" (John 16:7, 14).

The crucified Christ was to be glorified on the throne of heaven. And out of that glory He would send down the Holy Spirit into the hearts of His disciples to glorify Him in them. The Spirit of the crucified and glorified Christ would be their life in fellowship with Him and their power for His service. The Spirit comes to us as the Spirit of the Divine glory; as such we are to welcome Him and yield ourselves absolutely to His leading.

Yes, the Spirit that searcheth the deep things of God, that dwells in the very roots of the Divine Being, that had been with Christ through all His life and in His death upon the cross, the Spirit of the Father and the Son was to come and dwell in them and make them the conscious possessors of the presence of the glorified Christ. It was this blessed Spirit who was to be their power for a life of loving obedience, to be their Teacher and Leader in praying down from heaven the blessing that they needed. And it was in His power that they were to conquer God's enemies and carry the Gospel to the ends of the world.

It is this Spirit of God and of Christ that the Church lacks so sadly; it is this Spirit she grieves so unceasingly. It is owing to this that her work is so often feeble and fruitless. And what can be the reason of this?

The Spirit is God. He claims as God to have possession of our whole being. We have thought too much of Him as our help in the Christian life; we have not known that heart and life are to be entirely and unceasingly under His control; we are to be led by the Spirit every day and every hour. In His power our life is to be a direct and continual abiding in the love and fellowship of Jesus. No wonder that we have not believed in the great promise that, in a love that keeps the commandments, we can always abide in Christ's love. No wonder that we have not the courage to believe that Christ's mighty power will work in us and through us. No wonder that His Divine prayer-promises are beyond our reach. The Spirit that searcheth the deep things of God claims the very depths of our being, there to reveal Christ as Lord and Ruler.

The promise waits for its fulfillment in our life: *"He shall glorify Me; for He shall take of Mine, and shall declare it unto you."*

Blessed Father, we have thought of Thy Holy Spirit as a help in our lives, today we know that our hearts and lives are to be entirely and unceasingly under His control. Amen.

In Christ

*"In that day ye shall know that I am in My Father,
and ye in Me, and I in you" (John 14:20).*

Our Lord had spoken of His life in the Father: "Believe Me that I am in the Father, and the Father in Me." He and the Father were not two persons next each other; they were in each other; though on earth as man, He lived in the Father. All He did was what the Father did in Him.

This Divine life of heaven, of Christ in God and God in Christ, is the picture and the pledge of what our life in Christ is to be here upon earth. It is in the very nature of the Divine life that the Son is in the Father. Even so we must know and ever live in the faith that we are in Christ. Then we shall learn that even as the Father worked in Christ, so Christ will also work in us if we but believe that we are in Him and yield ourselves to His power.

And even as the Son waited on the Father and the Father worked through Him, so the disciples would make known to Him in prayer what they wanted done on earth, and He would do it. Their life in Him was to be the reflection of His life in the Father. *As the Father worked in Him, because He lived in the Father, so Christ would work in them as they lived in Him.*

But this would not be until the Holy Spirit came. It was for this they had to wait until they were endued with the power from on high. It was for this that they would abide in Him by daily fellowship and prayer that He might so do in them the greater works He had promised.

How little the Church understands that the secret of her power is to be found in nothing less than where Christ found it, abiding in the Father and His love. How little ministers understand to make this their one great object, daily and hourly to abide in Christ, as the only possible way of being fitted and used by Him in the great work of winning souls to Him. If anyone asks what the lost secret of the pulpit is, we have it here: "In that day"—when the Spirit fills your heart—"ye shall know that I am in My Father, and ye in Me."

Blessed Lord, we beseech Thee, teach us to surrender ourselves unreservedly to the Holy Spirit and so daily above everything to wait for His teaching, that we too may know the blessed secret, that *as Thou art in the Father and the Father worketh through Thee, so we are in Thee, and Thou workest through us.*

Gracious Lord, we beseech Thee humbly and fervently, be pleased to pour down upon all Thy children who are seeking to work for Thee such a Spirit of grace and of supplication that we may not rest until we too are filled with the Holy Spirit. Amen.

Abiding in Christ

"Abide in Me, and I in you" (John 15:4).

What our Lord had taught in John 14 of the union with Him in the likeness of His being in the Father, He seeks to enforce and illustrate by the wonderful Parable of the Branch and the Vine, and all for the sake of bringing home to the Apostles, and to all His servants in the Gospel, the absolute necessity of a life daily in full communion with Him. *"Abide in Me."*

On the one hand He points to Himself and to the Father: Just as truly and fully as I am in the Father, *so you are in Me*; and then, pointing to the vine: Just as truly as the branch is in the vine, *you are in Me*. And now, just as the Father abides in Me, and works in Me, and I work out what He works in Me; and just as truly as the branch abides in the vine, and the vine gives its life and strength to the branch, and the branch receives it and puts it forth in fruit—even so do you abide in Me, and receive My strength; and I will work with an almighty power My work in you and through you. Abide in Me!

Dear child of God, you have often meditated on this blessed passage. But do you not feel how much there is still to learn if you are to have Christ's almighty power working in you as He would wish you to have? The great need is to take time in waiting on the Lord Jesus in the power of His Spirit, until the two great truths get the complete mastery of your being. As Christ is in God—this is the testimony from heaven; as the branch is in the vine—this is the testimony of all nature. The law of heaven and the law of earth combine in calling to us: "Abide in Christ." *"He that abideth in Me, bringeth forth much fruit."* Fruit, more fruit, much fruit is what Christ seeks, is what He works, is what He will assuredly give to the soul that trusts Him.

To the feeblest of God's children Christ says: Ye are in Me. "Abide in Me. Ye shall bear much fruit." To the strongest of His messengers He still has the word, there can be nothing higher: "Abide in Me, and ye shall bear much fruit." To one and all the message comes: daily, continuous, unbroken abiding in Christ Jesus is the one condition of a life of power and of blessing. Take time and let the Holy Spirit so renew in you the secret abiding in Him that you may understand the meaning of His words: "These things have I spoken unto you that My joy might remain in you, and that your joy might be full."

Dear Father, I hear, "Believest Thou that I can do this, to keep thee abiding in My love?" "Yea, Lord"—"Fear not, only believe." Amen.

The Power of Prayer

"If ye abide in Me, and My words abide in you, ask whatsoever ye will, and it shall be done unto you" (John 15:7 R.V.).

Before our Lord went to heaven He taught His disciples two great lessons in regard to their relation to Him in the great work they had to do.

The one was that in Heaven He would have much more power than He had upon earth and that He would use that power for the salvation of men, solely through them, their word and their work.

The other was that they without Him could do nothing, but that they could count upon Him to work in them and through them and so carry out His purpose. Their first and chief work would therefore be to bring everything they wanted done to Him in prayer. In the Farewell Discourse He repeats the promise seven times: "Abide in Me, pray in My name"; you can count upon it, "you can ask what you will; it shall be done to you."

With these two truths written in their heart, He sent them out into the world. They could confidently undertake their work. The Almighty, glorified Jesus ready to do in and with and through them greater things than He Himself had ever done upon earth. The weak, helpless disciples on earth unceasingly looking up to Him in prayer with the full confidence that He would hear that prayer; the first and only condition, an unflinching confidence in the power of His promise. The chief thing in all their life and in the work of their ministry was to be the maintenance of a spirit of prayer and supplication.

Alas, how little the Church has understood and believed this! And why? Simply because believers live so little in the daily abiding in Christ that they are powerless in believing His great and precious promises. Let us learn the lesson, both for our life and work, that as the members of Christ's body, the chief thing every day must be that close abiding fellowship with Christ which ever first takes its place of deep dependence and unceasing supplication, Only then can we do our work in the full assurance that He has heard our prayer and will be faithful in doing His part in giving the power from on high as the source of strength and abundant blessing. Take time, oh, take time, ye servants of the Lord, and with your whole heart believe the word Christ has spoken. Christ asks: "Believest thou this?" Yea, Lord, I believe. "Abide in Me, Abide in My love." *"If ye abide in Me, ye shall ask what ye will, and it shall be done unto you."*

Dear Father, teach me to take time to abide, abide in Christ. Amen.

The Mystery of Love

"I pray that they may all be one; even as Thou, Father,
art in Me, and I in Thee; that they may be one, even as we
are one; I in them, and Thou in Me" (John 17:21–23).

In what Christ spoke in the last evening, He had especially pressed the thought of the disciples being in Him and abiding in Him. He had also mentioned His *being in them* but had not given such prominence to this as the first thought, their being in Him. But in His prayer as High Priest, He gives larger place to the thought of His *being in them*, just as the Father was in Him. "That they may be one, even as we are one; *I in them*, and Thou in Me, that they may be perfected into one; that the world may know that Thou didst send Me, and lovedst them, even as Thou lovedst Me."

The power to convince the world that God loved the disciples as He loved His Son could only come as believers lived out their life of having Christ in them and proving it by loving their brethren as Christ loved them. The feebleness of the Church is owing to this—that our life in Christ and His life in us is not known and not proved to the world by the living unity in which our love manifests that Christ is in us. Nothing less than this is needed: such an indwelling of Christ in the heart, such a binding together of believers because they know and see and love each other as those who together have Christ dwelling in them. As we have it in the very last words of the prayer, "I have made known Thy name, that the love wherewith Thou lovest Me may be in them, and I in them." The Divine indwelling has its chief glory in that it is the manifestation of Divine love. The Father's love to Christ is brought by Christ to us and flows out from us to our fellow believers and the world.

Christ had given (John 14:21, 23) the great promise to the loving, obedient disciple, "My Father will love him, and I will love him, and we will come and make our abode with him." It is to live this life of love to Christ and the brethren, that the Holy Spirit, in whom the Father and the Son are one, longs to live in our heart. Let nothing less than this, child of God, be what you seek, what you believe, what you claim with your whole heart and strength—the indwelling of the Lord Jesus in the "love that passeth knowledge," with which He can fill your heart. So shall the world indeed be constrained by the love God's children bear to each other to acknowledge that the word is being fulfilled, *"that the love wherewith Thou, Father, lovedst Me, may be in them, and I in them."*

Dear Father, I hear Thee ask, "Believest thou that I can do this?" I answer, "Yea, Lord." Amen.

Christ Our Righteousness

*"Justified freely by His grace through the redemption
that is in Christ Jesus" (Rom. 3:24).*

The first three Evangelists spoke of redemption as a pardon of sin or Justification. John spoke of it as a Life which Christ is to live in us or Regeneration. In Paul we find both truths in their beautiful connection and harmony.

So in Romans he first speaks of Justification, Romans 3:21–5:11. Then he goes on from 5:12 to 8:39 to speak of the Life that there is in union with Christ. In Romans 4 he tells us that we find both these things in Abraham. First, verses 3–5, "Abraham believed God, Him that *justifieth the ungodly*; his faith is reckoned for righteousness." Then, verse 17, "Abraham believed God, who *quickeneth the dead*." Just as God first of all counted to Abraham his faith as righteousness and then led him on to believe in Him as the God who can give life to the dead, even so with the believer.

Justification comes at the commencement full and complete, as the eye of faith is fixed upon Christ. But that is only the beginning. Gradually believers begin to understand that they were at the same time born again, *that they have Christ in them, and that their calling now is to abide in Christ, and let Christ abide and live and work in them.*

Most Christians strive, by holding fast their faith in justification, to stir and strengthen themselves for a life of gratitude and obedience. But they fail sadly because they do not know, do not in full faith yield themselves to Christ, to maintain His life in them. They have learned from Abraham the first lesson, to believe in God who justifies the ungodly. But they have not gone on to the second great lesson, to believe in God who quickeneth the dead and daily renews that life through Christ who lives in them and in whose life alone there is strength and fullness of blessing. The Christian life must be "from faith to faith." The grace of pardon is but the beginning; growing in grace leads on to the fuller insight and experience of what it is to be in Christ, to live in Him, and to grow up in Him in all things as the Head.

Blessed Father, lead us on to the fuller insight and experience of what it is to be in Christ. Amen.

Christ Our Life

*"Much more they which receive abundance of grace
and of the gift of righteousness, shall reign in life by
one, Jesus Christ" (Rom. 5:17).*

*"Reckon ye also yourselves to be dead unto sin, but
alive unto God in Christ Jesus" (Rom. 6:11 R.V.).*

We said that Paul teaches us now that our faith in Christ as our righteousness is to be followed by our faith in Him as our life from the dead. He asks (Rom. 6:3), "Know ye not that all we who were baptized into Christ Jesus were *baptized into His death?*" We were buried with Him and raised from the dead with Him. Just as in Adam all his children died, so all believers in Christ actually died too in Him. "Our old man was crucified with Him," with Him we were raised from the dead. And now we are to count ourselves as actually "dead to sin and alive unto God."

In very deed, just as the new life in us is an actual participation in and experience of the risen life of Christ, so our death to sin in Christ is also an actual spiritual reality. It is when, by the power of the Holy Spirit, we are enabled to see how really we were one with Christ on the cross in His death and in His resurrection, that we shall understand that in Him sin has no power over us. We present ourselves unto God "as alive from the dead."

Just as the old Adam lives in the sinner, even in the believer too who does not know of the new death in Christ which he has died, even so those who knows that they died in Christ and now are alive in Him can confidently count upon the word, "sin shall not have dominion over you," not even for a single moment. *"Reckon yourselves indeed dead to sin, and alive to God in Christ Jesus."* This is the true life of faith.

As what our Lord said about our being in Him and having Him living His life in us could only come true as the full power of the Holy Spirit is experienced, so it is here too. Paul says (Rom. 8:2), "The law of the Spirit of life in Christ Jesus hath made me free from the law of sin and death," of which he had been complaining that it had kept him in captivity. And he then adds "that the requirements of the law might be fulfilled in us who walk not after the flesh, but after the Spirit." Through the Spirit we enter into the glorious liberty of the children of God.

---

*Blessed Father, open the eyes of Thy children to see what the power is
of Christ living in them for a life of holiness and fruitfulness, when
they reckon themselves indeed dead unto sin and alive unto Thee in
Christ Jesus. Amen.*

Crucified with Christ

*"I have been crucified with Christ; yet I live; and yet
no longer I, but Christ liveth in me" (Gal. 2:20).*

As in Adam we died out of the life and the will of God into sin and corruption, so in Christ we are made partakers of a new spiritual death, a death to sin and into the will and the life of God. Such was the death Christ died; such is the death we are made partakers of in Him. To Paul this was such a reality that he was able to say: "I have been crucified with Christ; yet I live; and yet no longer I, but Christ liveth in me." The death with Christ had had such power that he no longer lived his own life; Christ lived His life in him. He had indeed died to the old nature and to sin and been raised up into the power of the living Christ dwelling in him.

It was the crucified Christ who lived in him and made him partaker of all that the cross had meant to Christ Himself. The very mind that was in Christ—His self-emptying and taking the form of a servant, His humbling Himself to become obedient unto death—these dispositions worked in him because the crucified Christ lived in him. He lives in very deed as a crucified man.

Christ's death on the cross was His highest exhibition of His holiness and victory over sin. And the believer who receives Christ is made partaker of all the power and blessing that the crucified Lord has won. As the believer learns to accept this by faith, he yields himself as now crucified to the world and dead to its pleasure and pride, its lusts and self-pleasing. He learns that the mystery of the cross, as the crucified Lord reveals its power in him, opens the entrance into the fullest fellowship with Christ and the conformity to His sufferings. And so he learns, in the full depth of its meaning, what the Word has said: "Christ crucified, the power of God and the wisdom of God." He grows into a fuller apprehension of the blessedness of daring to say: *"I am crucified with Christ, I live no more; Christ the crucified liveth in me."*

Heavenly Father, we thank Thee for the blessedness of the power of faith given by Thee that enables us to live all the day counting ourselves and yielding ourselves to Thee, as indeed dead to sin and alive to Thee in Christ Jesus. Amen.

The Faith Life

*"That life which I now live in the flesh, I live in faith,
the faith which is in the Son of God, who loved me
and gave Him self up for me" (Gal. 2:20 R.V.).*

If we ask Paul what he meant by saying that he no longer lives but that Christ lives in him, what now is his part in living that life? He gives us the answer: *"The life that I now live in the flesh is the life of faith in the Son of God, who loved me and gave Himself up for me."* His whole life, day by day and all the day, was an unceasing faith in the wonderful love that had given itself for him. Faith was the power that possessed and permeated his whole being and his every action.

Here we have the simple but full statement of what the secret of the true Christian life is. It is not faith only in certain promises of God or in certain blessings that we receive from Christ. It is a faith that has got a vision of how entirely Christ gives Himself to the soul to be, in the very deepest and fullest sense of the word, his life and all that that implies for every moment of the day. As essential as continuous breathing is to the support of our physical life is the unceasing faith in which the soul trusts Christ and counts upon Him to maintain the life of the Spirit within us. Faith ever rests on that infinite love in which Christ gave Himself wholly for us, to be ours in the deepest meaning of the word and to live His life over again in us. In virtue of His Divine omnipresence whereby He fills all things, He can be to each what He is to all, a complete and perfect Savior, an abiding Guest, in very deed taking charge and maintaining our life in us and for us, as if each of us were the only one in whom He lives. *Just as truly as the Father lived in Him and worked in Him all that He was to work out, just as truly will Christ live and work in each one of us.*

Faith, led and taught by God's Holy Spirit, gets such a confidence in the omnipotence and the omnipresence of Christ that it carries in the depth of the heart the abiding unbroken assurance all the day: He that loved me and gave Himself for me, He lives in me; He is in very deed my life and my all. *"I can do all things through Christ who strengthened me."*

Heavenly Father, reveal to us that inseparable union between Christ and us in which the consciousness of Christ's presence may become as natural to us as the consciousness of our existence. Amen.

Full Consecration

"Yea, verily, and I count all things to be loss for the excellency of the knowledge of Christ Jesus my Lord" (Phil. 3:8).

In studying the promises Jesus gave to His disciples in the last night, the question comes, What was it that made just these men fit and worthy of the high honor of being baptized with the Holy Spirit from heaven? The answer is simple. When Christ called them, they forsook all and followed Him. They denied themselves, even to the hating of their own life, and gave themselves to obey His commands. They followed Him to Calvary, and amid its suffering and death their hearts clung to Him alone. It was this that prepared them for receiving a share in His resurrection life and so becoming fitted here on earth to be filled with that Spirit, even as He received the fullness of the Spirit from the Father in glory.

Just as Jesus Christ had to sacrifice all to be wholly an offering to God, so all His people, from Abraham and Jacob and Joseph downward to His twelve disciples, have had to be those who had given up all to follow the Divine leading and lived separated unto God, before the Divine power could fulfill His purposes through them.

It was thus with Paul too. To count all things but loss for Christ was the keynote of His life, as it must be that of ours if we are to share fully in the power of His resurrection. But how little the Church understands that we have been entirely redeemed from the world, to live wholly and only for God and His love. As the merchantman who found the treasure in the field had to sell all he had to purchase it, Christ claims the whole heart and the whole life and the whole strength, if we are indeed to share with Him in the victory through the power of the Holy Spirit. The law of the kingdom is unchangeable—*all things loss for the excellency of the knowledge of Christ Jesus my Lord.*

The disciples had to spend years with Christ to be prepared for Pentecost. Christ calls us to walk every day in the closest union with Himself, to abide in Him without ceasing, and so to live as those who are not their own but wholly His. It is in this we shall find the path to the fullness of the Spirit.

Blessed Father, let our faith boldly believe that such a life is meant for us. Let our heart's fervent desire reach out after nothing less than this. Let us love Thee as Lord and Christ as our Savior with our whole heart. We shall be more than conquerors through Thee for Thou lovest us. Amen.

Entire Sanctification

"And the God of peace Himself sanctify you wholly; and may your spirit and soul and body be preserved entire, without blame at the coming of our Lord Jesus Christ. Faithful is He that calleth you, who will also do it" (1 Thess. 5:23–24. R.V.).

What a promise! One would expect to see all God's children clinging to it, claiming its fulfillment. Alas, unbelief does not know what to think of it, and but few count it their treasure and joy.

Just listen. God, the God of peace—the peace He made by the blood of the cross, the peace that passeth all understanding, keeping our hearts and thoughts in Christ Jesus—none other but Himself can and will do it. This God of peace Himself promises to sanctify us, to sanctify us wholly in Christ our sanctification, in the sanctification of the Spirit. It is God who is doing the work. It is in close, personal fellowship with God Himself that we become holy.

Ought not each of us to rejoice with exceeding joy at the prospect? But it is as if the promise is too great, and so it is repeated and amplified. *May your spirit*—the inmost part of our being, created for fellowship with God—*and your soul*, the seat of the life and all its powers—*and body*, through which sin entered, in which sin proved its power even unto death, but which has been redeemed in Christ: *spirit, soul, and body be preserved entire, without blame, at the coming of our Lord Jesus Christ.*

To prevent the possibility of any misconception, as if it is too great to be literally true, the words are added: *"Faithful is He that calleth you, who will also do it."* Yes, He hath said: "I the Lord have spoken it; and I, in Christ and through the Holy Spirit, will do it." All that He asks is that we shall come and abide in close fellowship with Himself every day. As the heat of the sun shines on the body and warms it, the fire of His holiness will burn in us and make us holy. Child of God, beware of unbelief. It dishonors God, it robs your soul of its heritage. Take refuge in the word: *"Faithful is He that calleth you, who will also do it."* Let every thought of your high and holy calling wake the response: *"Faithful is He that calleth you, who will also do it."* Yes, He will do it; and He will give me grace so to abide in His nearness that I can ever be under the cover of His perfect peace and of the holiness which He alone can give. O my soul, He will do it.

"All things are possible to him that believeth."

Blessed Lord Jesus, I believe, Lord; help my unbelief. Amen.

The Exceeding Greatness of His Power

"I cease not to make mention of you in my prayers; that the God of our Lord Jesus Christ, the Father of glory, may give unto you a spirit of wisdom and revelation; having the eyes of your heart enlightened, that ye may know what is the exceeding greatness of His power to us-ward who believe, according to that working of the strength of His might which He wrought in Christ, when He raised Him from the dead" (Eph. 1:16–20 R.V.).

Here we have again one of the great texts in regard to which faith has to be exercised—words that will make our faith large and strong and bold. Paul is writing to those who had been sealed with the Holy Spirit. And yet he felt the need of unceasing prayer for the enlightening of the Spirit, that they might know in truth what the mighty power of God was that was working in them. It was nothing less than the very same power, the working of the strength of His might, by which He raised Christ from the dead.

Christ died on the tree under the weight of the sin of the world and its curse. When He descended into the grave, it was under the weight of all that sin, and the power of that death which had apparently mastered Him. What a mighty working of the power of God, to raise that Man out of the grave to the power and the glory of His throne. And now it is that very same power, in the exceeding greatness of it toward us who believe, that by the teaching of the Holy Spirit we are to know as working in us every day of our life. The Lord who said to Abraham, "I am God Almighty, nothing is too hard for Me," comes to us with the message that what He did, not only in Abraham but in Christ Jesus, is *the pledge of what He is doing every moment in our hearts and will do effectually, if we learn to trust Him.*

It is by that Almighty power that the risen and exalted Christ can be revealed in our hearts as our life and our strength. How little believers *believe this*! Oh, let us cry to God, let us trust God for His Holy Spirit to enable us to claim nothing less every day than the exceeding greatness of this resurrection power working in us.

Blessed Father, let us very especially pray for all believers around us and throughout the Church that they may have their eyes opened to the wonderful vision of God's Almighty resurrection power working in them. And let ministers, like Paul, make this a matter of continual intercession for those among whom they labor. What a difference it would make in their ministry, the unceasing prayer for the Spirit to reveal the power that dwells and works in them. Amen.

The Indwelling Christ

"That Christ may dwell in your heart by faith" (Eph. 3:14–19).

The great privilege that separated Israel from other nations was this: they had God dwelling in their midst, His Home in the Holiest of all, in the tabernacle and the temple. The New Testament is the dispensation of the indwelling God in the heart of His people. As Christ said (John 14:21, 23), "If a man keep My words, he it is that loveth me; and My Father will love him, and I will love him, and we will come to him, and make our abode with him"—what Paul calls "The riches of the glory of this mystery among the Gentiles, which is Christ in you, the hope of glory." Or, as he says of himself, "Christ liveth in me".

The Gospel—the dispensation of the indwelling Christ. How few Christians there are who believe or experience it! Come and let us listen to Paul's teaching as to the way into the experience of this crowning blessing of the Christian life.

1. *"I bow my knees to the Father, that He would grant you."* The blessing must come from the Father to the supplicant on the bended knee, for himself or for those for whom he labors. It is to be found in much prayer.

2. *"That He would grant you according to the riches of His glory,"*—something very special and Divine—*"to be strengthened with might by His Spirit in the inner man,"* to separate from sin and the world, to yield to Christ as Lord and Master, and to live that life of love to Christ and keeping His commandments to which the promise has been given: "The Father and I will come to him, and make our abode with him."

3. *"That Christ may dwell in your heart by faith."* It is in the very nature of Christ, in His Divine omnipresence and love, to long for the heart to dwell in. As faith sees this and bows the knee and pleads with God for this great blessing, it receives grace to believe that the prayer is answered and in that faith accepts the wonderful gift so long thirsted for—Christ dwelling in the heart by faith.

4. *"That ye being rooted and grounded in love may be filled with all the fullness of God,"* as far as it is possible for man to experience it.

Child of God, feed on the words the Holy Spirit has given here. Meditate, with strong desire and childlike faith, on what the Father and the Son and the Holy Spirit have undertaken to work in you. Hold fast the confident assurance that God will do abundantly above what we can ask or think.

Blessed Father, I hear Christ speak to me: "According unto your faith be it unto you." Amen.

Christian Perfection

"The God of peace make you perfect in every good work to do His will, working in you that which is well-pleasing in His sight, through Jesus Christ" (Heb. 13:20–21).

Prepare your heart, my reader, for a large and strong faith, here again to take in one of those promises of God as high above all our thoughts as the heaven is above the earth.

You know what a wonderful exposition we have in the Epistle to the Hebrews of that eternal redemption which Christ our great High Priest, the Mediator of the new covenant, worked out for us through the shedding of His precious blood. The writer of the Epistle closes his whole argument and all its deep spiritual teaching with the benediction—"The God of peace"—listen, "make you perfect in every good work to do His will." Does not that include everything? Can we desire more? Yes, listen—"working in you that which is well-pleasing in His sight," and that through Jesus Christ.

The great thought here is that all that Christ had wrought out for our redemption and all that God had done in raising Him from the dead was just with the one object that He might now have free scope for working out in us that everlasting redemption which Christ had brought in. He Himself as God the Omnipotent ever-working will make us perfect in every good work. And if we want to know in what way, we have the answer: By His working within us that which is well-pleasing in His sight. And that through Jesus Christ.

All that we have been taught about the completeness of the salvation in Christ and our call to look on Him, to follow Him is here crowned and finds its consummation in the blessed assurance God Himself takes such an entire charge of the man who really trusts Him, that He Himself will through Jesus Christ work all that is well-pleasing in His sight.

The thought is too high, the promise is too large; we cannot attain to it. And yet there it is, claiming, stimulating our faith. It calls us just to take hold of the one truth—the everlasting God works in me every hour of the day through Jesus Christ. I have just one thing to do, to yield myself into God's hands for Him to work. Not to hinder Him by my working, but in a silent adoring faith to be assured that He Himself through Jesus Christ will work in me all that is well-pleasing in His sight.

"Lord, increase our faith!" Amen.

The God of All Grace

"The God of all grace, who called you unto His eternal glory in Christ, shall Himself perfect, stablish, strengthen you, after ye have suffered a little while" (1 Peter 5:10).

We know how the Epistle to the Hebrews gathers up all its teaching in that wonderful promise, "the God of peace perfect you in every good work." Peter does the same thing here: "The God of all grace perfect, stablish, strengthen you." God Himself is to be the one object of our trust day by day; as we think of our work, of our needs, of our life and all our hearts' desire, God Himself must be the one object of our hope and trust.

Just as God is the center of the universe, the one source of its strength, the one Guide that orders and controls its movements, so God must have the same place in the life of the believer. With every new day the first and chief thought ought to be—God, God alone, can fit me this day to live as He would have me.

And what is now to be our position toward this God? Do we not feel that the first thought of every day ought to be the humble placing of ourselves in His hands to confess our absolute helplessness and to yield ourselves in childlike surrender to receive from Him the fulfillment of such promises as these: *"The God of peace perfecting you in every good work"*: *"the God of all grace perfecting, stablishing, strengthening you"*?

Some of us have learned in the section on *The Secret of Adoration*, how absolutely indispensable it is to meet God every morning and give Him time to reveal Himself and to take charge of our life for the day. Is not this just what we have to do with these wonderful words of Peter until it is an understood thing between God and ourselves? Blessed Father, in view of the life and work of this new day, my heart is resting on Thee; my hope is in Thy Word. *"The God of peace perfect you in every good work"; "the God of all grace perfect, stablish, strengthen you."*

By Thy grace may this henceforth be the spirit in which I awake every morning to go out to my work, humbly trusting in the word: *"God shall Himself perfect you. The Lord will perfect that which concerneth me."*

Ever blessed Father, be pleased, I beseech Thee, to open the eyes of Thy children to the vision that even as Thy Son was perfected forevermore, so Thou art waiting to work in each of us that work of perfecting Thy saints in which Thy glory will be seen. Amen.

Not Sinning

"Ye know that He was manifested to take away sins;
and in Him is no sin. Whosoever abideth in Him
sinneth not" (1 John 3:5–6).

John had taken deep into his heart and life the words that Christ had spoken in the last night on abiding in Him. He ever remembered how the Lord had six times over spoken of loving Him and keeping His commandments as the way to abiding in His love and receiving the indwelling of the Father and the Son. And so in this Epistle in his old age the abiding in Christ is one of the key-words of the life it promises (John 2:6, 24, 28; 3:6, 24; 4:13, 16).

In our text John teaches how we can be kept from sinning: "He that abideth in Christ sinneth not." Though there is sin in our nature, the abiding in Christ, in whom is no sin, does indeed free us from the power of sin and enables us day by day to live so as to please God. Of the Lord Jesus it is written that He had said of the Father (John 8:29): "I do always those things that please Him." And so John writes in the Epistle: "Beloved, if our heart condemn us not, we have boldness toward God; and whatsoever we ask, we receive of Him, *because we keep His commandments and do the things that are pleasing in His sight.*"

Let the soul that longs to be free from the power of sin take these simple but far-reaching words: "In Him is no sin," and "of God I am in Him." "He that establisheth us in Christ is God." As I seek to abide in Him in whom there is no sin, Christ will indeed live out His own life in me in the power of the Holy Spirit and fit me for a life in which I always do the things that are pleasing in His sight.

Dear child of God, you are called to a life in which faith, great faith, strong faith, continuous and unbroken faith in the Almighty power of God is your one hope. As you day by day take time and yield yourself to the God of peace who perfects you in every good work to do His will, you will experience that what the heart has not conceived is what God indeed works in them that wait for Him.

"He that abideth in Him, sinneth not." The promise is sure: God the Almighty is pledged that He will work in you what is well-pleasing in His sight through Christ Jesus. In that faith, abide in Him.

"Whosoever abideth in Him, sinneth not."

"Have I not said unto thee that, if thou believest, thou shalt see the glory of God?"

Lord, work in my heart as I wait for Thee. Amen.

Overcoming the World

"Who is he that overcometh the world, but he that believeth that Jesus is the Son of God" (1 John 5:5).

Christ had spoken strongly on the world hating Him. His Kingdom and the kingdom of this world were in deadly hostility. John had understood the lesson and summed up all in the words: "We know that we are of God, and the whole world lieth in wickedness." "Love not the world, nor the things that are of the world." "If any man love the world, the love of the Father is not in him."

John also teaches us what the real nature and power of the world is: *the lust of the flesh*, with its self-pleasing; *the lust of the eyes*, with its seeing and seeking what there is in the glory of the world; and *the pride of life*, with its self-exaltation. We find these three marks of what the World is in Eve in Paradise. She "saw that the tree was good for food, and that it was pleasant to the eyes, and a tree to be desired to make one wise." Through the body and the eyes and the pride of wisdom, the world acquired the mastery over her and over us.

The world still exerts a terrible influence over the Christian who does not know that in Christ he has been crucified to the world. In the pleasure in eating and drinking, in the love and enjoyment of what there is to be seen of its glory, and in all that constitutes the pride of life, the power of this world proves itself. And most Christians are either utterly ignorant of the danger of a worldly spirit or feel themselves utterly powerless to conquer it.

Christ left us with the great far-reaching promise: *"Be of good cheer, I have overcome the world."* As the child of God abides in Christ and seeks to live the heavenly life in the power of the Holy Spirit, he may confidently count on the power to overcome the world. *"Who is he that overcometh the world, but he that believeth that Jesus is the Son of God?" "I live by the faith of the Son of God, who loved me, and gave Himself for me"*; this is the secret of daily, hourly victory over the world and all its secret, subtle temptation. But it needs a heart and a life entirely possessed by the faith of Jesus Christ to maintain the victor's attitude at all times. Oh, my brothers and sisters, take time to ask whether you do with your whole heart believe in the victory that faith gives over the world. Put your trust in the mighty power of God, in the abiding presence of Jesus as the only pledge of certain and continual victory.

"Believest thou this?"

Yea, Lord, I believe. Amen.

Jesus: The Author and Perfector of Our Faith

"Lord, I believe; help Thou mine unbelief" (Mark 9:24).

What a treasure of encouragement these words contain. Our Lord had said to the father of the possessed child, who had asked for His help: "If thou canst believe, all things are possible to him that believeth." The father felt that Christ was throwing the responsibility on him. If he believed, the child could be healed. And he felt as if he had not such faith. But as he looked in the face of Christ, he felt assured that the love which was willing to heal, would also be ready to help with his faith and graciously accept even its feeble beginnings. And he cried with tears: "Lord, I believe; help Thou mine unbelief." Christ heard the prayer, and the child was healed.

What a lesson for us who have so often felt, as we listened to the wonderful promises of God, that our faith was too feeble to grasp the precious gift. And here we receive the assurance that the Christ who waits for our faith to do its work is a Savior *who Himself will care for our faith.* Let us come, however feeble our faith may be and, though it be with tears, cry: "Lord, I believe; help Thou mine unbelief." And Christ will accept the prayer that puts its trust in Him. Let us bring it into exercise, even though it be but as a mustard seed; in contact with Christ the feeblest faith is made strong and bold. Jesus Christ is the Author and Perfector of our faith.

Dear Christian, I pray you as you read God's wonderful promises and long to have them fulfilled, remember the grain of mustard seed. However small, if it be put into the ground and allowed to grow, it becomes a great tree. Take the hidden feeble seed of the little faith you have with the Word of promise on which you are resting; plant it in your heart. Give utterance to it in the contact with Jesus Christ and fervent prayer to Him; He will in very deed accept of the feeble trembling faith that clings to Him and will not let Him go. A feeble faith in an Almighty Christ will become the great faith that can remove the mountains.

We saw in Abraham how God took charge of his faith and trained him to become strong in faith, giving glory to God. Count most confidently on the desire of Christ to strengthen your faith. And in answer to the question that each time comes again, "Believest thou that I can do this?" let your heart confidently say: "Yea, Lord, I do believe." Praise God! I have a Christ who not only waits to give the full possession of the heavenly life and the blessings of the covenant, but a Christ who secretly works in me the faith that can claim it all.

"Yea, Lord, I do believe." Amen.

The Lost Secret

"Wait for the promise of the Father. . . . ye shall be baptized with the Holy Spirit not many days hence" (Acts 1:4–5).

After our Lord had given the great command: "Go into all the world and preach the Gospel to every creature," He again added another, His very last command: "Tarry till ye be endued with power from on high." "Wait for the promise of the Father." "Ye shall be baptized with the Holy Spirit not many days hence."

All Christians agree that the great command to preach the Gospel to every creature was not only for the disciples but is binding on us too. But all do not appear to consider that the very last command, not to preach until they had received the power from on high, is equally binding on us as it was on the disciples. The Church appears to have lost possession of that which ought to be to her a secret of secrets—the abiding consciousness, day by day, that it is only as she lives in the power of the Holy Spirit that she can preach the Gospel in demonstration of the Spirit and of power. It is owing to this that there is so much preaching and working with so little of spiritual result. It is owing to nothing but this that the universal complaint is heard that there is so little prayer, and especially that there is so little of that much-availing prayer that brings down the Power from on high on her ministrations.

In this book we desire to study the Secret of Pentecost as it is to be found in the words and the deeds of our blessed Master and in the words and the deeds of His disciples as they took Him at His word and continued with one accord in prayer and supplication, until the promise was fulfilled and they became full of the Holy Spirit and proved what the mighty power of their God could do through them.

Let us seek earnestly the grace of the Holy Spirit, who alone can Himself reveal to us what eye hath not seen, nor ear heard, nor hath entered into the heart of man to conceive—the things which God hath done and loves to do for them that wait upon Him.

Blessed Father, we pray that the lost secret may be found—the sure promise that in answer to fervent prayer, the power of the Holy Spirit will indeed be given. Amen.

The Kingdom of God

"Jesus showed Himself to His disciples, being
seen of them forty days, and speaking of the things
pertaining to the Kingdom of God" (Acts 1:3).

When Christ began to preach He took up the message of John: "the Kingdom of heaven is at hand." Later on He spoke: "There are some of them that stand here which shall not taste of death till they have seen the Kingdom of God come with power." That could not be until the King had ascended His throne. Then first He and His disciples were ready to receive from the Father the great gift of the Holy Spirit, bringing down the Kingdom of God in its heavenly power into their hearts.

Our text tells us that all the teaching of Jesus, during the forty days after the Resurrection, dealt with the Kingdom of God, and it is remarkable how Luke, in the last verses of Acts, sums up all the teaching of Paul at Rome; he testified to the Kingdom of God, he preached the Kingdom of God (Acts 28:23, 31).

Christ seated upon the throne of God was now King and Lord of all. To His disciples He had entrusted the announcement of the Kingdom which is righteousness and peace and joy in the Holy Spirit. The prayer He had taught them: "Our Father, which art in heaven, Thy Kingdom come," had now for them a new meaning. The rule of God as seen in heaven came down in the power of the Spirit, and the disciples were full of the one thought—to preach the coming of the Spirit into the hearts of all people. There was now on earth good tidings of the Kingdom of God, a Kingdom of God ruling and dwelling with those on earth, even as in heaven.

In the last command our Lord gave to His disciples (Acts 1:4, 8) we shall find the great essential characteristics of the Kingdom put in great power.

1. The King—the crucified Christ. 2. The disciples—His faithful followers. 3. The power for their service—the Holy Spirit. 4. Their work—testifying for Christ as His witnesses. 5. Their aim—the ends of the earth. 6. Their first duty—waiting on God in united, unceasing prayer.

Blessed Father, give us a clear and full impression of all that Christ spoke to the disciples in that last moment and what it meant for their inner life and all their service. Amen.

Christ as King

"And He said: 'Verily, I say unto you, that there be some of them which stand here, which shall not taste of death, till they have seen the Kingdom of God come with power'" (Mark 9:1).

The first mark of the Church: *Christ as King.*

Christ and John had both preached that the Kingdom of God was at hand. In our text Christ said that it would be in the lifetime of some who heard Him that the Kingdom would come in power. That could mean nothing else but that when He, as King, had ascended the throne of the Father, the Kingdom would be revealed in the hearts of His disciples by the power of the Holy Spirit. In the Kingdom of heaven, God's will was always being done; in the power of the Holy Spirit, Christ's disciples would do His will even as it was done in heaven.

The mark of what a Kingdom is, is to be seen in *the King.* Christ now reigns as God and man on the throne of the Father. On earth there is no embodiment or external manifestation of the Kingdom; its power is seen in the lives of those in whom it rules. It is only in the Church, the members of Christ, that the united Body can be seen and known. Christ lives and dwells and rules in their hearts. Our Lord Himself taught how close the relationship would be. "In that day ye shall know that I am in My Father, and ye in Me, and I in you." Next to the faith of His oneness with God and His omnipotent power would be the knowledge that they lived in Him and He in them.

This must be our first lesson if we are to follow in the steps of the disciples and to share their blessing, that we must know that Christ actually as King dwells and rules in our hearts. We must know that we live in Him and in His power are able to accomplish all that He would have us do. Our whole life is to be devoted to our King and the service of His Kingdom.

Blessed Father, this blessed relationship to Christ means above all a daily fellowship with Him in prayer. The prayer life is to be a continuous and unbroken exercise. It is thus that His people can rejoice in their King and in Him can be more than conquerors. Amen.

Jesus the Crucified

*"God hath made that same Jesus, whom ye have
crucified, both Lord and Christ" (Acts 2:36).*

We have spoken of Christ as King in more than one respect. But there is one word more that may not be lacking. This King is none other than *the crucified Jesus*. All that we have to say of Him, His divine power, His abiding presence, His wonderful love does not teach us to know Him aright unless we maintain the deep consciousness: This our King is the crucified Jesus. God has placed Him in the midst of His throne as a Lamb, as it had been slain, and it is thus that the hosts of heaven adore Him. It is thus that we worship Him as a King.

Christ's cross is His highest glory. It is through this that He has conquered every enemy and gained His place on the throne of God. And it is this that He will impart to us too if we are to know fully what the victory over sin is to mean. When Paul wrote: "I have been crucified with Christ, Christ liveth in me," he taught us that it was as the crucified One that Christ ruled on the throne of His heart and that the spirit of the cross would triumph over us as it did in Him.

This was true of the disciples. This was their deepest preparation for receiving the Holy Spirit. They had with their Lord been crucified to the world. The old man had been crucified; in Him they were dead to sin and their life was hid with Christ in God. Each one of us needs to experience this fellowship with Christ in His cross if the Spirit of Pentecost is really to take possession of us. It was through the Eternal Spirit that Christ gave Himself as a sacrifice and became the King on the throne of God. It is as we become "comformable to His death," in the entire surrender of our will, in the entire self-denial of our old nature, in the entire separation from the spirit of this world, that we can become the worthy servants of a crucified King, and our hearts the worthy temples of His glory.

Lord Jesus Christ, make us Thy worthy servants and our hearts, worthy temples of Thy glory. Amen.

The Apostles

"Being assembled together with them, He charged
them not to depart from Jerusalem to wait for the
promise of the Father" (Acts 1:4 R.V.).

The second mark of the Church is to be found in *the disciples* whom the Lord had prepared to receive His Spirit and to be His witnesses.

If we would understand aright the outpouring of the Spirit answer to the prayer of the disciples, we must above all ask: What was there in these men that fitted them for such powerful, effectual prayer and the wonderful fulfillment of the promise that came to them? They were simple, unlearned men with many faults, whom the Lord had called to forsake all and follow Him. They had done this, as far as they could; they followed Him in the life He led and the work He did. Though there was much sin in them and they had as yet no power fully to deny themselves, their hearts clung to Him in deep sincerity. In the midst of much stumbling they yet followed Him to the cross. They shared with Him His death; unconsciously, but most really, they died with Him to sin and were raised with Him in the power of a new life. It was this that fitted them for the power in prayer and the being clothed with the power from on high.

Let this be the test by which we try ourselves whether we have indeed surrendered to the fellowship of Christ's sufferings and death, and whether we have hated our own life and crucified it—and have received the power of Christ's life in us. It is this that will give us liberty to believe that God will hear our prayer too and give us His Holy Spirit to work in us what we and He desire, if we are indeed with one accord to take up the disciples' prayer and to share in the answer.

Blessed Father, make us willing learners in the school of Jesus, seeking above everything that intimate fellowship with Him that will fit us for praying the prayer of Pentecost and receiving its answer. Amen.

Not of This World

*"They are not of the world even as I am not
of the world" (John 17:14, 16).*

In the last night our Lord took pains to make clear to His disciples the impassable gulf between Him and the world and between them and the world too (John 16:16-21). He had said of the Spirit: "The world cannot receive Him, because it seeth Him not, neither knoweth Him." "Because ye are not of the world, therefore the world hateth you."

One great mark of the disciples was thus to be that as little as Christ was of the world, so little were they to be of the world. Christ and they had become united in the cross and the resurrection; they both belonged to another world, the Kingdom of heaven. This separation from the world is to be the mark of all disciples who long to be filled with the Spirit.

How is it that faith in the Holy Spirit is so little preached and practiced in Christendom? The world rules too much in the life of Christians. Christians live too little the heavenly life to which they are called in Christ Jesus. The "love of the world" (1 John 2:15–16); "The lust of the flesh," pleasure in eating and drinking, in ease and comfort; "The lust of the eyes," delight in all that the world offers of beauty and possession; the vain glory of life, the self-exaltation in what the wisdom and power of man has accomplished—all this robs the heart of its susceptibility and desire for that true self-denial that fits for receiving the Holy Spirit.

Blessed Heavenly Father, let each one who would take up the Pentecostal prayer for the power of the Holy Spirit examine himself whether the spirit of the world is not the secret of that lack of love of prayer which is absolutely necessary in all who would plead the promise of the Thee. Write this deep in every heart, the world cannot receive the Holy Spirit! "Ye are not of the world, even as I am not of the world." Amen.

Obedience

"If ye love Me, ye will keep my commandments. And I will pray the Father, and He shall give you another Comforter" (John 14:15–16).

We have learned to know the disciples in their training for the baptism of the Spirit and seen what was needed for their continuing "with one accord" in the prayer for the power of the Spirit. Christ was everything to them. Even before the cross but much more after it, and with the resurrection, He was literally their life, their one thought, their only desire.

Such a devotion to Christ, was this something special and not to be expected of all? Or was it indeed something that the Lord asked from all who desired to be filled with the Spirit? God expects it of all His children; the Lord has need of such now, as much as then, to receive His Spirit and His power, to minister then, here on earth, and as intercessors to link the world to the throne of God.

Is Christ something or nothing or everything to us? For the unconverted, Christ is nothing; for the half converted—the average Christian—Christ is something; for the true Christian, Christ is all. Each one who prays for the power of the Spirit must be ready to say: "I yield myself with my whole heart this day to the leading of the Spirit"; a full surrender is the question of life or death, an absolute necessity.

My dear brothers and sisters, you have heard the word of our text: "If ye love Me, *keep My commandments.*" The surrender to live every day, all the day, abiding in Christ and keeping His commandments is to be the one mark of your discipleship. It is when the child of God learns that it is only as the heart longs in everything to do God's will that the Father's love and Spirit can rest upon it. This was the disposition in which the disciples continued with one accord in prayer. This will be the secret of power in our intercession as we plead for the Church and the world.

Heavenly Father, I surrender to live every day, all the day, abiding in Christ and keeping His commandments as a mark of Thy discipleship. Amen.

The Holy Spirit

"Ye shall be baptized with the Holy Spirit" (Acts 1:5).

"Ye shall receive power when the Holy Spirit
is come upon you" (Acts 1:8).

The third mark of the Church—*the power for service through the Holy Spirit*. Since the time of Adam's fall when he lost the spirit God had breathed into him, God's Spirit had striven with people, and worked in some with power, but He had never been able to find His permanent home in them.

It was only when Christ had come and by His death had broken the power of sin and had won in the resurrection a new life for all to live in Himself, that the Spirit of God could come and take possession of the whole heart and make it a dwelling place for Christ and for God.

Nothing less than this could be the power in the disciples and in us by which sin could be overcome and the prisoners set free. This Spirit is the *Holy Spirit*. In the Old Testament He was called the Spirit of God. But now that in the cross of Christ the holiness of God had been magnified and Christ had sanctified us that we might be sanctified like Him, the Spirit of God's holiness descends to dwell in believers and take possession of them as God's Holy temple.

He is *the Spirit of the Son*. On earth He led the Son first into the desert to be tempted of Satan, then to the Synagogue in Nazareth to proclaim Himself as the fulfillment of what the prophets had spoken (Isa. 61:1; Luke 4:18). And so on the cross, Christ yielded Himself implicitly to the leading of the Spirit.

The Spirit now reveals Christ in us as first of all our life and then our strength for a perfect obedience and the preaching of the Word in the power of God.

Amazing mystery! The Spirit of God, our life; the Spirit of Christ, our light and strength. It is as men and women who are led by this Spirit of the first disciples, that we shall have the power to pray the effectual prayer of the righteous that availeth much.

Blessed Father, we thank Thee for the Holy Spirit who decends to dwell in believers and take possession of them as God's Holy temple. Amen.

The Power from on High

"Tarry ye until ye be clothed with power from on high" (Luke 24:49).

The Lord had said to the disciples: "Without Me ye can do nothing." And now, why is it that He has chosen these weak, helpless men to send them out to conquer the world for Him? It was that in their feebleness they might yield themselves and give Him as Lord on His throne the opportunity to show His power working through them. As the Father had done all the work in Christ when He was upon earth, so Christ in heaven would now be the Great Worker, proving in them that all power had been given to Him in heaven and on earth. Their place would be to pray, to believe, and yield themselves to the mighty power of Christ.

The Holy Spirit would not be in them as a power of which they could have possession. But He would possess them, and their work would be in very deed the work of the Almighty Christ. Their whole posture each day would be that of unceasing dependence and prayer and of confident expectation.

The Apostles had indeed learned to know Christ intimately. They had seen all His mighty works; they had received His teaching; they had gone with Him through all His sufferings, even to the death of the cross. And they had not only seen Him but known Him in the power of His resurrection and the experience of that resurrection life in their own hearts. Yet they were not capable of making Him known aright until He Himself, from the throne of heaven, had taken possession of them by His Spirit dwelling in them.

Everything calls the Gospel minister to rest content with nothing less than the indwelling life and power of the Holy Spirit revealing Jesus in the heart as the only fitness for preaching the Gospel in power.

Blessed Father, nothing less than having Christ speaking through us in the power of His omnipotence will make us able ministers of the New Testament, bringing salvation to them that hear us. Amen.

My Witnesses

"Ye shall be My Witnesses" (Acts 1:8).

The fourth mark of Christ's Church—*His servants are to be witnesses to Him, ever testifying of His wonderful love, of His power to redeem,* of His continual abiding presence, and of His wonderful power to work in them.

This is the only weapon that the King allows His redeemed ones to use. Without claiming authority or power, without wisdom or eloquence, without influence or position, each one is called, not only by his words but by his life and action, to be a living *proof and witness of what Jesus can do.*

This is to be the only weapon they are to use in conquering souls and bringing them to the feet of Christ. This is what the first disciples did. When they were filled with the Spirit, they began to speak of the mighty things that Christ had done.

It was in this power that those who were scattered abroad by persecution went forth, even as far as Antioch, preaching in the name of Jesus, so that a multitude of the heathen believed. They had no commission from the Apostles; they had no special gifts or training; but out of the fullness of the heart, they spoke of Jesus Christ. They could not be silent; they were filled with the life and the love of Christ and could not but witness to Him.

It was this that gave the Gospel its power of increase; every new convert became a witness for Christ.

A heathen writer tells later in regard to the persecutions that if the Christians were only content to keep the worship of Jesus to themselves, they would not have to suffer. But in their zeal they wanted Christ to rule over all.

Here we have the secret of a flourishing Church: *every believer a witness for Jesus.* Here we have the cause of the weakness of the Church: so few who are willing in daily life to testify that Jesus is Lord.

Blessed Father, what a call to prayer! Lord, teach Thy disciples the blessedness of so knowing Jesus and the power of His love, that they may find their highest joy in witnessing to what He is and has done for them. Amen.

The Gospel Ministry

"The Spirit of truth, He shall testify of Me, and ye
shall also bear witness, because ye have been with
Me from the beginning" (John 15:26–27).

My witnesses—that not only refers to all believers, but very especially to all ministers of the Gospel. This is the high calling and also the only power of the preacher of the Gospel—in everything to be *a witness for Jesus.*

This gives us two great truths. The first, that with all that the preacher teaches from the Word of God or according to the need of his congregation, he must first of all place *the preaching of Christ Himself.* This is what the first disciples did. "They ceased not in every house to teach and to preach Jesus Christ." This was what Philip did at Samaria. "He preached Christ unto them." And so Paul writes: "I determined not to know anything among you, save Jesus Christ and Him crucified."

The minister of the Gospel may never forget that it is for this especially that he has been set apart, to be with the Holy Spirit a witness for Christ. It is as he does this that sinners will find salvation, that God's children will be sanctified and fitted for His service. It is thus alone that Christ can have His place in the heart of His people and in the world around.

But there is a second thought of not less importance. And that is, that the teaching must ever be a personal testimony from experience to what Christ is and can do. As this note is sounded, the Holy Spirit carries the message as a living reality to the heart. It is this that will build up believers so that they can walk in such fellowship with Jesus Christ that He can reveal Himself through them. And it is this that will lead them to the knowledge of the indispensable secret of spiritual health—the prayer life in daily fellowship, in childlike love and true consecration with the Father and the Son.

Heavenly Father, what abundant matter for prayer union, to cultivate among believers and ministers that joy of the Holy Spirit in which out of the abundance of the heart, the mouth speaks to the praise and glory of our ever-blessed Redeemer, Jesus Christ our Lord. Amen.

The Whole World

"My witnesses unto the uttermost parts of the earth" (Acts 1:8).

Here we have the fifth mark of Christ's Church—*the whole world*.

What words are these for the Man who in His absolute weakness had been crucified by His enemies to speak of *the ends of the earth as His dominion*. What folly on the part of those who speak of Christ as being nothing but a man. How could it have entered the mind of any writer to venture the prophecy that a Jew who had been crucified, whose whole life had been proved by that cross to be an utter failure, and whose disciples had at the last utterly forsaken Him—that by them He should conquer the world? No human mind could have formed such a conception. It is the thought of God; He alone could plan and execute such a purpose.

The word that Jesus spoke to His disciples: "Ye shall receive power after that the Holy Spirit is come upon you," gives them the assurance that the Holy Spirit would maintain in them Christ's divine power. As Christ did His works only because the Father worked in Him, so Christ assured His disciples that He Himself from the throne of Heaven would work all their works in them. They might ask what they would and it should be done unto them. In the strength of that promise the Church of Christ can make the ends of the earth its one aim.

Oh, that Christian people might understand that the extension of God's Kingdom can only be effected by the united continued prayer of men and women who give their hearts wholly to wait upon Christ in the assurance that what they desire He will do for them.

Oh, that God would grant that His children proved their faith in Christ by making His aim their aim and yielding themselves to be His witnesses in united, persevering prayer, waiting upon Him in the full assurance that He will most surely and most gloriously give all that they can ask.

Heavenly Father, help us believe that in answer to our prayer, the crucified Jesus will do far more than we can ask or think. Amen.

The Whole Earth Filled
with His Glory

*"Blessed be His glorious name forever: and let the whole earth be
filled with His glory; Amen, and Amen" (Ps. 72:19).*

What a prospect! This earth now under the power of the Evil One renewed and *filled with the glory of God*—a new earth wherein righteousness dwells. Though we believe it so little, it will surely come to pass; God's Word is the pledge of it. God's Son by His blood and death conquered the power of sin, and through the Eternal Spirit the power of God is working out His purpose. What a vision, the whole earth filled with His glory!

But what a great and difficult work. It is near two thousand years since Christ gave the promise and ascended the throne, and yet more than one-half of the human race have never learned to know even the name of Jesus. And of the other half, what millions are called by His name yet know Him not. This great work of bringing the knowledge of Christ to every creature has been entrusted to a Church that thinks little of her responsibility and of what the consequence of her neglect will be. We may indeed ask: Will the work ever be done? Blessed be His name, His power and His faithfulness are pledges that one day we shall see it, the whole earth filled with the glory of God.

What a wonderful prayer! For in our text it is a prayer—"Let the whole earth be filled with His glory; Amen, and Amen." It is to this prayer that every believer is called, and can count upon the Holy Spirit for inspiration and strength. It is to this prayer that we desire to strengthen each other so that every day of our life, with all the power there is in us, we with one accord and continually desire to pray in the faith of the name of Jesus and the power of His Spirit.

What blessedness to know that true prayer will indeed help and be answered! What blessedness every day of our lives to seek God's face, with confidence to lay hold of Him and give Him no rest till the earth is full of His Glory!

---

*Heavenly Father, what blessedness to unite in this the day of Thy power
with all Thy willing children who are seeking to prepare the way for
our King! Amen.*

The First Prayer Meeting

"These all with one accord continued steadfastly in prayer,
with the women" (Acts 1:14).

The sixth mark of the early Church—*waiting on the promise of the Father in united prayer.*

It is difficult to form a right conception of the unspeakable importance of this first prayer meeting in the history of the Kingdom, a prayer-meeting which was the simple fulfilling of the command of Christ. It was to be for all time the indication of the one condition on which His Presence and Spirit would be known in Power. In it we have the secret key that opens the storehouse of heaven with all its blessings.

Christ had prayed that the disciples might be one even as He and the Father were one—perfect in one—that the world might know that God loved them as He loved Christ. How far the disciples were from such a state when Christ prayed the prayer, we see in the strife that there was among them at the Lord's Table as to who would be chief. It was only after the resurrection and after Christ had gone to heaven, that they would be brought, in the ten days of united supplication, to that holy unity of love and of purpose which would make them the one Body of Christ prepared to receive the Spirit in all His power.

What a prayer meeting! The fruit of Christ's training during His three years with them. Adam's body was first created, before God breathed His spirit into him. And so the Body of Christ had first to be formed before the Spirit took possession.

This prayer meeting gives us the law of the Kingdom for all time. Where Christ's disciples are linked to each other in love and yield themselves wholly to Him in undivided consecration, the Spirit will be given from heaven as the seal of God's approval, and Christ will show His mighty power. One of the great marks of the new dispensation is the united unceasing prayer that availeth much and is crowned with the power of the Holy Spirit. Have we not here the reason why, if our prayers are confined in great measure to our own church or interests, the answer cannot come in such power as we expected?

Heavenly Father, help us to unite in unceasing prayer that availeth much and is crowned with the power of Thy Holy Spirit. Amen.

The Unity of the Spirit

"Endeavoring to keep the unity of the Spirit.
There is one body and one Spirit" (Eph. 4:3–4).

It is from Paul that we learn how the Christian communities in different places ought to remember each other in the fellowship of prayer. He points out how in such prayer God is glorified. So he writes more than once (2 Cor. 1:11; 4:15, 9:12–13) of how the ministry of intercession abounds to the glory of God.

In our days there is very great need that the children of God throughout the world should be drawn close together in the consciousness of their being chosen by God to be a holy priesthood ministering continually the sacrifice of praise and prayer. There is too little distinction between the world and the Body of Christ; in the life of many of God's children there is very little difference from what the world is. It is a question of the deepest importance: What can be done to foster the unity of the Spirit?

Nothing will help so much as the separation to a life of more prayer, with the definite intercession that God's people may prove their unity in a life of holiness and love. That will be a living testimony to the world of what it means to live for God. When Paul wrote: "Praying always with all prayer and supplication in the Spirit, and watching thereunto with all perseverance and supplication for all saints," he names one of the essential characteristics of the difference between God's people and the world.

You say you long to bear this mark of the children of God and to be able so to pray for them that you may prove to yourself and to others that you are indeed not of the world. Resolve in your life to bear about with you this one great distinctive feature of the true Christian—a life of prayer and intercession. Join with God's children who are seeking with one accord and unceasingly so to maintain the unity of the Spirit and the Body of Christ that they may be strong in the Lord and in the power of His might, to pray down a blessing upon His Church. Let none of us think it too much to give a quarter of an hour every day for meditation on some word of God connected with His promises to His Church—and then to plead with Him for its fulfillment. Slowly, unobservedly, and yet surely, you will taste the blessedness of being one, heart and soul, with God's people and receive the power to pray the effectual prayer that availeth much.

Blessed Father, we thank Thee that slowly, unobservedly, and yet surely, we will taste the blessedness of being one, heart and soul, with Thy people and receive the power to pray the effectual prayer that availeth much. Amen.

Union Is Strength

"And when they had prayed, they were all filled with
the Holy Spirit, and they spake the Word of God with
boldness. And the multitude of them that believed
were of one heart and one soul" (Acts 4:31–32).

The power of union we see everywhere in nature. How feeble is a drop of rain as it falls to earth. But when the many drops are united in one stream and thus become one body, how speedily the power is irresistible. Such is the power of true union in prayer. In Psalm 34:5 the English margin has, instead of "They looked unto Him," "They flowed unto Him." The Dutch translation is, "They rushed toward Him like a stream of water." Such was the prayer in the upper room. And such can our prayer be if we unite all our forces in pleading the promise of the Father. And when the world "comes in like a flood," it can be overcome in the power of united prayer.

In Natal, owing to the many mountains, the streams often flow down with great force. The Zulus are accustomed, when they wish to pass through a stream, to join hands. The leader has a strong stick in the right hand and gives his left hand to some strong man who comes behind him. And so they form a chain of twelve or twenty and help each other to stem and cross the current. Let us believe that when in Spirit God's people reach out their hands to each other, there will be power to resist the terrible influence that the world can exert. And in that unity God's children, when they have overcome the power of the world and the flesh, will have power to prevail with God.

It was in the upper room that they abode the ten days until they had truly become one heart and one soul. When the Spirit of God descended, He not only filled each individual but took possession of the whole company as the Body of Christ.

Do believe, O Christians, that in this twentieth century the prayer of our Lord Jesus is still being offered: "Father, that they may be one as We are one." It is in the fellowship of loving and believing prayer that our hearts can be melted into one and that we shall become strong in faith to believe and to accept what God has promised us.

Lord Jesus, we hear Thy prayer: "Father, that they may be one as We
are one." Amen.

Prayer in the Name of Christ

*"Whatsoever ye shall ask in My Name, that will I do, that the
Father may be glorified in the Son" (John 14:13).*

How wonderful the link between our prayers and Christ's glorifying the
Father in heaven. Much prayer on earth brings Him much glory in heav-
en. What an incentive to much prayer, to unceasing intercession. Our prayer
is indispensable to the glorifying of the Father.

So deep was the desire of Christ in the last night that His disciples
should learn to believe in the power of His Name and to avail themselves
of His promise of a sure and abundant answer, that we find the promise
repeated seven times over. He knew how slow we are to believe in the wonderful promise of answer to prayer in His name. He longs to rouse a large
and confident faith and to free our prayer from every shadow of a doubt
and to teach us to look upon intercession as the most certain and most
blessed way of bringing glory to God, joy to our own souls, and blessing
to the perishing world around us.

And if the thought comes to us that such prayer is not easy of attainment, we only need to remember what Christ told them. *It was when the
Holy Spirit came that they would have power thus to pray.* It is to draw us
on to yield ourselves fully to the control of the blessed Spirit that He holds
out to us the precious promise, "Ask and ye shall receive, that your joy
may be full." As we believe in the power of the Spirit working in us in
full measure, intercession will become to us the joy and the strength of all
our service.

When Paul wrote (Col 3:17), "Whatsoever you do in word or deed, do
all in the name of the Lord Jesus," he reminds us how in daily life everything is to bear the signature of the name of Jesus. It is as we learn to do
this that we shall have the confidence to say to the Father that as we live
in that Name before men we come to Him with the full confidence that
our prayer in that name will be answered. The life in communion with others is to be one with the life in communion with God. It is when the name
of Jesus rules all in our life that it will give power to our prayer too.

---

*Heavenly Father, it is our prayer that everything in daily life bears the
signature of the name of Jesus. Amen.*

Your Heavenly Father

"Our Father which art in heaven" (Luke 11:2).

How simple, how beautiful, this invocation which Christ puts upon our lips! And yet how inconceivably rich in its meaning, in the fullness of the love and blessing it contains.

Just think what a book could be written of all the memories that there have been on earth of wise and loving fathers. Just think of what this world owes to the fathers who have made their children strong and happy in giving their lives to seek the welfare of their fellowmen. And then think how all this is but a shadow—a shadow of exquisite beauty, but still but a shadow—of what the Father in heaven is to His children on earth.

What a gift Christ bestowed on us when He gave us the right to say: "Father!" "The Father of Christ," "Our Father," "My Father."

And then, "Our Father in heaven," our heavenly Father. We count it a great privilege as we bow in worship to know that the Father comes near to us where we are upon earth. But we soon begin to feel the need of rising up to enter into His Holy presence in heaven, to breathe its atmosphere, to drink in its spirit, and to become truly heavenly-minded. And as we in the power of thought and imagination leave earth behind, and in the power of the Holy Spirit enter the Holiest of all where the seraphs worship, the word "heavenly Father" gets a new meaning, and our hearts come under an influence that can abide all the day.

And as we then gather up our thoughts of what fatherhood on earth has meant and hear the voice of Christ saying: "How much more"—we feel the distance there is between the earthly picture and the heavenly reality, and can only bow in lowly, loving adoration, "Father, our Father, my Father." And only thus can full joy and power come to us as we rest rejoicingly in the word: "How much more shall your heavenly Father give the Holy Spirit to them that ask Him?"

Blessed Father: Oh, for grace to cultivate a heavenly spirit and daily to prove that we are children who have a Father in heaven and who love, day by day, to dwell in His Holy presence! Amen.

The Power of Prayer

"The effectual fervent prayer of a righteous
man availeth much" (James 5:16).

Prayer availeth much. It avails much with God. It avails much in the history of His Church and people. Prayer is the one great power which the Church can exercise in securing the working of God's omnipotence in the world.

The prayer *of a righteous man availeth much.* That is, a man who has the righteousness of Christ, not only as a garment covering him but as a life-power inspiring him, as a new man "created in righteousness and true holiness" (Eph. 4:24), a man that lives as "the servant to righteousness" (Rom. 6:16,19), these are the righteous whom the Lord loveth and whose prayer hath power (Ps. 66:18–19; 1 John 3:22). When Christ gave His great prayer promises in the last night, it was to those who keep His command-ments. "If ye love Me, ye will keep My commandments; and I will pray the Father, and He will give you another Comforter" (John 14:15–16). "If ye keep My commandments, ye shall abide in My love; and ye shall ask whatsoever ye will, and it shall be done unto you" (John 15:7, 10).

"The *effectual fervent prayer* of a righteous man availeth much." It is only when the righteous man stirs up himself and rouses his whole being to take hold of God that the prayer availeth much. As Jacob said: "I will not let thee go"; as the importunate widow gave the just Judge no rest, so it is that the effectual fervent prayer effects great things.

And then comes the effectual fervent prayer of many righteous. When two or three agree, there is the promise of an answer. How much more when hundreds and thousands unite with one accord to cry to God to dis-play His mighty power on behalf of His people.

Heavenly Father: Let us join those who have united themselves to call
upon Thee for the mighty power of Thy Holy Spirit in Thy Church.
What a great and blessed work, and what a sure prospect, in Thy time,
of an abundant answer! We pray individually and unitedly for the grace
of the effectual fervent prayer which availeth much. Amen.

Prayer and Sacrifice

*"I would that ye knew what great conflict
I have for you" (Col. 2:1).*

As those who are undertaking a great thing have to prepare themselves and summon all their powers to their aid, so Christians need to prepare themselves to pray, "with their whole heart and strength." This is the law of the Kingdom. Prayer needs sacrifice of ease, of time, of self. The secret of powerful prayer is sacrifice. It was thus with Christ Jesus, the great Intercessor. It is written of Him, "When thou shalt *make his soul an offering for sin*, He shall see His seed." "He shall see of the *travail of His soul.*" He shall divide the spoil with the strong, because he hath poured out his soul unto death." In Gethsemane "He offered up prayers and supplications with strong crying and tears." Prayer is sacrifice. David said: "Let my prayer be set forth before me as incense; and the lifting up of my hands as the evening sacrifice."

Prayer is sacrifice. Our prayer has its worth alone from being rooted in the sacrifice of Jesus Christ. As He gave up everything in His prayer: "Thy Will be done," our posture and disposition must ever be the offering up of everything to God and His service.

A pious Welsh miner had a relative whom the doctor ordered to Madeira. But there was no money. The miner resolved to take the little money that he had and ventured to use it all. He procured a comfortable lodging per day for the invalid. He was content with an out-room for a small sum for himself and lived on ten-pence a day. He spent much time in prayer until he got the assurance that the invalid would recover. On the last day of the month the sick one was well. When the miner reached home he said that he had now learned more than ever that the secret law and the hidden power of prayer lay in self-sacrifice.

Need we wonder at the lack of power in our prayer where there is so much reluctance to make the needful sacrifice in waiting upon God. Christ, the Christ we trust in, the Christ that lives in us offered Himself a sacrifice to God. It is as this spirit lives and rules in us that we shall receive power from Him as intercessors to pray the effectual prayer that availeth much.

Lord Jesus: Help us to learn that the secret of powerful prayer is sacrifice—sacrifice of ease, of time, of self. Amen.

The Intercession of the Spirit for the Saints

"He that searcheth the hearts knoweth what is the mind of the Spirit, because He maketh intercession for the saints according to the Will of God" (Rom. 8:27).

What a light these words cast upon the life of prayer in the hearts of the saints! We know not what we should pray for as we ought. How often this hinders our prayer or hinders the faith that is essential to its success. But here we are told for our encouragement, that the Holy Spirit maketh intercession for us with groanings that cannot be uttered: "He maketh intercession for the saints according to the Will of God."

What a prospect is here opened up to us! Where and how does the Spirit make intercession for the saints? In no other way than that, in the heart which knows not what to pray, He secretly and effectually prays what is according to the Will of God. This of course implies that we trust Him to do His work In us and that we tarry before God even when we know what to pray, in the assurance that the Holy Spirit is praying in us. This implies further that we take time to tarry in God's presence, that we exercise an unbounded dependence upon the Holy Spirit who has been given us to cry "Abba Father" within us, even when we have nothing to offer but groanings and sighs that cannot be uttered.

What a difference it would make in the life of many of God's saints if they realized this! They have not only Jesus the Son of God, the great High Priest, ever living to intercede for them, they have not only the liberty of asking in faith what they desire and the promise that it shall be given them, but they have actually and in very deed the Holy Spirit, "the Spirit of grace and supplication," to carry on, in the depths of their being, His work of interceding for them according to the Will of God.

Heavenly Father: What a call to separate ourselves from the world, to yield ourselves wholeheartedly to the leading and praying of the Spirit within us, deeper than all our thoughts or expectations! What a call to surrender ourselves in stillness of soul, resting in the Thee and waiting patiently for Thee, as the Holy Spirit prays within us not only for ourselves, but especially for all saints according to Thy Will. Amen.

That They All May Be One

*"Holy Father, keep them in Thy Name which Thou hast
given me, that they may be one, even as we are. Neither pray
I for these alone; but for them also which believe on me
through their word; that they may all be one, even as Thou,
Father, art in me, and I in Thee, that they also may be one in us.
And the glory which Thou hast given me I have given unto
them; that they may be one, even as we are one; I in them, and
Thou in me, that they may be perfected into one; that the world
may know that Thou didst send me" (John 17:11, 20–23).*

Notice carefully how the Lord used the expression, *"that they may be one,"* five times over. It is as if He felt the need of laying the emphasis strongly upon these words, if we are really to realize the chief thought of His High Priestly prayer. He longs that the words and the thought shall in very deed have the same place in our hearts that they have in His. As He was on the way to go to the Father through the cross, He would have us understand that He took the thought and the desire with Him to heaven, to make it the object of His unceasing intercession there. And He entrusted the words to us that we should take them into the world with us and make them the object of our unceasing intercession too. That alone would enable us to fulfill the last, the new command which He gave, that we should love the brethren as He loved us that our joy might be full.

How little the church has understood this. How little its different branches are marked by a fervent affectionate love to all the saints of whatever name or denomination. Shall we not welcome heartily the invitation to make this prayer, *"that they may be one"* a chief part of our daily fellowship with God? How simple it would be when once we connected the two words, "Our Father," with all the children of God throughout the world. Each time we used these sacred words we would only have to expand this little word *"Our"* into all the largeness and riches of God's Father Love, and our hearts would soon learn as naturally as we say "Father" with the thought of His infinite love and our love to Him, to say "Our" with the childlike affection to all the saints of God, whoever and wherever they may be.

---

*Heavenly Father: The prayer that "they may be one" becomes a joy
and a strength, a deeper bond of fellowship with Christ Jesus and all
His saints and an offer of a sweet savor to Thee, the Father of love.
Amen.*

The Disciples' Prayer

*"These all continued with one accord in
prayer and supplication" (Acts 1:14).*

*"They continued steadfastly in
fellowship and in prayers" (Acts 2:42).*

What a lesson it would be to us in the school of prayer to have a clear apprehension of what this continuing with one accord in prayer meant to the disciples.

Just think of the object of their desire. However defective the thoughts were that they had of the Blessed Spirit, this they knew, from the words of Jesus, "it is expedient for you that I go away," that the Spirit would give the glorified Christ into their very hearts in a way they had never known Him before. And it would be He Himself, in the mighty power of God's Spirit, who would be their strength for the work to which He had called them.

With what confidence they expected the fulfillment of the promise. Had not the Master, who had loved them so well, given them the assurance of what He would send upon them from the throne of the Father in Heaven?

And with what intensity and persistency they pleaded; in the midst of the praise and thanksgiving that filled their hearts as they worshiped their Lord in heaven, remembering all He had taught them about importunity, in the full assurance that however long the answer might be delayed, He would most assuredly fulfill their desires. Let us nourish our hearts with thoughts such as these, until we realize that the very same promise that was given to the disciples is given to us and that we too, even though we have to cry day and night to God, can count upon the Father to answer our prayers.

And then, and this is not the least—let us believe that as they continued with one accord in prayer, we also may unite as one in presenting our petitions even though we cannot be together in one place. We can—in the love wherewith His Spirit makes us one and in the experience of our Lord's presence with each one who joins with other believers in pleading the blessed Name—we can claim the promise that we too shall be filled with the Holy Spirit.

Heavenly Father: We claim the promise that we too shall be filled with the Holy Spirit and unite as one in presenting our petitions before Thee even though we cannot be together in one place. Amen.

Paul's Call to Prayer

"With all prayer and supplication, praying at all seasons in the Spirit, and watching thereunto in all perseverance and supplication for all the saints and on my behalf" (Eph. 6:18–19 R.V.).

What a sense Paul had of the deep divine unity of the whole body of Christ and of the actual need of unceasing prayer for all the members of the body by all who belong to it. That he did not mean this to be an occasional thing, but the unceasing exercise of the life union in which they were bound together is evident from the words he uses, "with *all prayer* and supplication, praying *at all seasons* in the Spirit and watching thereunto, in *all perseverance* and supplication *for all the saints*." He expects believers to be so filled with the consciousness of their being in Christ and through Him united consciously to the whole body, that in their daily life and all its engagements, their highest aim would ever be the welfare of the body of Christ of which they had become members. He counted upon their being filled with the Spirit so that it would be perfectly natural to them, without the thought of burden or constraint, to pray for all who belong to the body of Jesus Christ. As natural as it is for each member of my body to be ready every moment to do what is needful for the welfare of the whole, even so, where the Holy Spirit has entire possession, the consciousness of union with Christ will ever be accompanied by consciousness of the union and the joy and the love of all the members.

Is not this what we need in our daily life, that every believer who is yielded undividedly to Christ Jesus shall day by day, every day, and all the day live in the consciousness of oneness with Christ and His body? Just as this war has brought to light the intensity and the readiness with which millions of the subjects of the King sacrifice their all for the King and his service, so the saints of God shall live for Christ their King and also for all the members of that Body of which He is the Head.

Blessed Father, may Thy people be willing for this sacrifice of prayer and intercession at all times and for all saints! Amen.

Paul's Request for Prayer

"And for me, that utterance may be given unto me, that I may open my mouth boldly, to make known the mystery of the Gospel, that therein I may speak boldly, as I ought to speak" (Eph. 6:19–20).

"And for me"—what light these words cast on the deep reality of Paul's faith in the absolute necessity and the wonderful power of prayer. Just listen for what he asks that they should pray. "That utterance may be given unto me, that I may open my mouth boldly, that therein I may speak boldly as I ought to speak." Paul had now been a minister of the Gospel for more than twenty years. One would say that he had such experience of preaching and utterance that it would come naturally to him to speak boldly as he ought to speak. But so deep is his conviction of his own insufficiency and weakness, so absolute is his dependence on Divine teaching and power, that he feels that without the direct help of God he cannot do the work as it ought to be done. The sense of his total and unalterable dependence upon God who was with him, teaching him what and how to speak, is the ground of all his confidence and the keynote of his whole life.

But there is more. He had in all these twenty years, times without number, been in circumstances where he had to throw himself upon God alone, with no one to help him in prayer. And yet, such is his deep spiritual insight into the unity of the body of Christ and of his own actual dependence on the prayers of others, that he pleads for their praying with all prayer and supplication in the Spirit and watching thereunto with all prayer and perseverance and asks that they shall not forget to pray for him. As little as a wrestler can afford to dispense with the help of the weakest members of his body in the struggle in which he is engaged, so little could Paul do without the prayers of the believers.

What a call to us in this twentieth century to awake to the consciousness that Christ our Intercessor in heaven and all saints here upon earth are engaged in one mighty contest, and that it is our duty to call out and to cultivate the gift of unceasing supplication for the power of God's Spirit in all His servants, that all may have divine utterance given them and that all may speak boldly and as they ought to speak.

Heavenly Father, by the power of Thy Holy Spirit in all Thy servants, may we speak boldly and as we ought to speak. Amen.

Prayer for All Saints

*"To the Saints and faithful brethren in Christ, which are at
Colosse. We give thanks to God, praying always for you, since we
heard of the love which ye have to all the saints" (Col. 1:1–4).*

*"Continue in prayer, and watch in the same with
thanksgiving, withal praying also for us" (Col. 4:2–3).*

Prayer for all saints: let this be our first thought. It will need time and
thought and love to realize what is included in that simple expression. Think
of your own neighborhood and the saints you know; think of your whole
country and praise God for all who are His saints; think of all Christian
nations of the world and the saints to be found in each of these; think of
all the heathen nations and the saints of God to be found among them in
ever-increasing numbers.

Think of all the different circumstances and conditions in which these
are to be found and all the very varying needs which call for God's grace
and help. Think of many, oh, so many, who are God's saints and yet through
ignorance or sloth, through worldly-mindedness or an evil heart of unbelief are walking in the dark and bringing no honor to God. Think of so
many who are in earnest and yet conscious of a life of failure, with little
or no power to please God or to bless man. And then think again of those
who are to be found everywhere, in solitary places or in companies, whose
one aim is to serve the Lord who bought them and to be the light of those
around them. Think of them especially as joining, often unconscious of
their relation to the whole body of Christ, in pleading for the great promise of the Holy Spirit and the love and oneness of heart which He alone
can give.

This is not the work of one day or one night. It needs a heart which
will set itself from time to time to do serious thinking in regard to the state
and the need of that body of Christ to which we belong. But when once
we begin, we shall find what abundant reason there is for our persevering
and yielding to God's Spirit, that He may fit us for the great and blessed
work of day by day praying the twofold prayer, for the love of God and
Christ to fill the hearts of His people and for the power of the Holy Spirit
to come down and accomplish God's work in this sinful world.

---

*Blessed Father, may we pray day by day for the love of God and Christ
to fill our hearts and for the power of the Holy Spirit to come down
and accomplish Thy work in this sinful world. Amen.*

Prayer by All Saints

"We trust in God that He will yet deliver us; you also helping together by prayer for us" (2 Cor. 1:10–11).

"Some preach Christ of contention supposing to add affliction to my bonds. For I know that this shall turn to my salvation, through your prayer, and the supply of the Spirit of Christ Jesus" (Phil. 1:16, 19).

This subject calls us once again to think of all saints throughout the world but leads us to view them from a different standpoint. If we are to ask God to increase the number and the power of those who do pray, we shall be led to form some impression of what the hope is that our circle of intercessors may gradually increase in number and power.

Our first thoughts will naturally turn to the multitude of the saints who think and know very little about the duty or the blessedness of pleading for the body of Christ or for all the work which has to be done to perfect its members. We shall then have to remember how many there are for whom we may praise God that they do intercede for the power of His Spirit, but their thoughts are chiefly limited to spheres of work that they are acquainted with or directly interested in.

That will leave us with what is, comparatively speaking, a very limited number of those who will be ready to take part in the prayer which ought to be sent up by the whole Church, for the unity of the Body and the power of the Spirit. And even then the number may be but small who really feel themselves drawn and urged to take part in this daily prayer for the out-pouring of the Spirit on all God's people.

And yet many may be feeling that the proposal meets a long-felt need and that it is an unspeakable privilege, whether with few or many, to make Christ's last prayer, "that they may be one," the daily supplication of our faith and love. It may be that in time believers will stand together in small circles, or throughout wider districts, in helping to rouse those around them to take heart in the great work that the prayer *for all saints* may become *one by all saints.*

This message is sent out like radio waves to all who desire to be in touch with it and to seek to prove their consecration to their Lord in the unceasing daily supplication for the Power of His love and Spirit to be revealed to all His people.

Blessed Father, we pray Christ's last prayer, "that they may be one," will be the daily supplication of our faith and love. Amen.

Prayer for All the Fullness of the Spirit

"Bring ye all the tithes unto mine House, and prove me now therewith, saith the Lord of Hosts, if I will not open you the windows of heaven and pour you out a blessing that there shall not be room enough to receive it" (Mal. 3:10).

This last promise in the Old Testament tells us how abundant the blessing is to be. Pentecost was only the beginning of what God was willing to do. The promise of the Father, as Christ gave it, still waits for its perfect fulfillment. Let us try and realize what the liberty is that we have to ask and expect great things.

Just as the great command to go and preach the Gospel was not only meant for the disciples but for us too, so the very last command, "Tarry till ye be endued with power from on high," "Wait for the promise of the Father," "Ye shall be baptized with the Holy Spirit," is also for us and is the ground for the confident assurance that our prayer with one accord will be heard.

Take time to think of what a cry of need there is throughout the whole Church and throughout all our mission fields. Let us realize that the only remedy to be found for inefficiency or weakness to enable us to gain the victory over the powers of this world or of darkness is in the manifested presence of our Lord in the midst of His hosts and in the power of His Spirit. Let us take time to think of the state of all the churches throughout Christendom until we are brought deeper than ever to the conviction that nothing will avail except the supernatural, Almighty intervention of our Lord Himself to rouse His hosts for the great battle against evil. Can anyone conceive or suggest any other matter for prayer that can at all compete with this: for the power of God on the ministers of the Gospel and on all His people to endue them with power from on High to make the Gospel in very deed the power of God unto salvation?

As we connect the prayer for the whole Church on earth with the prayer for the whole power of God in heaven, we shall feel that the greatest truths of the heavenly world and the Kingdom of God have possession of us and that we are in very deed asking what God is longing to give, as soon as He finds hearts utterly yielded to Himself in faith and obedience.

Heavenly Father, may our hearts be utterly yielded to Thee in faith and obedience so that we ask only for what Thou art longing to give. Amen.

Every Day

"Give us day by day our daily bread" (Luke 11:3).

There are some Christians who are afraid of the thoughts of a promise to pray every day as altogether beyond them.

They could not undertake it, and yet they pray to God to give them their bread day by day. Surely if the children of God themselves once yielded themselves with their whole lives to God's love and service, they should count it a privilege to avail themselves of any invitation that would help them *every day* to come into God's Presence with the great need of His Church and Kingdom.

Are there not many who confess that they desire to live wholly for God? They acknowledge that Christ gave Himself for them, and that His love now watches over them and works in them without ceasing. They admit the claim that nothing less than the measure of the love of Christ to us is to be the measure of our love to Him. They feel that if this is indeed to be the standard of their lives, they ought surely to welcome every opportunity for proving day by day that they are devoting their heart's strength to the interests of Christ's Kingdom and to the prayer that can bring down God's blessing.

Our invitation to daily united prayer may come to some as a new and perhaps unexpected opportunity of becoming God's remembrancers who cry day and night for His power and blessing on His people and on this needy world. Think of the privilege of being thus allowed to plead every day with God on behalf of His saints, for the outpouring of His Spirit and for the coming of His Kingdom that His Will may indeed be done on earth as it is in Heaven. To those who have to confess that they have but little understood the high privilege and the solemn duty of waiting on God in prayer for His blessing on the world, the invitation ought to be most welcome. And even to those who have already their special circles of work for which to pray, the thought that the enlargement of their vision and their hearts to include all God's saints and all the work of His Kingdom and all the promise of an abundant outpouring of His Spirit should urge them to take part in a ministry by which their other work will not suffer, but their hearts be strengthened with a joy and a love and a faith that they have never known before.

Heavenly Father, enlarge our vision to include daily united prayer for all Thy saints and all the work of Thy Kingdom. Amen.

With One Accord

"They were all with one accord in one place . . . . and they were all filled with the Holy Spirit" (Acts 2:1, 4).

Our last chapters have opened to us wonderful thoughts of the solidarity of the whole body of Christ and the need of the deliberate cultivation of the slumbering or buried talents of intercession. We may indeed thank God, for we know of the tens of thousands of His children who in daily prayer are pleading for some portion of the work of God's kingdom in which they are personally interested. But in many cases there is a lack of that large-hearted and universal love that takes up all the saints of God and their service into its embrace. There is not the boldness and the strength that comes from the consciousness of being part of a large and conquering army under the leadership of our conquering King.

We said that a wrestler in the games gathers up his whole strength and counts upon every member of his body doing its very utmost. In the British Army in the present war, with its millions of soldiers, each detachment not only throws its whole heart into the work that it has to do, but it is ready to rejoice and take new courage from every tiding of the bravery and enthusiasm of the far-distant members of the one great army. And is not this what we need in the Church of Christ, such an enthusiasm for the King and His Kingdom and such a faith in His purpose that His name shall be made known to every human being, that our prayers shall rise up every day with a large-hearted love that grasps the whole body of Christ and pleads daily for the power of the Holy Spirit on all its members, even to the very feeblest?

The strength unity gives is something inconceivable. The power of each individual member is increased to a large degree by the inspiration of fellowship with a large and conquering host. Nothing can so help us to an ever-larger faith as the consciousness of being one body and one spirit in Christ Jesus. It was as the disciples were all with one accord in one place in the Day of Pentecost that they were all filled with the Holy Spirit.

Heavenly Father, may we be ever mindful that united prayer brings the answer to prayer. Amen.

A Personal Call

"We trust not in ourselves, but in God who delivered us,
and will yet deliver us" (2 Cor. 1:9–10).

"Some preach Christ of contention, supposing to add
affliction to my bonds. For I know that this shall
turn to my salvation, through your prayer, and the
supply of the Spirit of Jesus Christ" (Phil. 1:16–19).

Texts like these prove that there were still Christians in the churches under the full power of the Holy Spirit on whom Paul could count for effectual, much-availing prayer. When we plead with Christians to pray without ceasing, there are a very large number who quietly decide that such a life is not possible for them. They have not any special gift for prayer; they have not that intense desire for glorifying Christ in the salvation of souls; they have not yet learned what it is, under the power of the constraining love of Christ, to live not unto themselves but unto Him who died for them and rose again.

And yet it is to such that we bring the call to offer themselves for a whole-hearted surrender to live entirely for Christ. We ask them whether they are not ashamed of the selfish life that simply uses Christ as a convenience to escape from hell and to secure a place in heaven. We come to them with the assurance that God can change their lives and fill their hearts with Christ and His Holy Spirit. We plead with them to believe that with God all things are possible. He is able and willing, yea rather, most anxious to restore them to the Father's house, to the joy of His presence and service.

One step on the way to the attainment of this will be that they listen to the call for men and women who will every day and all the day, in the power of Christ's abiding presence, live in the spirit of unceasing intercession for all saints, that they receive the power of the Holy Spirit and acknowledge that this is nothing less than a duty, a sacrifice that Christ's love has a right to claim and that He by His Spirit will indeed work in them. Those, however far they may have come short, who accept the call as coming from Christ and draw near to God in humble prayer for the needed grace will have taken the first step in the path that leads to fellowship with God, to a new faith and life in Christ Jesus, and to the surrender of whole being to that intercession of the Spirit that will help to bring Pentecost again into the hearts of God's people.

Heavenly Father, we hear Thy call to offer ourselves for whole-hearted
surrender to live entirely for Christ. Amen.

The Redemption of the Cross

"Christ redeemed us from the curse of the law,
having become a curse for us" (Gal. 3:13).

Scripture teaches us that there are two points of view from which we may regard Christ's death upon the cross.

The one is *the redemption of the cross*: Christ dying for us as our complete deliverance from the curse of sin. The other, *the fellowship of the cross*: Christ taking us up to die with Him and making us partakers of the fellowship of His death in our own experience.

In our text we have three great unsearchable thoughts. The law of God has pronounced a curse on all sin and on all that is sinful. Christ took our curse upon Him, yea, became a curse and so destroyed its power, and in that cross we now have the everlasting redemption from sin and all its power. The cross reveals to us man's sin as under the curse, Christ becoming a curse and so overcoming it, and our full and everlasting deliverance from the curse.

In these thoughts the lost and most hopeless sinner finds a sure ground of confidence and of hope. God had indeed in Paradise pronounced a curse upon this earth and all that belongs to it. On Mount Ebal, in connection with giving the law, half of the people of Israel were twelve times over to pronounce a curse on all sin. And there was to be in their midst a continual reminder of it. "Cursed is every one that hangeth on a tree" (Deut. 21:23; 27:15–20). And yet who could ever have thought that the Son of God Himself would die upon the accursed tree and become a curse for us? But such is in very deed the Gospel of God's love and the penitent sinner can now rejoice in the confident assurance that the curse is forever put away from all who believe in Christ Jesus.

The preaching of the redemption of the cross is the foundation and center of the salvation the Gospel brings us. To those who believe its full truth, it is a cause of unceasing thanksgiving. It gives us boldness to rejoice in God. There is nothing which will keep the heart more tender toward God, enabling us to live in His love and to make Him known to those who have never yet found Him. God be praised for the redemption of the cross!

Blessed Father, we praise Thee for the redemption of the cross! Amen.

The Fellowship of the Cross

*"Have this mind in you, which was
also in Christ Jesus" (Phil. 2:5).*

Paul here tells us what that mind was in Christ: He emptied Himself; He took the form of a servant; He humbled Himself, even to the death of the cross. It is this mind that was in Christ, the deep humility that gave up His life to the very death, that is to be the spirit that animates us. It is thus that we shall prove and enjoy the blessed fellowship of His cross.

Paul had said (v. 1): "If there is any comfort in Christ,"—the Comforter was come to reveal His real presence in them—"if any fellowship of the Spirit,"—it was in this power of the Spirit that they were to breathe the Spirit of the crucified Christ and manifest His disposition in the fellowship of the cross in their lives.

As they strove to do this, they would feel the need of a deeper insight into their real oneness with Christ. They would learn to appreciate the truth that they had been crucified with Christ, that their "old man" had been crucified, and that they had died to sin in Christ's death and were now living to God in His life. They would learn to know what it meant that the crucified Christ lived in them and that they had crucified the flesh with its affections and lusts. It was because the crucified Jesus lived in them that they could live crucified to the world.

And so they would gradually enter more deeply into the meaning and the power of their high calling to live as those who were dead to sin and the world and self. Each in his own measure would bear about in his life the marks of the cross with its sentence of death on the flesh, with its hating of the self life and its entire denial of self, with its growing conformity to the crucified Redeemer in His deep humility and entire surrender of His will to the life of God.

It is no easy school and no hurried learning—this school of the cross. But it will lead to a deeper comprehension and a higher appreciation of the redemption of the cross through the personal experience of the fellowship of the cross.

Blessed Father, may we ever gain a higher appreciation of the redemption of the cross through the personal experience of the fellowship of the cross. Amen.

Crucified with Christ

*"I have been crucified with Christ; yet I live; and yet
no longer I, but Christ liveth in me" (Gal. 2:20).*

The thought of fellowship with Christ in His bearing the cross has often led to the vain attempt in our own power to follow Him and bear His image. But this is impossible to us until we first learn to know something of what it means to say, "I have been crucified with Christ."

Let us try to understand this. When Adam died, all his descendants died with him and in him. In his sin in Paradise and in the spiritual death into which he fell, I had a share; I died in him. And the power of that sin and death, in which all his descendants share, works in every child of Adam every day.

Christ came as the second Adam. In His death on the cross, all who believe in Him had a share. Each one may say in truth, "I have been crucified with Christ." As the representative of His people, He took them up with Him on the cross, and me too. The life that He gives is the crucified life in which He entered heaven and was exalted to the throne, standing as a Lamb as it had been slain. The power of His death and life work in me, and as I hold fast the truth that I have been crucified with Him and that now I myself live no more but Christ liveth in me, I receive power to conquer sin; the life that I have received from Him is a life that has been crucified and made free from the power of sin.

We have here a deep and very precious truth. Most Christians have but little knowledge of it. That knowledge is not gained easily or speedily. It needs a great longing in very deed to be dead to all sin. It needs a strong faith, wrought by the Holy Spirit, that the union with Christ crucified, that the fellowship of His cross can day by day become our life. The life that He lives in heaven has its strength and its glory in the fact that it is a crucified life. And the life that He imparts to the believing disciple is even so a crucified life with its victory over sin and its power of access into God's presence.

It is in very deed true that I no longer live but Christ lives in me as the Crucified one. As faith realizes and holds fast the fact that the crucified Christ lives in me, life in the fellowship of the cross becomes a possibility and a blessed experience.

---

*Heavenly Father, I long in very deed to be dead to all sin that the union
with Thy Son crucified and the fellowship of His cross can day by day
become my life. Amen.*

Crucified to the World

*"Far be it from me to glory, save in the cross of
our Lord Jesus Christ, through which the world hath
been crucified unto me, and I unto the world" (Gal. 6:14).*

What Paul had written in Galatians 2 is here in the end of the Epistle confirmed and expressed still more strongly.

He speaks of his only glory being that in Christ he has in very deed been crucified to the world and entirely delivered from its power. When he said: "I have been crucified with Christ," it was not only an inner spiritual truth, but an actual, practical experience in relation to the world and its temptations. Christ had spoken about the world hating Him and His having overcome the world. Paul knows that the world which nailed Christ to the cross had in that deed done the same to him. He boasts that he lives as one crucified to the world, and that now the world as an powerless enemy was crucified to him. It was this that made him glory in the cross of Christ. It had wrought out a complete deliverance from the world.

How very different the relation of Christians to the world in our day! They agree that they may not commit the sins that the world allows. But further they are good friends with the world and have liberty to enjoy as much of it as they can, if they only keep from open sin. They do not know that the most dangerous source of sin is the love of the world with its lusts and pleasures.

O Christian, when the world crucified Christ, it crucified you with Him. When Christ overcame the world on the cross, He made you an overcomer too. He calls you now, at whatever cost of self-denial, to regard the world in its hostility to God and His Kingdom as a crucified enemy over whom the cross can ever keep you conqueror.

What a different relationship to the pleasures and attractions of the world the Christian has who by the Holy Spirit has learned to say: "I have been crucified with Christ; the crucified Christ liveth in me"!

Heavenly Father, we pray fervently that the Holy Spirit, through whom Christ offered Himself on the cross, may reveal to us in power what it means to "glory in the cross of our Lord Jesus Christ, through which the world has been crucified unto me." Amen.

The Flesh Crucified

"They that are in Christ Jesus have crucified the flesh with the passions and the lusts thereof" (Gal. 5:24).

Of the flesh Paul teaches us (Rom. 7:18), "In me, that is, *in my flesh, dwelleth no good thing*." And again (Rom. 8:7), "The mind of the flesh in *enmity against God*; for it is not subject to the law of God, *neither indeed can it be*." When Adam lost the Spirit of God, he became flesh. Flesh is the expression for the evil, corrupt nature that we inherit from Adam. Of this flesh it is written, "Our old man was crucified with Him" (Rom. 7:6). And Paul puts it here even more strongly, "They that are in Christ Jesus have crucified the flesh."

When the disciples heard and obeyed the call of Jesus to follow Him, they honestly meant to do so, but as He later on taught them what that would imply, they were far from being ready to yield immediate obedience. And even so those who are Christ's and have accepted Him as the Crucified One little understand what that includes. By that act of surrender they actually have crucified the flesh and consented to regard it as an accursed thing, nailed to the cross of Christ.

Alas, how many there are who have never for a moment thought of such a thing! It may be that the preaching of Christ crucified has been defective. It may be that the truth of our being crucified with Christ has not been taught. They shrink back from the self-denial that it implies, and as a result, where the flesh is allowed in any measure to have its way, the Spirit of Christ cannot exert His power.

Paul taught the Galatians: "Walk in the Spirit, and ye shall not fulfill the lusts of the flesh." "As many as are led by the Spirit of God, they are the children of God." And the Spirit can alone guide us in living faith and fellowship with Christ Jesus as the flesh is kept in the place of crucifixion.

Blessed Lord, how little I understood when I accepted Thee in faith that I crucified once for all the flesh with its passions and lusts! I beseech Thee humbly, teach me so to believe and so to live in Thee, the Crucified One, that with Paul I may ever glory in the cross on which the world and the flesh are crucified. Amen.

Bearing the Cross

"He that doth not take his cross and follow after Me,
is not worthy of Me. He that loseth his life for
My sake shall find it" (Matt. 10:38–39).

We have had some of Paul's great words to the Galatians about the cross and our being crucified with Christ. Let us now turn to the Master Himself to hear what He has to teach us. We shall find that what Paul could teach openly and fully after the crucifixion was given by the Master in words that could at first hardly be understood and yet contained the seed of the full truth.

It was in the ordination charge, when Christ sent forth His disciples, that He first used the expression that the disciple must take up His cross and follow Him.

The only meaning the disciples could attach to these words was from what they had often seen when an evil-doer who had been sentenced to death by the cross was led out bearing his cross to the place of execution. In bearing the cross, he acknowledged the sentence of death that was on him. And Christ would have His disciples understand that their nature was so evil and corrupt that it was only in losing their natural life that they could find the true life. Of Himself it was true, all His life He bore His cross, the sentence of death that He knew to rest upon Himself on account of our sins. And so He would have His disciple bear his cross, the sentence of death upon himself and his evil, carnal nature.

The disciples could not at once understand all this. But Christ gave them seed words which would germinate in their hearts and later on begin to reveal their full meaning. The disciple was not only to carry the sentence of death in himself but to learn that in following the Master to His cross, he would find the power to lose his life and to receive instead of it the life that would come through the cross of Christ.

Christ asks of His disciples that they should forsake all and take up their cross, give up their whole will and life, and follow Him. The call comes to us too to give up the self life with its self-pleasing and self-exaltation and bear the cross in fellowship with Him, and we shall be made partakers of His victory.

Dear Lord Jesus, I hear Thy call to give up the self life and bear the cross in fellowship with Thee that I shall partake of Thy victory. Amen.

Self-Denial

*"Then said Jesus unto His disciples, 'If any man will
come after Me, let him deny himself, and take up
his cross, and follow Me'" (Matt. 16:24).*

Christ had for the first time definitely announced that He would have
to suffer much and be killed and be raised again. "Peter rebuked him, saying, 'Be it far from Thee, Lord: this shall never be unto Thee.'" Christ's
answer was, "Get thee behind Me, Satan." The spirit of Peter, seeking to
turn Him away from the cross and its suffering, was nothing but Satan
tempting Him to turn aside from the path which God had appointed as our
way of salvation.

Christ then adds the words of our text in which He uses for the second
time the words "take up the cross." But with that He uses a most significant expression revealing what is implied in the cross: "If any man come
after Me, *let him deny himself*, and take up his cross." When Adam sinned,
he fell out of the life of Heaven and of God into the life of the World and
of Self. Self-pleasing, self-sufficiency, self-exaltation became the law of
his life. When Jesus Christ came to restore man to his original place, "being in the form of God, *He emptied Himself*, taking the form of a servant,
and *humbled Himself* even to the death of the cross." What He has done
Himself He asks of all who desire to follow Him: "If any man will come
after Me, let him deny himself."

Instead of denying himself, Peter denied his Lord: "I know not the Man."
When a man learns to obey Christ's commands, he says of himself: "I know
not the man." It is the secret of true discipleship, to bear the cross, to acknowledge the death sentence that has been passed on self, and to deny
any right that self has to rule over us.

Death to self is to be the Christian's watchword. The surrender to Christ
is to be so entire, the surrender for Christ's sake to live for those around
us so complete, that self is never allowed to come down from the cross to
which it has been crucified but is ever kept in the place of death.

Let us listen to the voice of Jesus, "Deny self," and ask that by the grace
of the Holy Spirit, as the disciples of Christ who denied Himself for us,
we may ever live as those in whom self has been crucified with Christ and
in whom the crucified Christ now lives as Lord and Master.

---

*Dear Lord Jesus, let us hear Thy voice, "Deny self," and ask that by
the grace of the Holy Spirit we may live crucified with Thee and that
Thou wilt live in us as Lord and Master. Amen.*

He Cannot Be My Disciple

"If any man cometh unto Me, and hateth not his own life, he cannot be My disciple. Whosoever doth not bear his own cross, and come after Me, cannot be My disciple. Whosoever he be of you that renounceth not all that he hath, he cannot be My disciple" (Luke 14:26–33).

For the third time Christ speaks about bearing the cross. He gives new meaning to it when He says that we must hate our own life and renounce all that we have. Three times over He solemnly repeats the words that without this we cannot be His disciples.

"If a man hate not his own life." And why does Christ make such an exacting demand the condition of discipleship? Because the sinful nature we have inherited from Adam is indeed so vile and full of sin, that if our eyes were only opened to see it in its true nature, we would flee from it as loathsome and incurably evil. "The flesh is enmity against God"; the soul that seeks to love God cannot but hate the old man which is corrupt through its whole being. Nothing less than this, the hating of our own life, will make us willing to bear the cross and carry within us the sentence of death on our evil nature. It is not till we hate this life with a deadly hatred that we will be ready to give up the old nature to die the death that is its due.

Christ has one word more: "He that renounceth not all that he hath," whether in property or character, "cannot be My disciple." Christ claims all. Christ undertakes to satisfy every need and to give a hundredfold more than we give up. It is when by faith we become conscious what it means to know Christ and to love Him and to receive from Him what can in very deed enrich and satisfy our immortal spirits, that we shall count the surrender of what at first appeared so difficult, our highest privilege. As we learn what it means that Christ is our life, we shall count all things but loss for the excellency of the knowledge of Christ Jesus our Lord.

Blessed Lord Jesus, in the path of following Thee and ever learning to know and to love Thee better, we shall willingly sacrifice all, self with its life, to make room for Thee who is more than all. Amen.

Follow Me

"Then Jesus, beholding him, loved him, and said: 'One thing thou lackest: go thy way, sell whatsoever thou hast, and come, take up the cross, and follow Me'" (Mark 10:21).

When Christ spoke these words to the young ruler, he went away grieved. Jesus said: "How hardly shall they that have riches enter into the Kingdom of God!" The disciples were astonished at His words. When Christ repeated once again what He had said, they were astonished out of measure. "Who then can be saved?" "Jesus looking upon them said, 'With men it is impossible, but not with God; for with God all things are possible.'"

Christ had spoken about bearing the cross from the human side as the one condition of discipleship. Here with the rich young ruler He reveals from the side of God what is needed to give men the will and the power thus to sacrifice all, if they were to enter the Kingdom. He said to Peter, when he had confessed Him as Christ, the Son of God, that flesh and blood had not revealed it unto him, but his Father in heaven, to remind him and the other disciples that it was only by Divine teaching that he could make the confession. So here with the ruler, He unveils the great mystery that it is only by Divine power that a man can take up his cross, can lose his life, can deny himself and hate the life to which he is by nature so attached.

What multitudes have sought to follow Christ and obey His injunction and have found that they have utterly failed! What multitudes have felt that Christ's claims were beyond their reach and have sought to be Christians without any attempt at the wholehearted devotion and the entire self-denial which Christ asks for!

Heavenly Father, let us in our study of what the fellowship of the cross means take today's lesson to heart and believe that it is only by putting our trust in Thee, the living God, and the mighty power in which Thou art willing to work in the heart, that we can attempt to be disciples who forsake all and follow Christ in the fellowship of His cross. Amen.

A Grain of Wheat

*Verily, verily, I say unto you, Except a grain of wheat fall into
the earth and die, it abideth by itself alone; but if it die, it beareth
much fruit. He that loveth his life loseth it; and he that hateth his life
in this world shall keep it unto life eternal" (John 12:24–25 R.V.).*

All nature is the parable of how the losing of a life can be the way of
securing a truer and a higher life. Every grain of wheat, every seed throughout the world, teaches the lesson that through death lies the path to beautiful and fruitful life.

It was so with the Son of God. He had to pass through death in all its
bitterness and suffering before He could rise to heaven and impart His life
to His redeemed people. And here under the shadow of the approaching
cross, He calls His disciples: "If any man will serve Me, let him follow
Me." He repeats the words: "He that hateth his life in this world shall keep
it unto life eternal."

One might have thought that Christ did not need to lose His holy life
before He could find it again. But so it was: God had laid upon Him the
iniquity of us all, and he yielded to the inexorable law: Through death to
life and to fruit.

How much more ought we, in the consciousness of that evil nature and
that death which we inherited in Adam, be willing, yea, most grateful that
there is a way open to us by which, in the fellowship of Christ and His
cross, we can die to this accursed self! With what gratitude ought we to
listen to the call to bear our cross, to yield our "old man" as crucified with
Christ daily to that death which he deserves! Surely the thought that the
power of the eternal Life is working in us ought to make us willing and
glad to die the death that brings us into the fellowship and the power of
life in a risen Christ.

---

*Heavenly Father: Alas, how little this is understood! Let us believe that
what is impossible to man is possible to Thee. Let us believe that the
law of the Spirit of Christ Jesus, the Risen Lord, can in very deed make
His death and His life the daily experience of our souls. Amen.*

Thy Will Be Done

"O My Father, if it be possible, let this cup pass away from Me: nevertheless, not as I will, but as Thou wilt" (Matt. 26:39 R.V.).

The death of Christ on the cross is the highest and the holiest that can be known of Him even in the glory of heaven. And the highest and the holiest that the Holy Spirit can work in us is to take us up and to keep us in the fellowship of the cross of Christ. We need to enter deeply into the truth that Christ the beloved Son of the Father could not return to the glory of heaven until He had first given Himself over unto death. As this great truth opens up to us, it will help us to understand how in our life and in our fellowship with Christ, it is impossible for us to share His life until we have first in very deed surrendered ourselves every day to die to sin and the world and so to abide in the unbroken fellowship with our crucified Lord.

And it is from Christ alone that we can learn what it means to have fellowship with His sufferings and to be made conformable unto His death. When in the agony of Gethsemane He looked forward to what a death on the cross would be, He got such a vision of what it meant to die the accursed death under the power of sin, with God's countenance so turned from Him that not a single ray of its light could penetrate the darkness, He prayed that the cup might pass from Him. But when no answer came and He understood that the Father could not allow the cup to pass by, He yielded up His whole will and life in the word: "Thy will be done." O Christian, in this word of thy Lord in His agony, thou canst enter into fellowship with Him, and in His strength thy heart will be made strong to believe most confidently that God in His omnipotence will enable thee in very deed with Christ to yield up everything, because thou hast in very deed been crucified with Him.

"Thy will be done"; let this be the deepest and the highest word in thy life. In the power of Christ with whom thou hast been crucified and in the power of His Spirit, the definite daily surrender to the ever-blessed will of God will become the joy and the strength of thy life.

Heavenly Father, in the power of Christ with whom I, too, have been crucified, and in the power of His Spirit I pray, "Thy will be done." Amen.

The Love of the Cross

"Then said Jesus: 'Father, forgive them; for
they know not what they do'" (Luke 23:34).

The seven words on the cross reveal what the mind of Christ is and show the dispositions that become His disciples. Take the three first words, all the expression of His wonderful love.

"Father, forgive them, for they know not what they do." He prays for His enemies. In the hour of their triumph over Him and of the shame and suffering which they delight in showering on Him, He pours out His love in prayer for them. It is the call to everyone who believes in a crucified Christ to go and do likewise, even as He has said, "Love your enemies, bless them that curse you, Do good to them that hate you, and pray for them which Persecute you." The law of the Master is the law for the disciple; the love of the crucified Jesus, the only rule for those who believe in Him.

"Woman, behold thy son!" "Behold thy mother!" The love that cared for His enemies, cared too for His friends. Jesus felt what the anguish must be in the heart of His widowed mother and commits her to the care of the beloved disciple. He knew that for John there could be no higher privilege and no more blessed service, than that of taking His place in the care of Mary. Even so we who are the disciples of Christ must not only pray for His enemies, but prove our love to Him and to all who belong to Him, by seeing to it that every solitary one is comforted, and that every loving heart has some work to do in caring for those who belong to the blessed Master.

"Verily I say unto thee, today shalt thou be with Me in Paradise." The penitent thief had appealed to Christ's mercy to remember him. With what readiness of joy and love Christ gives the immediate answer to his prayer! Whether it was the love that prayed for His enemies, or the love that cared for His friends, or the love that rejoices over the penitent sinner who was being cast out by man—in all Christ proves that the Cross is a Cross of love, that the Crucified One is the embodiment of a love that passeth knowledge.

Blessed Father: With every thought of what we owe to that love, with every act of faith in which we rejoice in its redemption, let us prove that the mind of the crucified Christ is our mind and that His love is not only what we trust in for ourselves, but what guides us in our loving involvement with the world around us. Amen.

The Sacrifice of the Cross

"My God, My God, why hast Thou forsaken Me?" (Matt. 27:46).

"I thirst" (John 19:28).

"It is finished" (John 19:30).

The three first words on the cross reveal love in its outflow to men. The next three reveal love in the tremendous sacrifice that it brought to deliver us from our sins and give the victory over every foe. They will still reveal the very mind that was in Christ, and that is to be in us as the disposition of our whole life.

"My God, My God, why hast Thou forsaken Me?" How deep must have been the darkness that overshadowed Him, when not one ray of light could pierce and He could not say, "My Father"! It was this awful desertion, breaking in upon that life of childlike fellowship with the Father in which He had always walked, that caused Him the agony and the bloody sweat in Gethsemane. "O My Father, let this cup pass from Me"—but it might not be, and He bowed His head in submission: "Thy will be done." It was His love to God and love to man, yielding Himself to the very uttermost. It is as we learn to believe and to worship that love, that we too shall learn to say: "Abba, Father, Thy will be done."

"I thirst." The body now gives expression to the terrible experience of what it passed through when the fire of God's wrath against sin came upon Christ in the hour of His desertion. He had spoken of Dives crying: "I am tormented in this flame." Christ utters His complaint of what He had suffered. Physicians tell us that in crucifixion the whole body is in agony with a terrible fever and pain. Our Lord endured it all and cried: "I thirst"; soul and body was the sacrifice He brought the Father.

And then comes the great word: "It is finished." All that there was to suffer and endure had been brought a willing sacrifice; He had finished the work the Father gave Him to do. His love held nothing back. He gave Himself an offering and a sacrifice. Such was the mind of Christ, and such must be the disposition of everyone who owes Himself and his life to that sacrifice. The mind that was in Christ must be in us ready to say: "I am come to do the will of Him that sent Me and to finish His work." And every day, our confidence growing fuller in Christ's finished work, must see our heart more entirely yielding itself like Him, a whole burnt offering in the service of God and His love.

Heavenly Father, each day may our yielded hearts be a whole burnt offering in service to Thee and Thy love. Amen.

The Death of the Cross

"'Father, into Thy hands I commit My spirit.' And
having said this, He gave up the ghost" (Luke 23:46).

Like David (Ps. 31:5), Christ had often committed His spirit into the hands of His Father for His daily life and need. But here is something new and very special. He gives up His spirit into the power of death, gives up all control over it, to sink down into the darkness and death of the grave where He can neither think, nor pray, nor will. He surrenders Himself to the utmost into the Father's hands, trusting Him to care for Him in the dark and in due time to raise Him up again.

If we have indeed died in Christ and are now in faith every day to carry about with us the death of our Lord Jesus, this word is the very one that we need. Just think once again what Christ meant when He said that we must hate and lose our life.

We died in Adam; the life we receive from him is death; there is nothing good or heavenly in us by nature. It is to this inward evil nature, to all the life that we have from this world, that we must die. There cannot be any thought of any real holiness without totally dying to this self or "old man." Many deceive themselves because they seek to be alive in God before they are dead to their own nature—a thing as impossible as it is for a grain of wheat to be alive before it dies. This total dying to self lies at the root of all true piety. The spiritual life must grow out of death.

And if we ask how we can do this, we find the answer in the mind in which Christ died. Like Him we cast ourselves upon God without knowing how the new life is to be attained; but as we in fellowship with Jesus say, "Father, into Thy hands I commit my spirit," and depend simply and absolutely upon God to raise us up into the new life, there will be fulfilled in us the wonderful promise of God's Word concerning the exceeding greatness of His power in us who believe, according to the mighty power which He wrought in Christ when He raised Him from the dead.

This indeed is the true rest of faith that lives every day and every hour in the absolute dependence upon the continual and immediate quickening of the Divine life in us by God Himself through the Holy Spirit.

Heavenly Father, as my spiritual life can only grow out of death, I too,
pray, "Father, into Thy hands I commit my spirit." Amen.

It Is Finished

"When Jesus had received the vinegar,
He said: 'It is finished'" (John 19:30).

The seven words of our Lord on the cross reveal to us His mind and disposition. At the beginning of His ministry He said (John 4:34): "My meat is to do the will of Him that sent Me, and *to finish His work*." In all things, the small as well as the great, He should accomplish God's work. In the High-Priestly prayer at the end of the three years' ministry, He could say (John 17:4): "I have glorified Thee on the earth, *I have finished the work* which Thou gavest Me to do." He sacrificed all and in dying on the cross could in truth say: "It is finished."

With that word to the Father, He laid down His life. With that word He was strengthened, after the terrible agony on the cross, in the knowledge that all was now fulfilled. And with that word He uttered the truth of the gospel of our redemption, that all that was needed for man's salvation had been accomplished on the cross.

This disposition should characterize every follower of Christ. The mind that was in Him must be in us—it must be our meat, the strength of our life, *to do the Will of God in all things and to finish His work*. There may be small things about which we are not conscientious and so we bring harm to ourselves and to God's work. Or we draw back before some great thing which demands too much sacrifice. In every case we may find strength to perform our duty in Christ's word: "It is finished." His finished work secured the victory over every foe. By faith we may appropriate that dying word of Christ on the cross and find the power for daily living and dying in the fellowship of the crucified Christ.

Child of God, study the inexhaustible treasure contained in this word: "It is finished." Faith in what Christ accomplished on the cross will enable you to manifest in daily life the spirit of the cross.

Blessed Father, may the mind of Christ be in me, to do Thy will in all things and to finish Thy work. Amen.

Dead to Sin

"We who died to sin, how shall we
any longer live therein?" (Rom. 6:2).

After having, in the first section of the Epistle to the Romans (1:16 to 5:11), expounded the great doctrine of justification by faith, Paul proceeds, in the second section (5:12 to 8:39), to unfold the related doctrine of the new life by faith in Christ. Taking Adam as a figure of Christ, he teaches that just as we all really and actually died in Adam so that his death reigns in our nature, even so in Christ, those who believe in Him actually and effectually died to sin, were set free from it, and became partakers of the new holy life of Christ.

He asks the question: "We who died to sin, how shall we any longer live therein?" In these words we have the deep spiritual truth that our death to sin in Christ delivers us from its power so that we no longer may or need to live in it. The secret of true and full holiness is by faith and in the power of the Holy Spirit to live in the consciousness I am dead to sin.

In expounding this truth He reminds them that they were baptized *into the death of Christ*. We were buried with Him through baptism into death. We became *united with Him* by the likeness of His death. Our "old man" was crucified with Him that the body of sin might be done away—rendered void and powerless. Take time and, asking for the teaching of the Holy Spirit, quietly ponder these words until the truth masters you: I am indeed dead to sin in Christ Jesus. As we grow in the consciousness of our union with the crucified Christ, we shall experience that the power of His life in us has made us free from the power of sin.

Romans 6 is one of the most blessed portions of the New Testament of our Lord Jesus, teaching us that our "old man," the old nature that is in us, was actually crucified with Him so that now we need no longer be in bondage to sin. But remember, it is only as the Holy Spirit makes Christ's death a reality within us that we shall know, not by force of argument or conviction but in the reality of the power of a Divine life, that we are in very deed dead to sin. It only needs the continual living in Christ Jesus.

Heavenly Father, I quietly ponder this truth: I am indeed dead to sin in Christ Jesus, His life in me makes me free from the power of sin. Amen.

The Righteousness of God

*"Abraham believed God, and it was counted unto
him for righteousness." "He believed God, who
quickeneth the dead" (Rom. 4:3,17).*

Let us now, after listening to the words of our Lord Jesus about our fellowship with Him in the cross, turn to St. Paul and see how through the Holy Spirit he gives the deeper insight into what our death in Christ means.

You know how the first section of Romans is devoted to the doctrine of justification by faith in Christ. After speaking (1:18–32) of the awful sin of the heathen and then (2:1–29) of the sin of the Jew, he points out how Jew and Gentile are "guilty before God." "All have sinned and come short." And then he sets forth that free grace which gave the redemption that is in Christ Jesus (3:21–31). In chapter 4, he points to Abraham as having, when he believed, understood that God justified him freely by His grace and not for anything that he had done.

Abraham had not only believed this, but something more. "He believed in God, who quickeneth the dead, and calleth the things that are not, as though they were." The two expressions are most significant, as indicating the two essential needs there are in the redemption of man in Christ Jesus. There is the need of justification by faith, to restore man to the favor of God. But there is more needed. He must also be quickened to a new life. Just as justification is by faith alone, so is regeneration also. Christ died for our sins; He was raised again out of or through our justification.

In the first section (5:11) Paul deals exclusively with the great thought of our justification. But in the second section (5:12 to 8:39) he expounds that wonderful union with Christ through faith by which we died with Him, by which we live in Him, and by which through the Holy Spirit we are made free not only from the punishment but also from the power of sin and are enabled to live the life of righteousness, of obedience, and of sanctification.

Heavenly Father, we thank Thee that we are free not only from the punishment but also from the power of sin and are enabled to live the life of righteousness, of obedience, and of santification. Amen.

Dead with Christ

"If we died with Christ, we believe that
we shall also live with Him" (Rom. 6:8).

The reason that God's children live so little in the power of the resurrection life of Christ is because they have so little understanding of or faith in their death with Christ. How clearly this appears from what Paul says: "If we died with Christ, we believe that we shall also live with Him"; it is the knowledge and experience that gives us the assurance of the power of His resurrection in us. "Christ died unto sin once; but the life that He liveth, He liveth unto God" (v. 10). It is only because and as we know that we are dead with Him that we can live with Him.

On the strength of this, Paul now appeals to his readers. "Even so reckon ye also yourselves to be dead unto sin, but alive unto God in Christ Jesus" (v. 11). The words "even so reckon yourselves" are a call to an act of bold and confident faith. Reckon yourselves to be indeed dead unto sin as much as Christ is and alive to God in Christ Jesus. The word gives us a Divine assurance of what we actually are and have in Christ. And this is not a truth that our minds can master and appropriate, but a reality which the Holy Spirit will reveal within us. In His power we accept our death with Christ on the cross as the power of our daily life.

Then we are able to accept and obey the command: "Let not sin reign in your mortal body; but present yourself unto God, as alive from the dead; for sin shall not have dominion over you" (vv. 12–14). "Being made free from sin, ye became servants of righteousness; present your members as servants to righteousness unto sanctification. Being now made free from sin, ye have your fruit unto sanctification" (vv. 18–19, 22).

The whole chapter is a wonderful revelation of the deep meaning of its opening words: "How shall we, *who died to sin*, live any more therein?" Everything depends upon our acceptance of the Divine assurance: if we died with Christ as He died and now lives to God, we too have the assurance that in Him we have the power to live unto God.

Heavenly Father, we accept Thy Divine assurance that we shall live
with Christ. Amen.

Dead to the Law

*"Ye were made dead to the law, through the body
of Christ." "Having died to that wherein we were holden,
so that we serve in newness of the spirit" (Rom. 7:4, 6).*

The believer is not only dead to sin but dead to the law. This is a deeper truth, giving us deliverance from the thought of a life of effort and failure and opening the way to the life in the power of the Holy Spirit. "Thou shalt" is done away with; the power of the Spirit takes its place. In the remainder of this chapter (7:7–24) we have a description of the Christian as he still tries to obey the law, but utterly fails. He experiences that "in him, that is in his flesh, dwelleth no good thing." He finds that the law of sin, notwithstanding his utmost efforts, continually brings him into captivity and compels the cry: "O wretched man that I am, who shall deliver me from the body of this death?" In the whole passage, it is everywhere "I," without any thought of the Spirit's help. It is only when he has given utterance to his cry of despair that he is brought to see that he is no longer under the law, but under the rule of the Holy Spirit (8:1–2). "There is therefore now no condemnation," such as he had experienced in his attempt to obey the law "to them that are in Christ Jesus. For the law of the Spirit of life in Christ Jesus has made me free from the law of sin and death." As chapter 7 gives us the experience that leads to being a captive under the power of sin, chapter 8 reveals the experience of the life of a man in Christ Jesus who has now been made free from the law of sin and death. In the former we have the life of the ordinary Christian doing his utmost to keep the commandments of the law and to walk in His ways but ever finding how much there is of failure and shortcoming. In the latter we have the man who knows that he is in Christ Jesus, dead to sin and alive to God, and by the Spirit has been made free and is kept free from the bondage of sin and of death.

Heavenly Father: Oh that we understood what the deep meaning is of Romans 7, where we learn that in ourselves, that is in our flesh, there is no good thing and that there is no deliverance from this state but by yielding to the power of the Spirit making free from the power of bondage of the flesh, and so fulfilling the righteousness of the law in the power of the life of Christ! Amen.

The Flesh Condemned on the Cross

"What the law could not do, in that it was weak through the flesh, God, sending His own Son in the likeness of sinful flesh, and for sin, condemned sin in the flesh" (Rom. 8:3).

In Romans 8:7 Paul writes: "The mind of the flesh is enmity against God; for it is not subject to the law of God, neither indeed can it be." Here Paul opens up the depth of sin that there is in the flesh. In chapter 7 he had said that in the flesh there is no good thing. Here he goes deeper and tells us that it is enmity against God; it hates God and His law. It was on this account that God condemned sin in the flesh on the cross; all the curse that there is upon sin is upon the flesh in which sin dwells. It is as the believers understand this that they will cease from any attempt at seeking to perfect in the flesh what is begun in the Spirit. The two are at deadly, irreconcilable enmity.

See how this lies at the very root of the true Christian life (vv. 3–4): "God condemned sin in the flesh, that the righteousness of the law might be fulfilled in us who walk, not after the flesh, but after the Spirit." All the requirements of God's law will be fulfilled, not in those who strive to keep and fulfill that law—a thing that is utterly impossible—but who walk by the Spirit and in His power live out the life that Christ won for us on the cross and imparted to us in the resurrection.

Would God that His children might learn the double lesson. In me, that is in my flesh, in the old nature which I have from Adam, there dwells literally no good thing that can satisfy the eye of a holy God! And that flesh can never by any process of discipline, or struggling, or prayer, be made better than it is! But the Son of God in the likeness of sinful flesh—in the form of a man—condemned sin on the cross. "There is now no condemnation to them which are in Christ Jesus, who walk, not after the flesh, but after the Spirit."

Our prayer, Dear Heavenly Father, is that we, Thy children, learn that in us, in our flesh, dwells no good thing that can satisfy Thy Holy eye, but that in Thy Son we walk not after the flesh but after Thy Spirit. Amen.

Jesus Christ and
Him Crucified

*"I determined not to know anything among you, save
Jesus Christ and Him crucified. And my preaching was in
demonstration of the Spirit and of power" (1 Cor 2:2, 4).*

This text is very often understood of Paul's purpose in his preaching to
know nothing but Jesus Christ and Him crucified. But it contains a far deeper thought. He speaks of his purpose, not only in the matter of his preaching but in his whole spirit and life, to prove how he in everything seeks to
act in conformity to the crucified Christ. Thus he writes (2 Cor. 13:4–5):
"Christ was crucified through weakness, yet He liveth through the power
of God. For we also are weak in Him, but we shall live with Him through
the power of God toward you." His whole ministry and conversation bore
the mark of Christ's likeness—crucified through weakness, yet living by
the power of God.

Just before the words of our text Paul had written (1:17–24): "The word
of the cross is to them that are perishing foolishness; but unto us which
are being saved it is the power of God." It was not only in his preaching
but in his whole disposition and deportment that he sought to act in harmony with that weakness in which Christ was crucified. He had so identified himself with the weakness of the cross and its shame, that in his whole
life and conduct he would prove that in everything he sought to show forth
the likeness and the spirit of the crucified Jesus. Hence he says (2:3): "I
was with you in weakness, and in fear, and in much trembling."

It is on this account that he spoke so strongly (1:17): "Christ sent me
to preach the gospel, not in wisdom of words, lest the cross of Christ should
be made void"; (2:4): "My preaching was not with enticing words of man's
wisdom, but in demonstration of the Spirit and of power." Have we not
here the great reason why the power of God is so little manifested in the
preaching of the Gospel? Christ the crucified may be the subject of the
preaching and yet there may be such confidence in human learning and
eloquence that there is nothing to be seen of that likeness of the crucified
Jesus which alone gives preaching its supernatural, its divine power.

---

*God help us to understand how the life of every minister and of every
believer must bear the hallmark, the stamp of the sanctuary—Nothing
but Jesus Christ, and Him crucified. Amen.*

Temperate in All Things

*"Every man that striveth in the games exerciseth
self-control in all things . . . . I buffet my body, and
bring it into bondage" (1 Cor. 9:25, 27 R.V.).*

Paul here reminds us of the well-known principle that anyone competing for a prize in the public games is "temperate in all things." Everything, however attractive, that might be a hindrance in the race is given up or set aside. And this in order to obtain an earthly prize. And shall we who strive for an incorruptible crown and that Christ may be Lord of all—shall we not be temperate in all things that could in the very least prevent our following the Lord Jesus with an undivided heart?

Paul says: "I buffet my body, and bring it into bondage." He would allow nothing to hinder him. He tells us: "This one thing I do; I press toward the mark for the prize." No self-pleasing in eating and drinking, no comfort or ease should for a moment keep him from showing the spirit of the cross in his daily life or from sacrificing all, like his Master. Read the following four passages which comprise his life-history: 2 Cor. 4:11–13, 2 Cor. 4:8–12; 6:4–10; 11:23–27. The cross was not only the theme of his preaching, but the rule of his life in all its details.

We need to pray God that this disposition may be found in all Christians and preachers of the Gospel, through the power of the Holy Spirit. When the death of Christ works with power in the preacher, then Christ's life will be known among the people. Let us pray that the fellowship of the cross may regain its old place and that God's children may obey the injunction: "Let this mind be in you that was in Christ Jesus." He humbled Himself and became obedient unto the death of the cross. For, "if we have been planted together in the likeness of His death, we shall be also in the likeness of His resurrection" (Rom. 6:5).

Blessed Heavenly Father, we pray that this disposition may be found in all Christians and preachers of the Gospel and that the mind of Christ Jesus may be in us. Amen.

The Dying of the Lord Jesus

*"Always bearing about in the body the dying of Jesus, that
the life also of Jesus may be manifested in our body . . . . So
then death worketh in us, but life in you" (2 Cor. 4:10, 12).*

Paul here is very bold in speaking of the intimate union that there was
between Christ living in him and the life he lived in the flesh with all its
suffering. He had spoken (Gal. 2:20) of his being crucified with Christ and
Christ living in him. Here he tells how he was always bearing about in the
body the dying of Jesus; it was through that that the life also of Jesus was
manifested in his body. And he says that it was because the death of Christ
was thus working in and through him, that Christ's life could work in them.

We often speak of our abiding in Christ. But we forget that that means
the abiding in a crucified Christ. Many believers appear to think that when
once they have claimed Christ's death in the fellowship of the cross and
have counted themselves as crucified with Him, that they may now consider it as past and done with. They do not understand that it is in the crucified Christ and in the fellowship of His death that they are to abide daily
and unceasingly. The fellowship of the cross is to be the life of a daily
experience, the self-emptying of our Lord, His taking the form of a servant, His humbling Himself and becoming obedient unto death, even the
death of the cross—this mind that was in Christ is to be the disposition
that marks our daily life.

"Always bearing about in the body the dying of Jesus." This is what
we are called to as much as Paul. If we are indeed to live for the welfare
of others around us, if we are to sacrifice our ease and pleasure to win
souls for our Lord, it will be true of us as of Paul, that we are able to say:
Death worketh in us, but life in those for whom we pray and labor. It is in
the fellowship of the sufferings of Christ that the crucified Lord can live
out and work out His life in us and through us.

---

*Heavenly Father: Let us learn the lesson that the abiding in Christ
Jesus for which we have so often prayed and striven is nothing less
than the abiding of the Crucified in us and we in Him. Amen.*

The Cross and the Spirit

*"How much more shall the blood of Christ, who through
the Eternal Spirit offered Himself without blemish unto
God, cleanse your conscience?" (Heb. 9:14 R.V.).*

The cross is Christ's highest glory. The glory which He received from the Father was entirely owing to His having humbled Himself to the death of the cross. "Wherefore also God highly exalted Him." The greatest work which the Holy Spirit could ever do in the Son of God was when He enabled Him to yield Himself a sacrifice and an offering for a sweet-smelling savor. And the Holy Spirit can now do nothing greater or more glorious for us than to lead us into the fellowship and likeness of that crucified life of our Lord.

Have we not here the reason that our prayers for the mighty working of the Holy Spirit are not more abundantly answered? We have prayed too little that the Holy Spirit might glorify Christ in us in the fellowship and the conformity to His sufferings. The Spirit, who led Christ to the cross, is longing and is able to maintain in us the life of abiding in the crucified Jesus.

The Spirit and the cross are inseparable. The Spirit led Christ to the cross; the cross brought Christ to the throne to receive the fullness of the Spirit to impart to His people. The Spirit taught Peter at once to preach Christ crucified; it was through that preaching that the three thousand received the Spirit. In the preaching of the Gospel, in the Christian life, as in Christ so in us, the Spirit and the cross are inseparable. It is the sad lack of the mind and disposition of the crucified Christ sacrificing self and the world to win life for the dying, that is one great cause of the feebleness of the Church. Let us beseech God fervently to teach us to say: We have been crucified with Christ; in Him we have died to sin, "always bearing about in the body the dying of Jesus." So shall we be prepared for that fullness of the Spirit which the Father longs to bestow.

Heavenly Father, we beseech Thee fervently to teach us: We have been crucified with Christ, in Him we have died to sin, "always bearing about in the body the dying of Jesus." Amen.

The Veil of the Flesh

"Having therefore, brethren, boldness to enter into the
holy place by the blood of Jesus, by the way which He
dedicated for us, a new and living way, through the veil,
that is to say, His flesh" (Heb. 10:19–20).

In the temple there was a veil between the holy place and the most holy. At the altar in the court the blood of the sacrifice was sprinkled for forgiveness of sins. That gave the priest entrance into the holy place to offer God the incense as part of a holy worship. But into the most holy, behind the veil, the High Priest alone might enter once a year. That veil was the type of sinful human nature; even though it had received the forgiveness of sin, full access and fellowship with God was impossible.

When Christ died, the veil was rent. Christ dedicated a new and living way to God through the rent veil of His flesh. This new way, by which we now can enter into the holiest of all, ever passes through the rent veil of the flesh. Every believer "has crucified the flesh with the passions and the lusts thereof" (Gal. 5:24). Every step on the new and living way for entering into God's holy presence maintains the fellowship with the cross of Christ. The rent veil of the flesh has reference not only to Christ and His sufferings but to our experience in the likeness of His sufferings.

Have we not here the reason why many Christians can never attain to close fellowship with God? They have never yielded the flesh as an accursed thing to the condemnation of the cross. They desire to enter into the holiest of all and yet allow the flesh with its desires and pleasures to rule over them. God grant that we may rightly understand, in the power of the Holy Spirit, that Christ has called us to hate our life, to lose our life, to be dead with Him to sin that we may live to God with Him. There is no way to a full abiding fellowship with God but through the rent veil of the flesh, through a life with the flesh crucified in Christ Jesus.

Heavenly Father: We praise Thee that the Holy Spirit ever dwells in us to keep the flesh in its place of crucifixion and condemnation and to give us the abiding victory over all temptations. Amen.

Looking unto Jesus

"Let us run with patience the race that is set before
us, looking unto Jesus, the Author and Perfector of our
faith, who for the joy that was set before Him endured
the cross, despising the shame" (Heb. 12:1–2 R.V.).

In running a race the eye and heart are ever set upon the goal and the prize. Christians are here called to keep their eyes fixed on Jesus enduring the cross as the one object of imitation and desire. In our whole life we are ever to be animated by His Spirit as He bore the cross. This was the way that led to the throne and the glory of God. This is the new and living way which He opened for us through the veil of the flesh. It is as we study and realize that it was for His bearing the cross that God so highly exalted Him, that we shall walk in His footsteps bearing our cross after Him with the flesh condemned and crucified.

The weakness of the Church is greatly owing to the fact that this cross-bearing mind of Jesus is so little preached and practiced. Most Christians think that as long as they do not commit actual sin, they are at liberty to possess and enjoy as much of the world as they please. There is so little insight into the deep truth that the world and the flesh that loves the world is enmity against God. Hence it comes that many Christians seek and pray for years for conformity to the image of Jesus and yet fail so entirely. They do not know, they do not seek with the whole heart to know, what it is to die to self and the world.

It was for the joy set before Him that Christ endured the cross—the joy of pleasing and glorifying the Father, the joy of loving and winning souls for Himself. We have indeed need of a new crusade with the proclamation: This is the will of God, that as Christ found His highest happiness and received from the Father the fullness of the Spirit to pour down on His people through His endurance of the cross, so it is only *in our fellowship of the cross* that we can really become conformed to the image of God's Son. As believers awake to this blessed truth and run the race ever looking to the crucified Jesus, they will receive power to win for Christ the souls He has purchased on the cross.

Heavenly Father, we fix our eyes on Jesus enduring the cross as the one object of imitation and desire. Amen.

Without the Gate

*"The bodies of those beasts, whose blood is brought into the
Holy Place, are burned without the camp. Wherefore Jesus
also, that He might sanctify the people through His own blood,
suffered without the gate. Let us go forth therefore unto Him
without the camp, bearing His reproach" (Heb. 13:11–13).*

The blood of the sin offering was brought into the Holy Place; the body
of the sacrifice was burnt without the camp. Even so with Christ, His blood
was presented to the Father; but His body was cast out as an accursed thing,
without the camp.

And so we read in Hebrews 10: "Let us enter into the Holy Place by
the blood of Jesus." And in our text: "Let us go forth unto Him without
the camp, bearing His reproach." The deeper my insight is into the boldness which His blood gives me in God's presence, so much greater will
be the joy with which I enter the Holy Place. And the deeper my insight is
into the shame of the cross which He on my behalf bore without the camp,
the more willing shall I be in the fellowship of His cross to follow Him
without the camp, bearing His reproach.

There are many Christians who love to hear of the boldness with which
we can enter into the Holy Place through His blood, who yet have little
desire for the fellowship of His reproach and are unwilling to separate themselves from the world with the same boldness with which they think to
enter the sanctuary. Christians suffer inconceivable loss when they think
of entering into the Holy Place in faith and prayer and then feel themselves
free to enjoy the friendship of the world so long as they do nothing actually sinful. But the Word of God has said: "Know ye not that the friendship of the world is enmity against God?" "Love not the world, neither
the things that are in the world; if any man love the world, the love of the
Father is not in him." "Be not conformed to this world."

To be a follower of Christ implies a heart given up to testify for Christ in
the midst of the world if by any means some may be won. To be a follower
of Christ means to be like Him in His love of the cross and His will to sacrifice self that the Father may be glorified and that others may be saved.

---

*Blessed Savior, teach me what it means that I am called to follow Thee
without the camp, bearing Thy reproach, and so to bear witness to Thy
holy redeeming love as it embraces those who are in the world to win
them back to the Father. Blessed Lord, let the spirit and the love that
was in Thee be in me too, that I may at any cost seek to win the souls
for whom Thou hast died. Amen.*

Alive unto Righteousness

*"Who His own self bare our sins in His own body on
the tree, that we, having died unto sins, might live unto
righteousness" (1 Peter 2:24 R.V.).*

Here we have in the Epistle of Peter the same lessons that Paul has
taught us. First, *the atonement of the cross*: "Who His own self bare our
sins in His own body upon the tree." And then, *the fellowship of the cross*:
"That we, having died unto sins, might live unto righteousness."

In this last expression we have the great thought that Christians cannot
live unto righteousness, except as they know that they have died unto sin.
We need the Holy Spirit to make our death to sin in Christ such a reality
that we know ourselves to be forever free from its power and so yield our
members to God as instruments of righteousness. The words give us a short
summary of the blessed teaching of Romans 6.

Dear Christian, it cost Christ much to bear the cross and then to yield
Himself for it to bear Him. It cost Him much when He cried: "Now is My
soul troubled, and what shall I say? Father, save Me from this hour. But
for this cause came I unto this hour."

Let us not imagine that the fellowship of the cross of which Peter speaks
here, "that we, having died to sins, might live unto righteousness," is easily understood or experienced. It means that the Holy Spirit will teach us
what it is to be identified with Christ in His cross. It means that we realize by faith how actually we shared with Christ in His death and now, as
He lives in us, abide in unceasing fellowship with Him, the Crucified One.
This costs self-sacrifice; it costs earnest prayer; it costs a whole-hearted
surrender to God and His will and the cross of Jesus; it costs abiding in
Christ and unceasing fellowship with Him.

---

*Blessed Lord, discover to us day by day through the Holy Spirit the
secret of our life in Thee: "We in Thee and Thou in us." Let Thy Spirit
reveal to us that as truly as we died in Thee, Thou now livest in us the
life that was crucified and now is glorified in heaven. Let Thy Spirit
burn the words deep into our hearts. Having died unto sin and being
forever set free from its dominion, let us know that sin can no more
reign over us or have dominion. Let us in the power of Thy redemption
yield ourselves unto God as those who are alive from the dead, ready
and prepared for all His will. Amen.*

Followers of the Cross

"Hereby know we love, because He laid down His life for us: and we ought to lay down our lives for the brethren" (1 John 3:16 R.V.).

"Greater love hath no man than this, that a man lay down his life for his friend." Here our Lord reveals to us the inconceivable love that moved Him to die for us. And now under the influence and in the power of that love dwelling in us comes the message: *"We ought to lay down our lives for the brethren."* Nothing less is expected of us than a Christ-like life and a Christ-like love proving itself in all our fellowship with believers.

The cross of Christ is the measure by which we know how much Christ loves us. That cross is the measure too of the love which we owe to the Christians around us. It is only as the love of Christ on the cross possesses our hearts and daily animates our whole being, that we shall be able to love one another. Our fellowship in the cross of Christ is to manifest itself in our sacrifice of love not only to Christ Himself but to all who belong to Him.

The life to which John calls us here is something entirely supernatural and divine. It is only the faith of Christ Himself living in us that can enable us to accept this great command in the assurance that Christ Himself will work it out in us. It is He Himself who calls us: "If any man will come after Me, let him deny himself, and take up his cross, and follow Me." Nothing less than this, a dying to our own nature, a faith that our "old man," our flesh, has been crucified with Christ, so that we no longer need to sin— nothing less than this can enable us to say: We love His commandments; this commandment too is not grievous.

But for such fellowship and conformity to the death of Christ, nothing will avail but the daily, unbroken abiding in Christ Jesus which He has promised us. By the Holy Spirit revealing and glorifying Christ in us, we may trust Christ Himself to live out His life in us. He who proved His love on the cross of Calvary, He Himself, He alone can enable us to say in truth: He laid down His life for us; we ought to lay down our lives for one another. It is only as the great truth of the indwelling Christ obtains a place in the faith of the Church which it has not now, that the Christ-like love to one another will become the mark of true Christianity by which the world shall know that we are Christ's disciples. This is what will bring the world to believe that God has loved us even as He loved Christ.

Heavenly Father, as we daily abide in Thee, may we lay down our lives for one another as Christ laid down His life for us. Amen.

Following the Lamb

"These are they which follow the Lamb whithersoever He goeth" (Rev. 14:4).

It may not be easy to say exactly what is implied in this following of the Lamb in the heavenly vision. But of this we may be sure, that it will be the counterpart in glory of what it is to follow in the footsteps of the Lamb here upon earth. As the lamb on earth reveals what the Lamb in heaven would be, so His followers on earth can show forth something of the glory of what it is to follow Him in heaven.

And how may the footsteps of the Lamb be known? "He humbled Himself." "As a Lamb that is led to the slaughter, He opened not His mouth" (Isa. 53:7). It is the meekness and gentleness and humility that marked Him which calls for His followers to walk in His footsteps.

Our Lord Himself said: "Learn of Me, that I am meek and lowly of heart, and ye shall find rest unto your souls." Paul writes: "Have this mind in you, which was also in Christ Jesus" (Phil. 2:5). And then he teaches us in what that mind consisted: Being in the form of God, He emptied Himself; He was made in the likeness of men; He took the form of a servant; He humbled Himself; He became obedient unto death, even the death of the cross. The Lamb is our Lord and Lawgiver. He opened the only path that leads to the throne of God. It is as we learn from Him what it means to be meek and lowly, what it means to empty ourselves, to choose the place of the servant, to humble ourselves and become obedient even unto death, the death of the cross, that we shall find the new and living way that leads us through the rent veil into the Holiest of All.

"Wherefore also God highly exalted Him, and gave unto Him the name which is above every name" (v. 9). It is because Christians so little bear the mark of this self-emptying and humiliation even unto death, that the world refuses to believe in the possibility of a Christ-filled life.

Children of God oh, come and study the Lamb who is to be your model and your Savior. Let Paul's words be the keynote of your life: "I have been crucified with Christ; yet I live; and yet no longer I, but Christ liveth in me." Here you have the way to follow the Lamb even to the glory of the Throne of God in Heaven.

Heavenly Father: Let us learn from the Lamb what it means to be meek and lowly, to empty ourselves, to choose the place of the servant, to be obedient even unto death and thus find the way that leads to the Holiest of All. Amen.

To Him Be the Glory

*"Unto Him that loved us, and washed us from our sins
in His own blood, and hath made us kings and priests
unto God and His Father; to Him be glory and
dominion forever and ever. Amen." (Rev. 1:5–6).*

Some of my readers may feel that it is not easy to understand the lesson of the cross or to carry it out in their lives. Do not think of it as a heavy burden or yoke that you have to bear. Christ says: "My yoke is easy, and My burden is light." *Love makes everything easy.* Do not think of your love to Him but of His great love to you, given through the Holy Spirit. Meditate on this day and night until you have the assurance: He loves me unspeakably. It is through the love of Christ on the cross that souls are drawn to Him.

We have here the answer as to what will enable us to love the fellowship of the crucified Jesus: Nothing less than His love poured out through the continual inspiration of the Holy Spirit into the heart of every child of God.

"Unto Him that loved us"—Be still, O my soul, and think what this everlasting love is that seeks to take possession of you and fill you with joy unspeakable.

"And washed us from our sins in His own blood"—Is that not proof enough that He will never reject me, that I am precious in His sight and through the power of His blood am well-pleasing to God?

"And hath made us kings and priests unto God and His Father"—and now preserves us by His power and will strengthen us through His Spirit to reign as kings over sin and the world and to appear as priests before God in intercession for others. O Christian, learn this wonderful song, and repeat it until your heart is filled with love and joy and courage and turns to Him in glad surrender day by day—"To Him be glory and dominion forever and ever. Amen."

Yes, to Him who has loved me and washed me from my sins in His blood and made me a king and a priest—to Him be the glory in all ages. Amen.

The Blessing of the Cross

*"But God forbid that I should glory, save in the cross
of our Lord Jesus Christ, by whom the world is crucified
unto me, and I unto the world" (Gal. 6:14).*

One of the blessings of the cross consists in this, that it teaches us to know the worthlessness of our efforts and the utter corruption of our own nature. The cross does not offer to improve human nature or to supply what we are unable to do. Many people, indeed, use it in this way, like patching a new cloth on an old garment. But this rends the garment, and such persons walk about in torn clothes and go from one minister to another without finding what they seek. No, the old garment, our old self, must be laid aside and given over to the death of the cross. And the cross causes all that is of the lost nature of each of us to die the accursed death, and the "I" takes the place of a malefactor; it breaks the staff over all that is of the old nature.

Whosoever has been brought to the cross through the Spirit has learned to pronounce the death sentence on his old nature; he has broken the staff over himself, for whatever does not bear the mark of the cross lies under the curse. We who would save our lives remain under the curse. If we have learned through the Spirit to understand the cross, then we have lost our life and will no longer expect any good from our old nature and will not judge others but ourselves only.

But as long as we have not been taught this lesson through the Spirit, we shall try to find good in ourselves, something of worth in God's sight and upon which the sentence of death need not be passed. And if we find nothing at all, we fall into a false grief which the Evil One eagerly uses to make us despair by saying: "You may as well give up; God will not trouble about you; there is nothing for you but failure."

But this is not what God desires. What we possess by nature must be nailed to the cross, and we must put on the new nature. The cross brings us to utter bankruptcy of ourselves, and then God can come to our aid. The cross brought the disciples of Jesus once to such an end of themselves which even the words of the Master had failed to do. It took from them the aureole of holiness which they thought they had won in the three years that they followed Jesus, and it taught them to know themselves. And so they were prepared to receive the Holy Spirit who would impart a new nature and a new life. For we cannot separate the cross from the Spirit. We can have no Easter and no Pentecost until we have first had a Good Friday.

Heavenly Father, through the cross alone we are prepared for life in the fullness of Thee, only as we are crucified with Christ can we be a vessel unto honor. Amen.

The Abiding Presence

*"Lo, I am with you alway, even unto
the end of the world" (Matt. 28:20).*

When the Lord chose His twelve disciples, it was "that they should be with Him and that He might send them forth to preach" (Mark 3:14). A life in fellowship with Himself was to be their preparation and their fitness for the work of preaching.

So deeply were the disciples conscious of this having been their great privilege, that when Christ spoke of His leaving them to go to the Father, their hearts were filled with great sorrow. The presence of Christ had become indispensable to them; they could not think of living without Him. To comfort them, Christ gave them the promise of the Holy Spirit with the assurance that they then would have Himself in His heavenly presence in a sense far deeper and more intimate than they ever had known on earth. The law of their first vocation remained unchanged: to be with Him, to live in unbroken fellowship with Him would be the secret of power to preach and to testify of Him.

When Christ gave them the Great Commission to go into all the world and to preach the Gospel to every creature, He added the words: "Lo, I am with you alway, even unto the end of the world."

For all time the principle is to hold good for all His servants that without the experience of His presence ever abiding with them, their preaching would have no power. The secret of their strength would be the living testimony that Jesus Christ was every moment with them, inspiring and directing and strengthening them. It was this that made them so bold in preaching Him as the Crucified One in the midst of His enemies. They never for a moment regretted His bodily absence; they had Him with them and in them in the divine power of the Holy Spirit.

In all the work of the minister and the missionary, everything depends on the consciousness, through a living faith, of the abiding presence of the Lord with His servant, the living experience of the presence of Jesus as an essential element in preaching the Gospel. If this is clouded, work becomes a human effort without the freshness and the power of the heavenly life. And nothing can bring back the power and the blessing but a return to the Master's feet, for Him to breathe into the heart in divine power His blessed word: "Lo, I am with you alway!"

Dear Lord Jesus, I thank Thee for Thy abiding presence, for the freshness and power of the heavenly life. Amen.

The Omnipotence of Christ

"All power is given unto Me in heaven and on earth" (Matt. 28:18).

Before Christ gave His disciples their Great Commission to begin that great world conquest which should aim at bringing His Gospel to every creature, He first revealed Himself in His divine power as a partner with God Himself, the Almighty One. It was the faith of this that enabled the disciples to undertake the work in all simplicity and boldness. They had begun to know Him in that mighty resurrection power which had conquered sin and death; there was nothing too great for Him to command or for them to undertake.

Every disciple of Jesus Christ who desires to take part in the victory that overcometh the world needs time and faith and the Holy Spirit to come under the full conviction that it is as the servant of the omnipotent Lord Jesus that one is to take part in the work. We are to count literally upon the daily experience of being "strong in the Lord and in the power of His might." The word of promise gives the courage to obey implicitly the word of command.

Just think of what the disciples had learned to know of the power of Christ Jesus here on earth. And yet that was but a little thing as compared with the greater works that He was now to do in and through them. He has the power to work even in the feeblest of His servants with the strength of the Almighty God. He has power even to use their apparent weakness to carry out His purposes. He has the power over every enemy and every human heart, over every difficulty and danger.

But let us remember that this power is never meant to be experienced as if it were our own. It is only as Jesus Christ as a living Person dwells and works with His divine energy in our own heart and life that there can be power in our preaching as a personal testimony. It was when Christ had said to Paul, "My strength is made perfect in weakness," that he could say, what he never learned to say before, "When I am weak, then am I strong." It is the disciple of Christ who understands aright that all the power has been entrusted to Him to be received from Him hour by hour, who will feel the need and experience the power of that precious word: "Lo, I am with you alway," the Almighty One.

Dear Lord Jesus, although I am unable to carry out Thy purposes, I trust in Thy power over every enemy and every human heart, over every difficulty and danger. Amen.

The Omnipresence of Christ

"Certainly I will be with thee" (Ex. 3:12).

Our first thought in our conception of a God is that of power, however limited. The first thought of the true God is His omnipotence: "I am God Almighty." The second thought in Scripture is His omnipresence. God ever gave His servants the promise of His unseen presence with them. To His "I am with thee," their faith responded: "Thou art with me."

When Christ had said to His disciples, "All power is given unto Me in heaven and on earth," the promise immediately follows, "I am with you always." The Omnipotent One is surely the Omnipresent One.

The writer of Psalm 139 speaks of God's omnipresence as something beyond his comprehension: "Such knowledge is too wonderful for me; it is high, I cannot attain unto it."

The revelation of God's omnipresence in the man Christ Jesus makes the mystery still deeper. It also makes the grace that enables us to claim this presence as our strength and our joy something inexpressibly blessed. And yet how many a servant of Christ, when the promise is given, finds it difficult to understand all that is implied in it and how it can become the practical experience of daily life.

Here, as elsewhere in the spiritual life, everything depends upon faith, accepting Christ's word as a divine reality and trusting the Holy Spirit to make it true to us from moment to moment. When Christ says "always" (Gr. "all the days"), He means to give us the assurance that there is not to be a day of our life in which that blessed presence is not to be with us. And that "all the days" implies "all the day." There need not be a moment in which that presence cannot be our experience. It does not depend upon what we can effect but upon what He undertakes to do. The omnipotent Christ is the omnipresent Christ, the ever-present is the everlasting, the unchangeable One. As sure as He is the unchangeable One will His presence, as the power of an endless life, be with each of His servants who trusts Him for it.

Our attitude must be that of a quiet, restful faith, of a humble, lowly dependence in accordance with the word: "Rest in the Lord, and wait patiently for Him."

"Lo, I am, with you alway." Let our faith in Christ, the Omnipresent One, be in the quiet confidence that He will every day and every moment keep us as the apple of His eye, keep us in perfect peace and in the sure experience of all the light and the strength we need in His service.

Thank you, Lord Jesus, for Thy words, "Lo, I am, with you alway."
Amen.

Christ: The Savior of the World

This is indeed the Christ, the Savior of the world" (John 4:42).

Omnipotence and Omnipresence are what are called natural attributes of God. They have their true worth only when linked to and inspired by His moral attributes, holiness and love. When our Lord spoke of the omnipotence having been given to Him—all power on earth and in heaven—and the omnipresence—His presence with each of His disciples—His words pointed to that which lies at the root of all—His divine glory as the Savior of the world and Redeemer of men. It was because He humbled Himself and became obedient to death, the death of the Cross, that God so highly exalted Him. His share as the man Christ Jesus in the attributes of God was owing to the work He had done in His perfect obedience to the will of God and the finished redemption He had wrought out for the salvation of the world.

It is this that gives meaning and worth to what He says of Himself as the omnipotent and omnipresent One. Between His mention of these two attributes, He gives His command that they should go out into all the world and preach the Gospel and teach others to obey all that He has commanded. It is as the Redeemer who saves and keeps from sin, as the Lord Christ who claims obedience to all that He has commanded, that He promises His divine presence to be with His servants.

It follows as a matter of necessity that it is only when His servants in their lives show that they obey Him in all His commands, that they can expect the fullness of His power and His presence to be with them. It is only when they themselves are living witnesses to the reality of His power to save and to keep from sin that they can expect the full experience of His abiding presence, and that they will have power to train others to the life of obedience that He asks.

Yes, it is Jesus Christ who saves His people from their sin, who rules over a people willing in the day of His power and proves in them that He enables them to say, "I delight to do Thy will, O my God," who says, "Lo, I am with you alway." The abiding presence of the Savior from sin is promised to all who have accepted Him in the fullness of His redeeming power and who preach by their lives as well as by their words what a wonderful Savior He is.

Dear Lord Jesus, Thou art the Savior of the world and Redeemer of men. We hear and obey Thy command to go into all the world and preach the Gospel and obey all that Thou hast commanded. Amen.

Christ Crucified

*"God forbid that I should glory, save in the Cross of
our Lord Jesus Christ, through which the world hath been
crucified unto me, and I unto the world" (Gal. 6:14).*

Christ's highest glory is His Cross. It was in this that He glorified the
Father, and the Father glorified Him. It was as the Lamb slain in the midst
of the throne that in that wonderful fifth chapter of Revelation He receives
the worship of the ransomed and the angels and all creation. And it is as
the Crucified One that His servants have learned to say: "God forbid that
I should glory save in the Cross of our Lord Jesus Christ, through which I
am crucified to the world." Is it not reasonable that Christ's highest glory
should be our only glory too?

When the Lord Jesus said to His disciples, "Lo, I am with you alway,"
it was as the Crucified One, who had shown them His hands and His feet,
that He gave the promise. And to each one of us who seeks to claim the
promise, it is of the first importance that we should realize: It is the crucified Jesus who promises, who offers, to be with me every day.

May not this be one reason why we find it so difficult to expect and
enjoy the abiding presence?—because we do not glory in the Cross by
which we are crucified to the world. We have been crucified with Christ;
our "old man was crucified with Him"; "they that are Christ's have crucified the flesh with its affections and lusts"—and yet how little we have
learned that the world has been crucified to us and that we are free from
its power. How little we have learned, as those who are crucified with
Christ, to deny ourselves, to have the mind that was in Christ when He
emptied Himself and took the form of a servant and humbled Himself and
became obedient even to the death of the Cross.

---

*Precious Lord Jesus: Oh, let us learn the lesson, it is Thee, the crucified
Christ, who comes to walk with us every day, and in whose power we
too are to live the life that can say: "I have been crucified with Christ";
"Christ crucified lives in me." Amen.*

Christ Glorified

"The Lamb which is in the midst of the throne shall
be their shepherd." "These are they which follow
the Lamb whithersoever He goeth" (Rev. 7:17; 14:4).

"Lo, I am with you always." Who is this that thus speaks? We must take time to know Him well if we are to understand what we may expect from Him as He offers to be with us all the day. Who is He? None else than the Lamb as it had been slain in the midst of the throne! The Lamb in His deepest humiliation enthroned in the glory of God. This is He who speaks and invites me to the closest fellowship and likeness to Himself.

It needs time and deep reverence and adoring worship to come under the full impression—He who dwelleth in the glory of the Father before whom all heaven bows in prostrate adoration—it is none other than He who offers to be my companion, to lead me like a shepherd who cares for each individual sheep, and so to make me one of those who follow the Lamb whithersoever He goeth.

Read often that wonderful fifth chapter of Revelation until the heart is possessed by the one great thought of how all heaven falls prostrate, and the elders cast their crowns before the throne, and the Lamb reigns amidst the praises and the love of His ransomed ones and the praises of all creation. And if this is He who comes to me in my daily life and offers to walk with me and to be my strength and my joy and my almighty Keeper, surely I cannot expect Him to abide with me except as my heart bows, if possible, in a still deeper reverence and in a surrender to a life of praise and service such as may be worthy of the love that has redeemed me.

Oh, Christian, do believe that the Lamb in the midst of the throne is in very deed the embodiment of the omnipotent glory of the everlasting God and of His love. And do believe that to have this Lamb of God as your almighty Shepherd and your faithful Keeper does indeed make it possible that the thoughts and the cares of earth shall indeed not prevail to separate you from His love for a single moment.

Heavenly Father, I believe that the Lamb is the embodiment of Thee,
the everlasting God, and of Thy love, and is my Shepherd and Keeper.
Amen.

The Great Question

"Believe ye that I am able to do this? They said
unto Him, Yea, Lord" (Mark. 9:28).

If thou canst believe, all things are possible to him that believeth. And straightway the father of the child said with tears: "Lord, I believe, help Thou mine unbelief" (Mark 9:23–24). "Jesus said, He that believeth in Me, though he were dead, yet shall he live. Believeth thou this? She saith unto Him, Yea, Lord, I believe" (John 11:25–27).

To what we have seen and heard of Christ Jesus, our heart is ready to say with Martha in answer to Christ's question: "Yea, Lord, I have believed that Thou art the Christ, the Son of God." But when it comes to the point of believing that what Christ promises to us of the power of the resurrection life, of His abiding presence every day and all the day, we do not find it so easy to say, "I do believe that this omnipotent, omnipresent, unchangeable Christ, our Redeemer God will in very deed walk with me all the day and give me the unceasing consciousness of His holy presence"—it almost looks too much to venture. And yet it is just this faith that Christ asks and is waiting to work within us.

It is well that we understand clearly what the conditions are on which Christ offers to reveal to us in experience the secret of His abiding presence. God cannot force His blessings on us against our will. He seeks in every possible way to stir our desire and to help us to realize that He is able and most willing to make His promises true. The resurrection of Christ from the dead is His great plea, His all-prevailing argument. If He could raise that dead Christ who had died under the burden of all our sin and curse, surely He can, now that Christ has conquered death and is to us the Resurrection and the Life, fulfill in our hearts His promise that Christ can be so with us and so in us that He Himself should be our life all the day.

And now the great question comes, whether in view of what we have said and seen about Christ as our Lord, as our redeeming God, whether we are willing to take His word in all simplicity in its divine fullness of meaning and to rest in the promise: "Lo, I am with you all the day." Christ's question comes to us: "Believest thou this?" Let us not rest until we have bowed before Him and said: "Yea, Lord, I do believe."

Heavenly Father, I do believe Thou canst walk with me all the day and
give me the unceasing consciousness of Thy holy presence. Amen.

Christ Manifesting Self

"He that hath My commandments, and keepeth them, he it is that loveth Me: and he that loveth Me shall be loved of My Father, and I will love him, and will manifest Myself unto him" (John 14:21).

Christ had promised the disciples that the Holy Spirit would come to reveal His presence as ever with them. When the Spirit thus came, He through the Spirit would manifest Himself to them. They should know Him in a new, divine spiritual way; in the power of the Spirit they should know Him and have Him far more intimately and unceasingly with them than they ever had upon earth.

The condition of this revelation of Himself is comprised in the one word—love: "He that keepeth My commandments, he it is that loveth Me: and he that loveth Me shall be loved of My Father, and I will love him." It is to be the meeting of Divine and human love. The love with which Christ had loved them had taken possession of their hearts and would show itself in the love of a full and absolute obedience. The Father would see this, and His love would rest upon the soul; Christ would love him with the special love drawn out by the loving heart and would manifest Himself. The love of heaven shed abroad in the heart would be met by the new and blessed revelation of Christ Himself.

But this is not all. When the question was asked, "What is it?" the answer came in the repetition of the words, "If a man love Me, he will keep My word"; and then again, "My Father will love him, and We will come unto him and make Our abode with him." In the heart thus prepared by the Holy Spirit, showing itself in the obedience of love in a fully surrendered heart, the Father and the Son will take up their abode.

And now, nothing less is what Christ promises them: "Lo, I am with you alway." That "with" implies "in"—Christ with the Father, dwelling in the heart by faith. Oh, that everyone who would enter into the secret of the abiding presence—"Lo, I am with you alway"—would study and believe and claim in childlike simplicity the blessed promise: "I will manifest Myself unto him."

Dear Lord Jesus, I claim Thy promise: "I will manifest Myself unto him." Abide in my heart. Amen.

Mary: The Morning Watch

"Jesus saith unto her, Mary! She turned herself, and saith unto Him, Rabboni! which is to say, Master" (John 20:16).

Here we have the first manifestation of the risen Savior to Mary Magdalene, the woman who loved much.

Think of what the morning watch meant to Mary. Is it not a proof of the intense longing of a love that would not rest until it had found the Lord it sought? It meant a separation from all else, even from the chief of the apostles, in her longing to find Christ. It meant the struggle of fear against a faith that refused to let go its hold of its wonderful promise. It meant Christ's coming and fulfilling the promise: "If a man love Me, he will keep My words, and I will love him and manifest Myself to him." It meant that her love was met by the love of Jesus, and she found Him, the living Lord, in all the power of His resurrection life. It meant that she now understood what He had said about ascending to the Father, to the life of divine and omnipotent glory. It meant too that she received her commission from her Lord to go and tell His brethren of what she had heard from Him.

That first morning watch, waiting for the risen Lord to reveal Himself, what a prophecy and a pledge of what the morning watch has been to thousands of souls! In fear and doubt and yet with a burning love and strong hope, they waited until He whom they had known but little, by reason of their human feeble apprehension, should breathe upon them in the power of His resurrection life and manifest Himself as the Lord of Glory. And there they learned, not in words or thought but in the reality of a divine experience, that He, to whom all power had been given on earth and in heaven, and had taken them up into the keeping of His abiding presence.

And what are we now to learn? That there is nothing that can prove a greater attraction to our Lord than the love that sacrifices everything and rests satisfied with nothing less than Himself. It is to such a love that Christ manifests Himself. He loved us and gave Himself for us. Christ's love needs our love in which to reveal itself. It is to our love that He speaks the word: "Lo, I am with you alway." It is love that accepts and rejoices in and lives in that word.

Lord Jesus Christ, manifest Thy love to the world through me, for I am satisfied with nothing less than sacrificing everything and resting completely in Thy love. Amen.

Emmaus: The Evening Prayer

*"They constrained Him, saying, Abide with us. . . . And He went in
to tarry with them. And . . . as He sat at meat with them . . . their
eyes were opened, and they knew Him" (Luke 24:29–31).*

If Mary teaches us what the morning watch can be for the revelation of
Jesus to the soul, Emmaus reminds us of the place that the evening prayer
may have in preparing for the full manifestation of Christ in the soul.

To the two disciples the day had begun in thick darkness. When at length
the woman told of the angel who had said that He was alive, they knew
not what to think. When "Jesus Himself drew near," their eyes were hold-
en, and they knew Him not. How often Jesus does come near with the one
object of manifesting Himself but is hindered because we are so slow of
heart to believe what the Word has spoken. But as the Lord spoke with
them, their hearts began to burn within them, and yet there never was a
thought that it might be Himself. It is often even so now. The Word becomes precious to us in the fellowship of the saints; our hearts are stirred
with the new vision of what Christ's presence may be, and yet—the eyes
are holden, and we see Him not.

When the Lord made as though He would have gone farther, their prayer,
"Abide with us," constrained Him. Christ had given in the last night a new
meaning to the word "Abide." They did not yet understand that but in the
use of it received far more than they expected, a foretaste of that life of
abiding which the resurrection had now made possible. Let us learn the
lesson of how needful it is that toward the close of the day there should
be a pause, perhaps in fellowship with others, when the whole heart takes
up anew the promise of the abiding presence and prays with the urgency
that constrains Him: "Abide, abide with us."

And what is now the chief lesson of the story? What was it that led our
Lord to reveal Himself to these two men? Nothing less than this, their intense devotion to their Lord. There may be much ignorance and unbelief,
but if there is a burning desire that above everything longs for Him, a desire that is ever fostered as the Word is heard or spoken, we may count
upon it, He will make Himself known to us. To such intense devotion and
constraining prayer, the Lord's message will be given in power: "Lo, I am
with you alway"; our eyes will be opened, and we will know Him and the
blessed secret of the abiding presence always. It is to strong desire and
constraining prayer that Christ will most assuredly manifest Himself.

---

*Lord Jesus, open our eyes to know Thee and Thy abiding presence
always. Amen.*

The Disciples: Their Divine Mission

"The same day at evening . . . when the doors were shut
where the disciples were assembled for fear of the Jews,
came Jesus and stood in the midst, and saith unto
them, Peace be unto you" (John 20:19).

The disciples had received the message of Mary. Peter had told them that he had seen the Lord. Late in the evening the men from Emmaus told how He had been made known to them. Their hearts were prepared for what now came, when Jesus stood in the midst of them and said, "Peace be unto you," and showed them His hands and His feet. This was not only to be a sign of recognition, but the deep eternal mystery of what would be seen in heaven when He was in the midst of the throne, "a Lamb as it had been slain."

"Then were the disciples glad when they saw the Lord." And He spoke again: "Peace be unto you! As the Father sent Me, so send I you." With Mary He revealed Himself to the fervent love that could not rest without Him. With the men at Emmaus it was their constraining prayer that received the revelation. Here He meets the willing servants whom He had trained for His service and hands over to them the work He had done on earth. He changes their fear into the boldness of peace and gladness. He ascends to the Father; the work the Father had given Him to do He now entrusts to them. The Divine Mission is now theirs to make known and carry out to victory.

For this divine work they need nothing less than divine power. He breathes upon them the resurrection life He had won by His death. He fulfills the promise He gave: "I live, and ye shall live also." The exceeding greatness of the mighty power of God by which He raised Christ from the dead, none other than that spirit of holiness by which He, as the Son of God, was raised from the dead, will henceforth work in them. And all that was bound or loosed in that power would be bound in heaven.

The story comes to every messenger of the Gospel with wonderful power. To us too the word is spoken: "As the Father sent Me, so send I you." For us too is the word: "Receive ye the Holy Spirit." For us too the personal manifestation of Jesus as the Living One, with the pierced hands and feet. If our hearts are set on nothing less than the presence of the living Lord, we may count confidently it will be given us.

Lord Jesus, thank you for sending out Thy servants with the promise
of Thy abiding presence and Thy almighty power. Amen.

Thomas: The Blessedness of Believing

*"Jesus saith unto him, Thomas, because thou hast seen
Me, thou hast believed: blessed are they that have not
seen, and yet have believed" (John 20:29).*

We all count the blessedness of Thomas as something very wonderful—
Christ manifesting Himself and allowing Thomas to touch His hands and
His side. No wonder that this blessedness can find no words but those of
holy adoration: "My Lord and my God." Has there ever been higher expression of the overwhelming nearness and glory of God?

And yet Christ said: "Because thou hast seen Me, thou hast believed:
blessed are they that have not seen and yet have believed." True, living
faith gives a sense of Christ's divine nearness far deeper and more intimate than even the joy that filled the heart of Thomas. Here, even now,
after the lapse of all these centuries, we may have experienced the presence and power of Christ in a far deeper reality than Thomas did. To those
who see not, yet believe, simply, only, truly, fully, believe in what Christ
is and can be to them every moment, He has promised that He will manifest Himself and that the Father and He will come and dwell in them.

Have we not often been inclined to think of this full life of faith as something beyond our reach? Such a thought robs us of the power to believe.
Let us turn to take hold of Christ's word: "Blessed are they that have not
seen, and yet believe." This is indeed the heavenly blessing filling the whole
heart and life, the faith that receives the love and the presence of the living Lord.

You ask how to come to this childlike faith. The answer is very simple.
Where Jesus Christ is the one object of our desire and our confidence, He
will manifest Himself in divine power. Thomas had proved his intense devotion to Christ when he said, "Let us go, that we may die with Him." To
such a love, even when it is struggling with unbelief, Jesus Christ will manifest Himself. He will make His holy promise an actual reality in our conscious experience: "I am with you alway."

---

*Heavenly Father: Let us see to it that our faith in Christ's blessed word,
in His divine power, in His holy abiding presence is the one thing that
masters our whole being—Christ will in very deed manifest Himself,
abide with us, and dwell in our hearts as His home. Amen.*

Peter: The Greatness of Love

*"Peter was grieved because He said unto him the third time,
Lovest thou Me? He said unto Him, Lord, Thou knowest all
things; Thou knowest that I love Thee. Jesus saith unto
him, Feed My sheep" (John 21:17).*

It was to Mary who loved much that Christ first revealed Himself. Then in Peter's first vision of the Lord, in His making Himself known in the upper room at Emmaus, in His appearance to the ten, and in the revelation of Himself to Thomas, it was ever to the intense devotion of the prepared heart that Christ manifested Himself. And now in His manifestation of Himself to Peter, it is again love that is the keynote.

We can easily understand why Christ asked the question thrice, Lovest thou Me? It was to remind Peter of the terrible self-confidence in which he had said: "Though I should die with Thee, I will not deny Thee"; of the need of quiet, deep heart-searching before he could be sure that his love was real and true; of the need of deep penitence in the consciousness of how little he could trust himself; and then of love being the one thing needful for the full restoration to his place in the heart of Jesus, the first and highest condition for feeding His sheep and caring for His lambs.

God is love. Christ is the Son of His love. Having loved His own, He loved them to the uttermost and said: "As the Father loved Me, so love I you." He asked that they should prove their love to Him by keeping His commandments and loving each other with the love with which He loved them. In heaven and on earth, in the Father and in the Son and in us and in all our work for Him and our care for souls, the greatest thing is love.

To everyone who longs to have Jesus manifest Himself—"I am with you alway"—the chief, the essential requisite is love. Peter teaches us that such love is not in our power to offer. But such love came to him through the power of Christ's death to sin and that power of His resurrection life of which Peter became partaker. As he puts it in his first Epistle: "Whom having not seen, we love; in whom, though now ye see Him not, yet believing, ye rejoice with joy unspeakable and full of glory." Thank God, if Peter the self-confident could be so changed, shall not we believe that Christ will work in us the wondrous change too and manifcst Himself to a loving heart in all the fullness of His precious word: "Lo, I am with you alway." It is to love that Christ will manifest Himself as the only fitness for feeding His sheep and tending His lambs.

Dear Lord Jesus, may our hearts ever be intensely devoted to caring for Thy lambs and fully prepared for the manisfestation of Thy love in us to others. Amen.

John: Life from the Dead

*"And when I saw Him, I fell at His feet as one dead. And
He laid His right hand upon me, saying, Fear not; I am
the First and the Last, and the Living One; and I was dead,
and behold, I am alive forevermore" (Rev. 1:17–18).*

Here we have, sixty or more years after the resurrection, Christ's manifesting Himself to the beloved disciple. John fell as dead at His feet. God
had said to Moses in answer to his prayer "Show me Thy glory:" "Thou
canst not see My face: for man cannot see Me and live." Man's sinful nature cannot receive the vision of the Divine glory and live; it needs the
death of the natural life for the life of God in glory to enter in. When John
fell as dead at Christ's feet, it proved how little he could endure the wonderful heavenly vision.

When Christ laid His right hand upon him and said, "Fear not; I am He
that liveth, and was dead, and behold, I am alive forevermore," He remind-
ed him that He Himself too had passed through death before He could rise
to the life and the glory of God.

The lesson is a deep and most needful one to all who long that Jesus shall
manifest Himself unto them. The knowledge of Jesus, fellowship with Him,
and the experience of His power is not possible without the sacrifice of all
that there is in us of the world and its spirit. The disciples had experience of
this. Christ had from His first ordination charge (Matt. 10:37–39)—where
He had spoken about forsaking father and mother, about taking up the cross,
about losing our life for His sake down to the days before His death, when
He said: "Except a corn of wheat die, it abideth alone, but if it die, it bringeth
forth much fruit"; "He that loveth his life shall lose it"—made this the one
great charge: Deny self; bear the cross, and follow Me.

We are seeking to find out the secret of getting into such touch with
the Lord Jesus that His abiding presence shall be our portion every day.
Let us accept the lesson—through death to life. In the power of Christ Jesus
with whom we have been crucified and whose death now works in us, if
we will yield ourselves to it, death to sin, death to the world with all its
self-pleasing and self-exaltation is to be the deepest law of our spiritual
life. Peter said to Christ: "Spare Thyself" (Matt. 16:22 marg.); Jesus said
to him: "Deny thyself." The disciples had followed Christ even to the Cross.
That was what fitted them to receive the Master's word: "Lo, I am with
you alway."

Lord Jesus, I accept the lesson—through death to life. Amen.

Paul: Christ Revealed in Him

"It was the good pleasure of God . . . to reveal
His Son in Me" (Gal. 1:15–16).

In all our study and worship of Christ we find our thoughts ever gathering round these five points: The Incarnate Christ, the Crucified Christ, the Enthroned Christ, the Indwelling Christ, and Christ coming in glory. If the first be the seed, the second is the seed cast into the ground, and the third the seed growing up to the very heaven. Then follows the fruit through the Holy Spirit, Christ dwelling in the heart and then the gathering of the fruit into the garner when Christ appears.

Paul tells us that it pleased God to reveal His Son in Him. And he gives his testimony to the result of that revelation: "Christ liveth in me" (Gal. 2:20). Of that life he says that its chief mark is that he is crucified with Christ. It is this that enables him to say, "I live no longer"; in Christ he had found the death of self. Just as the Cross is the chief characteristic of Christ Himself—"A lamb as it had been slain in the midst of the throne"— so the life of Christ in Paul made him inseparably one with his crucified Lord. So completely was this the case that he could say: "Far be it from me to glory save in the Cross of our Lord Jesus Christ, through which I am crucified to the world."

If you had asked Paul, if Christ so actually lived in him that he no longer lived, what became of his responsibility? The answer was ready and clear: "I live by the faith of the Son of God, who loved me and gave Himself for me." His life was every moment a life of faith in Him who had loved him and given Himself so completely that He had undertaken at all times to be the life of His willing disciple.

This was the sum and substance of all Paul's teaching. He asks for intercession that he might speak "the mystery of Christ"; "even the riches of the glory of this mystery among the Gentiles, which is Christ in you, the hope of glory" (Col. 2:2; 1:27). The indwelling Christ was the secret of his life of faith, the one power, the one aim of all his life and work, the hope of glory.

Heavenly Father: Let us believe in the abiding presence of Christ as the sure gift to each one who trusts Him fully. Amen

Why Could We Not?

*"The disciples came to Jesus apart, and said, Why could
not we cast it out? He saith unto them, Because of your
little faith. Howbeit this kind goeth not out but by
prayer and fasting" (Matt. 17:19–21).*

The disciples had often cast out devils. But here they had been powerless. They asked the Lord what the reason might be. His answer is very
simple: "Because of your little faith."

We have here the reply to the great question so often asked, How is it
that we cannot live that life of unbroken fellowship with Christ which the
Scripture promises? Simply, because of our unbelief. We do not realize that
faith must accept and expect that God will, by His almighty power, fulfill
every promise He has made. We do not live in that utter helplessness and
dependence on God alone which is the very essence of faith. We are not
strong in the faith, fully persuaded that what God has promised He is able
and willing to perform. We do not give ourselves with our whole heart simply to believe that God by His almighty power will work wonders in our
hearts.

But what can be the reason that this faith is so often lacking? "Howbeit this kind goeth not out but by prayer and fasting." To have a strong faith
in God needs a life in close touch with Him by persistent prayer. We cannot call up faith at our bidding; it needs close communion with God. It
needs not only prayer but fasting too in the larger and deeper meaning of
that word. It needs the denial of self, the sacrifice of that pleasing of the
flesh and the eye and the pride of life which is the essence of a worldly
spirit. To gain the prizes of the heavenly life here on earth needs the sacrifice of all that earth can offer. Just as it needs God to satisfy the human
heart and work His mighty miracles in it, it needs the whole man, utterly
given up to God, to have the power of that faith which can cast out every
evil spirit. "Prayer and fasting" are essential.

---

*Heavenly Father: Keep our faith strong and our lives in close touch
with Thee by persistent prayer and fasting. Amen.*

The Power of Obedience

*"He that hath sent Me is with Me; He hath not left Me alone; for
I do always the things that are pleasing to Him" (John 8:29).*

In these words Christ not only tells what His life with the Father was
but reveals at the same time the law of all communion with God—simple
obedience.

How strongly He insisted upon it we see in the Farewell Discourse. In
chapter 14 He says three times: "If ye love Me, keep My commandments.
And then I will pray the Father, and He will give you the Holy Spirit, and
the Father will love you, and I will love you and manifest Myself to you,
and then we will make Our abode with you." And so three times over in
chapter 15: "If My words abide with you, ye shall ask what ye will, and it
shall be done unto you"; "If ye keep My commandments, ye shall abide
in My love; even as I kept My Father's commandments and abide in His
love"; "Ye are My friends, if ye do the things which I command you."

Obedience is the proof and the exercise of the love of God that has been
shed abroad in our hearts by the Holy Spirit. It comes from love and leads
to love, a deeper and a fuller experience of God's love and indwelling. It
assures us that what we ask will be given us. It assures us that we are abiding in the love of Christ. It seals our claim to be called the friends of Christ.
And so it is not only a proof of love but of faith too, as assuring us that
we "ask and receive because we keep His commandments, and do the
things that are pleasing in His sight."

For the abiding enjoyment of the Holy Presence, simple, full obedience
is necessary. The New Covenant has made full provision for this: "I will
write My law in their hearts; I will put My fear in their heart, that they
may not depart from Me"; "I will cause them to walk in My statutes and
to keep them."

Blessed obedience, that enables us to abide in His love and gives the
full experience of His unbroken presence. Christ did not speak of an impossibility; He saw what in the power of the Spirit we might confidently
expect.

---

*Heavenly Father: Let the thought take deep hold of us. It is to the
obedient that the word comes, "Lo, I am with you alway," and to whom
all the fullness of its meaning will be revealed. Amen.*

The Power of Intercession

"We will continue steadfastly in prayer" (Acts 6:4).

"Prayer was made earnestly of the Church unto God for him" (Acts 12:5).

Dr. Mott* urges us to believe in the unlimited power of united intercession. In traveling in Asia he was charged by men who have penetrated most deeply into the heart of the problem to press upon the missionary societies the *imperative need of more intercession—above all, of united intercession.* "We can in no way better serve the deepest interest of the Churches than by multiplying the number of real intercessors, and by focusing the prayers of Christendom upon those great situations which demand the almighty working of the Spirit of God. Far more important and vital than any service we can render to missions is that of helping to release the superhuman energy of prayer and, through uniting in this holy ministry true intercessors of all lands, to help the ushering in of a new era abounding in signs and wonders characteristic of the working of the living Christ. Immeasurably more important than any other work is the linking of all we do to the fountain of Divine life and energy. The Christian world has not only a right to expect mission leaders to set forth the facts and methods of the work, but also a larger discovery of superhuman resources and a greater irradiation of spiritual power."

And where is there a greater need of focusing the united intercession of Christendom than on the great army of missionaries? They confess the need of the presence and the power of God's Spirit in their life and work. They long for the experience of the abiding presence and power of Christ every day. They need it; they have a right to it—shall we not, those of us reading this book, make a part of that great army that pleads with God for that enduement of power which is so absolutely necessary for effective work? Shall we not, like the early Apostles, "continue steadfastly in prayer," until God sends an abundant answer?

Dear Heavenly Father, we thank Thee that as we give ourselves continually to prayer, the power of the promise, "Lo, I am with you alway," will be proved in our lives. Amen.

---

* John Raleigh Mott (1865-1955), General Secretary of the Y.M.C.A. and Chairman of the Student Volunteer Movement for Foreign Missions.

The Power of Time

"My times are in Thy hand" (Ps. 31:15).

The plural implies the singular: "My time is in Thy hand. It belongs to Thee; Thou alone hast a right to command it. I yield it wholly and gladly to Thy disposal." What mighty power time can exert if wholly given up to God!

Time is lord of all things. What is all the history of the world but a proof of how, slowly but surely, time has made us what we are today? All around us we see the proofs. In the growth of the child, both physically and mentally, in the success in every pursuit, in all our labors and all our attainments, it is under the law of time and its inconceivable power that we spend our lives.

This is especially true in religion and communion with God. Time here too is master. What fellowship with God! What holiness and blessedness! What likeness to His image and what power in His service for blessing to others!—all on the one condition: that we have sufficient time with God for His holiness to shine on us with its light and its heat and to make us partakers of His Spirit and His life. The very essence of religion lies in the thought: Time with God. And yet how many of God's servants there are who, while giving their lives to His service, frankly confess that the feebleness of their spiritual life as missionaries and the inadequate results of mission work as a whole are due to the failure to make the leisure and, when secured, rightly to use it for daily communion with God,

What can be the cause at the back of this sad confession? Nothing but a lack of faith in the God-given assurance that time spent alone with God will indeed bring into the lives of His servants the power to enable them to use all their time in His fellowship that His abiding presence will be with them all the day.

Oh, my brothers and sisters who complain that overwork or too much zeal in doing the work is hindering your spiritual efficiency, do you not see that if you would but submit your time-table to the inspection of Christ and His Holy Spirit, you would find that a new life would be yours if you fully believed and put into daily practice the word: "My time is in Thy hand"?

Lord Jesus Christ, I submit my time-table to Thy inspection and fully believe "my time is in Thy hand." Amen.

The Power of Faith

"All things are possible to him that believeth" (Mark 9:23).

Scripture teaches us that there is not one truth on which Christ insisted more frequently, both with His disciples and with those who came seeking His help, than the absolute necessity of faith and its unlimited possibilities. And experience has taught us that there is nothing in which we come so short as the simple and absolute trust in God to fulfill literally in us all He has promised. A life in the abiding presence must of necessity be a life of unceasing faith.

Think for a moment of what the marks of a true faith are. First of all, faith counts upon God to do all He has promised, as the only measure of its expectation. It does not rest content with taking some of the promises; it seeks nothing less than to claim every promise that God has made in its largest and fullest meaning. Under a sense of its own nothingness and utter powerlessness, it trusts the power of an Almighty God to work wonders in the heart in which He dwells.

It does this with the whole heart and all its strength. Faith yields itself to the promise that God will take full possession and all through the day and night inspire its hope and expectation. It recognizes the inseparable link that unites God's promises and His commands and yields itself to do the one as fully as it trusts the other.

In the pursuit of the power which such a life of faith can give, there is often a faith that seeks and strives but cannot grasp. This is followed by a faith that begins to see that waiting on God is needed and that quietly rests in the hope of what God will do. This should lead on to an act of decision in which the soul takes God at His word and claims the fulfillment of the promise and then looks to Him, even in utter darkness, to perform what He has spoken.

The life of faith to which the abiding presence will be granted must needs have complete mastery of the whole being. It is such a wonderful privilege, Christ's presence actually keeping us all day in its blessed experience, that it needs a parting with much that was formerly thought lawful if He is indeed to be the Lord of all, the blessed Friend who companies with us, the joy and light of our life. This faith will be able to claim and to experience the words of the Master: "Lo, I am with you alway."

Lord Jesus, show me those things in my life that I formerly thought lawful which now are keeping me from the full joy and light of Thy presence. Amen.

John's Missionary Message

*"That which we have seen and heard declare we unto you, that ye
also may have fellowship with us: and truly our fellowship is with
the Father, and with His Son Jesus Christ" (1 John 1:3).*

What a revelation of the calling of the preacher of the Gospel! His message is nothing less than to proclaim that Christ has opened the way for
us simple souls to have day by day living, loving fellowship with the holy
God. He is to preach this as a witness to the life he himself lives in all its
blessed experience. In the power of that testimony, he is to prove its reality and to show how a sinful person upon earth can indeed live in fellowship with the Father and the Son.

The message suggests to us that the very first duty of the minister or
the missionary every day is to maintain such close communion with God
that he can preach the truth in the fullness of joy and with the consciousness that his life and conversation are the proof that his preaching is true,
so that his words appeal with power to the heart: "These things write we
unto you that your joy may be full."

In an October 1914 article, on the influence of the Keswick Conven-
tion on mission work, the substance of Keswick teaching is given in these
words: "It points to a life of communion with God through Christ as a reality to be entered upon, and constantly maintained, by the unconditional
and habitual surrender of the whole personality to Christ's control and gov-
ernment, in the assurance that the living Christ will take possession of the
life thus yielded to Him." It is such teaching, revealing the infinite claim
and power of Christ's love as maintained by the power of the Holy Spirit,
that will encourage and compel us to make the measure of Christ's surrender for us the only measure of our surrender to Him and His service.

It is this intimate fellowship with Christ as the secret of daily service
and testimony that has power to make Christ known as the deliverer from
sin and the inspiration of a life of whole-hearted devotion to His service.

It is this intimate and abiding fellowship with Christ that the promise,
"I am with you alway," secures to us. This is what every missionary needs,
what every missionary has a right to claim, and by which alone he maintains that spiritual efficiency that will influence the workers and the converts with whom he comes in contact.

---

*Lord Jesus, may we see the measure of our surrender to Thee and Thy
service only by the measure of Christ's surrender for us. Amen.*

Paul's Missionary Message

"Continue in prayer . . . withal praying also for us, that God would open unto us a door of utterance, to speak the mystery of Christ . . . that I may make it manifest, as I ought to speak" (Col. 4:2–4).

"The mystery now made manifest to His saints: to whom God would make known what is the riches of the glory of this mystery among the Gentiles; which is Christ in you, the hope of glory" (Col. 1:26–27).

To Paul's mind, the very center and substance of his Gospel was the indwelling Christ. He spoke of the "riches of the glory of this mystery—Christ in you, the hope of glory." Though he had been so many years a preacher of this Gospel, he still asked for prayer, that he might make known that mystery aright.

The complaint is often made in regard to native Churches, that after a time there appears to be no further growth and very little of the joy and power for bearing witness to Christ Jesus. The question comes whether the Church at home is living in the experience of this indwelling Christ, so that the sons and daughters whom she sends out know the secret and make it the substance of their teaching and preaching.

Some years ago one of our ministers went to the foreign mission field to do deputation work. Before he left there was a little gathering for prayer at which he asked what his message should be. The thought was expressed that in speaking to Christians it was desirable that a message of a full salvation should be pressed home, and the hearts roused to believe in and to accept of an indwelling Christ. On his return he told with what deep interest the presentation of this truth had been received, many saying that they had never before understood this aright.

Has the Church lost the truth of the indwelling Christ? We speak of Paul's missionary methods, but is there not a greater need of Paul's missionary message as it culminates in the one word: "Christ in you, the hope of glory"? Paul felt the need of much prayer to enable him to give the message aright. Is there not a call to all missionary intercessors and to our beloved missionaries themselves to make it a matter of first importance to obtain the power and from a living experience to lead Christians into the enjoyment of their rightful heritage? "If a man love Me, he will keep My words, and My Father will love him, and we will make our abode with him." And it may be the Church at home will also share in the blessing, the restoration to its right place of this truth: "Christ in you, the hope of glory."

Lord Jesus Christ: Dwell in me. Amen.

219

The Missionary's Life

*"Ye are witnesses, and God also, how holily and
righteously and unblameably we behaved ourselves
toward you that believe" (1 Thess. 2:10 R.V.).*

Paul more than once appeals to what his converts had seen of his own life. So he says (2 Cor. 1:12): "Our glorying is this, the testimony of our conscience, that in holiness and sincerity of God, not in fleshly wisdom but in the grace of God, we behaved ourselves in the world, and more abundantly to you-ward." Christ had taught His disciples as much of His life as by His teaching. Paul had sought to be a living witness to the truth of all that he had preached about Christ—as able to save and to keep from sin, as renewing the whole nature by the power of His Holy Spirit, as Himself becoming the life of those who believe in Him.

In a recent missionary report one finds this expression: "It has come to pass that our representatives on the field, just because they are what we have made them, have far too often hidden the Christ whom they are giving their lives to reveal. It is only in proportion as the missionary can manifest the character of Christ in and through his own life that he can gain a hearing for the Gospel. Only as far as he can live Christ before their eyes can he help them to understand his message."

See how Paul's appeal to his life, as holy and righteous and unblameable, gave him courage to put a high standard before his converts. In the same Epistle he calls them to trust God, to establish their hearts unblameable in holiness before God (1 Thess. 3:13). And later in the Epistle (5:23–24): "The God of peace Himself sanctify you wholly, who also will do it." In Philippians 4:9 he writes: "The things which ye both heard and saw in me, these things do, and the God of peace shall be with you." And in 1 Timothy 1:14–16: "The grace of our Lord abounded exceedingly with faith and love which is in Christ Jesus, . . . for an example of them which should hereafter believe on Him unto eternal life." Let us believe that when Paul said, "Christ liveth in me," "I live no more," he spoke of an actual, divine, unceasing, abiding of Christ in him, working in him from hour to hour all that was well-pleasing to the Father. And let us not rest until we can say, "The Christ of Paul is my Christ! His missionary enduement is mine too."

Lord Jesus Christ, forgive me for hiding Thee whom it is my purpose to reveal, manifest Thyself through me to others. Amen.

The Holy Spirit

*"The Comforter shall glorify Me: for He shall receive
of Mine, and shall show it unto you" (John 16:14).*

When our Lord spoke the words to the disciples, "Lo, I am with you alway," they did not at first understand or experience their full meaning.

It was when at Pentecost they were filled with the Holy Spirit and the Spirit from heaven brought down into their hearts the glorified Lord Jesus that they began the new life in the joy of the abiding presence.

All our attempts to claim to live that life of continuous, unbroken communion will be in vain unless we too yield ourselves wholly to the power and the indwelling of the ever blessed Spirit.

Throughout the Church of Christ what a lack of faith is apparent in what the Spirit is as God, and of what He can enable us to be, and of how completely He demands full and undisturbed possession of our whole being. All our faith in the fulfillment of Christ's glorious promises of the Father and Son making their abode in us is subject to the one essential and indispensable condition   a life utterly and unceasingly yielded to the rule and leading of the Spirit of Christ.

Let no one say: "The experience of Christ's being with us every day and all the day is impossible." Christ meant His word to be a simple and eternal reality. He meant the promises to be accepted—"He that loveth Me shall be loved of My Father, and I will love him, and will manifest Myself to him," and "We will come unto him and make our abode with him"— as absolute divine truth. But this truth could only be experienced where the Spirit in His power as God was known and believed in and obeyed. What Christ speaks of in John 14 is what Paul testifies to when he says, "Christ liveth in me," or, as John expresses it, "Hereby know we that we abide in Him and He in us, because He hath given us of His Spirit."

Christ came as God to make known the Father, and the Spirit came as God to make known the Son in us. We need to understand that the Spirit as God claims absolute subjection and is willing to take possession of our whole being and enable us to fulfill all that Christ asks of us. It is the Spirit who can deliver us from all the power of the flesh, who can conquer the power of the world. It is the Spirit through whom Christ Jesus will manifest Himself to us in nothing less than His abiding presence: "Lo, I am with you alway."

---

*Heavenly Father, through Thy Spirit deliver us from all the power of
the flesh and conquer the power of the world. Amen.*

Filled with the Spirit

"Be filled with the Spirit; speaking one to another in
psalms and hymns and spiritual songs, singing and making
melody with your heart to the Lord; giving thanks always
for all things" (Eph. 5:18–20 R.V.).

If we had the expression, "filled with the Spirit," only in regard to the story of Pentecost, we might naturally think that it was something special and not meant for ordinary life. But our text teaches us the great lesson that it is meant for every Christian and for everyday life.

To realize this more fully, think of what the Holy Spirit was in Christ Jesus and what the conditions were under which He, as man, was filled with the Spirit. He received the Spirit when He was praying and had yielded Himself as a sacrifice to God in going down into the sinner's baptism. And full of the Holy Spirit He was led to the forty days' fasting, sacrificing the needs of the body to be free for fellowship with the Father and the victory over Satan. He even refused, when He was an hungered, to listen to the temptation of the Evil One to use His power to make bread to supply His hunger. And so He was led by the Spirit all through life until He, by the Eternal Spirit, offered Himself without blemish unto God. In Christ the Spirit meant prayer, obedience, and sacrifice.

Even so we, if we are to follow Christ, to have His mind in us, to live out His life, must seek to regard the fullness of the Spirit as a daily supply, as a daily provision, if we are to live the life of obedience, of joy, of self-sacrifice, and of power for service. There may be occasions when that fullness of the Spirit will become especially manifest, but every day and all the day it is only as we are led by the Spirit that we can abide in Christ Jesus, conquer the flesh and the world, and live the life with God in prayer and with those around us in humble, holy, fruitful service.

Above all, it is only as we are filled with the Spirit that the words of Jesus can be fully understood and experienced: "Lo, I am with you alway." "Lo, I am with you alway," was meant for daily life and that not without but with the sure and all-sufficient aid of that blessed Spirit of whom Jesus said: "He that believeth in Me, out of him shall flow rivers of living water." Our faith in Christ will be the measure of our fullness of the Spirit. The measure of the power of the Spirit in us will be the measure of our experience of the presence of Christ.

Lord Jesus, my prayer is that out of me will "flow rivers of living water."
Amen.

The Christ Life

"Christ liveth in me" (Gal. 2:20).

"Christ is our life" (Col. 3:4).

Christ's life was more than His teaching, more than His work, more even than His death. It was His life in the sight of God and man that gave value to what He said and did and suffered. And it is this life, glorified in the resurrection, that He imparts to His people and enables them to live out before others.

"Hereby shall all men know that ye are My disciples, if ye love one another." It was the life in the new family of the Holy Spirit that made both Jews and Greeks feel that there was some super-human power about Christ's disciples; they gave living proof of the truth of what they said, that God's love had come down and taken possession of them.

It has often been said of the missionary, that unless he lives out the Christ life on an entirely different level from that on which others live, he misses the deepest secret of power and success in his work. When Christ sent His disciples forth, it was with the command: "Tarry till ye be endued with power from on high." "Wait, and ye shall receive the power of the Holy Spirit, and be My witnesses to the ends of the earth." Many a missionary has felt that it is not learning and not zeal and not the willingness for self-sacrifice in Christ's service, but the secret experience of the life hid with Christ in God that enables him to meet and overcome every difficulty.

Everything depends upon the life with God in Christ being right. It was so with Christ, with the disciples, with Paul. It is the simplicity and intensity of our life in Christ Jesus and of the life of Christ Jesus in us, that sustains us in the daily drudgery of work, that makes us conquer over self and everything that could hinder the Christ life, and gives the victory over the powers of evil and over the hearts from which the evil spirits have to be cast out.

The life is everything. It was so in Christ Jesus. It must be so in His servants. It can be so because Christ Himself will live in us. When He spoke the word, "Lo, I am with you alway," He meant nothing less than this: "Every day and all the day I am with you, the secret of your life, your joy, and your strength."

Heavenly Father, Oh, to learn what hidden treasures are contained in the blessed words we love to repeat: "Lo, I am with you all the days." Amen.

223

The Christlike Life

"Have this mind in you, which was also in Christ Jesus" (Phil. 2:5).

And what was the mind that was in Christ Jesus? "Being in the form of God, He emptied Himself, taking the form of a servant, being made in the likeness of men; He humbled Himself, becoming obedient even unto death, yea, the death of the Cross." Self-emptying and self-sacrifice, obedience to God's will, and love to the world, even unto the death of the Cross— such was the character of Christ for which God so highly exalted Him. Such is the character of Christ that we are to imitate. He was made in the likeness of human flesh, that we might be conformed into the likeness of God.

Self-effacement, self-sacrifice, that God's will might be done and that we might be saved—such was the life of Christ. "Love seeketh not her own." This was His life; He lived only to please God and to bless people.

Let no one say that this is an impossibility. "What is impossible with men is possible with God." We are called to work out this salvation of a Christlike character with fear and trembling; for "it is God that worketh in us both to will and to do of His good pleasure." He of whom Christ said, "It is the Father in Me that doeth the works," is He who works in us to will and to do.

It has been said that the "missionary who is to commend the Gospel must first embody it in a character fully conformed to the likeness of Jesus Christ. It is only as far as he can live Christ before the eyes of the converts that he can help them to understand his message. It has at times come to pass that our representatives on the field, just because they are what we have made them, have far too often hidden the Christ whom they are giving their lives to reveal."

As the Church aims at making some marked degree of likeness to Christ's character the standard for Christian teachers, our missionaries will be able to pass this on to their converts and say to them: "Be ye followers of us, even as we are of Christ."

Let us not rest until our faith lays hold of the promise, "It is God that worketh in us." The confidence will be aroused, that as the character of Christ is the revelation with which every missionary has been entrusted, so the power will be given to fulfill this high and holy calling. Let ministers and missionaries and all intercessors make this their one great plea and aim to have this mind that was in Christ Jesus.

Heavenly Father, my one great plea and aim is to have this mind that was in Christ Jesus. Amen.

Christ: The Nearness of God

"Draw nigh to God, and He will draw nigh to you" (James 4:8).

It has been said that the holiness of God is the union of God's infinite distance from sinful man with God's infinite nearness in His redeeming grace. Faith must ever seek to realize both the distance and the nearness.

In Christ God has come near, so very near to man, and now the command comes: If you would have God come still nearer, you must draw nigh to Him. The promised nearness of Christ Jesus expressed in the promise, "Lo, I am with you alway," can only be experienced as we draw near to Him.

That means, first of all, at the beginning of each day afresh to yield ourselves for His holy presence to rest upon us. It means a voluntary, intentional, and whole-hearted turning away from the world to wait on God to make Himself known to our souls. It means giving time and all our heart and strength to allow Him to reveal Himself. It is impossible to expect the abiding presence of Christ with us through the day, unless there is the definite daily exercise of strong desire and childlike trust in His word: "Draw nigh to God, and He will draw nigh to you."

And that means, further, the simple, childlike offering of ourselves and our lives in everything to do His will alone and to seek above everything to please Him. His promise is sure: "If a man love Me he will keep My words, and My Father will love him, and we will make our abode in him."

Then comes the quiet assurance of faith, even if there is not much feeling or sense of His presence, that God is with us, and that as we go out to do His will, He will watch over us and keep us and, what is more, strengthen us in the inner man with divine strength for the work we have to do for Him.

Precious Heavenly Father, as Thy child I pray that these words come to me with a new meaning each morning: "Draw nigh to God, and He will draw nigh to you." Wait patiently, and He will speak in divine power: "Lo, I am with you alway." Amen.

Love

*"Jesus, having loved His own which were in
the world, loved them unto the end" (John 13:1).*

These are the opening words of that holy, confidential talk of Christ with His disciples, as out of the depths of eternity He discoursed with them in the last hours before He went to Gethsemane (John 13 to 17). They are the revelation and full display of that divine love which was manifested in His death on the Cross.

He begins with the new commandment: "That ye love one another as I have loved you" (John 13:34). A little later follows: "If ye love Me, keep My commandments. . . . He that loveth Me shall be loved of My Father, and I will love him, and will manifest Myself unto him . . . and We will come unto him, and make Our abode with him" (14:15, 21, 23). The new life, the heavenly life in Christ Jesus is to be the unfolding of God's love in Christ. Then, farther on: "As the Father hath loved Me, so have I loved you: continue ye in My love. If ye keep My commandments, ye shall abide in My love. . . . This is My commandment, That ye love one another, as I have loved you. Greater love hath no man than this, that a man lay down his life for his friends" (John 15:9–13); "That the world may know that Thou hast sent Me, and hast loved them, as Thou hast loved Me. . . . I have declared unto them Thy name . . . that the love wherewith Thou hast loved Me may be in them, and I in them" (John 17:23, 26).

Can words make it plainer that God's love to Christ is given to pass into us and to become our life, that the love wherewith the Father loved the Son is to be in us? If the Lord Jesus is to manifest Himself to us, it can only be to the loving heart. If we are to claim His daily presence with us, it can only be as a relationship of infinite tender love between Him and us, love rooted in the faith of God's love to Christ coming into our hearts and showing itself in obedience to His commandments and in love to one another.

We see how in the early Church the first love was forsaken after a time, and confidence was put in all the activities of service (Rev. 2:2–4).

It is only in the atmosphere of a holy, living love that the abiding presence of the loving Christ can be known, and the depth of the Divine Love expressed in Christ's promise, "Lo, I am with you alway," will be realized.

Heavenly Father: Thy love becomes my life and I turn to Thee with a loving heart for others and a willingness to obey Thy commandments. Amen.

The Trial and
Triumph of Faith

"Jesus said unto him, If thou canst believe, all things
are possible to him that believeth. And straightway the
father of the child cried out, and said with tears, Lord,
I believe; help Thou mine unbelief" (Mark 9:23–24).

What a glorious promise: "All things are possible to him that believeth"! And yet it is just the greatness of the promise that constitutes the trial of faith. At first we do not really believe its truth. But when we have grasped it, then comes the real trial in the thought: Such a wonder-working faith is utterly beyond my reach.

But what constitutes the trial of faith soon becomes its triumph. How can this be? When Christ said to the father of the child, "If thou canst believe, all things are possible to him that believeth," he felt that this was only casting him into deeper despair. How could his faith be able to work the miracle? But as he looked into the face of Christ and the love of the tender eye touched his heart, he felt sure that this blessed Man not only had the power to heal his child, but the power too to inspire him with the needed faith. The impression Christ produced upon him made not only the one miracle of the healing possible, but the second miracle too that he should have so great a faith. And with tears he cried, "Lord, I believe; help Thou mine unbelief." The very greatness of faith's trial was the greatness of faith's triumph.

What a lesson! Of all things that are possible to faith, the most impossible is that I should be able to exercise such faith. The abiding presence of Christ is possible to faith. And this faith is possible to the soul that clings to Christ and trusts Him. As surely as He will lead us into His abiding presence all the day, so surely will He strengthen us with divine power for the faith that claims and receives the promise. Blessed the hour when the believer sees how entirely he is dependent on Christ for the faith as well as the blessing and, in the consciousness of the unbelief that is still struggling within, he casts himself on the power and the love of Jesus: "Lord, I believe; Lord, I believe."

Through such trial and through such triumph, sometimes the triumph of despair, we enter upon our inheritance, the abiding presence of Him who speaks to us now: "Lo, I am with you alway."

Lord Jesus Christ, we tarry at Thy feet until we know that Thou hast has blessed us. "I can do all things in Him that strengtheneth me" (Phil. 4:13 R.V.). Amen.

Exceeding Abundantly

"Now unto Him that is able to do exceeding abundantly above all that we ask or think, according to the power that worketh in us, unto Him be glory in the Church by Christ Jesus throughout all ages, world without end. Amen" (Eph. 3:20–21).

In the great prayer which Paul had just indited, he had apparently reached the highest expression possible of the life to which God's mighty power could bring the believer. But Paul is not content. In this doxology he rises still higher and lifts us up to give glory to God as "able to do exceeding abundantly above all that we can ask or think." Pause a moment to think what that "exceeding abundantly" means.

Think of the words, "the exceeding great and precious promises." Think of "the exceeding greatness of His power toward us who believe, according to the working of the strength of His might which He wrought in Christ when He raised Him from the dead." Think of the grace of our Lord as exceeding abundant with faith and love which is in Christ Jesus, so that where sin abounded grace did abound more exceedingly. He lifts our hearts to give glory to God as able to do "exceeding abundantly above all that we ask or think," according to the greatness of that power which worketh in us, nothing less than the exceeding greatness of the power that raised Christ from the dead. And as our hearts begin to feel that there is here a prospect of something that God will work in us beyond all our imagination, He lifts our hearts to join in the universal chorus: "Unto Him be the glory in the Church and in Christ Jesus, unto all generations, forever and ever. Amen."

Paul began his great prayer, "I bow my knees to the Father." He ends it by bringing us to our knees, to give glory to Him as able to fulfill every promise, to reveal Christ dwelling in our hearts and keep us in that life of love which leads to being filled with all the fullness of God.

Child of God, bow in deep adoration, giving glory to God, until your heart learns to believe; the prayer will be fulfilled, Jesus Christ will dwell in my heart by faith. Faith in this Almighty God and the exceeding abundance of His grace and power will teach us that the abiding indwelling of Christ in the heart is the secret of the abiding presence.

Heavenly Father, we lift our hearts to give Thee glory to do "exceedingly abundantly above all that we ask or think." Amen.

The One Thing Needful

"An Humble, Earnest and Affectionate Address to the Clergy," was the dying legacy of William Law to the Church. He had corrected the proofs of the greater part when he was taken away. He invites the clergy to its perusal with the assurance that he desires "not to call their attention to any thing but *the one thing needful, the one thing essential, and alone available* to our rising out of our fallen state, and becoming as we were at our creation, an holy offspring of God, and real partakers of the Divine nature."

"If it be asked, What this one thing is; *It is the Spirit of God brought again to His first power of life in us.*"

"Everything else, however glorious and divine in outward appearance, everything that churches or reformations can do for us, is dead and helpless, but so far as it is the immediate work of the Spirit of God breathing and living in it. The end and design of all that is written in Scripture is only to call us back from the spirit of Satan, the flesh, and the world, to be again under the *full Dependence upon and Obedience to the Spirit of God,* who out of free love and thirst after our souls, seeks to have His first power of life in us. All love and delight in Scripture, which is merely human, is but the self-love of fallen Adam, and can have no better a nature till it proceeds from the inspiration of God, quickening His own life and nature within us, which alone can bring forth a godly love. For if it be an immutable truth, that 'no man can call Jesus, Lord, but by the Holy Spirit,' it must be a truth equally immutable, that no one can have any Christlike temper, or power of goodness, but so far as he is immediately led and governed by the Holy Spirit."†

Let us remember that it is of little profit to know the meaning of what we read; the great question is, whether we have taken the instruction to heart. Do we indeed believe that this is the one thing needful for the Church and ourselves, the deep conviction that God's one desire is that the Holy Spirit should have the place in us that He had in Adam before the Fall, so that the only thing that gives value to our religion is that it is the immediate work of the Spirit of God.

Blessed Father, we now take Thy instruction into our hearts, acknowledging that no one can have any Christlike temper, or power of goodness, but so far as he is immediately led and governed by the Holy Spirit. Amen.

---

* William Law (1686-1761), English devotional writer.
† William Law, *A Serious Call to a Devout and Holy Life* (1728).

Our Total Dependence on God Alone

"All that is called Divine goodness and virtue in the creature is nothing else but the one goodness of God manifesting a discovery of itself in the creature. This is the unalterable state between God and the creature, according as its created nature is fitted to receive it. Goodness, forever and ever, can only belong to God as essential to Him, and inseparable from Him, as His own unity.

"But if now all that is glorious and happy in the spirit and enjoyment of the creature is only so much of the glory and blessedness of God dwelling in it, then we may infallibly see the true nature of all true religion. For the creature's true religion is its *'rendering to God all that is God's'*; its true continual acknowledging that all which it is and has, is in and from God alone.

"The one relation, which is the ground alone of all true religion, is this; it is *a total unalterable dependence on God, an immediate continual receiving of every degree of goodness and happiness from God alone.*

"The angels are ever abiding flames of pure love, always ascending up to and uniting with God, because the glory, the love and goodness of God alone is all that they see and know, either within or without themselves. Their adoration in spirit and in truth never ceases, because they never cease to acknowledge *the all* of God—*the all* of God in themselves, and *the all* of God in the whole creation. This is the one religion of heaven, and nothing else is the truth of religion on earth.

"Nothing can be the good of religion, but the power and presence of God *really and essentially living and working in it.* So that the creature must have all its religious goodness as wholly and solely from God's immediate operation, as it had its first goodness at its creation."*

Ever Blessed Father! we thank Thee for that wonderful relationship to Thyself for which Thou didst create us. And we thank Thee still more for that wonderful Redemption which has restored us by the gift of the Holy Spirit into that blessed union and communion with Thyself in which Thou wilt enable us always to live. We humbly pray Thee ever to keep this in the thought of the heart of Thy people. Amen.

---

* William Law, *A Serious Call.*

Continual Inspiration

"All true religion is, or brings forth, an essential union and communion of the spirit of the creature with the Spirit of the Creator; God in it, and it in God, one Life, one Light, one Love. *Divine, immediate inspiration* and Divine religion are inseparable in the nature of the thing.

"All that the natural or uninspired man does or can do, has no more of the truth or power of Divine worship in it, than that which he does in the field or shop. Self love, self-esteem, self-seeking, and living wholly to self are the whole of all that can be in the natural man. Nor can any creature be in a better or higher state than this, till something supernatural is found in it; and this supernatural something, called in Scripture *the Word*, or *Spirit*, or *Inspiration of God*, is that alone from which man can have the first good thought about God, or the least power of having heavenly desires in his spirit.

"No man can reach God with his love or have union with Him by it, *but he who is inspired with that one same Spirit of Love* with which God Himself loved from all eternity. Infinite hosts of new-created heavenly beings can begin no new kind of love to God, nor have the least power of beginning to love Him at all, but so far as *His own Holy Spirit of Love* is brought to life

"This love can be the only love in creatures that can draw them to God; they have no power of cleaving to Him or adoring Him, but by partaking of that Eternal Spirit of Love. *Therefore the continual inspiration or operation of the Holy Spirit is the one only possible ground of our continually loving God.*"*

Heavenly Father: Let us meditate and pray, until this blessed truth begins to get possession of our heart—the immediate, continual inspiration of Thee, as actually our only power of goodness, is our birthright and must be our experience, if we are to live out Thy will. To an extent which we have very little realized, the Holy Spirit waits in very deed to fill our life all the day with Thy love. Amen.

---

* William Law, *A Serious Call.*

The Spirit of God in Adam

"Divine inspiration was *essential* to man's first created state. The Spirit of the Triune God, breathed into him, was that alone which made him a holy creature in the image and likeness of God. Had he not been thus at the first, God in him and he in God, a true offspring of the Holy Spirit, no dispensation of God to *fallen man* would have directed him to the Holy Spirit or ever made mention of His inspiration in man.

"Hence it plainly appears, that the Gospel state could not be God's *last dispensation*, or the finishing of man's redemption, unless its whole work was a work of the Spirit of God in man so as to bring *the thing itself* or the substance of all former types and shadows into real enjoyment. Now the thing itself, and for the sake of which all God's dispensations have been, is *that first life of God which was essentially born in the soul of the first man, Adam*, and to which he died. This makes it plain that the work of this dispensation must be *solely and immediately* the work of the Holy Spirit. Therefore *immediate inspiration* is as necessary to make fallen man alive again unto God as it was to make man at first a living soul after the image of God.

"And *continual inspiration* is as necessary as man's continuance in his redeemed state. That alone which begins or gives life must of all necessity be the only continuance or preservation of life. No life can continue in the goodness of its first created or redeemed state but by its continuing under the influence of and working with that powerful Root or Spirit which at first created or redeemed it. Because without Christ we can do nothing, therefore we ought *to believe, expect, wait for, and depend upon His continual immediate operation in everything that we do*, through His Spirit dwelling in us."*

Heavenly Father, we pause to consider how little this immediate continual inspiration of the Holy Spirit in the heart of Thy child is believed or accepted. And let us, from the very beginning of our readings, make this the one object of our desire and prayer—the full experience of what the Holy Spirit is meant to be to us. Amen.

---

* William Law, *A Serious Call.*

The Ministration of the Spirit

"A Natural life can subsist no longer than while it is *immediately and continually* under the working power of that root or source from which it sprang. Hence nothing but obedience to the Spirit, trusting to the Spirit, walking in the Spirit, praying with and for its continual inspiration can possibly keep men from sin. The truth and perfection of the Gospel state could not show itself till it became solely *a ministration of the Spirit* or a kingdom in which the Holy Spirit of God had the doing of all that was done in it.

"When Christ taught His disciples: 'I tell you the truth, it is expedient for you that I go away,' He taught them to believe what the want was of their present condition, and joyfully to expect the coming of a higher and more blessed state, which they could not have till *His outward teaching* in human language *was changed into the inspiration and operation of His Spirit in their souls.*

"Here two most fundamental truths are fully demonstrated. First, that the truth and perfection of the Gospel state could not take place till Christ was glorified and His Kingdom among men made wholly and solely *a continual, immediate ministration of the Spirit*, which carried man into the real possession and enjoyment of a Divine life.

"Secondly, that as the Apostles could not, so no man, from their time to the end of the world, can have any true and real knowledge of the spiritual blessings of Christ's redemption or have a Divine capacity of fitness to preach and bear witness of them to the world, *but solely by that same Divine Spirit* opening all the mysteries of a Redeeming Christ in their inward part, as it did in the Apostles and first ministers of the Gospel."*

Heavenly Father: Let us confess how much we have thought of the working of the Spirit as an occasional thing, for certain times or duties. Let us remember that it will be no easy thing for us to be delivered from this thought, and to yield ourselves wholly to the great truth that the immediate and continual inspiration of the Holy Spirit is what is absolutely needed, is promised by Thee, and made possible to us. Let us make this the one aim of our desire and prayer. Amen.

---

* William Law, *A Serious Call.*

Our Death and Life in Christ

"Why could not the Apostles, who had been eye-witnesses to the whole process of Christ, testify with their human apprehension the truth of such things, till they were baptized with fire and born again of the Spirit? It is because the truth of such things, or the mysteries of Christ's process as knowable by man, are nothing else in themselves, *but those very things* which are done by this heavenly fire and Spirit of God in our souls. Therefore every man, however able in all kinds of human literature, must be an entire stranger to all the mysteries of Gospel redemption till they are verified, fulfilled, and witnessed to by that which *is found and enjoyed of the whole process of Christ in his soul.* As the work of the Spirit consists in altering that which is the most radical in the soul, bringing forth a new spiritual death and a new spiritual life, it must be true that no one can know or believe the mysteries of Christ's redeeming power, but only and solely *by an inward and experimental finding and feeling the operation of them in that new death and new life, both* of which must be effected in the soul of man, or Christ is not known as its salvation.

"Behmen* prefixed as a motto to most of his epistles the words of Scripture: that our salvation is in the life of Jesus Christ in us. This truth of truths fully possessed and firmly adhered to, turns the whole faith of man to a Christ that can nowhere be a Savior to him but *as essentially born in the inmost spirit of his soul by the immediate inspiration and working power of the Holy Spirit within him.* To such a man the words of Christ and His Apostles fall like a fire into him. And what is it they kindle there? A holy flame of love, to be always with, always attending to, that Christ and his Holy Spirit within Him, which alone can make him to be and do all that which the words of Christ and His Apostles have taught. For there is no possibility of being like-minded with Christ in anything that He taught, or having the truth of one Christian virtue, but *by the nature and Spirit of Christ essentially living in us.*"†

Heavenly Father: We need ever to remember that the great work of the Holy Spirit is to reveal Christ in us. Not to the mind as a matter of knowledge, but in the heart and life, communicating to us the very death and life of our Lord. It is thus that Christ is formed in us, has His abode in us and works in us and through us all that is well-pleasing to Thee. I yield myself to this blessed truth; in it lies the true secret of the Christian life. Amen.

---

* Jacob Behmen (1575-1624), German mystic whose writings were held in high estimation by William Law.

† William Law, *A Serious Call.*

Humility

After writing what we have given extracts from, Law goes on to prove how in the Church of Christ the gifts of human learning and wisdom speedily asserted themselves instead of that entire dependence upon the Holy Spirit of which Christ had spoken. And with that learning came, as a natural consequence, the exaltation of self and the whole difference became the question between Pride, in the power of human learning and wisdom, and Humility, in the absolute dependence on the teaching of the Holy Spirit.

"Man's intellectual faculties are, by the Fall, in a much worse state than his natural animal appetites, and want a much greater self-denial. To realize this we only need to know two things: 1. That our salvation consists wholly in *being saved from ourselves*, or that which we are by nature; 2. That in the whole nature of things nothing could be this salvation or Savior to us, but such *a humility of God* manifested in human nature as is beyond all expression. Hence, the first unalterable Term of this Savior to fallen man is this, 'Except a man deny himself, forsakes all that he has, yea, and his own life, he cannot be My disciple.' And to show that this is but the beginning or ground of man's salvation the Savior adds: 'Learn of Me for I am meek and lowly of heart.' What a light is here for those who can bear or love the light: Self is the whole evil of fallen nature; self-denial is our capacity of being saved, humility is our Savior.

"All the vices of fallen angels and men have their birth and power in the Pride of self, or I may better say, in the atheism and idolatry of self, for Self is both Atheist and Idolater. It is Atheist because it has rejected God, it is an Idolater because it is its own idol. On the other hand, all the virtues of the heavenly life are the virtues of humility. Not a joy, or glory, or praise in heaven but is what it is through humility. It is humility alone that makes the unpassable gulf between heaven and hell. This is the most plain and capital truth of the Gospel, namely, that there never was, nor never will be, but one humility in the whole world, and that is, the one humility of Christ."*

In the life of faith, humility has a far deeper place than we think. It is not only one among other virtues, but is the first and chief need of the soul. It leads us to know our absolute and entire inability in ourselves to do any good.

Dear Lord Jesus, we look to the humility of Thee, as being what Thou hast prepared in Thy life for us and will most surely work in us in response to our faith. Amen.

---

* William Law, *A Serious Call.*

The Kingdom of Heaven

That one Light and Spirit, which was only one from all eternity before angels or any heavenly beings were created, must to all eternity be that one only Light and Spirit by which angels or men can ever have any union or communion with God. What, therefore, can have the least share of power toward man's redemption but the Light and Spirit of God making again a birth of themselves in Him, as they did in His first glorious creation.

"Hence it is that the Gospel state is by our Lord affirmed to be *a kingdom of heaven at hand, or come among men*, because it has the nature of no worldly thing or creaturely power, receives nothing from man but man's full denial of himself, has no existence, but in that working power of God that created and upholds heaven and earth, and is *a kingdom of God become man, and a kingdom of men united to God through a continual, immediate Divine illumination.* What Scripture of the New Testament can you read that does not prove this to be the Gospel state, a kingdom of God into which none can enter but by being born of the Spirit, none can continue to be alive in it but by being led by the Spirit, and which not a thought, or desire, or action can be allowed to have any part in it but as it is a fruit of the Spirit?

"'Thy Kingdom come, Thy will be done on earth as it is in heaven.' What is God's Kingdom in heaven but *the manifestation of what God is* and what He does in His heavenly creatures? How is His will done there, but because His Holy Spirit is the life, the power, and mover of all that live in it. We daily read this prayer, reminding us that nothing but a *continual, essential, immediate, Divine illumination* can do that which we pray may be done. For where can God's Kingdom become, but where every other power but His is at an end and driven out of it? How can His will only be done, but where the Spirit that wills in God, wills in the creature?

"This is the truth of the Kingdom of God, come unto men, and this is the birthright privilege of all that are living members of it, to be delivered from their own natural spirit which they had from Adam, from the spirit and wisdom of this world, and through the whole course of their lives only to say, and do, and be that which the Spirit of their Father worketh in."*

How much has been written about what the Kingdom of heaven means, but here we have what it really is. As God rules in His Kingdom in heaven, so when the kingdom comes into our hearts He lives and rules there. The Kingdom of God consists of those in whom God rules as He does in heaven.

Heavenly Father, rule in my heart. Amen.

---

* William Law, *A Serious Call.*

The Nature of Love

"The Spirit of Love has this original God, as considered in Himself, in His Holy Being, before anything is brought forth by Him, or out of Him, is only *an eternal Will to all Goodness*. This is the *one eternal, immutable God* that, from Eternity to Eternity, changeth not, that can be neither more nor less, but *an eternal Will to all the Goodness* that is in Himself and comes from Him. The creation of ever so many worlds adds nothing to, nor takes anything from, this immutable God: He always was and always will be the same immutable Will to all Goodness. So that as certainly as He is the Creator, so certainly is He the Blesser of every created thing and can give nothing but Blessing, Goodness, and Happiness from Himself, because He has in Himself nothing else to give.

"Now this is the ground and original of the Spirit of love in the creature. It is and must be a *will to all goodness*, and you have not the Spirit of Love till you have this will to all goodness at all times and on all occasions. You may indeed do many works of love and delight in them, because they are not contradictory to your state and temper. But the Spirit of Love is not in you till it is the Spirit of your life, till you live freely, willingly, and universally according to it. It knows no difference of time, place, or person; but whether it gives or forgives, bears or forbears, it is equally doing its own delightful work. For the Spirit of Love, wherever it is, is its own blessing and happiness, because it is the truth and the reality of God in the soul. For as love has no by-ends, wills nothing but its own increase, so everything is as oil to its flame. The Spirit of Love does not want to be rewarded or honored; its only desire is to propagate itself and become the blessing and happiness of everything that wants it. The wrath of an enemy, the treachery of a friend, only helps the Spirit of Love to be more triumphant, to live its own life and find all its own blessing in a higher degree. The infinitely perfect and happy God is mere love, an unchangeable Will to all Goodness, and therefore every creature must be corrupt and unhappy so far as it is led by any other will than the one will to all goodness."*

Heavenly Father, teach us that as glorious and holy as is Thy love to us, is the love with which Thou promises by Thy Holy Spirit to fill our hearts. Amen.

---

* William Law, *A Serious Call.*

The Necessity of Love

"This necessity is absolute and unchangeable. No creature can be a child of God, but because the Goodness of God is in it; nor can it have any union or communion with the Goodness of the Deity, till its Life is a Spirit of Love. This is the one only bond of union between God and the creature. For as God is an immutable Will to all goodness, so the Divine Will can unite or work with no creaturely will but that which wills with Him only that which is good. For as the will to all goodness is *the whole Nature of God*, so it must be *the whole Nature* of every service or religion that can be acceptable to Him, for nothing serves God or worships and adores Him, but that which wills and works with Him. For God can delight in nothing but His own will and His own Spirit, because all goodness is included in it and can be nowhere else. And therefore everything that follows an own will, or an own spirit, forsakes the one Will to all Goodness and, while it does so, has no capacity for the Life and Spirit of God.

"The necessity therefore of the Spirit of Love is what God Himself cannot dispense with in the creature any more than He can deny Himself or act contrary to His own holy being. But as it was His Will to all Goodness that brought forth angels and the spirits of men, so He can will nothing in their existence but that they should live and work and manifest that same spirit of Love and Goodness which brought them into being.

"There is no peace, nor ever can be, for the soul of man but in the purity and perfection of its first created nature; nor can it have its purity and perfection in any other way than in and by the Spirit of Love. For as Love is the God that created all things, so Love is the purity, the perfection, and blessing of all created things; and nothing can live in God but as it lives in love. So that Love alone is, and only can be, the cure of every evil; and he that lives in the purity of love is risen out of the power of evil into the freedom of the one Spirit of heaven."*

Let us take time to ponder this blessed truth and promise: the God and Father of all love is longing to fill the heart of His children with nothing less than His own Divine, Eternal Love!

Heavenly Father: Fill my heart with nothing less than Thy Divine, Eternal love. Amen.

---

* William Law, *A Serious Call.*

Love: A New Birth from Above

"Your coming calls me to the most delightful subject in the world, to help both you and myself to rejoice in that adorable Deity whose infinite Being is an infinity of mere love, an unbeginning, never-ceasing, and for-ever-flowing Ocean of Meekness, Sweetness, Delight, Blessing, Goodness, Patience and Mercy; and all this as so many streams breaking out of the Abyss of the universal Love, Father, Son, and Holy Spirit, a triune Infinity of Love and Goodness, forever and ever giving forth nothing but the same gifts of Light and Love, of Blessing and Joy, whether before or after the Fall, either of angels or of men.

"Hold it therefore for a certain truth that you can have no good come into your soul, but only by the one way of a birth from above, from the *Entrance of the Deity* into the properties of your own soulish life. Nature must be set right; its properties must enter into the process of a new birth, it must work to the production of life before the Spirit of Love can have a birth in it. For Love is Delight, and Delight cannot arise in any creature until its nature is in a delightful state or is possessed of that in which it must rejoice. And this is the reason why God must become man; it is because a birth of the Deity must be found in the soul, giving to nature all that it wants, or the soul can never find itself in a delightful state and only working with the Spirit of Love.

"And now you also see the absolute necessity of the Gospel doctrine of the cross, viz. of *dying to self as the only way to life in God*. This Cross, or Dying to self, is the one morality that does us any good. The one work therefore of morality is the one doctrine of the cross, viz., *to resist and deny nature*, that a supernatural power or Divine goodness may take possession of it and bring a new life into it. Goodness is only a sound and virtue a mere strife of natural passions, till the Spirit of Love is the breath of everything that lives and moves in the heart. For Love is the one only blessing and goodness and God of nature; and you have no true religion or no worship of the one true God but in and by that Spirit of Love which is *God Himself living and working in you*."*

Heavenly Father, we bow in deep humility to adore Thee for this wonderful love, and ask for grace in very deed to yield ourselves to the denial and the death of self. Amen.

---

* William Law, *A Serious Call.*

The Twofold Life

"No intelligent creature, whether angel or man, can be good and happy, but by partaking of and having in himself a twofold life. Now there is in the nature of things, an absolute necessity of this twofold life in every creature that is to be good and happy. The twofold life is this: it must have the life of nature and the life of God in it. It cannot be a creature and intelligent but by having the life and properties of nature, that is, by finding itself to be a life of various sensibilities that has a power of Understanding, Willing, and Desiring. This is its creaturely life which, by the creating power of God, it has in and from nature. God Himself cannot make a creature to be in its self or as to its own nature anything else but a state of emptiness, of want, of appetite. The highest life, therefore, that is natural and creaturely can go no higher than this; it can only be a bare capacity for goodness and happiness and cannot possibly be a good and happy life but by *the life of God dwelling in and in union with it.*

"There can be no goodness and happiness for any intelligent creature but in and by this twofold life; and therefore the union of the Divine and human life, or the Son of God incarnate in man, to make man again a partaker of the Divine nature, is the one only possible salvation for all the sons of fallen Adam, that is, of Adam dead to, or fallen from, his first union with the Divine life.

"A plain demonstration that there can be no happiness, blessing, and goodness for any creature in heaven or on earth but by having, as the Gospel says, Jesus Christ made unto it Wisdom, Righteousness, Sanctification, and Peace with God. The reason is this: it is because *goodness and happiness are absolutely inseparable from God* and can be nowhere but in God.

"This great truth clearly gives the solid distinction between inward holiness and all outward, creaturely practices. All the dispensations of God whether by the law or the prophets, by the Scriptures or ordinances of the Church are only helps to a holiness which they cannot give but are meant to turn the creaturely life from itself and its own working to a faith and hope, a hunger and thirst after that first union with the life of the Deity, which was lost in the fall of the first father of mankind."*

Heavenly Father, bring us to be possessed by the great truth that because goodness and happiness are absolutely inseparable from Thee, our only hope is to be found in the unceasing fellowship with Thyself and that Love which longs to have complete possession of us. Let this be our one desire and continual prayer—the life and the love of Thee dwelling in our hearts. Amen.

---

* William Law, *A Serious Call.*

Perpetual Inspiration

"How unreasonable is it to call perpetual inspiration fanaticism or enthusiasm when there cannot be the least degree of goodness or happiness in any intelligent being but *what is in its whole nature merely and truly the Breathing, the Life, and the Operation of God in the life of the creature*. For if goodness can only be in God, if it cannot exist separate from Him, if He can only bless and sanctify *not by a creaturely gift but* by *Himself becoming the Blessing and Sanctification of the creature*, then it is the highest degree of blindness to look for any goodness and happiness from anything but the *immediate in dwelling union and operation of the Deity in the life of the creature*. Perpetual inspiration therefore is in the nature of the thing as necessary to a life of Goodness, Holiness, and Happiness, as the perpetual respiration of the air is necessary to animal life.

"What a mistake it is to confine inspiration to particular times and occasions, to prophets and apostles when the common Christian looks and trusts *to be continually led and inspired by the Spirit of God*. For though all are not called to be prophets or apostles, yet all are called to be holy as He who has called them is holy, to be perfect as their heavenly Father is perfect, to be like-minded with Christ, to will only as God wills, to do all to His glory and honor, to renounce the spirit of the world, to love God with all their heart, soul, and spirit, and their neighbor as themselves.

"Behold a work as great, Divine, and supernatural as that of a prophet and an apostle. Now the holiness of the common Christian is *not an occasional thing* that is only for a time, but is the holiness of that which is always alive and stirring in us, namely, of our thoughts, wills, desires, and affections. If we are all called to this inward holiness and goodness, then *a perpetual, always-existing operation of the Spirit of God within us is absolutely necessary*. If our thoughts and affections are to be always holy and good, then the Holy and Good Spirit of God is to be always operating as a principle of life within us."*

Ever blessed God and Father, we beseech Thee, reveal to us in power this blessed truth that the immediate and continual leading and working of Thy Holy Spirit is in very deed what Thou longest to give and what we may confidently claim. Amen.

---

* William Law, *A Serious Call.*

Two Kinds of Knowledge

"Every kind of virtue and goodness may be brought into us by two different ways. They may be taught us outwardly by men, by rules and precepts; and they may be inwardly born in us as the genuine birth of our own renewed spirit. In the former way, they at best only change our outward behavior, putting our passions under a false restraint. Now this way of learning and attaining goodness, though thus imperfect, is yet absolutely necessary and must have its time and work in us; yet it is only for a time, as the law was a schoolmaster to the Gospel. But of all this outward instruction, whether from good men or the letter of Scripture, it must be said as the Apostle says of the law, that 'it maketh nothing perfect.' And yet it is highly necessary in order to perfection. All the Scriptures have no other good or benefit in them but as they lead to a salvation, not to be had in themselves, but from faith in Christ Jesus. Their teaching is only to teach us where to seek and to find the fountain and source of all light and knowledge. They can only direct us to something that is better than themselves, that can be the true Light, Life, and Power of Holiness in us.

"From this twofold life or teaching there naturally arises a twofold state of virtue and goodness. If you learn virtue and goodness only from outward means, from men or books, you will be virtuous or good according to time and place and outward forms. You may do works of humility, works of love, use times and forms of prayer; all this goodness is suitable to this kind of teaching and may very well be had in it. But the Spirit of Prayer, the Spirit of Love, the Spirit of Humility are only to be obtained by the operation of *the Light and Spirit of God*, not outwardly teaching but *inwardly bringing forth a new-born spirit within us.*"*

Heavenly Father: Alas, how much there is in the Church of the outward teaching with its intermittent states of goodness. Let us with our whole heart believe in that immediate teaching and working of the Holy Spirit which brings the life of heaven as a new-born spirit within us. Amen.

---

* William Law, *A Serious Call.*

The Monster of Self

"Until this birth of the Spirit of Divine Love is found in you, you cannot know what Divine Love is in itself. For Divine Love is perfect Peace and Joy, it is a Freedom from all disquiet, it is all Content and mere Happiness and makes everything to rejoice in itself. Love is the Christ of God; wherever it comes, it comes as the Blessing and Happiness of every natural life, as the Restorer of every lost perfection, a Fulfiller of all righteousness, and a Peace of God which passes all understanding.

"When the intelligent creature turns from God to self, he finds nature only as it is in himself and without God. Nothing is to be had from it or found in it but the working of every kind of evil. Covetousness, envy, pride, and wrath are the four elements of self or nature, all of them inseparable from it. Were we truly affected with things as they are, our real Good or real Evil, we should be much more afraid of having the serpents of Covetousness, Envy, Pride, and Wrath well nourished and kept alive in us, than of being shut up in a Pest-house or cast into a Dungeon of venomous beasts. This monster of self can hide himself under all forms of goodness, can watch and fast, pray much and preach long, and yet often gets more life and strength and more immovable abode in these forms of virtue than he has in publicans and sinners.

"*To die to self or to come from under its power* cannot be done by any act of resistance we can make to it by the powers of nature. The one only way of dying to self is most simple and plain; it is equally practicable by everybody; it is always at hand; it meets you in everything and is never without success.

"If you ask what is this one true simple, plain, immediate, and unerring way, *it is the way of Patience, Meekness, Humility, and Resignation to God.* This is the truth and perfection of dying to self."*

There is not a more difficult lesson in the Christian life than to attain a true knowledge of what self is. Its terrible power, its secret and universal rule, and the blinding influence it exerts in keeping us from the knowledge of what it is are the cause of all our sin and evil. Hence it comes that so few really believe in their absolute inability to obey God or to believe in His love.

Heavenly Father: There is nothing that can deliver us from self but that entire willingness to die to self which comes when by faith we understand that we died in Christ Jesus. It is that alone that can make us partakers through faith and the Holy Spirit of that meekness and gentleness and humility and surrender to Thee which gave Christ's death its worth and its beauty in the sight of Thee, Our Father. Amen.

---

* William Law, *A Serious Call.*

Dying to Self

"Many will ask how this way of overcoming self is to be so simple, plain, and immediate. Is it not the doctrine of almost all people that much length of time and practice are scarce sufficient for the attainment of any one of these four virtues? I have referred you to Patience, Meekness, Humility as the one plain and immediate way of dying to self, because you can as easily and immediately by the mere turning and faith of your mind have all the benefit of these virtues, as publicans and sinners by their turning to Christ could be helped and saved by Him. The reason that you or others are vainly endeavoring after these virtues is because you seek them in a multitude of human rules and methods and not in that simplicity of faith in which those who applied to Christ immediately obtained that which they asked of Him.

"'Come unto Me, all ye that labor and are heavy laden, and I will give you rest.' How short and simple and certain a way to peace and comfort. What becomes now of your rules and methods to be delivered from self and the power of sin and find the redeeming power and virtue of Christ? What a folly it would be to suppose that Christ, after having finished His great work and ascended into heaven with all power in heaven and on earth, was become less a Savior and gave less immediate help than when He lived as man upon earth.

"You say that it is not the question whether my giving up myself to Christ in faith would do me as much good as it did to them who came to Him on earth; but whether my turning in faith to Patience, Meekness, Humility, and Resignation to God would do to me all that faith in Christ did for those who became His disciples.

"When I exhort you to give up yourself in faith and hope to these virtues, what else do I do but turn you directly to so much faith and hope in the true Lamb of God. What is the Lamb of God but the perfection of patience, meekness, humility and resignation to God? And consequently, is not every sincere wish and desire, every inclination of your heart that longs to be governed by these virtues an immediate, direct application to Christ, a worshiping and falling down before Him, a giving up of yourself unto Him, and the very perfection of faith in Him."*

We too often think of faith in Christ only as connected with the work He did for us on the Cross. But its meaning is far larger and richer. It is by faith that we can claim all the grace and the mind there were in Him and receive it through the Spirit as ours.

Heavenly Father, help us to see that faith then becomes the daily exercise by which the virtues and the graces that there are in Christ can become ours. And so we get the mind of Christ. Amen.

---

* William Law, *A Serious Call.*

Of Faith in Christ

"In the words of Christ, 'Learn of Me, for I am meek and lowly of heart, and ye shall find rest unto your souls,' you have two truths asserted. First that to be given up to Patience, Meekness, Humility, and Resignation to God is strictly the same thing as to learn of Christ or to have faith in Him. And that because the inclination of your heart toward these virtues is truly giving up all that you are and all that you have from fallen Adam, it is perfectly leaving all that you have and your highest act of faith in Him. Therefore all the blessing and deliverance from sin from any degree of faith and hope in Christ are sure of being led and governed by His Spirit of Patience, Meekness, Humility, and Resignation to God. While you shut up yourself in these, you are in the very arms of Christ, your whole heart is His dwelling place, and He lives and works in you. *When these tempers live and abide in you as the spirit and aim of your life, then Christ is in you of a truth*, and the life that you then lead is not yours, but it is Christ that liveth in you. The Spirit of Divine Love can have no place or possibility of birth in any fallen creature till it wills and chooses to be dead to all self in a patient, meek, humble, resignation to the good power and mercy of God. And when your own impatience or pride attacks you, stand turned to this humble resignation and leave and give up yourself to be helped by the mercy of God. The greater the perplexity of your distress is, the nearer you are to the greatest and best relief, provided you have the patience to expect it all from God. And be assured that we have neither more nor less of the Divine operation within us but just and strictly in that degree as our faith and hope and trust are upon God more or less.

"These are short but full articles of true religion which carry salvation along with them, which make a true and full offering and oblation of our whole nature to the Divine operation and are also a true and full confession of the Holy Trinity in Unity."*

Blessed Father, it is now my one thought: It is now the whole bent and design of my soul to seek for my salvation alone through the mediation of the meek, humble, patient, resigned Lamb of God, who alone has power to bring forth the blessed birth of these heavenly virtues in my soul. Amen.

---

* William Law, *A Serious Call.*

The Lamb of God

"The Lamb of God is the Eternal Love and Meekness that left the bosom of His Father to be Himself the resurrection of Meekness and Love in the darkened souls of fallen men. What a comfort it is to think that this Lamb of God, who is the glory of heaven, is as near to us, as truly in the midst of us, as He is in the midst of heaven.

"*Oh, sweet resignation of myself to God*! Happy death of every self-desire; blessed unction of a holy life; the only driver of all evil out of my soul, be thou my guide and governor wherever I go. Nothing but thou canst take me from myself, nothing but thou canst lead me to God; hell has no power where thou art nor can heaven hide itself from thee. Oh, may I never indulge a thought, bring forth a word, or do anything for myself or others but under the influence of thy blessed inspiration. The sight, though distant, of this Sabbath of the soul, freed from the miserable labor of self to rest in Meekness, Humility, Patience, and Resignation under the Spirit of God is like the joyful voice of the Bridegroom to my soul and leaves no wish in me but to be at the marriage-feast of the Lamb.

"This marriage-feast signifies the entrance into the highest state of union that can be between God and the soul in this life. In other words, it is the birthday of the Spirit of Love in our souls which, whenever we attain it, will feast our souls with such peace and joy in God as will blot out the remembrance of everything that we called joy or peace before.

"Thither you must certainly come if you keep to this path of Meekness, Humility, and Patience under a full Resignation to God. But if you go aside from it, let the occasion seem ever so glorious, it is only preparing you for a harder death. For *die you must to all and everything that you have worked or done* under any other spirit but that of the Meekness of the Lamb.

"As the Lamb of God He has all power to bring forth in us a weariness of our fallen state and a willingness to fall from it into His Meekness and Humility."*

Blessed Lord Jesus, Lamb of God, as Thou calleth us: "Learn of Me, for I am meek and lowly of heart." It was for His humility that God so highly exalted Him. It is only as our life becomes the unceasing expression of a longing for His humility and meekness that we shall find rest to our souls. I listen as Thou sayest to me: "Learn of Me, for I am meek and lowly of heart." Amen.

---

* William Law, *A Serious Call.*

Prayer: The Key to the Treasures of Heaven

"Man has been sent into the world on no other errand but by prayer to rise out of the vanity of time into the riches of eternity. For poor and miserable as this life is, we have all of us free access to all that is great and good and happy and carry within ourselves *a key to all the treasures that Heaven has to bestow upon us.*

"God, the only good of all intelligent nature, is not an absent or distant God but is more present in and to our souls than our bodies; and we are strangers to heaven and without God in the world for this only reason because we are *void of that Spirit of prayer*, which alone can and never fails to unite us with *the one only good* and to open heaven and the Kingdom of God within us. A root set in the finest soil in the best climate is not in so sure a way of its growth to perfection as every man may be whose spirit aspires after all that which God is ready and infinitely desirous to give him. For the sun meets not the springing bud that stretches toward him with half that certainty as God, the source of all good, *communicates Himself to the soul that longs to partake of Him.*

"We are all of us by birth the offspring of God, *more nearly related to Him than we are to one another.* For in Him we live and move and have our being. The first man that was brought forth from God had the breath and spirit of Father, Son, and Holy Spirit breathed into him, and so he became a living soul. He was the image and likeness of God, not with any regard to his outward shape or form, for no shape has any likeness to God, but he was in the image and likeness to God because *the Holy Trinity had breathed their own nature and spirit into Him.* And as the Deity, Father, Son, and Holy Spirit, are always in heaven and make heaven to be everywhere, so this spirit breathed by Them into man brought heaven into man along with it. And so man was in heaven as well as on earth, that is, in Paradise which signifies a heavenly state or birth of life."*

The lesson that we find here in regard to the sun is one of the deepest truths of God's Word. As willing as the sun is unceasingly to shine forth its light and warmth on the waiting earth, is the living God waiting unceasingly to work in the heart of His child. Or, rather, He is ever actually working within us except as we hold Him back and hinder Him by our unbelief for our surrender to the spirit of the world.

Blessed Father: As sure as the sun shines on this earth, Thou art sending forth Thy light and Thy love into my heart for me to receive and to rejoice in. Amen.

---

* William Law, *A Serious Call.*

The Goodness of God

"The goodness of God breaking forth into a desire to communicate good was the cause and the beginning of the Creation. Hence it follows that to all eternity God can have no thought or intent toward the creature but to communicate good because He made the creature for this sole end, to receive good. He must always will that to it which He willed at the creation of it. As the sun hath but one nature and can give forth nothing but the blessings of life, so the holy triune God has but one nature and intent toward all the creation, which is to pour forth the riches and sweetness of the Divine perfection upon everything that is capable of them and according to its capacity to receive them.

"This is the amiable nature of God; He is the Good, the unchangeable overflowing fountain of good, that sends forth nothing but good to all eternity. He is Love itself, the unmixed immeasurable Love, doing nothing but from love, giving nothing but gifts of love to everything that He has made, requiring nothing of all His creatures but the spirits and fruits of that Love which brought them into being. Oh, how sweet is this contemplation of the heighth and depth of the riches of Divine Love! With what attractions must it draw every thoughtful person to return Love for Love to this overflowing fountain of boundless goodness! What charms has that religion which discovers to us our existence in relation to and dependence upon this ocean of Divine Love! View every part of our redemption from Adam's first sin to the resurrection of the dead, and you will find nothing but successive mysteries of that first love which created angels and men. All the mysteries of the Gospel are only so many marks and proofs of God's desiring to make His love triumph in the removal of sin and disorder from all nature and creatures."*

With what joy an invalid on a winter's day yields himself to bask in the bright sunshine. What journeys are undertaken to the heights in Switzerland where the sun gives its warmth best. And, alas! how little God's children understand that this is just the one thing they need, to wait before God in quiet till His light shines upon them and into them and through them. How little it is understood that unless we take time, time enough with God for His light to shine into the depths of our hearts, it is in vain for us to expect that His immeasurable love can enter our hearts and fill our lives.

Oh, our Father, teach us, we pray Thee, to believe in Thy love and not to rest until our hearts are filled with it! Amen.

---

* William Law, *A Serious Call.*

The Kingdom of Self

"Man by his fall had fallen from a life in God into *a life of self*, an animal life of self-love, self-esteem, and self-seeking in the poor perishing enjoyments of the world. All sin, death, and hell are nothing else but this kingdom of self or the various operations of self-love, self-esteem, and self-seeking.

"On the Day of Pentecost a new dispensation of God came forth. On God's part it was the operation of the Holy Spirit in gifts and graces upon the whole Church. On man's part it was the adoration of God in spirit and in truth. All this was to make way for *the immediate and continual operation of God* in the soul; that man, baptized with the Holy Spirit, *should absolutely renounce self* and give up his whole soul to use the faculties of his mind and all the outward things of the world as enlightened and inspired by the Holy Spirit.

"The kingdom of self is the fall of man and the great apostasy from the life of God in the soul. The Kingdom of Christ is the Spirit and Power of God manifesting itself in the birth of a new inward man. When the call of God to repentance first arises in thy soul, be retired, silent, passive, and humbly attentive to the new risen life within thee, disregarding the working of thine own will and reason.

"Hence is to be seen the true ground and necessity of that *universal mortification and self-denial* with regard to all senses, appetites, tempers, passions, and judgments. Our own life is to be hated; and the reason is plain, because there is nothing lovely in it. By this knowing and owning our own nothingness and inability that we have *no other capacity for good but that of receiving it from God alone*, self is wholly denied and its kingdom destroyed.

"You know now to what it is that you are daily to die and daily to live; and therefore look upon every day as lost that does not help forward both this death and this life in you. Casting yourself with a broken heart at the feet of the Divine Mercy, desire nothing but that every moment of your life may be given to God, and pray from the bottom of your heart that the seed of eternity, the spark of life that had so long been smothered under earthly rubbish, might breathe and come to life in you."*

Let us take hold of the central thought here that to make way for the immediate and continual operation of God in our souls, we need in the power of the Holy Spirit absolutely to renounce self and yield our whole being for God to dwell and work in. The universal mortification and self-denial is indispensable if God's redeeming love is to display its power and shed forth all its blessing.

Heavenly Father, we cast ourselves with a broken heart at the feet of the Divine mercy and desire nothing but that every moment of our life may be given to Thee. Amen.

---

* William Law, *A Serious Call.*

Continual Self-Denial

"A spiritual look is a call to as real and total a death to the life of corrupt nature as that which Adam died in Paradise was to the life of heaven. To the end of our lives every inch of our road is to be made up of denial and dying to ourselves. To think of anything but *the continual total denial of our earthly nature* is to overlook the very thing on which all depends.

"You rejoice in thinking that now in knowing these truths you have found the Pearl of great price. But notice, it is not yours till you sell all that you have and buy it. Now *self* is all that you have; you have no good of your own, nothing is yours but this self; and all this self is to be parted with before the pearl is yours. That is, die to all thy possession of self; all of it is to be given up; it is an apostate nature, a continual departure from God; it corrupts everything that it touches. All evil tempers are born and nourished in self. Die to this self, to this inward nature, then all outward enemies are overcome.

"The true ground of all true religion is: it means nothing but *to overcome that earthly life which overcame Adam in the Fall.* Therefore you must know that the one thing needed is to die to all the life that we have from this world. The Son of God calls us to die to this life and take up His cross. When the human soul turns from itself and turns to God, *dies to itself and lives to God* in the Spirit and tempers of the holy Jesus, then only it is delivered from covetousness and sensuality, from a worldly spirit, from all self-interest and self-exaltation, from all hatred and envy.

"To think of anything in religion or to pretend to real holiness *without totally dying to this old man* is building castles in the air. To think of being alive in God before we are dead to our own nature is as impossible as for a grain of wheat to be alive before it dies.

"The total dying to self is the only foundation of a solid piety. Thus alone does the spiritual life begin at the true root, grows out of death, and is born in a broken heart, a heart broken off from all its own natural life."*

Our blessed Lord Jesus could not be raised from the dead into the glory of the Father's right hand until He had died on the Cross. This is the new and living way which He opened up through the rent veil of the flesh into the Holiest of All. And it is in this new and living way with our flesh also crucified and given over to the death, that we can enter into the life and the joy of God's presence here upon earth.

Heavenly Father: The continual denial of self is one of the secrets of the continual enjoyment of Thy presence and power working in our hearts. Amen.

---

* William Law, *A Serious Call.*

Prayer: A State of the Heart

"Our Savior, though He had all wisdom, yet gives but a small number of moral teachings to mankind. It is because He knew that our whole malady lies in this, that the will of our mind, the lust of our life is turned into this world and that nothing can set us right but the turning the will of our mind and the desire of our hearts to God and that heaven which we had lost. And hence it is that He calls us to nothing but *a total denial of ourselves and the life of this world* and to a faith in Him as the worker of a new birth and a new life in us. He teaches us every reason for *renouncing ourselves* and loving the whole nature of our redemption as the greatest joy and desire of our heart.

"We see thus that our will and our heart is all; that nothing either finds or loses God; and that all our religion is only the religion of the heart. We see with open eyes that as a spirit of longing after the life of this world made Adam and us to be the poor pilgrims on earth that we are, so the Spirit of prayer or *the longing desire of the heart after Christ and God and heaven* breaks all our bonds asunder and raises us out of the miseries of time into the riches of eternity. Thus seeing and knowing our first and our present state, everything calls us to prayer; and the desire of our heart becomes the spirit of prayer. When the spirit of prayer is born in us, then prayer is no longer considered as only the business of this or that hour but is *the continual breathing of the heart after God*. The spirit of prayer *as a state of the heart* becomes the governing principle of the soul's life.

"An honest man may prove his honesty by acts. At other times there is no special call to show his honesty. But it is all the same the inward living principle of his heart. Just so the Spirit of prayer may possess the heart without interruption and yet at other times may have its hours of prayer. But its own life and spirit is vastly superior to, independent of, and stays for no particular hours or forms of work."*

It would be worthwhile making a study of the place that, according to Law, the word "continual" ought to have in our life. First there is the continual streaming forth of the infinite love of God toward us. Then the continual unalterable dependence upon God every hour of our life. Then the continual receiving of goodness and happiness from God alone. Then comes the continual mortification of our evil nature; then again the continual and immediate inspiration of the Holy Spirit maintaining the life of Christ in us. Then the continual breathing of the heart after God in prayer. And then the continual loving of Him with our whole heart.

Heavenly Father: May we be found to be continually abiding in Thee. Amen.

---

* William Law, *A Serious Call.*

A Worldly Spirit

"From what has been said of the first state and fall of man, it plainly follows that the sin of all sin or the heresy of all heresies is a worldly spirit. We are apt to consider this temper only as an infirmity, but it is indeed *the great Apostasy from God and the Divine Life.*

"Choose any life but the life of God and heaven, and you choose death, for death is nothing else but the loss of the life of God. The spirit of the soul is in itself nothing else but a *spirit breathed forth from the life of God* and for this only end that the life of God, the nature of God, the working of God, the tempers of God might be manifested in it.

"Hence it is that all the religion of fallen man, all the methods of our redemption have only this one end, to take from us that strange and earthly life we have gotten by the Fall and to kindle again the life of God and heaven in our souls. 'All that is in the world, the lust of the flesh, the lust of the eyes, and the pride of life, is not of the Father, it is not that life that we had from God by creation but is of this world, is brought into us by our fall from God into the life of this world and therefore a worldly spirit is not to be considered as a single sin, but as *a state of real death to the kingdom of life and God in our souls.*

"Hold this therefore as a certain truth, that the heresy of all heresies is a worldly spirit. It is the whole nature and misery of our fall and keeps up the death of our souls. Of all things, therefore, detest the spirit of this world, or there is no help; you must live and die an utter stranger to all that is Divine and heavenly. *For a worldly, earthly spirit can know nothing of God.* All real knowledge is Life or a living sensibility of the thing that is known as far as our life reaches, so far we understand and know, and no further. All after this is only the play of our imagination amusing itself with the dead pictures of its own ideas."*

When our Lord spoke of the world, its prince, and its spirit, He ever laid stress on its hatred of Him and His Church. And so His Apostles, too, warned most earnestly against being conformed to the world. "If a man love the world, the love of the Father is not in Him."

Holy Spirit of God, we yield ourselves to Thee from heaven to discover the evil and the danger of the spirit of the world, to give us the victory over it, and to fill us with the life of heaven. Amen.

---

* William Law, *A Serious Call.*

Of the Despair of Self

"When the truth touches a man's heart, he feels that he cannot overcome the hardness of his heart and his pride by force of his reason. Nature becomes a torment and a burden to itself before it can willingly give up to that death through which alone it can pass into life. There is no true and real conversion from the life of sin and death till a man comes to know and feel that *nothing less than his whole nature is to be parted with and yet finds in himself no possibility of doing it.* This is the despair by which we lose all our own life to find a new one in God. For here it is that faith and hope and true seeking to God and Christ are born. But till all is despair in ourselves, faith and hope and turning to God in prayer are only things practiced by rule and method; they are not born in us, are not living qualities of a new birth till we have done feeling any trust or confidence in ourselves.

"A man must feel that he is still within the reach of Divine Love; God created him for Himself to be a habitation of His own life and Holy Spirit. In dealing with such souls, love must be our bait; it will put its hook into the heart and force men to know that of all strong things, nothing is so strong, so irresistible, as Divine Love.

"Ask what God is; His Name is Love; He is the Good, the Perfection of Peace, the Joy, the Glory and the Blessing of every life. Ask what Christ is. He is the universal Remedy of all evil broken forth in nature and creatures. He is the unwearied Compassion, the long-suffering Pity, the never-ceasing Mercifulness of God to every want and infirmity of human nature.

"Let us surround and encompass others with these frames of love until they become a willing victim to their power. All religion is the Spirit of Love, all its gifts and graces are love; it has no breath, no life but the life of love. Love is heaven revealed in the soul; it is light and truth, it is infallible. Love is the Christ of God; it is the resurrection and life of every Divine virtue, a fruitful mother of true humility, boundless benevolence, unwearied patience, and bowels of compassion."*

Let us seek above everything to believe that God is love and as such longs intensely to fill every heart with its blessedness. As the sun shines upon the earth with the one great object of shedding on it its light and its life, do let us believe that the great God of love is shining upon us every moment of the day. If we will but give Him time and patient waiting, that love will enter our hearts with all its gifts and graces and its unspeakable blessedness.

Heavenly Father, we willingly part utterly with self and yield ourselves a continual sacrifice to Thee who loves us. Amen.

---

* William Law, *A Serious Call.*

True Religion

"Here you should once for all mark where and what the true nature of religion is; its work and effect is *within*; its glory, its life, its perfection is all within. It is merely and solely the raising a new life, new love, and a new birth in the inward spirit of our heart. This was the spiritual nature of religion in its first beginning, and this alone is its whole nature to the end of time. It is nothing else *but the power and life and Spirit of God*, as Father, Son, and Holy Spirit working, creating, and reviving life in the fallen soul and driving all its evil out of it. Religion is no true Divine service, no proper worshiping of God, has no good in it, can remove no evil out of man, raise no Divine life in him but so far as it serves, worships, conforms, and gives itself up to this operation of the Holy Triune God as living and dwelling in the soul.

"Keep close to this idea of religion as an inward spiritual life in the soul; observe all its works within you, the death and life that are found there; seek for no good, no comfort but in the inward awakening of all that is holy and heavenly in your heart; and then so much as you have of this inward religion, so much you have of a real salvation. For *salvation is nothing but a victory over nature*; so far as you resist and renounce your own vain, selfish, and earthly nature, so far as you overcome all your own natural tempers of the old man, *so far God enters into you, lives and operates in you, He is in you* the Light, the Life, and the Spirit of your soul; and you are in Him, that new creature that worships Him in spirit and in truth.

"All Scripture brings us to the conclusion that our religious services are only so many ways of giving up ourselves more and more to the inward working, quickening, sanctifying Spirit of God in us; and all for this end, that a true, real, Christ-like nature be formed in us by the same Spirit by which it was formed in the holy Virgin Mary."*

How much there is of religion in which have our own thoughts of what it should be. Oh, let us seek to study what God counts true religion. Nothing less than this, that He Himself, by His Spirit, should live and work in us as the Light and the Life of our souls. As we take these thoughts of God into our hearts, we shall see that a continual depending upon Him, a continual receiving of His Holy Spirit breathing His life into us, and a continual breathing of our heart and its longing after Him is the life of Christ in us. It is this will enable us continually to worship, to pray, and to work in His holy presence.

Lord Jesus: We desire only to continually worship, pray, and work in Thy Holy presence. Amen.

---

* William Law, *A Serious Call.*

The Practice of Prayer

"The best instruction I can give you as helpful or preparatory to the Spirit of Prayer is already fully given where we have set forth the original perfection, the miserable fall, and the glorious redemption of man. It is the true knowledge of these great things which can do all for you which human instruction can do. These things must fill you with a dislike of your present estate, drive all earthly desires out of your soul, and create an honest longing after your first perfection. For prayer can only be taught you by awakening in you a true sense and knowledge of what you are and what you should be, and filling you with a continual longing desire of the heart after God, His life, and Holy Spirit. When you begin to pray, ask your heart what it wants and have nothing in your prayer but what the state of your heart puts you upon demanding, saying, or offering to God.

"The one and only infallible way to go safely through all the difficulties, trials, dryness, or opposition of our evil tempers is this: *to expect nothing from ourselves* but in everything expect and depend upon God for relief. Keep fast hold of this thread, and then let your way be what it will, temptation or the rebellion of nature, you will be led through all to a union with God. *For nothing hurts us in any state but an expectation of something in it and from it which we should only expect from God.* And thus it will be till the whole turn of our minds is so changed that we as fully see and know *our inability to have any goodness of our own as to have a life of our own.* When we are happily brought to this conviction, the whole spirit of our mind becomes a true faith and hope and trust in the sole operation of God's Spirit, looking no more to any other power to be formed in Christ new creatures, than we look to any other power for the resurrection of our bodies at the last day."*

What a universal confession there is that we pray too little. How strange that our highest privilege, holding fellowship with God in prayer, is to so many a burden and a failure and to so many more a matter of form without the power. Let us learn the lesson that to expect nothing from ourselves is the first step and then truly with the heart to expect everything from God. These two thoughts lie at the root of all true prayer.

Heavenly Father: Instead of our thoughts being centered on man, on ourselves, and our needs, let them become centered on Thee in Thy glory and His love, and prayer will become a joy and a power, and our trials will become our greatest blessing because they compel us to wait upon Thee. Amen.

---

* William Law, *A Serious Call.*

A Touchstone of Truth

"I will here give you an infallible touchstone that will tie all to the truth. It is this: retire from the world and all conversation; stop all the former workings of your heart and mind and with all the strength of your heart, stand all this month as continually as you can in this form of prayer to God. Offer it frequently on your knees; but whether sitting, standing, or walking, be always inwardly longing and earnestly praying this one prayer to God: 'That of His great goodness, He would make known to you and take from your heart every kind and form and degree of pride, whether it be from evil spirits or your own corrupt nature and that He would awaken in you the deepest depths and truth of that humility which can make you capable of His light and His Holy Spirit.'

"Reject every thought but that of wishing and praying in this matter from the bottom of your heart, with such truth and earnestness as people in torment wish and pray to be delivered from it.

"The painful sense and feeling of what you are, kindled into a working state of sensibility by the light of God within you, is the fire and light from which your spirit of prayer proceeds. In its first kindling nothing is found or felt but pain, wrath, and darkness, as is to be seen in the kindling of every heat or fire. And therefore its first prayer is nothing else but a sense of penitence, self-condemnation, confession, and humility. *It feels nothing but its own misery and so is all humility*.

"This prayer of humility is met by the Divine Love, the mercifulness of God embraces it; and then its prayer is changed into songs and thanksgiving. When this state of fervor has done its work, has melted away all earthly passions and affections, and left *no inclination in the soul but to delight in God alone*, then its prayer changes again.

"It is now come so near to God, has found such union with Him, that it does not so much pray as live in God. Its prayer is not any particular action, not confined to times, or words, or place, but is the work of the whole being *which continually stands in fullness of faith, in purity of love, in absolute resignation to do and be what and how the Beloved pleases*. This is the last state of the Spirit of Prayer and is its highest union with God in this life."*

Prayer is not merely bringing certain requests to God. Prayer is the highest revelation of our fitness for fellowship with God. It begins with the deep humility that knows that it is nothing, that has no desire but to meet God in the fellowship of His love and then with the whole being continually to live in absolute surrender to do and to be what and how the Beloved pleases.

Heavenly Father, help me to live in absolute surrender to do and to be what is pleasing to Thee. Amen.

---

* William Law, *A Serious Call*.

The Spirit of Prayer

"The spirit of the soul is in itself nothing else but a spirit breathed forth from the life of God and for this only end, that the life of God, the nature of God, the working of God, the tempers of God might be manifested in it.

"The Spirit of Prayer is a pressing forth of the soul out of this earthly life; it is a stretching with all its desires after the life of God; it is a leaving, as far as it can, all its own spirit to receive a Spirit from above, to be one Life, one Love, one Spirit with Christ in God. This prayer, which is an emptying itself of all its own lusts and natural tempers and an opening itself for the Light and Love of God to enter into it, is the prayer in the Name of Christ to which nothing is denied. For the love which God bears to the soul, His eternal, never-ceasing desire to enter into it, to dwell in it and open the birth of His Holy Word and Spirit in it stays no longer than till the door of the heart opens for it. For nothing does or can keep God out of the soul or hinder His Holy union with it but the desire of the heart turned from Him. For the life of the soul in itself is nothing else but a working will; wherever the will works, there and there only the soul lives, whether it be in God or in the creature.

"A will given up to earthly good is eating grass with Nebuchadnezzar and has one life with the beasts of the field, for *earthly desires keep up the same life in a man and an ox.* Earthly food only desired and used for the support of the earthly body is suitable to man's present condition and the order of nature. But when the desire, the delight and longing of the soul is set upon earthly things, then the humanity is degraded, is fallen from God; and the life of the soul is made as earthly and animal as the life of the body."*

Child of God, do let us rise to a right conception of what it means that the Eternal Father by the Holy Spirit breathes into us, is seeking to have the life of God, the nature of God, the working of God revealed within us. In earthly things we are not unwilling to take pains to make sacrifices for the object of our desire. Shall we not begin as never before to make the knowledge of God, the love of God, the will of God, the pleasing of God the great object of our study and our effort. God is waiting to bless us, to reveal Himself to us, to fill us with His life, to use us for His glory if we will but yield ourselves to the life of continual dependence and adoration. We shall then prove how possible it is for a man to walk in the footsteps of Christ Jesus, living His life on earth every day in the love of the Father and to His glory.

Heavenly Father, I yield myself to you in continual dependence and adoration. Amen.

---

* William Law, *A Serious Call.*

The Prayer of the Heart

"Turning to God according to the inward feeling, want, and motion of your own heart in love, in trust, in faith of having from Him all that you want and wish to have—this turning unto God, whether it be with or without words, is the best form of prayer in the world. For prayers not formed according to the real state of your heart are but like a prayer to be pulled out of a deep well when you are not in it.

"When the heart really pants and longs after God, its prayer is a praying moved and animated by the Spirit of God; it is *the breath or inspiration of God*, stirring, moving, and opening itself in the heart. It is a certain truth that nothing ever did or can have the least desire or tendency to ascend to heaven but that which came down from heaven. And therefore every time a good desire stirs in the heart, a good prayer goes out of it that reaches God as being the fruit and work of His Holy Spirit.

"It is when the heart stands continually in this state of wishing to have that which may be expressed in but few words—it is the Reality, the Steadiness, and the Continuity of the desire that is the goodness and perfection of the prayer.

"You have already rightly taken the first step in the spiritual life; you have devoted yourself absolutely to God, to live wholly to His will under the light and guidance of His Holy Spirit. Your next step is this, a looking to the continuance of this first resolution and donation of yourself to God. Now this second step cannot be taken but purely by prayer; nothing else has the least power here but prayer, prayer of the heart, a prayer of your own proceeding from the state of your heart and its tendency toward God. Of all things, look to this prayer of the heart; consider it an infallible guide to heaven. As a man who has some great worldly matter at heart stands turned from everything that has not some relation to it, *so our heart will carry on its own state of prayer as soon as God is its great object*, or it is wholly given up to Him as its one great Good."*

Our times of prayer are meant to lead us on to a life of prayer in which, just as the eye can all the day rejoice in the sunshine which gives it light, the heart will continually live and rejoice in God's presence.

Heavenly Father, we believe that Thou, who art able to do exceeding abundantly above all that we ask or think, is indeed able and willing by the power of Thy Holy Spirit to strengthen us for this life of unceasing prayer as we walk in the light of Thy countenance. Amen.

---

* William Law, *A Serious Call.*

The Proof of the Spirit

"The Holy Spirit of God is as necessary to our Divine life as the air of this world is necessary to our animal life and is as distinct from and as much without us as the air of this world is distinct from the creatures that live in it. And yet our own good spirit is the very Spirit of God moving and stirring in us, and yet not God, but the Spirit of God breathed into a creaturely form; and this good Spirit, Divine in its origin, and Divine in its nature, is that alone in us that can reach God, unite with Him, be moved and blessed by Him.

"You ask how you may know *in how far you are led by the Spirit of God.* As every man knows of himself when he is hungry or pleased, so too with regard to the Spirit of God, for the Spirit of God is more distinguishable from all other spirits and tempers than any of your natural affections are from one another. Let me show you this.

"'God is unwearied patience, a Meekness that cannot be provoked. He is an everduring Mercifulness; He is unmixed Goodness, universal Love; His delight is in the communication of Himself, His own happiness, to everything according to its capacity. He is the Good from which nothing but good comes and resisteth all evil only with goodness.' This is the nature and Spirit of God, and here you have your infallible proof whether you are moved and led by the Spirit of God. If it is the earnest desire and longing of your heart to be merciful as He is merciful, to be full of His unwearied Patience, to dwell in His unalterable Meekness; if you long to be like Him in universal impartial Love; if you desire to communicate every good to every creature that you are able, you have *the utmost certainty that the Spirit of God lives, dwells, and governs in you.* Now if you lack any of these tempers, if the whole bent of your heart and mind is not set upon them, all pretenses to an immediate inspiration and continual operation of the Spirit of God in your soul are vague and groundless. Keep within the bounds here set you; call nothing a proof of the Spirit or work of God in your soul but these tempers and the works which they produce, and then, and not till then, you may safely say with St. John, 'Hereby we know that He abideth in us, by the Spirit which He hath given us.'"*

Heavenly Father, we believe that the Spirit beareth witness with our spirit and gives us the assurance of His own presence. To we who yield ourself in childlike trust and obedience, the consciousness will not be withheld that we are indeed led by Him and transformed from glory to glory as by Thy Holy Spirit. Amen.

---

* William Law, *A Serious Call.*

Love and Faith

*"This is His commandment, that we should believe in
the name of His Son Jesus Christ, and love one another,
even as He gave us commandment" (1 John 3:23).*

At a Conference at Graaff Reinet, the closing service was held on Sunday night. At the afternoon meeting we decided to take as subject the five great lessons to be learned from the parable of the Vine and Branches in John 15. The subject of brotherly love fell to the lot of a certain minister. But he demurred saying: "I cannot speak on that subject, and I have never yet preached on it." In explanation he said: "You know that I studied in Holland and when there, the subject of love was left to the liberal section. They did not believe in God's stern justice nor in the redemption through Christ. God was love; that was enough. The orthodox party were not allowed to suggest that their opponents should be put out of the church. No, all should be borne in love! And so it came to pass that the orthodox party were strong in preaching faith but left the preaching of love to the liberal section."

The Church must learn not only to preach the love of God in redemption; it must go further and teach Christians to show that the love of Christ is in their hearts by love shown to the brethren. Our Lord called this a new commandment—a badge by which the world should recognize His disciples!

There is great need for this preaching of love. God sometimes allows bitterness to arise between Christians that they may view the terrible power of sin in their hearts and shrink back at the sight. How greatly a minister and his people should feel the importance of Christ's command: "Love one another." A life of great holiness will result if we really but love each other as Christ loves us.

Heavenly Father: May we understand the two manifestations of love: Thy wonderful love of Thee in Christ to us and the wonderful love in us, through the Holy Spirit, to Thee and to our brethren. Amen.

Faith and Love

*"And the grace of our Lord abounded exceedingly
with faith and love" (1 Tim. 1:14).*

"Your work of faith and labor of love" (1 Thess. 1:3).

"The breastplate of faith and love" (1 Thess. 5:8).

*"Your faith groweth exceedingly, and the love of each of you all
toward one another aboundeth" (2 Thess. 1:3).*

These expressions of the Apostle Paul show us the true connection between faith and love in the life of the Christian. Faith always comes first; it roots itself deeply in the love of God and bears fruit in love to the brethren. As in nature the root and the fruit are inseparable, so is it with faith and love in the realm of grace.

Too often the two are separated. On the Day of Pentecost they were one. There was a powerful faith toward the Lord Jesus with a fervent love to the brethren. The sum of the preaching on that day was: Believe in the Name of Jesus Christ, and ye shall receive the gift of the Holy Spirit. And the natural result followed: "And all that believed were together and had all things common." "And the multitude of them that believed were of one heart and of one soul."

Alas, that this should not have been wholly the case at the Reformation. A powerful reformation took place in regard to the doctrine of faith, but at the same time what a lack of love there was between the preachers and the leaders in that faith! So the world was not taught the lesson that God's love was all-powerful to sanctify the whole life of man!

Let this thought sink deep into our hearts: "The grace of our Lord abounded exceedingly with faith and love." As we cultivate *faith in God's love,* our hearts will be *filled with love to the brethren.* The genuineness of our faith in the love of God must be shown by love in our daily lives at home.

Heavenly Father, help us from day to day by faith to be rooted in this love, that we may at all times be living examples of its truth and power and so become a blessing to others. Amen.

261

The Love of God

*"God is love, and he that dwelleth in love dwelleth
in God, and God in him" (1 John 4:16).*

May God through His Holy Spirit grant us grace rightly to adore this unfathomable mystery.

Jesus said: "None is good save one, even God." The glory of God in heaven is that He has a Will to all that is good. That includes the two meanings of the word: *good*, all that is right and perfect: *good*, all that makes happy.

The God who wills nothing but good is a God of love. He does not seek His own; He does not live for Himself but pours out His love on all living creatures. All created things share in this love to the end that they may be satisfied with that which is good.

The characteristic of Love is that she "seeketh not her own." She finds her happiness in giving to others; she sacrifices herself wholly for others. Even so God offered Himself to mankind in the Person of His Son, and the Son offered Himself upon the cross to bring that love to us and to win our hearts. The everlasting love with which the Father loved the Son is the same love with which the Son has loved us. *This self-same love of God, Christ has poured into our hearts through the Holy Spirit* so that our whole life may be permeated with its vital power.

The love of God to His Son, the love of the Son to us, the love with which we love the Son, the love with which we in obedience to His command love the brethren and try to love all men and win them for Christ— all is the same eternal, incomprehensible, almighty love of God. Love is the power of the God-head in the Father, Son, and Holy Spirit. This love is the possession of all who are members of the body of Christ and streams forth from them to take the whole world within its compass.

Unsearchable, adorable wonder of love! "He that abideth in love, abideth in God, and God in him."

---

*O my soul, meditate on this wondrous love, and adore the great God
of Love! Amen.*

The Love of Christ

"The love of Christ constraineth us" (2 Cor. 5:14).

God sent His Son into the world to make known His everlasting love, even as it was known in heaven. God's existence there is in the glory of that love; all His angels are as tongues of fire overflowing with praise and worship through the power of the love that fills them. God's desire is that on this sinful earth, likewise, His love should take possession of our hearts.

And how was this accomplished? By sending Christ, the Son of His love, to earth to reveal as Man the love of the Father and win our hearts to Himself. The Lord Jesus became man and made Himself of no reputation. In His dealings with the poor and needy and those who were unbelieving and rebellious and through His miracles, He poured out His love into the hearts of all sinners.

With the same purpose our Lord chose the disciples to be always with Him and to be filled with His love. With this purpose He gave on the cross the greatest proof of love that the world has ever seen. He took our sins upon Him; He bore the suffering and the scorn of His enemies, that friend and foe alike might know God's eternal love.

And then, after He had ascended to heaven, *He gave the Holy Spirit to shed abroad this love in our hearts.* The disciples, impelled by the love of Christ, in turn offered their lives to make it known to others.

O Christians, think this over: God longs to have our hearts wholly filled with His love. Then He will be able to use us as channels for this love to flow out to others. Let us say with the Apostle Paul: "The love of Christ constraineth me" (Dutch Version—"urges").

Heavenly Father, I can be satisfied with nothing less, I will sacrifice everything to secure a place for this great love in the hearts of all people. Amen.

The Love of the Spirit

"The love of God hath been shed abroad in our hearts through the Holy Spirit, which was given unto us" (Rom. 5:5).

How many Christians must confess all their lives long that they know very little of a fervent, childlike love to their heavenly Father! They realize too that they cannot keep Christ's second great commandment, to love their neighbor as themselves. The thought of this lack of a joyful love to the Lord Jesus, or of a continual love to other believers, is so great a source of shame and sorrow.

What is the cause of this failure? Has the heavenly Father made no provision for His children on earth, enabling them to prove their love to Him and to each other? Certainly He has. But God's children have not learned the lesson, that there must be a constant renewal of faith in what God is able to do. One tries to stir up love toward God in one's heart, yet is conscious all the time that in one's own strength one cannot awaken the slightest love to God. O Christian, *believe that the love of God will work in your heart as a vital power to enable you to love God and to love the brethren.* Cease to expect the least love in yourself. Believe in the power of God's love resting on you and abiding in you, teaching you to love God and the brethren, with His own love.

Learn the lesson of our text: "The love of God hath been shed abroad in our hearts, through the Holy Spirit." The Spirit will enable us to love God and other Christians and even our enemies. Be assured of two things. First, that in your own strength you cannot love God or other Christians. And, second, that the Holy Spirit is within you every day and every hour, seeking to fill you with the Spirit of love. Each morning as you commit yourself into the keeping of the Holy Spirit for the day, let this prayer arise:

Grant me the assurance that Thou wilt pour forth the love of Christ into my own heart, and then let it stream forth to all around me! Amen.

The Power of Love

"We are more than conquerors through
Him that loved us" (Rom. 8:37).

In days of unrest and strong racial feeling, we need above all a new discovery and living experience of the love of God. Let us anchor our hope in the thought, "God is Love." God's power by which He rules and guides the world is the power of an undying, persistent love. He works through the hearts and spirits and wills of men and women wholly yielded to Him and His service; and He waits for them to open their hearts to Him in love and then, full of courage, to become witnesses for Him.

When this has been achieved, Christ's kingdom is manifested, and *His reign of love on earth* begun. Christ died in order to establish this kingdom. The only means He used to gain influence was through the manifestation of a great serving, suffering Love. He saw the possibility of redemption in the hearts of even the worst of sinners. He knew that our hearts could never resist the steady, continuous influence of love and that unbounded faith in God's love would be our strength and stay. It was in the fire and the fervor of that love that the disciples were able to expect and to do the impossible.

The spirit of hatred and bitterness can never be overcome by argument or by reproaches. Some think things can never be different, but if we really believe in the omnipotence of God's love, we may not distrust His power. God's children must learn to accept His love not only for themselves individually, but for the life of others. Gradually better feelings will prevail if believers will yield themselves unreservedly for God to work through them.

Our faith in Love, as the greatest power in the world, should prepare us for a life in communion with God in prayer and for a life of unselfish service among those around us.

Heavenly Father, let us examine our lives and pray for grace so that as servants of that all-powerful Love, we will let God's love work through us so that we may serve others. Amen.

The Sign of a True Church

"By this shall all men know that ye are My disciples,
if ye have love one to another" (John 13:35).

We are taught in most of our creeds that the true Church is to be found where God's Word is rightly preached and the holy sacraments dispensed as instituted by Christ. Christ Himself took a much broader view. Not merely what the Church teaches through her ministers was, to Him, the distinguishing mark of His followers, but a life lived in love to other believers.

It is most important that we should understand this. In God, love reaches its highest point and is the culmination of His glory. In the man Christ Jesus on the cross, love is at its highest. We owe everything to this love. Love is the power that moved Christ to die for us. In love, God highly exalted Him as Lord and Christ. Love is the power that broke our hearts, and love is the power that heals them. Love is the power through which Christ dwells in us and works in us. Love can change my whole nature and enable me to surrender all to God. It gives me strength to live a holy, joyous life, full of blessing to others. Every Christian should show forth, as in a mirror, the love of God.

Alas, how seldom do Christians realize this! They seek, in the power of human love, to love Christ and other believers. And then they fail. They are sure it is impossible to lead such a life, and they do not even greatly desire it or pray for it. They do not understand that we may and can love with *God's own love*, which is poured forth unto our hearts by the Holy Spirit.

Oh, that this great truth might possess us: *the love of God is shed abroad in our hearts by the Holy Spirit*. If we fully believe that the Holy Spirit dwelling within us will maintain this heavenly love from hour to hour, we shall be able to understand the word of Christ: "All things are possible to him that believeth," and to love God and Christ with all our hearts; and, what is even harder, to love other Christians and even our enemies, while love flows from us as a stream of living water, "through the Holy Spirit."

Heavenly Father, our prayer is that we love Thee with all our hearts and that Thy love through the Holy Spirit flows through us to other Christians and even our enemies. Amen.

Race-Hatred

*"For we also were sometimes foolish, living in malice
and envy, hateful, and hating one another" (Titus 3:3).*

What a dark picture of the state of human nature and of human society! Whence comes such a sad condition of things, worse even than we
see among animals? The answer is: "From Adam's Fall." Just think how
Cain, the first child born on earth, born of man whom God had created,
shed the blood of his brother Abel. Yes, the first child born on earth was
the murderer of his own brother and came under the power of the devil
who "was a murderer from the beginning." "God saw that the wickedness
of man was great on the earth, and that every imagination of the thoughts
of his heart was only evil continually." No wonder that He destroyed mankind by a flood. Yet soon after the flood there were signs that man was
still under the power of sin.

No wonder that man's love of his own people, implanted in his heart
by nature, soon changed to hatred of other peoples. Love of country became the fruitful source of race-hatred, war, and bloodshed. Note how, here
in South Africa, God has placed the two races side by side, as in a school,
to see if our Christianity will enable us to overcome race-hatred and in
the power of Christ's love prove that "in the new creature there is neither
Greek nor Jew, barbarian nor Scythian, bond nor free, but are all one in
Christ Jesus."

What an opening there is for the Church of Christ and her ministers to
preach and proclaim the love of God and to prove its might to change race-
hatred into brotherly love! God has abundant power to bring this to pass.

What a call to all Christians to pray for themselves and all believers,
that we may not make the Word of God of none effect by our unbelief!

---

*O God, make known to us Thy love in heavenly power, and let it take
full possession of our lives that it might change race-hatred into
brotherly love. Amen.*

"Love Your Enemies."
"Me No' Love Fingo."

"Ye have heard that it hath been said: Thou shalt love thy neighbor and hate thine enemy" (Matt. 5:43).

It was the Jewish Rabbis in Christ's earthly day who said this. They deemed they had a right to say it because of what was written in Leviticus 19:17–18: "Thou shalt not hate thy brother in thine heart; thou shalt not bear any grudge against the children of thy people; but thou shalt love thy neighbor as thyself." From this they argued that it was only the children of their own people whom they might not hate; it was all right to hate their enemies. But our Lord said: "Love your enemies: bless them that curse you."

How often the Christian follows the example of the Jewish teachers! The command of our Lord is too strict and narrow for us; we have not yielded ourselves to God in obedience to the new commandment to love other Christians with Christ's love, believing that this love will flow out to all around, even to those who hate us. This will require much grace and will cost time and trouble and much earnest prayer.

When I was a minister in Cape Town, I met a German deaconess who was working in connection with the English Church at Woodstock. She had a class every evening for ten or twelve Kaffirs who were preparing for admission to the Church. One evening she spoke about loving our enemies. She asked one man if his people had enemies. "Oh, yes!" "Who were they?" "The Fingoes." (The Kaffirs count the Fingoes as dogs.) She asked the man if he could love a Fingo. His answer was quite decided: "Me no' love Fingo. Me no' love Fingo." It was an indisputable fact; there could be no question about it. He could not love a Fingo. She told him that in that case he could not go to the Communion. He went home very thoughtful and the next evening at class seemed very downcast. But he still had only one answer: "Me no' love Fingo." He was not received into the church with the others, but continued to attend the class. He was always in earnest, and there was evidently a struggle going on; until one evening he appeared with a bright face and said: "Me *now* love Fingo." He had prayed about it, and God had heard his prayer.

Heavenly Father, Day by day we learn there is only one way to love our enemies: by the love of Christ sought and found in prayer. Amen.

Forgive, but Not Forget

"I will forgive their iniquity, and I will remember
their sin no more" (Jer. 31:34).

At the unveiling of the Women's Monument at Bloemfontein in 1913, I happened to be sitting in the front row on the platform at the foot of the Monument. After a while the sun became very hot. Suddenly I noticed that someone behind me was holding an umbrella over my head. When the speaker had finished, I asked my nephew beside me: "Who is so friendly as to hold an umbrella over my head?" His answer was: "General de Wet." I was surprised, and turning round, thanked him heartily. My nephew told me afterward that he had said: "But I would gladly have paid for the privilege of doing it." I thought, what a generous nature to speak in that way. Presently his turn came to give an address. I could agree with all he said except his last words which were: "Forgive—yes, but forget—never." When the ceremony was over and I shook hands with him again, it was in my heart to say to him: "You say, 'I can never forget.' Be careful to what that may lead."

Many have allowed themselves to be deceived by these words. On the farms, I have often seen a dog come in at the front door to seek coolness and shade. He would be driven out, and the door closed. Then he would go through the back door and would soon be inside the house again. The front door is: "I will forgive." One wishes to put away all thought of hatred or ill-feeling. But see how quickly and quietly these evil thoughts come back through the back door of "I will never forget." Many a one trusts in God's forgiving love, but does not remember that when God forgives, He forgets. "I will forgive their iniquity, and will remember their sins no more."

Heavenly Father, Let us ever remember the advice of St. Paul in Colossians 3:13: **"Forgiving one another, even as Christ forgave you, so also do ye."** *Amen.*

As God Forgives

*"And forgive us our sins; for we also forgive every
one that is indebted to us" (Luke 11:4).*

The forgiveness of sins is the great all-embracing gift by which, in His mercy, God sets the sinner free and receives him back into His love and favor. The forgiveness of sins gives us boldness toward God and is the source of our salvation. The forgiveness of sins gives us cause for thankfulness every day of our lives. It is God's will, and our souls feel the need of it, that we should each day walk with Him, as those whose sins are forgiven and who are living in the light of His countenance.

As we walk with God in the full assurance of sins forgiven, He desires that in our fellowship with those around us, too, we should live as those who have been freely forgiven. And we can only prove our sincerity by forgiving those who have offended us as freely and as willingly as God has forgiven us.

How clearly and urgently our Lord speaks upon this! In the Lord's Prayer we are taught to pray each day: "Forgive us our debts, as we forgive our debtors," and then at the end: "If ye forgive not men their trespasses, neither will your heavenly Father forgive your trespasses" (Matt. 6:15). After the great promise of Mark 11:24 come the words: "And, whensoever ye stand praying, forgive, if ye have aught against any." In Matthew 18:21, we have the question of Peter: "Lord, how oft shall my brother sin against me, and I forgive him?" and our Lord's answer: "Unto seventy times seven." Then follows the parable of the servant whose Lord forgave him his debt but who would not show compassion on his fellow-servant. His Lord's question to him was: "Shouldest not thou also have had mercy on thy fellow-servant, even as I had mercy on thee?" So he was delivered to his tormentors. And our Lord gives the warning: *"So shall also My heavenly Father do unto you, if ye forgive not every one his brother from your hearts."*

Heavenly Father, Let us remember to realize daily: As I need Thy forgiveness each day, so let me be ready each day to forgive my brother. Grant us grace to do it! Amen.

The Preaching of Love

"The greatest of these is Love" (1 Cor. 13:13).

During the Boer War when there was much unrest in the country, a certain minister asked his brother-minister, who was a leader in the church, to do his best to calm the minds of those around him. His answer was: "I have enough trouble with myself; my own mind is unsettled. How can I quiet others?" If there were a revival of the preaching of love, more than one of our ministers would have to say: "There is such a lack of love in my own heart; how can I teach others?"

Yet there is a remedy. Let me tell you what I have learned from John Wesley. During the first fourteen years of his ministry he had no insight into what a free and full salvation by faith meant. After he had been convicted of the sin of unbelief by means of a conversation with one of the Moravian Brethren, he began to preach with such power that many were converted. But he felt that it was too much a matter of the intellect; he had not yet experienced the full joy and love which the Moravian possessed. He asked the Brother what he should do. The answer was: "Preach it because you believe that it is what God's Word teaches: you will soon find what you are seeking and will then preach it because you possess it."

This has been my own experience. Often in preaching or in writing, I have asked myself: But do you possess what you preach to others? And I have followed the advice: *Preach it because you believe it to be the teaching of God's Word, and heartily desire it.* Preach the truth by faith, and the experience will follow. Let the minister who feels impelled to preach about love not hesitate to do so, and he will soon he able to preach it because he has himself received that which he commends.

Heavenly Father, Help us to ever preach what Thy Word teaches knowing that as we seek Thy Truth, we will find that we possess it too. Amen.

The Two Leaders

*"I exhort, therefore, that first of all supplications, prayers,
intercessions, thanksgivings, be made for all men; for kings
and all that are in authority, that we may lead a quiet and
peaceable life in all godliness and honesty" (1 Tim. 2:1–2).*

At the time of the unveiling of the Women's Monument at Bloemfontein, before the procession took place, I spoke a few words in the Dutch
Church about the suffering, praying, all-conquering love of these women
who, they say, prayed earnestly that God would keep them from hatred or
want of love toward their enemies. I expressed the hope that this prayerful
love might be ours, and that nothing might be done to disturb the feeling
of peace and unity. I said that there were some who feared disunion not
only between the two races in the country, but between those who were
fellow-countrymen. Not long after, we heard that there had been a breach
between the leaders of the two parties.

I felt impelled to write an article on the question: "For whom do you
pray?" Some one answers: "I pray for the man at the head of the Govern-
ment and who, under God's guidance as General of the burghers in the
war, has now become the leader of all South Africa. I pray for him." And
another: "I pray especially for the man who has been serviceable in bringing the interests of his people into the foreground." But would it not be
sad if we came into God's presence divided into two camps, praying one
against the other? No, we must pray for both our leaders and for *all* who
are in authority. As leaders of the people, their influence for good or evil
is inexpressible. Their hearts are in God's hands, and He can turn them
whithersoever He wills. Let our prayers ascend to God in all sincerity, and
He will hear and grant that which is good for the whole land.

---

*Let us pray: "Lord, the hearts of rulers are in Thy hands; teach them
to do Thy will." Amen.*

Unfeigned Love of the Brethren

"Seeing ye have purified your souls through the Spirit,
unto unfeigned love of the brethren, see that ye love one
another with a pure heart fervently" (1 Peter 1:22).

In the beginning of this chapter, Peter had expressed a wonderful truth about our love to Christ: "Whom having not seen, ye love; in whom ye rejoice with joy unspeakable and full of glory" (v. 8). This was the fruit of the Spirit.

In our text he speaks of "the love of the brethren." "Ye have purified your souls in *obeying the truth through the Spirit unto the unfeigned love of the brethren.*" In the days of the Early Church it was clearly understood at conversion that, in confessing Christ, the new convert also promised unfeigned love to the brethren. So Peter continues: "See that ye love one another with a pure heart fervently." Unfeigned, fervent love through the Spirit should be the chief token of a true conversion.

We see how much stress Peter lays on this point in the three next chapters as he returns to the subject each time. (2:17), "Love the brotherhood. Fear God. Honor the king." (3:8), "Finally, be ye all like-minded, compassionate, loving as brethren, tender-hearted, humble-minded." These are all signs of the life of God in the soul. And then (4:7–8), "Watch unto Prayer, above all things being fervent in your love among yourselves; for love covereth a multitude of sins." Unfeigned, fervent love of the brethren was the indispensable sign of true godliness.

God's Word is a mirror into which the Church and each individual member must look, to see that we are truly Christian, showing by our conduct that we take God's Word as our rule of life. If our hearts condemn us, we must turn at once to God, confessing our sin. Let us believe that *the Spirit of love does indeed dwell in us* and will shed abroad God's love in our hearts and purify us from all hatred and selfishness, and *restore the image of Christ within us.*

Heavenly Father: Let us not rest content until we have surrendered ourselves wholly to Thee, that Thy Spirit of love may reign and rule within us. Amen.

The Spirit of Love

"The fruit of the Spirit is love" (Gal. 5:22).

"God hath given us the spirit of love" (2 Tim. 1:7).

Our love, which is the fruit of the Spirit, does not consist merely in the knowledge of and faith in God's love as revealed in our redemption. No, the matter goes far deeper. Our love has its origin in the fact that the love of God has been shed abroad in our hearts by the Holy Spirit, not only as an experience or feeling, but the spirit of love takes possession of us and directs and controls and inspires. This love becomes a heavenly life-power, a disposition of the soul whereby man tastes and knows that God is good. The Spirit gives to love such a form that it contains the commands of the divine love within itself and thus can keep the commandments without difficulty. "This is the love of God, that we keep His commandments, and His commandments are not grievous" (1 John 5:3). When God according to promise writes His law in our hearts, the summing up of that law is love. It governs the life of those wholly devoted to God and controls all thoughts and actions. This divine love in the heart of the believer is *a little sanctuary, whence the child of God receives power*, in obedience to the inner law of love, to live always in the love of God. This holy love includes Fellowship with God, Union with Christ, and Love to all Christians.

How can we attain to this experience? Through *faith alone*. The chief sign of faith in the blind and the lepers who came to Christ to be healed was the knowledge of their own inability to help themselves. When our eyes have been opened and we realize that the love of God has already been shed abroad in our hearts by His Spirit, enabling us to keep His commandments and to love the brethren—then let us bow in stillness of soul before God and adore the love which has taken possession of our hearts until our faith can firmly say: God has indeed given me the spirit of love in my heart.

Heavenly Father, in the power of the Spirit I can and will love Thee and those around me. Amen.

A Song of Love

"But now abideth faith, hope, love, these three;
but the greatest of these is love" (1 Cor. 13:13).

This chapter is wholly devoted to the praise of love. The first three verses speak of the absolute necessity of love as the chief thing in our religion. "If I speak with the tongues of angels, if I have the gift of prophecy, if I have all faith so as to remove mountains, and if I bestow all my goods on the poor, and if I give my body to be burned, but have not love"; then, three times repeated, "I am become sounding brass, I am nothing, it profiteth me nothing." If I have not love, it all profiteth me nothing.

Then follows the Song of Love (vv. 4–8). There are fifteen things said about love—what it is and what it is not. In this description one sentence sums up the whole nature of love: "It seeketh not its own." And again: "Love never faileth." Prophecies, tongues, and knowledge shall vanish away. Even faith and hope shall be changed into sight. But Love abides to all eternity, as long as God endures. *Love is the greatest thing* in the world.

We should read this chapter oftener than we do and commit the Song to memory so that the great words are imprinted on our hearts: "Love seeketh not her own." Think over it and pray over it. "Love never faileth." Consider all that means. "The greatest of these is love." Let this love rule in your life.

God is love. "He that dwelleth in love, dwelleth in God, and God in him." O Christian, are you living in a world that is uncharitable and selfish or full of bitterness and hatred? Take refuge under the wings of this everlasting love. Let your heart be filled with it so that by God's almighty power you may be a witness to the transforming power of love. Thus you will be a fountain of blessing to all around you.

Heavenly Father, I seek to live each day in fellowship with the triune
love of Father, Son, and Holy Spirit, and know I will learn the secret
of how to love. Amen.

The Obedience of Love

"If ye love Me, ye will keep My commandments" (John 14:15).

The love wherewith the Father loved the Son was a wonderful, never-ending love. All that the Father was and had, He gave to the Son. The Son responded to this love by giving the Father all. Cost what it might, He kept the Father's commandments and abode in His love.

Christ, in His great love to us, sacrificed all; His life and death were wholly at our service, and He asks of us that which is only reasonable, that we, out of love, should keep His commandments. Read verses 15, 21, 23 and see how the words are repeated three times, together with the great promise that follows. And chapter 15, verses 7, 10, 14, speak three times of the rich blessing connected with the keeping of the commandments.

"If ye love Me, keep My commandments." This precept loses its power because Christians say: "It is quite impossible; I cannot always keep His commandments." And so conscience is quieted, and the commandments are not kept. Yet our Lord really meant it, for in the last night with His disciples, He promised them definitely a new life in which the power of the Spirit would enable them to live a life of obedience.

"But what becomes of our sinful nature?" you ask. We keep our sinful nature to the end of life. "In me, that is, in my flesh, dwelleth no good thing." The Holy Spirit is the power of God that works within us, both to will and to do, and so prevents the flesh from gaining the upper hand. Think of the text in Hebrews (13:20–21), "The God of peace . . . make you perfect in every good thing to do His will, working in you that which is well-pleasing, through Jesus Christ."

O brothers and sisters, these are no mere idle words: "If ye love Me, keep My commandments," and "My Father will love him, and We will make our abode with him." Believe that the Holy Spirit will cause the love of Christ to work in your heart in such power that you will be *able to abide in the love of Jesus the whole day, and to keep His words with great joy.* Then you will understand the saying: "This is the love of God, that we keep His commandments; and His commandments are not grievous."

Heavenly Father, I do believe that the Holy Spirit will endue me with power to live this life of perfect love. Amen.

Love and Prayer

"Be sober, and watch unto prayer, above all things being fervent in your love among yourselves" (1 Peter 4:7–8).

In our text, watching unto prayer and fervent love are closely linked. This is true, too, in the spiritual life. The man who prays only for himself will not find it easy to be in the right attitude toward God. But where the heart is filled with fervent love to others, prayer will continually rise to God for those whom we love and even for those with whom we do not agree.

We must never neglect to indicate what an important place prayer holds in the life of love. These two fruits of the Spirit are inseparably connected. If you wish your love to grow and increase, forget yourself and pray, pray earnestly for God's children and His Church. And if you would *increase in prayerfulness*, give yourself in fervent love to the service of those around you, helping to bear their burdens.

What a great need there is at this time of earnest, powerful intercessors! Let those who complain that there is so little love among Christians acknowledge that one of the chief signs of love is lacking in themselves if they do not *pray much and often for their brethren*. I am deeply convinced that God desires His children, as members of one body, to present themselves each day before the Throne of grace to pray down the power of the Spirit upon all believers. Union is strength. This is true in regard to the Kingdom of Heaven. Real spiritual unity will help us to forget ourselves, to live unselfishly, wholly for God and those around us. And the word of Peter will be applied to our lives—"watching in prayer—fervent in love."

There can be no surer way of growing in the spirit of love than by uniting daily at the Throne of grace and finding our joy and life in the oneness of Spirit with the whole Body of Christ.

Let our thoughts on love be also on prayer. As we meditate on love among believers we shall be constrained to have fellowship with God. And we shall attain this not by reading or thinking, but by communion with the Father, and with the Lord Jesus through the Holy Spirit. Love impels to prayer; to believing prayer is granted the love of God.

Heavenly Father, may we be ever mindful that watching unto prayer and fervent love are closely linked. Amen.

The First and Great Commandment

"The Lord thy God will circumcise thine heart to love the Lord thy God with all thy heart and with all thy soul" (Deut. 30:6).

God greatly desires our love. It is the nature of all love to long to be acceptable and to meet with response. Yes, God longs with a never-ending, fervent desire to have our love, the love of the whole heart.

But how can I attain such a condition? Just in the same way that I receive salvation—*through faith alone*. Paul says: "I live through the faith of the Son of God, who loved me." When we take time to wait upon God and remember with what a burning desire God sought to win our love through the gift of His Son, we shall be able to realize that God has a strong and never-ceasing longing for the love of our heart.

Our hearts are blind and dark, and we are apt to forget that God longs each day for the love of His child. If I once begin to believe it, I shall feel constrained to tarry before God and ask Him to let His light shine into my heart. Just as the sun is willing to give me its light and heat if I will receive them, God is a thousand times more *willing to give me the light and glow of His love.*

In the Old Testament God gave us the promise of the new covenant (Ezek. 36:25–26), "I will cleanse you, a new heart will I give you, and put within you a new spirit." He gave His Son to die for us in order to win our love. Take time, O my soul, to grasp this, and wait silently upon God and become strong in the assurance of faith. God, who longs for my love, is Almighty, and will shed abroad His love in my heart through the Holy Spirit now dwelling within me.

Oh, that we could understand that there is nothing on earth to be compared to this experience! Shall I not take time each day and give God His desire and believe with firmer faith? God, who so greatly longs for my love, will work within me by His Spirit, granting the desire to love Him with my whole heart and enabling me to prove my love by keeping His commandments.

O Lord, I bow before Thee; fulfill my longing desire which is also Thy desire, that my heart may be filled with Thy love. Amen.

The Royal Law of Love

"If ye fulfill the royal law according to the scripture, Thou shalt love the neighbor as thyself, ye do well" (James 2:8).

When our Lord, in answer to the question, "Master, which is the great commandment in the law?" had answered: "Thou shalt love the Lord thy God with all thy heart," He added: "The second is like unto it, Thou shalt love thy neighbor as thyself." These two commandments both contain the one verb, love. In heaven where God is and on earth among all people, love is the royal law, love is supreme.

The Christian's love for others has more than one purpose:

1. It reveals to us our own nature implanted by God, that we should love ourselves, and it calls us to love our neighbors with the same love. Thus we have in our hearts the law to love our neighbors as ourselves.

2. Christianity teaches us to love our neighbors because God loves them. Everyone, howsoever vile, has a share in God's compassion and love because each one is made in God's image. I ought, then, to love my neighbors, not merely because they are people, but because I see God's likeness in them and because God loves them. As God loves everyone, even His enemies, even so, not more, nor less, I must love all. "Be ye merciful, even as your Father is merciful." From my Father in heaven I must learn how to love.

3. The Christian love of all people may rise still higher. In the realm of grace, God has reconciled us to Himself so that He can apportion to us His personal love. This is the law for each child of God; we must love one another *with the same love with which Christ has loved us.*

4. And then comes the last and the highest thought, that even as Christ in His great love redeemed a world dying in misery and sin, so all those who have received this love should give themselves, even as Christ did, to love everyone and devote their lives to making other partakers of this great blessedness.

Child of God, here are four reasons why we should love our neighbors. Have they not a Divine authority and irresistible power which will compel us to manifest this Christian love towards others in fullness of beauty?

May God write the royal law of love deep in our hearts! Amen.

National Feeling

"God hath made of one blood all nations of men" (Acts 17:26).

A former Prime Minister of England said in regard to the Boer War that it "served to maintain the principle that the smaller nationalities should not be oppressed. That is to say, that all these precious lives and the treasures of gold were offered up in vindication of nationality which may be regarded as a gift of God, as the divine right of each nation according to its special nature to preserve and develop its individuality in the service of the common life of all the world. This war will develop national feeling more intensely and will increase a national consciousness and arouse hope amongst the peoples who have hitherto been considered the most backward in the world. People will slowly learn that national feeling depends on character, and character depends on religion.

"In a struggle such as this we cannot expect the breach to be healed at once; but we can cultivate a spirit of Christian sympathy with those who differ from us and cease to regard each other with suspicion and distrust. We can trust the honesty of each other's convictions and take more trouble to understand one another."

This extract speaks most strongly of the divine right of national feeling, yet we must also clearly understand that the feeling, as a merely human force, is under the power of sin. Let us remember "every creature of God is good, for it is sanctified by the Word and by prayer." Without that sanctifying process, national feeling may become the prey of ambition and the source of hatred and aversion and contempt for other nations. God has, in Christ, placed everyone under the law of Heavenly love. It is the holy calling of every Christian, and more especially of every minister of the Gospel, under the guidance of the Holy Spirit to point out to others the way by which national feeling may attain its twofold aim: (1) the development and uplifting of the people themselves, and (2) the right attitude to other peoples in the upbuilding of all mankind.

Heavenly Father, as we seek to develop and uplift ourselves as a nation, may we at the same time seek to upbuild all the peoples of the world. Amen.

One Stream or Two Streams?

"The stick of Ephraim, and the stick of Judah, I will make them one stick, and they shall be one in Mine hand" (Ezek. 37:19).

If any one were to ask me: "In which of these two do you believe?" My answer would be: "In both." "And why?" "Because God has so willed it." When the small stream of the Africander people with less than one million souls was turned into the mighty stream of the British Empire, with its three hundred millions, it was God's will that this should happen. It was His will that in the great stream there should be two streams, side by side. The two nationalities, the smaller as well as the greater, have each their own history, their own national characteristics, and their own special virtues and shortcomings. In God's plan and council there was room for both.

Why has there been such terrible strife and discord over the question: One Stream or Two Streams? Because people would not accept both viewpoints and accord to each its right. They wanted one or the other, exclusively, in the foreground. They forgot that God had said: "What God hath joined together, let not man put asunder." One who is really desirous of knowing and doing God's will—in His dealings with our people—must try to understand the twofold calling: to be faithful in preserving one's own nationality; and at the same time to show one's love and appreciation of the second nationality with whom under God's Providence, one's lot has been cast.

God has given to His people in this land a great and holy calling, in submission to His will and in the power of His love, to prove what it is to be a true Africander and yet at the same time a faithful subject of the British Empire. Our love to God and to our neighbors will supply the right incentive.

When Ephraim and Judah became one in God's hand, the difference between the two was not destroyed. Each kept separate characteristics but also the oneness was that of true unity and mutual love. "Ephraim shall not envy Judah, and Judah shall not vex Ephraim." God will fulfill this promise to us but on one condition: We must place our people in God's hand by our prayers. "They shall be one in Mine hand." Let us, by means of intercession, place our people in God's hand. He can, and will, give the love and mutual forbearance that is needed.

Heavenly Father, we thank Thee that we can place our people in Thy hand, and Thou wilt give us the love and mutual forbearance that is needed. Amen.

Pray for Love

"The Lord make you to increase and abound in love one toward another, and toward all men, even as we also do toward you; to the end that He may stablish your hearts unblameable in holiness" (1 Thess. 3:12–13).

What a prayer! That the Lord would make them to abound in love toward each other, even as Paul did toward them, that He would strengthen their hearts to be unblameable in holiness. Without love this was impossible. Their hearts would be strengthened for a life of true holiness through the love of the brethren by the power of God. Let us use this prayer often, both for ourselves and for those around us. Do you pray for holiness? Then show it by a hearty love to all believers!

In 2 Thessalonians 3:5 we read: "The Lord direct your hearts into the love of God." Yes, that is what the Lord Jesus will do for us, give us a heart always directed to the love of God. *Lord, by Thy great love, grant me a heart of love!*

"Always in every prayer of mine for you all making request with joy. I pray that your love may abound yet more and more in knowledge . . . that ye may be filled with the fruits of righteousness" (Phil. 1:4–11). The Apostle, in his constant prayer for those in his charge, makes Love the chief thing. Let us do the same.

"I would that ye knew what great conflict I have for you, that your hearts may be comforted, being knit together in love, unto all riches of understanding" (Col. 2:1–2). Paul considers it indispensable for their growth in the knowledge of God that the hearts of the believers should be knit together in love. God is love—everlasting, endless love. That love can only be experienced when Christians are knit together in love and live for others and not only for themselves.

These four prayers of Paul give us abundant matter for meditation and prayer. Take time to let these heavenly thoughts grow in your heart. As the sun freely gives its light and heat to the grass and grain that they may grow and bring forth fruit, so God is far more willing to give His love to us in ever-increasing measure. O Christian, if you feel as if you cannot pray, take these words of divine love and ponder them in your heart. You will gain a strong and a joyous assurance of what God is able to do for you. He will make you to abound in love and strengthen your heart to live before Him in holiness and love of the brethren.

Lord, teach me so to pray! Amen.

Like Christ

*"I have given you an example, that ye should do
as I have done to you" (John 13:15).*

The love of Christ manifested in His death on the cross is the ground not only of our hope of salvation, but it is *the only rule for our daily life and conduct.* Our Lord says clearly: "Ye should do as I have done." The love of Christ is my only hope of salvation. A walk in that love is the way truly and fully to enjoy that salvation.

"Let each one of us please his neighbor for that which is good, unto edifying; for even Christ pleased not Himself. Wherefore receive ye one another, as Christ also received us" (Rom. 15:2, 7). God will work the power within us to "receive one another, as Christ received us." He will do it for every upright soul and for all who pray in confident faith.

"Be ye followers of God, as dear children; and walk in love, as Christ also hath loved us, and hath given Himself for us" (Eph. 5:1–2). Here, again, love is everything. We must realize that Christ loved us even unto death and that we are now God's dear children. It follows naturally that we should walk in love. Faith in Christ's wonderful love and in God's inconceivable love resting upon us, makes it not only possible but certain that those who keep close to Christ will walk in love.

"Put on therefore, as God's elect, holy and beloved, a heart of compassion; forbearing one another, and forgiving each other; even as the Lord forgave you, so also do ye. And *above all these things put on love*, which is the bond of perfectness" (Col. 3:12–14). What a blessed life in the love and the power that we have in Christ! What a blessed walk in His fellowship, when we are led by the Holy Spirit and strengthened for a life in His likeness!

O God, the Father of love, the Father of Christ, our Father, wilt Thou indeed strengthen us each day to love one another in Christ, even as He loved us! Amen.

The Power of God's Word

*"The words that I have spoken unto you are spirit
and are life" (John 6:63).*

*"Ye received the Word of God, as it is in truth, the Word of
God that worketh effectually in you that believe" (1 Thess. 2:13).*

"The Word of God is living and active" (Heb. 4:12).

The question constantly recurs: What is the reason that God's children so little realize the great value and absolute necessity of love to one another? One answer is: Because of unbelief. *Without faith*, great faith, persevering faith, there can be *no thought of the power of love* within us. But it is a different faith from what we usually mean when we say we believe in God's Word. This true faith is deeper and higher. It bows before God in the deep realization of His greatness, of His power to work wonders in our hearts, and of His loving care of us. The word of a king or a general has great influence over his soldiers. And how great beyond compare is the Word of the Infinite and Almighty One!

It is necessary to be deeply convinced of our utter inability to produce this love which is holy and can conquer sin and unbelief. We need *a burning desire to receive this heavenly love into our hearts* whatever the cost may be. Then at length we shall gain an insight into what God's Word is as a living power in our hearts. This supernatural power will be the love of God shed abroad in our hearts by the Holy Spirit living and working within us.

In the following portion we shall consider the verses from the first Epistle of John in which the love of God is promised to believers. As Christians let us ask ourselves, are we ready to acknowledge our deep sinfulness and want of power and to yield our hearts unreservedly for this love to take possession? And, above all, take time in God's presence to wait on Him in the confidence that His Word will work effectually in us as a seed of new life. Then we shall love our Lord Jesus and one another with a love like that with which God has loved us.

Heavenly Father, we acknowledge our deep sinfulness and want of power and now yield our hearts unreservedly for Thy love to take possession. Amen.

Perfect Love
According to 1 John

"These are the true sayings of God" (Rev. 19:9).

"He that loveth his brother abideth in the light" (1 John 2:10).

"Whosoever doeth not righteousness is not of God, neither he that loveth not his brother. For this is the message which ye heard from the beginning, that we should love one another" (3:10–11). "We know that we have passed out of death into life, because we love the brethren" (3:14). "Hereby know we love, because He laid down His life for us: and we ought to lay down our lives for the brethren" (3:16). "And this is His commandment, That we should believe on the Name of His Son Jesus Christ, and love one another" (3:23). "Beloved, let us love one another: for love is of God" (4:7). "Beloved, if God so loved us, *we ought also to love one another. If we love one another, God abideth in us, and His love is perfected in us.* We have known and believed the love that God hath to us. God is love; and he that abideth in love abideth in God, and God in him" (4:11–12, 16). "If a man say, I love God, and hateth his brother, he is a liar: for he that loveth not his brother whom he hath seen, cannot love God whom he hath not seen. *And this commandment have we from Him, that he who loveth God love his brother also*" (4:20–21).

Each of these words is a living seed and has within it a Divine power which is able to take root and grow and bear fruit in our hearts. But just as the seed requires the soil in which it grows to be kept free of all weeds, so the heart must be wholly surrendered to God and His service, that the seed of the Word may bear this heavenly fruit.

Read over again 3:23. As necessary as faith is for our salvation, so necessary is love one to another. And (4:21) love to God and love to one another are inseparable.

Heavenly Father, with wholly surrendered hearts to Thee and Thy service, we look for the seed of Thy Word to bear its heavenly fruit. Amen.

The Love That Suffers

"Walk in love, as Christ also hath loved us, and hath given Himself for us" (Eph. 5:2).

Is it not strange that love, which is the source of the greatest happiness, should also be the cause of the most intense suffering? Our life on earth is such that suffering always follows when love seeks to save the object of its love. Yes, it is only by means of suffering that love can gain its end and so attain the highest happiness.

What a wonderful thought! Even the almighty power of God's love could not achieve its purpose without suffering that passes understanding. By means of His sufferings, Christ bore and overcame the sins of the whole world, and the hard heart of man was softened and drawn to God. So love in the midst of suffering manifested the greatest glory and attained its end perfectly.

Let no one with such an Example before him imagine that love is self-sufficient. No; love worthy of the name manifests itself in a life of continual self-sacrifice. Love's strength lies in renunciation. Just think what a mother suffers when a beloved child is ill or when a son falls into evil ways. Love gives her strength to endure whatever the circumstances may be. Think, too, what one must undergo who is yielded wholeheartedly to work and to pray for others. It may mean tears and heartache and much wrestling in prayer. But love overcomes all obstacles.

O Christian, do you really long to know the love of Christ in all its fullness? Then yield yourself wholly to Him and His blessed service. Regard yourself as a channel through which the Highest Love can attain its aim. Take the souls around you into a sympathizing, loving heart and begin to suffer with them and intercede for them. Let it be your chief delight to live and to suffer for others in the love and fellowship of the Lord Jesus. Then at length you will realize what this life of love is, as a servant of God and even as God Himself and as Christ, to live wholly for the welfare and happiness of others.

O soul, dwell on this wondrous truth, that there can be no real fellowship in the love of Christ save in unreserved surrender, to seek always the glory of God in the salvation of others. "He that dwelleth in love, dwelleth in God, and God in him."

Heavenly Father, make me a channel through which Thy Highest Love can attain its aim. Amen.

The Works of the Flesh

"The works of the flesh are manifest; witchcraft, hatred, strife, jealousies, wrath, envyings, murders, and such like" (Gal. 5:19-21.

Paul in these three verses mentions seventeen of the terrible "works of the flesh." Nine of these are sins against love. And he says, elsewhere (Eph. 4:31), "Let all bitterness, and wrath, and anger, and clamor, and evil speaking, be put away from you, with all malice." He here answers the question, why there is so little love among Christians, and why it is so hard to arouse such love. All these sins are "works of the flesh."

Even the earnest Christian is still in the flesh. Paul says: "In me, that is in my flesh, dwelleth no good thing"; "Because the mind of the flesh is enmity against God." It is quite impossible for Christians by their own efforts to lead a life of love. Scripture says: "Walk in the Spirit, and ye shall not fulfill the lusts of the flesh." The Spirit will enable us to keep the flesh always in subjection. The "fruit of the Spirit" will be Christ's love poured into our hearts as a fountain of love. Paul adds to what was quoted above: "The law of the Spirit of life in Christ Jesus hath made me free from the law of sin." The grace of God will enable the Christian to walk, not after the flesh, but after the Spirit.

Learn these three great lessons: 1. Christians cannot in their own strength love God and all people. 2. The great reason of so much bitterness and want of love, is that Christians walk after the flesh. 3. The only sure way to abide in this life of love, to love God and Christ with the whole heart, to love one another fervently, and to have a tender compassionate love for all who do not yet know Christ—is an absolute surrender to the Holy Spirit, to be led and guided by Him each day of our lives. It is through the Holy Spirit that this love is shed abroad in our hearts.

Heavenly Father, as Thy child, may I learn the lesson that the Holy Spirit will take entire possession of me and will work continually within me a life of love to Christ and to all people. Help me to pray over this thought until it gains control of my whole being! Amen.

Passing the Love of Women

"My brother Jonathan: very pleasant hast thou been unto me: thy love to me was wonderful, passing the love of women" (2 Sam. 1:26).

God created man in order to show what the power of love is when a man strives for the welfare of others and even gives up his life for them. He created woman to show what tenderness and quiet endurance are when she sacrifices herself for the sake of others. A little child, during the first years of its life, is dependent on the mother. It is not only that the child may learn to love its mother, but that the mother herself may be trained in the school of self-sacrificing love, for her greatest adorning is "the ornament of a meek and quiet spirit, which is in the sight of God of great price" (1 Peter 3:4).

The tendency nowadays in public life is to place woman on an equal footing with man. This is only right in many cases. But one must not forget that the best ornament of a woman is a meek and quiet spirit which is of great price in the sight of God and of man and which makes her a blessing in her home. It is the suffering, prayerful, all-conquering love of the wife and the mother which secures the happiness of a people.

Dear sisters, preserve as a great treasure the precious jewel which God has entrusted to you—to reflect the love of God in all its tenderness and sympathy. "As one whom his mother comforteth, so will I comfort you." Let each one, as she reads this book, take time to meditate on God's wonderful love and pray for it earnestly in a receptive spirit. This will give her a heavenly influence and power over her husband and children; and in her dealings with her neighbors, she will be a living witness to what the love of God can do.

Think of Mary, the woman who loved much, and the other women to whom the Lord revealed Himself on the resurrection morning. It was the love of these women that gave them the right to be the first to meet the Lord and to take the message to the disciples.

God bless the mothers and wives and daughters of our land! May they prove in their lives how beautiful and powerful the love of women is! And the words from the time of David will still be true: "Wonderful as the love of women" is the love of God's children. Amen.

Stewards of the Love of God

"Let a man so account of us, as of the ministers of Christ, and stewards of the mysteries of God. Moreover it is required in stewards, that a man be found faithful" (1 Cor. 4:1–2).

A steward is the man to whom the king or master entrusts his treasures and goods to apportion to those who have a right to them. God in heaven needs people on earth to make known the treasures of His love and to give them to those who have need. The minister of the Gospel is a steward of the mystery of God and above all of the deep mystery of His everlasting love and all the blessings that flow from it.

It is required in stewards that a man be found faithful; he must devote himself wholly to his life task. He must be faithful at his work and always at his post in the palace or house where the treasures are stored up. So the minister of the Gospel must himself be faithful, living each day in the love and fellowship of God. He must be faithful not only to God, but to his congregation, caring for the needs of the souls entrusted to him and ready to recommend God's love and to share it with others. This divine love is a mystery and can only dwell in a heart set apart for God and satisfied with His love which flows from Him as a stream of living water.

O child of God, seek to have a deeper insight into what the office of a servant of God means, as a steward of the wonderful love of God to sinners. Pray much and often for your ministers that God may hide them in the secret of His tabernacle, so that they may be faithful stewards of the mystery of God and chiefly of the mystery of Divine Love.

And you, my beloved brethren to whom the love of God in heaven and of Christ on the cross is entrusted, remember that your congregation, your Church, and your people are dependent on your faithfulness in living a heavenly life in fellowship with God. Then you will be able with joy and in the power of the Holy Spirit to pass on the love of God to souls that so greatly need it.

Heavenly Father, help our pastors to ever remember that their congregation, their church and their people are dependent upon their faithfulness in living a heavenly life in fellowship with Thee. Amen.

Faith Working Through Love

"In Christ Jesus neither circumcision availeth anything, nor uncircumcision; but faith working through love" (Gal. 5:6).

Faith is the root; Love is the fruit. Faith becomes strong in the love of God and of Christ. Faith in God and love to the brethren must always go hand in hand. Faith in God's wonderful love, shed abroad in our hearts, enables us to live always in love towards those around us. This true faith gives us power for a life of fervent, all-embracing love.

Yet how little the Church realizes of all this! How seldom does the preacher lay stress on a Christlike love to one another, as the fruit and joy of the life of faith!

All of our life—in the home, between father and mother, parents and children, brothers and sisters, friends and servants—should be a life in the love of Christ. Do not say: "It is impossible." All things are possible to God, who through His Holy Spirit will shed His love in our hearts to be lived out in our daily lives. Let our faith cling to God's Word and to the unseen and wonderful things He will do for us each day. Let these thoughts about love impel us to accept with new and greater faith the Love of God. and then dedicate our lives to letting it radiate from us to all people, yes, even to our enemies and to the heathen at the uttermost parts of the earth.

O Christian, the whole of salvation lies in these two words—Faith and Love. Let our faith each day take deeper root in God's eternal love. And then each day the fruit of the Spirit will be love in all our dealings with those around us.

May God imprint these words deeply in our hearts and make them a joy and strength to us—In Jesus Christ nothing avails, but "love working through faith." Amen.

The Dispensation of the Spirit

"How much more shall your Heavenly Father give the Holy Spirit to them that ask Him" (Luke 11:13).

The writer of a little book on Prayer tells us that he has learned through his own experience the secret of a better prayer life and would gladly pass on that which has helped him. As he was meditating on prayer, the great thought came with power that we are now living in the dispensation of the Spirit. He says: "I felt deeply that in this time of the working of the Holy Spirit, all we may do in God's service is of little value unless it is inspired by the power of the Holy Spirit. This brought me to the well-known, precious, and inexhaustible text, 'How much more shall your Heavenly Father give the Holy Spirit to them that ask Him?'"

I felt anew that the main thing for each of us is to receive, afresh from the Father, the Holy Spirit for our daily needs and daily life. Without this we cannot please God, nor can we be of any real help to those around us. This brought the further thought that our prayers, if they are to raise our loves to fulfill God's purpose, must have their origin in God Himself, the highest source of power. Water cannot rise higher than its source. And so it happens that if the Holy Spirit prays through us, as human channels or conduits, our prayers will rise again to God who is their source, and the prayers will be answered by the Divine working in ourselves and in others. "I believe more and more," says the writer, "that the Christian life of each one of us depends chiefly on the quality of our prayers and not on the quantity."

What material for thought is here, for deep meditation, for earnest prayer! When you pray today, ask the Heavenly Father to give you the Holy Spirit afresh for this day. He yearns to do it.

Father, grant me now the working of Thy Holy Spirit, that I may learn to pray. Amen.

The Fruit of the Spirit

"The fruit of the Spirit is love, joy, peace, long-suffering, gentleness, goodness, faith, meekness, temperance" (Gal. 5:22-23).

We have seen what the two first lessons are on prayer. We must pray the Father every morning to give us the Spirit anew and then pray the Spirit to teach us and help us. Here is a third lesson—commit to memory the text at the head of this chapter.

Christians often think that they have only to ask God to teach them to pray, and He will do it at once. This is not always the case. What the Spirit does is so to strengthen our spiritual lives that we are able to pray better. When we ask Him to teach us, it is important that we open our hearts to His gracious influence, so that our desires are stirred and we first of all surrender ourselves to the working of the Spirit. This surrender consists in naming before Him the fruits of the Spirit, with the earnest prayer to be filled with these fruits. So that the benefit of learning the text by heart will be that as we pray for the teaching of the Spirit, we may say: "Here is my heart, fill it with the fruits of the Spirit."

Think of the first three fruits, *Love, Joy, Peace,* the three chief characteristics of a strong faith life. *Love* to God and to Christ, to other Christians and to all people. *Joy,* the proof of the perfect fulfillment of every need, of courage and faith for all the work we have to do. *Peace,* the blessed state of undisturbed rest and security in which the peace of God that passes all understanding can keep our hearts and minds.

In the last discourse with His disciples, Christ used these three words with the word "My" before them. "Abide in *My love.*" "That *My joy* might remain in you." "*My peace* I give unto you." Shall we not lay before the Spirit as the great desire of our hearts that He may make these fruits reach perfection within us? Then at last we shall be able to pray aright and always ask more and more of our Heavenly Father.

Blessed Father, through Thy Holy Spirit we long for these fruits to reach perfection within us. Amen.

Led by the Spirit

*"As many as are led by the Spirit of God, they
are the sons of God" (Rom. 8:14).*

Let us now consider four other fruits of the Spirit: *Long-suffering, Gentleness, Goodness, Meekness*. These four words all denote attributes of the Godhead. They will reach maturity in us through much prayer for the working of the Holy Spirit. Think of what they mean.

Long-suffering—In the Old Testament in the time of Moses, God's long-suffering was praised. All Scripture bears witness to the wonderful patience with which God dealt with sinners, until we come to the word in 2 Peter 3:9: "The Lord is long-suffering, not willing that any should perish, but that all should come to repentance." This attribute of God, the Spirit will make a characteristic of our lives, so that we too may exercise a divine patience with all sin and wrong, so that souls may be saved.

Gentleness—What wonderful things we read in the Psalms about God's goodness and gentleness, which are from everlasting to everlasting. "As the heavens are high above the earth, so great is His mercy toward them that fear Him." God works in our hearts this same goodness and mercy toward all the sin and wretchedness around us.

Goodness—"There is none good but God." All goodness comes from Him, and He gives to His children according as each heart asks and desires. And this goodness is manifested in sympathy and love to all who are in need.

Meekness—We read in Psalm 18:35: "Thy gentleness hath made me great." But it was chiefly in God's Son that the divine meekness was shown. Jesus says: "Learn of Me, for I am meek and lowly of heart." Paul entreats his readers "by the gentleness and meekness of Christ." The Holy Spirit, too, the gentle Dove, longs to impart the ripe fruit of meekness to our hearts.

Is it not a wonderful thought that these four attributes of God, which are the characteristics of God's work among sinners, may be brought to ripeness in our hearts by the Holy Spirit, so that we in all our ways and conversation may be like the Meek and Lowly One

---

Heavenly Father, may Thy long-suffering, gentleness, goodness and meekness be ripe in our hearts so that we may be like Thee. Amen.

The Spirit of Faith

"Having the same spirit of faith, we also believe" (2 Cor. 4:13).

Do you begin to realize why it is so important to commit to memory the text, Galatians 5:22? It will strengthen the desire in our hearts to have and to hold the fruits of the Spirit within us. Our expectation of the blessing God will give will be enlarged. Let us pause a while on the two last fruits of the Spirit—*Faith and Temperance.*

When the disciples asked the Lord: "Why could we not cast out the evil spirit?"—His reply was: "This kind goeth not out but by prayer and fasting." Their faith was not powerful enough, and even if they had prayed, they had not the zeal and self-sacrifice needed for prevailing prayer. Here we see the union of faith and temperance.

Faith is a fruit of the Spirit—and leads the seeking soul to depend on God alone. Faith believes God's Word and clings to Him and waits in perfect trust that His power will work within us all that He has promised. The whole life of the Christian each day is a faith life.

Let us now think of *Temperance.* This refers in the first place to eating and drinking and leads us to restraint, carefulness, and unselfishness in our conversation, our desires, in all our dealings with one another. Our motto should be: "Forsaking all worldly desires, to live righteously and godly and temperately in all things." Temperate in all our dealings with the world and its temptations. Righteous in the doing of God's will. Devout in the close communion with God Himself.

Faith and temperance are both fruits of the Spirit. When we ask the Spirit to teach us to pray, we open our hearts toward Him that He may grant us the fruits of the Spirit, faith and temperance, to influence our daily lives in our communion with God and man.

Learn this text by heart, and let the promptings of the Spirit in your heart each day lead you to the Father, that He may grant the fruits of the Spirit in your inner life which will be seen in all your actions.

Blessed Father, grant the fruits of the Spirit in my inner life such that they will be seen in all I do. Amen.

Worship God in Spirit

"We are the circumcision, which worship God in the Spirit, and rejoice in Christ Jesus, and have no confidence in the flesh" (Phil. 3:3).

The foregoing remarks serve as preparatory to the prayer itself. We have come to the Father with the prayer for the Holy Spirit. We have invoked the guidance of the Holy Spirit. Now we begin to pray.

First, we pray to God the Father, thanking Him for all the blessings of this life. We acknowledge our entire dependence and weakness and express our trust in His love and care for us. We wait before Him until we have the assurance that He sees and hears us. Then we direct our prayer to the Lord Jesus and ask for grace to abide in Him always, for without Him we can do nothing. We look to Him as our Lord, our Preserver, our Life and give ourselves into His keeping for the day. We give utterance to our faith in His infinite love and the reality of His presence with us.

Lastly, we pray to the Holy Spirit. We have already prayed to Him for guidance. We now ask Him to strengthen us in the faith, that what we have asked of the Father and the Son may be truly wrought in us. He is the Dispenser of the power and gifts of the Father and of the Lord Jesus; all the grace we need must be the result of the working of the Spirit within us.

Our text says: "We serve God in the Spirit, we glory in the Lord Jesus, and have no confidence in the flesh." We have no power to do the thing that is good. We count on the Lord Jesus through the Holy Spirit to work within us. Let us take time to think and meditate on these things. It will help to strengthen our faith if we repeat the text of Galatians 5:22, asking God to grant these fruits in our lives.

Heavenly Father, as we surrender ourselves wholly, we shall have boldness by faith to accept the working of the Holy Spirit in our hearts. Amen.

Intercession

"Pray one for another" (James 5:16).

There is much value in intercession, and it is an indispensable part of prayer. It strengthens our love and faith in what God can do and is a means of bringing blessing and salvation to others. Let us learn the lesson thoroughly: Prayer should not be for ourselves alone, but chiefly for others. Let us begin by praying for those who are near and dear to us, those with whom we live, that we may be of help to them and not a hindrance. Pray for divine wisdom, for thoughtfulness for others, for kindliness, for self-sacrifice on their behalf.

Pray for all your friends and all with whom you come into contact. Pray that you may watch in prayer for their souls. Pray for all Christians, especially for ministers and those in responsible positions.

Pray for those who do not yet know the Lord as their Savior. Make a list of the names of those whom God has laid upon your heart and pray for their conversion. You belong to Christ; He needs you to bring to Him in prayer the souls of those around you. The Holy Spirit will strengthen you to an active love in watching for souls. Pray, too, for all poor and neglected ones.

Pray for the heathen and for all mission work. Use a mission calendar with daily subjects of prayer and bear on your heart before God the missionaries, evangelists, teachers, and believers among the heathen.

Do you think this will take too much time? Just think what an inconceivable blessing it is to help souls through your prayers; and look to the Holy Spirit for further guidance. If this takes too much time in your morning watch, then take some time later in the day. Cultivate the feeling: "I am saved to serve." You will taste the great joy of knowing that you are living even as Jesus Christ lived on earth—to make God's love known to others.

Blessed Father, help me to learn day by day, "I am saved to serve." Amen.

Time

"What, could ye not watch with me one hour?" (Matt. 26:40).

One who wishes to pray as we have indicated in our previous meditations might say: "I think I could do all that in ten minutes' time." Very well; if ten minutes is all the time that you can give, see what you can do in that time. Most people can spare more time. If they will only persevere from day to day with their hearts set on prayer, time will come of its own accord.

Is it possible that Christians can say that they cannot afford to spend a quarter or half an hour alone with God and His Word? When a friend comes to see us, or we have to attend an important meeting, or there is anything to our advantage or pleasure, we find time easily enough.

And God, the great God, who has a right to us and who in His wondrous love longs for us to spend time with Him that He may communicate to us His power and grace—we find no time for fellowship with Him. Even God's own servants, who might consider it their special privilege to be much with Him in prayer to receive the fullness of power even His servants are so occupied with their own work that they find little time for that which is all-important—waiting on God to receive power from on high.

Dear child of God, let us never say, "I have no time for God." Let the Holy Spirit teach us that the most important, the most blessed, the most profitable time of the whole day is the time we spend alone with God. Pray to the Lord Jesus who in His earthly life experienced the need of prayer, pray to the Holy Spirit who will impress upon us this divine truth. As indispensable to me as the bread I eat and the air I breathe is communion with God through His Word and prayer. Whatever else is left undone, God has the first and chief right to my time. Then only will my surrender to God's will be full and unreserved.

Heavenly Father, let the Holy Spirit teach me that the most important, the most blessed, the most profitable time of the whole day is the time I spend alone with Thee. Amen.

The Word of God

"The Word of God is living and active" (Heb. 4:12).

I find it a great help to use much of God's Word in my prayers. If the Holy Spirit impresses a certain text upon my mind, I take it to the Throne of Grace and plead the promise. This habit increases our faith, reminds us of God's promises, and brings us into harmony with God's will. We learn to pray according to God's will and understand that we can only expect an answer when our prayers are in accordance with that will (1 John 5:14).

Prayer is like fire. The fire can only burn brightly if it is supplied with good fuel. That fuel is God's Word which must not only be studied carefully and prayerfully, but must be taken into the heart and lived out in the life. The inspiration and powerful working of the Holy Spirit alone can do this.

By thoughts such as these we gain a deeper insight into the value and power of God's Word as a seed of eternal life. We are all familiar with the characteristics of a seed—a small grain in which the life-power of a whole tree slumbers. If it is placed in the soil, it will grow and increase and become a large tree.

Each word or promise of God is a seed containing a divine life in it. If I carry it in my heart by faith, love it and meditate on it, it will surely but slowly spring up and bring forth the fruits of righteousness. Think over this until you gain the assurance: although my heart seems cold and dead, the Word of God will work within me the disposition promised in His Word.

The Holy Spirit uses both the Word and prayer. Prayer is the expression of our human need and desire. The Word of God is the means that the Holy Spirit teaches us to use as a guide to what God will do for us and the demonstration of the secret working of the Holy Spirit in our hearts by which God Himself fulfills His promise and gives us what we could not obtain without the help of the Spirit.

Blessed Father, I thank Thee that although my heart seems cold and dead, Thy Word is working in me the disposition promised in Thy Word. Amen.

In the Name of Christ

"Whatsoever ye do, in word or in deed, do all in the
Name of the Lord Jesus, giving thanks to God the
Father through Him" (Col. 3:17).

At the close of your prayer it is always well to add a request for the "Spirit of Remembrance"; "He shall bring all things to your remembrance" all through the day, so that the prayers of the morning may not be counteracted by the work of the day. Read the text at the head of this passage once more, prayerfully.

Have you ever realized that it is a command? Is it the aim of your life to obey it and to fulfill its injunctions? This may be difficult, but it is not impossible, or God would not have asked it of us. God's Word has a wonderful power to preserve the spirit of thanksgiving in our lives. When we rise in the morning, let us thank God for the rest of the night in "the Name of the Lord Jesus," and in His Name let us at night thank Him for the mercies of the day. The ordinary daily life, full of most ordinary duties, will thus be lightened by the thought of what God has done for us for Christ's sake. Each ordinary deed will lead to thankfulness that He has given us the power to perform it.

At first it may seem impossible to remember the Lord Jesus in everything and to do all in His Name, yet the mere endeavor will strengthen us. Even as a mother is conscious of her love for her little child all through the day's hard work, so the love of Christ will enable us to live all day in His Presence. We need to completely surrender ourselves—to live for God all the day.

I have often spoken and written of what it means to pray in the Name of Christ. On reading our text of today I thought: Here we have the right explanation. The man who does all in word and deed, in the Name of Jesus, may have the full, childlike confidence that what he asks in that Name, he will receive. Take the text into your heart, and you may count on the Holy Spirit to make it true in your life.

Blessed Father, we thank Thee that when we do all in word and deed
in the name of Jesus, we have the full, childlike confidence that what
we ask in Jesus' name, we well receive. Amen.

The Spirit Glorifies Christ

"He shall glorify Me, for He shall take of Mine, and shall declare it unto you" (John 16:14).

To understand the work of the Holy Spirit and truly to experience it, one must try to grasp the relationship of the Holy Spirit to the Lord Jesus. Our Lord said definitely, before His departure, that the Spirit would come as a Comforter to the disciples. *The Spirit* would reveal Him in their hearts in *heavenly glory*. The disciples were full of the thought. They would not miss their Lord but have Him with them always. This made them pray earnestly for the Holy Spirit, for they longed to have Jesus with them always. This was the promise of the Master: the Spirit should reveal Him to them.

This is the meaning of our text—"The Spirit shall glorify Me": even as I am in the glory of heaven, He will make Me known. "He shall take of Mine"—My love, My Joy, My Peace, and all My life—"and reveal it unto you." Where there is an earnest desire for the glory of Jesus in the heart of the believer, the Holy Spirit will preserve the holy Presence of Jesus in our hearts all the day. We must not weary ourselves with striving after God's Presence. We must quietly endeavor to abide in fellowship with Christ always, to love Him and keep His commandments, and to do anything, in word and deed, in the Name of Jesus. Then shall we be able to count upon the secret but powerful working of the Spirit within us.

We see again the value of remembering and meditating on the text in Galatians 5:22. If our thoughts are always occupied with the Lord Jesus, His love, His joy, His peace—then the Holy Spirit will graciously bring these fruits to ripeness within us.

The great desire of the Holy Spirit and of the Father is that Christ may be glorified in and through us. Let it be the earnest desire and prayer of our lives too!

Blessed Father, let it be the earnest desire and prayer of our lives that Christ may be glorified in and through us. Amen.

Praying in the Spirit

*"Praying in the Spirit, keep yourselves in
the love of God" (Jude 20–21).*

Paul began the last section of the Epistle to the Ephesians with the words: "Be strong in the Lord and the power of His might." He speaks of the whole armor of God and closes by saying that this armor must be put on with prayer and supplication, "praying always in the Spirit." As the Christian needs to be strong in the Lord all the day and to wear his armor against the foe the whole day, so he needs to live always praying in the Spirit.

The Holy Spirit will not come to us, nor work within us, just at certain times when we think we need His aid. The Spirit comes to be our life-companion. He wants us wholly in His possession at all times, otherwise He cannot do His work in us. Many Christians do not understand this. They want the Spirit to help and to teach them, but do not grasp the truth that He must dwell in them continually and have full possession of all their being.

When once this truth is grasped, we shall realize that it is possible to live always "praying in the Spirit." By faith we may have the assurance that the Spirit will keep us in a prayerful attitude and make us realize God's presence, so that our prayer will be the continual exercise of fellowship with God and His great love. But as long as we regard the work of the Spirit as restricted to certain times and seasons, it will remain an unsolved mystery and a possible stone of offense.

The Apostle Jude expresses the same thought as St. Paul when he says: "Praying in the Spirit, keep yourselves in the love of God." This is what each child of God desires and what the Spirit will do within him, keeping him in the love of God, even as I may keep in the sunlight all day long.

---

*Heavenly Father, it is this blessed nearness of Thee which can enable
me to abide in Thy love at all times, praying without ceasing, in entire
dependence on Thee. Amen.*

The Temple of God

"Know ye not, that ye are the temple of God, and that
the Spirit of God dwelleth in you? The temple of God
is holy, which temple ye are" (1 Cor. 3:16–17).

From eternity it was God's desire to create man for a dwelling in which to show forth His glory. Through man's sin this plan was a seeming failure. In His people Israel God sought a means of carrying out His plan. He would have a house in the midst of His people—first a tabernacle and then a temple—in which He could dwell. This was but a shadow and image of the true indwelling of God in redeemed mankind who would be His temple to eternity. So we are built up "into a holy temple, for a habitation of God through the Spirit" (Eph. 2:22).

In the meantime, since the Holy Spirit has been poured forth, He has His dwelling in each heart that has been cleansed and renewed by the Spirit. The message comes to each believer, however feeble he may be: "Know ye not? Know ye not?—that ye are a temple of God?" How little this truth is known or experienced. And yet how true it is, "The temple of God is holy, which temple ye are."

Paul testifies of himself: "Christ liveth in me."

This is the fullness of the Gospel which he preached: the riches of the glory of the mystery, Christ in you. This is what he prayed for so earnestly for believers, that God would strengthen them through His Spirit in the inner man; that Christ might dwell in their hearts by faith. Yes, this is what our Lord Himself promised: "He that loveth Me, and keepeth My words— the Father will love him; and *We will come* unto him, and *make Our abode* with him." Is it not strange that Christians are so slow to receive and to adore this wonder of grace?

It is through the Holy Spirit that you will be sanctified into a temple of God, and you will experience that Christ, with the Father, will take up His abode in your heart. Do you desire that the Holy Spirit should teach you to pray? He will do it on this one condition, that you surrender yourself wholly to His guidance.

Heavenly Father, as I surrender myself wholly to the guidance of Thy
Holy Spirit, I desire that the Holy Spirit will teach me to pray. Amen.

The Fellowship of the Spirit

"The Communion of the Holy Spirit be with you" (2 Cor. 13:14).

In this verse we have one of the chief characteristics and activities of the Holy Spirit. It is the Holy Spirit through whom the Father and Son are one and through whom they have fellowship with each other in the Godhead. For the Holy Spirit is the true life of the Godhead.

We have fellowship with the Father and the Son through the Spirit. "Our fellowship is with the Father and the Son." "Hereby know we that He abideth in us, by the Spirit which He has given us" (1 John 3:24). Through the Spirit we know and experience the fellowship of love in the life with the Father and Son.

Through the Spirit we, as God's children, have fellowship one with another. In the child of God there should be nothing of the selfishness and self-interest that seeks its own welfare. We are members of one Body. "It is one Body and one Spirit." And through the Spirit the unity of the Body must be maintained. One reason that the Spirit does not work with greater power in the Church is that the unity of the Spirit is too little sought after. At Pentecost, after ten days spent in united prayer, the one hundred and twenty seemed melted together into one body. They received the Spirit in fellowship with one another.

We have the fellowship in the bread and wine when we meet at the Communion table; we have also fellowship one with another in the trials of other members of the Body. Always it is: "The fellowship of the Spirit be with you now and evermore. Remember the words of the text in Galatians about the fruits of the Spirit and present it to the Spirit in prayer and so make manifest our love for all God's children.

In heaven there is an eternal fellowship of love between Father and Son through the Spirit. Do we really long to be filled with the Spirit?

Heavenly Father, let us offer ourselves to Thee, beseeching Thee to grant us the unity and the fellowship of the Spirit with all members of Christ's Body. Amen.

With the Whole Heart

"Ye shall seek Me, and find Me, when ye shall search for Me with all your heart" (Jer. 29:13).

You have often heard it said that if one seeks to perform any great work, he must do it *with his whole heart and with all his powers*. In worldly affairs this is the secret of success and of victory. And above all in divine things, it is indispensable, especially in praying for the Holy Spirit.

I cannot too earnestly or too urgently repeat that the Holy Spirit desires to have full possession of you. He can be satisfied with nothing less if He is to show His full power in your life. He has the right. Why? Because He is the Almighty God.

Have you ever realized when you pray for the Holy Spirit, *that you are praying for the whole Godhead to take possession of you*? Do you really understand this? Or have your prayers had a wrong motive? Were you expecting that God would do something in your heart, but for the rest you must be free to do your own will? That would be a great mistake. The Holy Spirit must have *full* possession.

You say, that is just the trouble. You do not feel such a burning, urgent desire as you ought, and you do not see any chance of its becoming true in your life. God knows about this weakness of yours; He has ordained in His divine Providence that the Holy Spirit shall work within you all you need. What God commands and demands of us, *He will Himself work within us*. On our part there must be the earnest prayer to the Father each day and an acceptance of the Holy Spirit as our Leader and Guide.

Child of God, the Holy Spirit longs to possess you wholly. Take time to give Him your answer and cast yourself in complete dependence on the word of His promise and on His Almighty power at work within you.

Heavenly Father, I know that the Holy Spirit longs to possess me wholly. I cast myself in complete dependence on the word of Thy promise and on Thy Almighty power at work in me. Amen.

The Love of God in Our Hearts

"The love of God hath been shed abroad in our hearts through the Holy Spirit, which is given unto us" (Rom. 5:5).

The Holy Spirit is shed abroad in our hearts by God the Father. The love of God is shed abroad in our hearts through the Holy Spirit. As truly as God has poured forth the Spirit, so truly is the love of God shed forth by the Spirit.

Why do we so seldom experience this? Simply because of our unbelief. It takes time to believe in the divine mighty working of the Holy Spirit through whom our hearts are filled with the love of God. We need time for retirement from the world and its interests for our souls to bask in the light of God so that the eternal love may take possession of our hearts. If we believe in the infinite love of God and the divine power with which He takes possession of the heart, then we will receive what we ask for—the love of God shed abroad in our hearts by the Holy Spirit. God desires His children to love Him with all their hearts and all their strength. He knows how weak we are. And for that very reason He has given the Spirit who searches the deep things of God and in these depths has found the fountain of eternal love to fill our hearts with His love to His Son.

If you long for this, draw nigh to God and abide with Him in quiet worship and adoration, and you will know the love of God in Christ which passes all knowledge.

The Holy Spirit wants to have you wholly. He will teach you each day to dwell with the Father in His great love as a little child and to abide in the love of Christ each day and to show forth that love toward the brethren and toward a perishing world. He will make your heart a fountain of everlasting love, springing up to life eternal and flowing forth in blessing to all around.

Heavenly Father, I say with a heart full of thanksgiving: "The love of God is shed abroad in my heart through the Holy Spirit." Amen.

Walk in the Spirit

"Walk in the Spirit . . . If we live in the Spirit, let us also walk in the Spirit" (Gal. 5:16, 25).

The word "walk" reminds us of daily life with those around us. The Christian's walk and conversation must follow the leading of the Spirit and be by the Spirit. That will be the sign of the spiritual person, who serves God in the Spirit and does not trust in the flesh.

People speak as though the Spirit were only needed in our communion with God when we pray or for our work in the service of the Kingdom. This is a great mistake. God gives us His Spirit to be in us the whole day. We need Him most in the midst of our daily work because the world has then such power to lead us away from God. We need to pray the Father every morning for a fresh portion of His Spirit for each day. During the course of the day let us remind ourselves that the Spirit is with us and lift up our hearts to God, remembering that the Spirit abides with us always.

Paul says: "As ye have received Christ Jesus our Lord, so walk ye in Him"; and again: "Put on the Lord Jesus Christ." As I put on my cloak when I go out, so Christians must put on the Lord Jesus and show by their conduct that Christ lives in them, and that they walk by the Spirit.

"Walk in the Spirit, and ye shall not fulfill the lusts of the flesh." As long as we are not under the guidance of the Holy Spirit, the flesh will rule over us. Oh, that we knew the unspeakable value of the grace that God has given! The Spirit of His Son in our hearts will cry "Abba, Father," so that we may walk the whole day in God's presence as His beloved children. Christian, learn this lesson: the Spirit is given you to teach you that you may walk by the Spirit at all times.

We thank Thee, Heavenly Father, continually for this Divine Leader who gives us daily renewal from heaven and enables us to walk and to abide in Christ. Amen.

The Spirit Promised to the Obedient

"If ye love Me, ye will keep My commandments.
And I will pray the Father, and He shall give you
another Comforter" (John 14:15–16).

Christ would ascend to heaven and pray the Father to send the Comforter, the Holy Spirit. He would not only do this once, but it would form part of His intercessory work. He would remain "ever living to make intercession." The continual communication of the Spirit of the Father comes through the Son.

The Lord tells us here on what conditions He will send the Spirit. If we love Him and keep His commandments: "I will pray the Father." This is a word of deep meaning, a searching word—a word of greatly needed and blessed teaching. The Holy Spirit is given us to enable us to do the will of the Father. The condition is reasonable and just, that as far as we have kept the commandments through the Spirit, the Spirit will be granted to us in fuller measure. As we heartily accept this truth and yield ourselves willingly to the Spirit's guidance, we shall receive from day to day the fullness of the Spirit. Let us say to God that we accept the condition with all our heart and will strive to keep His commands and ask for power to do His commandments more perfectly.

Do not listen to the whispers of Satan or give way to unbelief and sloth. Surrender yourself unreservedly to the Lord who has said: "If ye love me, ye will keep my commands." Love will enable you to do it. The Lord Jesus does not deceive us with a vain hope in this matter. No, He gives the grace, He gives His own love in our hearts, teaching us to say: "I delight to do Thy will." Let us trust Him with childlike faith and give ourselves wholly—that is all that is necessary—to do His will. Then the beauty of the divine agreement that He makes with us will dawn upon us: "If ye keep My commandments ye shall abide in My love," and the Father will send the Holy Spirit anew each day.

Heavenly Father, I delight to do Thy will. Amen.

Spiritual or Carnal?

"And I, brethren, could not speak unto you as unto spiritual, but as unto carnal, even as unto babes in Christ" (1 Cor. 3:1).

The Apostle here uses three words describing the spiritual condition of each person. There is *the natural man* in his unconverted state—one who cannot "receive the things of the Spirit of God" (1 Cor. 2:14). There is *"the spiritual man*, who can discern spiritual things" (1 Cor. 2:13, 14). And between the two there is *the carnal man*, who is called "a babe in Christ," and who lives in jealousy and strife (1 Cor. 3:3).

It is important for us to know whether we are carnal Christians, giving way to sin and the lusts of the flesh. With the thought that things cannot be otherwise, we are apt to be content to allow much that is sinful and wrong in our lives. God calls us and the Spirit draws us to be spiritual men and women—that is to say, people who pray each day to be led and guided each day into a truly spiritual life.

When the Lord Jesus promised the Spirit to His disciples, it was in the full expectation that they *would yield themselves wholly to the leading and power of the Spirit*. And it is in the same expectation that the Spirit will be granted anew each day, if we yield ourselves unreservedly to be sanctified in all our walk and conversation. Oh, that our eyes were open to see how right and how blessed this is!

Many Christians pray for the Holy Spirit but always with a certain reservation, for they intend in many things still to do their own will. Oh, Christian, when you pray, entrust yourself fully to the guidance of the Holy Spirit for the whole day. If there is true willingness on your part, then the Holy Spirit will take full possession of you and will preserve and sanctify your life. Do not serve God half-heartedly.

Heavenly Father, I pray for the enlightenment of the Spirit, that I may see the possibility and the blessedness of a life wholly surrendered to His service. Amen.

The Spirit of Wisdom

"That the Father may give unto you a spirit of wisdom and revelation in the knowledge of Him, having the eyes of your heart enlightened" (Eph. 1:17–18).

In the Word of God we find a wonderful combination of the human and the divine. The language is human. Anyone who has a good understanding can grasp the meaning of the words and the truths contained in them. Yet this is all that we, in the power of our human understanding, can do.

There is a divine side in which the holy God expresses His deepest thoughts to us. The carnal man cannot attain to them or comprehend them, for they must be "spiritually discerned." Only through the Holy Spirit can the Christian appropriate the divine truth contained in God's Word. Paul prays earnestly that God would grant the spirit of wisdom to his readers, eyes that are enlightened through the Holy Spirit to understand what is written and to know the exceeding greatness of His power working in all who believe.

Much of our religion is ineffectual because people accept the truths of God's Word with the intellect and strive to put them into practice in their own strength, but *it is only the Holy Spirit that can really reveal divine truth to us.* A young student in a theological seminary may accept the truths of God's Word as head knowledge, while the Word has little power in his heart to lead to a life of joy and peace in the Lord Jesus. Paul teaches us that when we read God's Word or meditate on it, we should pray *"Father, grant me the spirit of wisdom and revelation."* As we do this each day, we shall find that God's Word is living and powerful and will work experience in our hearts. God's commands will be changed into promises. His commands are not grievous, and the Holy Spirit will teach us to do lovingly and joyfully all that He has commanded.

Heavenly Father, through Thy Holy Spirit, teach us to do lovingly and joyfully all that Thou hast commanded. Amen.

The Spirit of Sanctification

"Elect, through sanctification of the Spirit, unto obedience and sprinkling of the blood of Christ" (1 Peter 1:2).

In the Old Testament God was revealed as the Thrice Holy One. The Spirit is mentioned more than a hundred times, but only three times as the Holy Spirit. But in the New Testament the word Holy is ascribed to the Holy Spirit, and Christ sanctified Himself for us, that we might be holy. The great work of the Holy Spirit is to glorify Christ in us as our Sanctification.

Has this truth ever taken hold of you—at the Pentecostal prayer-meetings or in your private devotions—that the great object for which the Holy Spirit is given is to sanctify you? If you do not accept this truth, then the Holy Spirit cannot do His purifying work. If you only want the Spirit to help you to be a little better and to pray a little more, you will not get very far. But when you once understand that He has the name of Holy Spirit in order definitely to impart God's holiness and will sanctify you wholly, then you will begin to realize that the Holy Spirit dwells in your heart.

And what will be the result? You will feel that He must have you wholly. He must rule and control the whole day. My whole life and conversation must be in the Spirit. My prayer, my faith, my fellowship with the Father, and all my work in God's service must be completely under His sway. As the Spirit of holiness, He is the Spirit of my sanctification.

Dear brothers and sisters, what I have just said is deep, eternal truth. Even if we are willing to accept this truth and meditate on it daily, it will be of no avail if we do not wait upon God to grant us the Spirit of heavenly wisdom and a vision of what God has intended for us in His wonderful gift—the Spirit of sanctification. Each morning say slowly and calmly: "Abba, Father, for this new day renew within me the gift of Thy Holy Spirit."

"Abba, Father, for this new day renew within me the gift of Thy Holy Spirit." Amen.

Rivers of Living Water

*"He that believeth on Me, out of him shall flow
rivers of living water" (John 7:38).*

Our Lord, in His conversation with the Samaritan woman, said: "The water that I shall give him shall be in him a well of water springing up to eternal life." In our text the promise is even greater: rivers of living waters flowing from him, bringing life and blessing to others. John says further that this refers to the Holy Spirit who should come when Christ had been glorified, for the Holy Spirit was not yet poured out. The Spirit of God was mentioned in the Old Testament, but the Holy Spirit had not yet been given. Christ must first be offered through the eternal Spirit (on the cross) (Heb. 9:14), and raised from the dead by the spirit of holiness (Rom. 1:4), and receive from the Father power to send forth the Holy Spirit. Then only would the Christian be able to say: Now the Holy Spirit of Christ is in me.

What do we need in order to experience these two wonderful promises of the well of water and the rivers of living water? Just one thing—*the inner attachment to Christ and the unreserved surrender to fellowship with Him and the firm assurance that His Spirit will work in us what we cannot do.* In one word: He that believeth on Me. We need a faith that rejoices in the divine might and love and depends on Him day by day to grant us grace that living water may flow forth from us.

If the water from a reservoir is to flow into a house all day, one thing is necessary—the connection must be perfect, then the water passes through the pipe of its own accord. So the union between you and Christ must be uninterrupted; your faith must accept Christ and depend on Him to sustain the new life.

Let your faith rejoice that Jesus Christ gives us the Holy Spirit, and may you have the assurance that the Holy Spirit is within you as a fountain of blessing.

Heavenly Father, I thank Thee that Thy Holy Spirit is within me as a fountain of blessing, working in me what I cannot do. Amen.

Joy in God

*"For the kingdom of God is righteousness and peace
and joy in the Holy Spirit" (Rom. 14:17).*

*"Now the God of hope fill you with all joy and peace in believing,
. . . through the power of the Holy Spirit" (Rom. 15:13).*

A Christian man said to me shortly after his conversion: "I always thought that if I became religious it would be impossible for me to do my worldly business. The two things seemed so contrary. I seemed to be a man trying to dig a vineyard with a bag of sand on his shoulders. But when I found the Lord, I was so filled with joy that I could do my work cheerfully from morning till night. The bag of sand was gone; the joy of the Lord was my strength for all my work."

Truly a significant lesson. Many Christians do not understand that the joy of the Lord will keep them and fit them for their work. Even slaves, when filled with the love of Christ, could testify to the happiness that He gave.

Read the two texts at the heading of this chapter and see how the kingdom of God is pure joy and peace *through the Holy Spirit*, and how God will "fill us with all joy and peace in believing," *"through the power of the Holy Spirit."* Then try to realize that the Holy Spirit will give this joy and peace of Christ in our hearts. To many the thought of the Holy Spirit is a matter of grief and self-reproach, of desire and disappointment, of something too high and holy for them. What a foolish thought, that the great gift of the Father, meant to keep us in the joy and peace of Christ, should be a matter of self-reproach and care!

Remember Galatians 5:22 and listen attentively to the voice of the Spirit each day as He points to Jesus Christ, who offers you this wonderful fruit: "My Love, My Joy, My Peace." "On whom, though now ye see Him not, yet believing, ye rejoice greatly with joy unspeakable and full of glory" (1 Peter 1:8). Pray in all humility to the Holy Spirit, believing firmly that He will lead you into the joy of the Lord.

Heavenly Father, through Thy Holy Spirit, lead me into Thy joy. Amen.

All the Day—Every Day

"Every day will I bless Thee" (Ps. 145:2).

It is a step forward in the Christian life when one definitely decides to seek to have fellowship with God in His Word each day without fail. His perseverance will be crowned with success, if one is really in earnest. The experience may be somewhat as follows:

On waking in the morning, God will be his first thought. He must set apart a time for prayer and resolve to give God time to hear his requests and to reveal Himself to him. Then he may speak out all his desires to God and expect an answer.

Later on in the day, even if only for a few minutes, he will take time to keep up the fellowship with God. And again in the evening, a quiet period is necessary to review the day's work and with confession of sin receive the assurance of forgiveness and dedicate himself afresh to God and His service.

Such an one will gradually get an insight into what is lacking in his life and will be ready to say. Not only "every day" but "all the day." He will realize that the Holy Spirit is in him unceasingly, just as his breathing is continuous. In the inner chamber he will make it his aim to gain the assurance through faith that the Holy Spirit and the Lord Jesus and the Father Himself will grant His presence and help all through the day.

All the day! Christian, the Holy Spirit says: "Today." "Behold, now is the accepted time!" A man who had undergone a serious operation asked his doctor, "How long will I have to lie here?" And the answer came: "Only a day at a time." And that is the law of the Christian life. God gave the manna daily, the morning and evening sacrifice on the altar—by these God showed that His children should live by the day. Seek this day to trust to the leading of the Holy Spirit the whole day. You need not care for the morrow, but rest in the assurance that He who has led you today will draw still nearer tomorrow.

Blessed Father, I trust Thee for leading one day at a time. Amen.

The Spirit and the Cross

"The blood of Christ, who through the Eternal Spirit offered Himself without blemish unto God, shall cleanse your conscience to serve the living God" (Heb. 9:14).

The connection between the cross and the Spirit is inconceivably close and full of meaning. The Spirit brought Christ to the cross and enabled Him to die there. The cross was to Christ and to the Spirit the culminating point of their desire on earth. The cross gave Christ the right to pray down the Holy Spirit on earth because He had there made reconciliation for sin. The cross gave Christ the right and the power to grant us the power of the Spirit because on it He freed us from the power of sin.

To put it briefly: Christ could not have attained to the heavenly life or have poured out the Holy Spirit if He had not first died to sin, to the world, and to His own life. He died to sin that He might live to God. And that is the way the Holy Spirit brings the cross into our hearts. It is only as those who have been crucified with Christ that we can receive the full power of the Spirit. It is because we do not realize how necessary it is to die to all earthly things that the Spirit cannot gain full possession of us.

How is it so few Christians understand or experience that the fellowship of the Spirit is a fellowship of the cross? Simply because they do not feel the need of praying for the Spirit of wisdom to give them a deep, spiritual insight into the oneness of the Spirit and the Cross. They try to use their human understanding, but there is too little waiting upon God to teach them divine truths through the Spirit.

My brothers and sisters, begin today to ask God to grant you a sight of how the Spirit will take you to the cross of Christ in fellowship with Him, to die to the world and to sin, so that all things may become new, and you will actually live and walk and work and pray in the Spirit, to the glory of God.

Heavenly Father, through Thy Holy Spirit, I bow at the cross of Christ, to die to the world and to sin, so that all things are new, and I live and walk and work and pray in Thy Spirit. Amen.

The Spirit and the Blood

"There are three who bear witness, the Spirit, and the water, and the blood: and these three agree in one" (1 John 5:8).

The water is external, a sign of the renewing and purifying through regeneration used in baptism. The Spirit and the blood are two spiritual expressions, working together in regeneration: the blood for the forgiveness of sins, the Spirit for the renewal of the whole nature. All through life the Spirit and the blood must agree.

The oneness is spiritual and true. Through the blood we obtain the Spirit, as through the blood we are redeemed and purified unto it to receive the Spirit. Only through the blood can we with confidence pray for and receive the Spirit. O Christian, would you have boldness each day to trust to the guidance of the Spirit, then let your faith in the precious blood be sure and strong.

There may be some sin in your life of which you are hardly conscious but which grieves the Spirit and drives Him away. The only way to avoid this is to believe that "the blood of Jesus Christ cleanses from all sin." Your only right to approach God is through the blood of the Lamb. Come with every sin, known or unknown, and plead the blood of Christ as your only claim on the love that accepts and forgives.

Nevertheless, do not rest content with the forgiveness of sins, but accept the fullness of the Spirit to which the blood gives you access. In the Old Testament the priest went into the Holy Place with the blood, and the High Priest into the Holiest of All. With the blood Christ entered the heavenly sanctuary and poured out thence the Holy Spirit. Do not for a moment doubt that you have a right through the blood to the fullness of the Spirit.

Heavenly Father, as one who has been redeemed by the blood of Christ, I make a complete surrender of myself to Thee as Thy purchased possession, a vessel ready for Thee to use, a dwelling-place of the Holy Spirit. Amen.

The Spirit in Preacher and Hearer

"Our Gospel came unto you . . . in power, and in the Holy Spirit, and in much assurance . . . Having received the Word . . . with joy of the Holy Spirit" (1 Thess. 1:5–6). (See also 1 Cor. 2:4–5.)

Paul more than once reminds his converts that the chief characteristic of his preaching was the power—*the supernatural power of the Holy Spirit.* The Holy Spirit was so imparted to his hearers that they received the Word "with joy of the Holy Spirit."

This is one of the most important lessons in the spiritual life. We, as hearers, are so accustomed to listen attentively to the sermon to see what it has to teach us, that we are apt to forget that the blessing of our church-going depends on two things. First, the prayer for the preacher that he may speak "in the demonstration of the Spirit and of power," and then the prayer for the congregation and for ourselves, that we may receive the Word, not from man, but as it is in truth, God's Word, "which effectually worketh in you that believe" (1 Thess. 2:13.) How often there is no manifestation of the Spirit when both the speaking and the hearing are mainly the work of human understanding or feeling. So often there is no power that raises the soul with spiritual insight into the life of faith that God has provided for His children.

How earnestly we should pray that God may reveal to us all, both minister and people, "*the Spirit of wisdom and revelation*," that we may discover what the place really is that the Holy Spirit should have in our lives, and what the perfect work is that He will do within us! God help us to learn this prayer! Then we shall understand what Christ meant when He said: "*Go not, preach not*—but wait for the promise of the Father, and ye shall receive the power of the Spirit, and ye shall be my witnesses unto the uttermost part of the earth" (Acts 1:4, 8).

Heavenly Father, we pray earnestly that Thou wilt teach us to pray down the power of the Holy Spirit upon ministers and missionaries and their congregations, that the preaching may be in the manifestation of the Spirit and of power for the conversion and sanctification of souls. Amen.

The Full Gospel

"Then Peter said: Repent, . . . for the remission of sins, and ye shall receive the gift of the Holy Spirit" (Acts 2:38).

When John the Baptist preached, "Repent, for the kingdom of heaven is at hand," he also said: "He that cometh after me shall baptize you with the Holy Spirit and with fire." When Christ preached the Gospel of the Kingdom, He said: "There are some standing here, who shall not see death till the kingdom of God has come in power." This is what happened at the outpouring of the Holy Spirit. Peter preached on the Day of Pentecost the full Gospel of repentance and forgiveness of sins *and the gift of the Holy Spirit*. This is indispensable in preaching the Gospel, for then only is it possible for a Christian to live in the will of God and to please Him in all things. The kingdom of God is righteousness (in Christ), and joy (in God) through the Holy Spirit. The continuous joy of which Christ speaks, "My joy," can only be obtained through the power of the Holy Spirit.

How often only half the Gospel is preached—conversion and forgiveness of sins, and souls are led no further into the truth   the knowledge and appropriation of the life of the Spirit within us is not mentioned. No wonder that so many Christians fail to understand that they must depend each day on the Spirit for the joy which will be their strength.

Dear Christian, accept this truth for yourself as well as for those among whom you labor—that the daily enjoyment of the leading of God's Spirit is indispensable for a joyous life of faith. If you feel that there has been a lack in your spiritual life, then begin at once to pray the Father to grant you the gift of the Holy Spirit anew each day. Then trust yourself to His leading and guidance all the day. Let the remembrance of the text (Gal. 5:22) give you courage for all that the Holy Spirit will do for you. Regard your heart constantly as a garden of the Lord in which the Holy Spirit will bear abundant fruit to the glory of God.

Heavenly Father, grant me the gift of the Holy Spirit anew each day. Amen.

The Ministry of the Spirit

"Ye are an epistle of Christ, ministered by us,
written with the Spirit of the living God, in
fleshly tables of the heart" (2 Cor. 3:3).

The Corinthians' Church was a "letter of recommendation" for Paul, showing how much he had done for them. Although he claimed nothing for himself, God had enabled him as a "minister of the Spirit," to write in their hearts "with the Spirit of the living God." He himself declared: "Not that we are sufficient of ourselves to think anything as of ourselves: but our sufficiency is from God; who also made us sufficient as ministers of a new covenant."

What a wonderful presentation of the work of a minister for his people! A preacher prepared to be a minister of the Spirit, with power to write in the hearts of his people the name and the love of Christ. No wonder that when (vv. 7–11), speaking of the glory that was upon the face of Moses when he communed with God, Paul says, "The ministration of the Spirit is more glorious by reason of the glory that excelleth." He then (v. 18) speaks of how "we all, with open face reflecting as in a mirror the glory of the Lord, are transformed into the same image from glory to glory, even as from the Lord, the Spirit."

Oh, that God would restore the ministry of the Gospel to its original power! Oh, that all ministers and church-members would unite in the prayer that God, by the mighty working of His Spirit, would give the ministry of the Spirit its right place and teach the people to believe that when Christ is preached to them, they are beholding as in a glass the glory of the Lord and may be changed into the same image by the Spirit of the Lord!

Heavenly Father, we are called to persevere in the prayer that the Holy Spirit may again have His rightful place in the ministry of the Word, so that the exceeding and abundant glory of this ministry may be manifested. Amen.

The Spirit from Heaven

"Them that preached the gospel unto you by the
Holy Spirit sent down from heaven" (1 Peter 1:12).

Christ has taught us to think of God as our own Father in heaven who is ready to bestow His blessings on His children on earth. Our Lord Himself was taken up into the glory of heaven, and we are told that we are seated with Him in the heavenly places in Christ. The Holy Spirit comes to us from heaven to pour into our hearts all the light and the love and the joy and the power of heaven.

Those who are truly filled with the Spirit have a heavenly life in themselves. Their walk and conversation are in heaven. They are in daily fellowship with the Father and with the Son. They seek the things that are above, for their life is hid with Christ in God. Their chief characteristic is heavenly-mindedness. They carry about with them the marks of their eternal, heavenly destiny.

How can one cultivate this heavenly disposition? By allowing the Holy Spirit, sent from heaven, to do His heavenly work in our hearts, and to bring to ripeness in our souls the fruits of the Spirit which grow in the Paradise of God. The Spirit will raise our hearts daily to fellowship with God in heaven and will teach us to dwell in the heavenlies with Him. The Spirit makes the glorified Christ in heaven present in our hearts and teaches us to dwell in His abiding presence.

O Christian, take time each day to receive from the Father the continual guidance of the Holy Spirit. Let Him overcome the world for you and strengthen you as a child of heaven to walk daily with your God and with the Lord Jesus. Do not be unbelieving. The Holy Spirit will do His part, if you in faith surrender yourself to His control. You will learn to speak to others with such heavenly joy that you will draw them, too, to give themselves to the leading of the Spirit and to walk in the heavenly joy of Christ's love.

Heavenly Father, may Thy Holy Spirit overcome the world for me and strengthen me as a child of heaven to walk daily with Thee and with the Lord Jesus. Amen.

The Spirit and Prayer

*"Verily, verily, I say unto you, If ye shall ask anything of
the Father, in My Name, He will give it you" (John 16:23).*

In our Lord's farewell discourse (John 13:17) He presented the life in
the dispensation of the Spirit in all its power and attractiveness. One of
the most glorious results of the day when the Holy Spirit should come
would be: the *new power that man should have* to pray down from heav-
en the power of God to bless the world. Seven times we have the promise
repeated: *"Whatsoever ye shall desire* in My Name, *that will I do* (John
14:13–14; 15:7, 16; 16:23–24, 26). Read these passages over, that you may
come to understand fully how urgently and earnestly our Lord repeated
the promise.

In the power of the perfect salvation that Christ accomplished, in the
power of His glory with the Father, in the power of the outpouring of the
third Person of the Godhead—the Holy Spirit—to dwell in the hearts of
His servants, they would have the unspeakable freedom to ask what they
desired of the fullness of the will of God, and it should be done. Everything was included in these few words: *"What ye desire, that will I do."*

During the ten days before Pentecost, the disciples put this to the proof.
In response to their continuous united prayer, the heavens were opened,
and the Spirit of God descended to earth to dwell in their hearts, filling
them with His life-power. They received the power of the Spirit that they
might impart it to thousands. That power is still *the pledge for all time of
what God will do*. If God's children will agree with one accord to wait for
the promise of the Father each day, there is no limit to what God will do
for them.

O Christian, remember that you are living in the dispensation of the Spirit. That means that the Holy Spirit will dwell in you with heavenly power,
enabling you to testify for Him.

---

*Heavenly Father, let us unite with God's children to ask in prayer
greater and more wonderful things than the heart has conceived. Amen.*

With One Accord in Prayer

*"These all with one accord continued
steadfastly in prayer" (Acts 1:14).*

*"And when the Day of Pentecost was now come, . . . they
were all filled with the Holy Spirit" (Acts 2:1, 4).*

Our Lord gave the command to His disciples: "Go ye into all the world
and preach the Gospel to every creature," and He added the promise: "Lo,
I am with you always." We may be fully assured that this command and
this promise were not meant alone for the disciples, *but also for us, their
followers.*

Just before His Ascension, Christ gave His very last command, also with
a promise attached to it. The command was: "Go not, preach not—*wait*
for the promise of the Father." And the promise was: "Ye shall receive power after that the Holy Spirit is come upon you; and ye shall be witnesses
to Me, unto the uttermost parts of the earth." *This very last command and
promise are also meant for us.* As irrevocable as the command: "*Preach
the Gospel,*" with its accompanying promise is this last command of all,
to wait for the promise of the Father—"Ye shall receive the power of the
Holy Spirit."

For ten days the disciples pled that promise with one accord, and their
prayer was wonderfully answered. Alas, that the church of our day has tried
to carry out the first command, "Preach the Gospel," but has too often forgotten the second, "Wait for the promise of the Father." The call comes to
each believer to *pray daily with one accord* for this great gift of the Holy
Spirit. Many Christians who pray for themselves and their own work forget to pray for the Church of Christ. The power of the first disciples lay in
the fact that they *as One Body* were prepared to forget themselves and to
pray for the Holy Spirit over all mankind.

O Christian, *daily prayer in fellowship with God's children is indispensable*, and it is a sacred duty if the Spirit is again to come in power. Let not
your knowledge of the working of God's Holy Spirit be limited to yourself alone nor even to your Church, but in a world-embracing love of Christ
for all God's children and His kingdom over the whole world, pray for power.

---

*Heavenly Father, give us power to pray for all Thy children and Thy
Kingdom over the whole world. Amen.*

God's Plan of Salvation

"When Christ, who is our life, shall be manifested, then shall ye also with Him be manifested in glory" (Col. 3:4).

After Adam had sinned and brought death upon himself and his descendants, God gave the promise that a man born of woman should conquer the power of Satan and Sin. This Man, who was the Son of God, the Bible calls the Second Adam—"Adam, who is the figure of Him that was to come" (Rom. 5:14). The second Adam was in every respect to be like the first.

Adam not only brought the curse of sin and death upon his descendants, but actually bequeathed to them a life which was the cause of their being wholly dominated by evil. In this way, the old sinful nature of Adam survived in his descendants. The old nature lived in them and held sway. Likewise Christ by His death not only delivered us from the power of sin and death, but He Himself lives in each of His redeemed ones and is their life.

We are too apt to think of Christ as in Heaven and from there living for and through us; but the last night He was on earth He taught that as His Father lived and worked in Him here on earth, even so would He dwell in us and work in us. The full Gospel is contained in these words: "Christ is our life." "Christ lives in me." "Know ye not that Jesus Christ is in you?"

Many Christians forget this. They believe Christ died on the cross for them and lives in Heaven for them, but hardly that Christ is in them. The powerlessness of the Church is mainly due to this. *We do not realize that the Almighty Christ dwells in us.* We must know and experience and testify to this great truth if there is to be a real and lasting revival in the Church of Christ. Then we shall know what it means to give ourselves wholly to Christ, always to abide in fellowship with Him, that His work may be accomplished through us. "Christ liveth in me, To me to live is Christ."

Heavenly Father, my daily prayer is to always remember, "Christ liveth in me, to me to live is Christ." Amen.

The Twofold Life

"I came that they may have life, and may
have it abundantly" (John 10:10).

Everyone can understand the difference between life that is weak and sickly and life that has abundant vitality. Thus St. Paul speaks of the Christian life of the Corinthians as not spiritual but carnal, as of young children in Christ incapable of assimilating strong meat or of understanding the deeper truths of the Gospel (see 1 Cor. 3 and Heb. 5). There are some, the majority of Christians, who never advance beyond first principles. They are dull of hearing and remain carnal Christians. There are others again, a minority, who indeed show forth the abundant riches of grace. All through the history of the Church we find this difference. In our day, too, the number is small of those who seek to live wholly for God and being spiritually minded have large thoughts of the abundant life there is in Christ. They witness to the glory of Christ "full of grace and truth." "For of His fullness we all received, and grace for grace" (John 1:16).

The preacher's aim should be so to declare the fullness of God's grace in Jesus Christ as to make Christians ashamed of the poverty of their spiritual life and to encourage them to believe that "life abundant" in the fullness of the Spirit is for them.

Dear Reader, ask yourself if you are living such an abundant life as Jesus came to bestow? Is it manifest in your love to the Savior and in the abundant fruit you bear to the glory of God in soul-winning? If not, pray God to strengthen your faith that He is able to make all grace abound toward you that you always having all sufficiency may abound in every good work. Let Jesus be precious to you, and daily communion with Him indispensable. He will teach you by His Holy Spirit to honor Him by an abundant life.

Blessed Father, strengthen my faith that I will abound in every good
work. Amen.

Life Abundant

"Where sin abounded, grace did abound more exceedingly:
that, as sin reigned in death, even so might grace reign
through Jesus Christ our Lord" (Rom. 5:20–21).

How little this truth is grasped or understood. That sin abounds we know full well. But do we believe that "grace abounds more exceedingly" and enables us to reign over sin? Yet it is absolutely necessary that we grasp this truth if we would have life abundant in Christ. Read 2 Corinthians 9:8 and observe the words "all" and "every," denoting abundance. "God is able to make *all grace* abound unto you; that ye, having *always* (without exception) *all* sufficiency in *every* thing (every possible need), may abound unto every good work." Dear Reader, say to yourself: "Is this abundant all-abounding life for me? Verily, if God is faithful it is possible for me! O God, write this truth upon my heart!"

Now take St. Paul's prayer in Col. 1:9–11, so that you may be able to pray it first for yourself and then for others—"We do not cease to pray and make request for you, that ye may be filled with the knowledge of His will in *all* spiritual wisdom and understanding, to walk worthily of the Lord unto *all* pleasing, bearing fruit in *every* good work, strengthened with *all* power, according to the might of His glory, unto *all* patience and long-suffering with joy" (cf. 1 John 3:22). These words of the Holy Spirit are almost beyond our grasp. Let us continually take them to God that He Himself through His Holy Spirit may make them to live in our hearts. By then, we shall attain to a firm and joyous faith. With such a God, with such abounding grace—much more abundant than the easily besetting sin—with such a Lord Jesus to give grace and cause grace to reign—thank God, I may believe that life abundant is for me!

Heavenly Father, I do believe that life abundant is for me. Amen.

"Christ Liveth in Me"

*"I have been crucified with Christ; yet I live: and yet
no longer I, but Christ liveth in me" (Gal. 2:20).*

In these words St. Paul expresses three great thoughts:

Firstly, "I am crucified with Christ." When Christ died on the cross, He identified all God's people with Himself in that death. As we all died in Adam and have inherited Adam's sinful nature, so we all have been crucified with Christ, and the power of His death works in us daily, that having died to sin in Christ we may live unto God. Our union with the crucified Christ is vital and complete. The power of His death and of His life is active in us.

St. Paul's second thought is, "I live, and yet no longer I." Having actually participated in the death of Christ he could say: "No longer do I live." My life has been yielded to death upon the Cross of Christ. By faith I see my life under sentence of death canceled. It is still mine, in my flesh wherein no good thing dwells, but I am free in Christ, so that I no longer serve sin as long as I abide in Christ.

His third thought, "Christ liveth in me," is the true secret of a Christlike life. Christ was not only crucified for me. He does not live only in heaven to intercede for me. No! *Christ liveth in me.* He Himself said that even as His Father dwelt and worked in Him, even so He dwells and works in us. He is truly the life in us by which we live.

Oh, Christian, I beseech you, take time to meditate and adore. Allow the Holy Spirit to make these words live in your heart. This is the work of the Holy Spirit, to manifest Christ in you, to glorify Him in you with the heavenly glory which fills all things. Do not imagine that Christ's life can be manifested in us unless we die to the world and to self. Christ had to die. You are crucified with Christ and must experience the crucified life. The rest will follow—"I live no longer, Christ lives in me."

"Thanks be to God for His unspeakable Gift!" Amen.

The Life of Faith

*"That life which I now live in the flesh I live in
faith, the faith which is in the Son of God, who
loved me, and gave Himself for me" (Gal. 2:20).*

These words are St. Paul's reply to the objection: "If you say, 'Christ lives in me'; where does your will come in?" If Christ does actually live in you, and holds Himself responsible for your life, what remains for you to do?

St. Paul's words contain the secret of the true life of faith. Elsewhere he prays for believers, "that Christ may dwell in your hearts by faith." Here we see the great work that faith has to accomplish in us and for us moment by moment, in order to allow the living Lord to work His will in us. Christ will accomplish the work in our hearts.

Because of His divinity, it is natural for the Lord Jesus to fill all things, to be all in all, and especially in the hearts of His children.

Christ's own words to His disciples best explain this. Even as the Father dwelt in Him and worked His work in Him, so our Lord dwells in us and works His work in us. The Son expressed the Father. We are to express Christ. The Father worked in the Son, and the Son worked out what the Father had wrought in Him. Christ works in us and enables us to carry on His work. This is His gift to us.

The only attitude that becomes us is one of trust, strengthening our faith in the assurance that "He loved me and gave Himself for me." He and I are eternally and inseparably one. "He lives in me."

This is almost too great to grasp or to believe, and yet it is God's truth. The child of God needs time for meditation and adoration, so that the Spirit of God may reveal to Him how completely He will fill our being, accomplishing the work in us. Oh, the depth of the riches of the wisdom and the knowledge of God! How unsearchable are His judgments and His Ways past finding out! Oh, the depth of the love of God in Christ!

Heavenly Father: We can hardly grasp the truth that Christ will accomplish His work in our hearts as we trust Him by faith. We freely give our hearts to Christ to live in us moment by moment. Amen.

The Ever-Abiding Spirit

*"The Father shall give you another Comforter, that He
may be with you forever . . . He abideth with you,
and shall be in you" (John 14:16–17).*

We usually think of the abiding Presence of the Lord as promised to
us. Christ distinctly says, "Abide in Me and I in you," "Abide ye in My
love" (John 15). In the above text He speaks of "abiding" as evidence of
the indwelling and work of the Holy Spirit. Read the text over again, and
you will see that Christ abiding in us and our abiding in Him—"ye in Me,
and I in you"—is altogether dependent upon the indwelling of the Holy
Spirit. Therefore it is of the greatest importance that we rightly grasp the
fact of the ever-abiding, indwelling of the Holy Spirit.

This can only be done each day as we appear in God's Presence by renewing and confessing our faith in the ever-abiding, indwelling of the Spirit.
It was as the Comforter that He was to compensate the disciples for the
absence of Christ's physical Presence, and with this heavenly comfort He
comforts us each hour. It is through Him we have Christ in our hearts, a
living mighty force, animating and enlightening us and filling our lives.
This can be ours if we come into touch with God in Christ each day, thus
receiving fresh power to influence and bless others.

Oh, my brothers and sisters! Begin the day with the Triune God. Take
time to worship God in Christ. Take time to yield yourself to the Holy Spirit
and to count upon Him to accomplish a great work in you by making Christ
ever present in you.

---

*Heavenly Father, I worship Thee, I yield myself to Thy Holy Spirit, I
know that Christ lives in me. Amen.*

Christ and the Spirit

"He that believeth on Me, out of his belly shall flow rivers of living water. This spake He of the Spirit, which they that believed on Him were to receive" (John 7:38–39).

Each Person of the blessed Trinity gives honor to the Other. The Father seeks the honor of the Son, and the Son seeks the honor of the Spirit, and the Spirit honors the Son. So in our text we hear Christ calling us to *believe in Him*, confident that the Holy Spirit will work powerfully in us according to the measure of our faith in Christ. On the other hand Christ says, "The Spirit shall not speak from Himself; but what things soever He shall hear, these shall He speak. He shall glorify Me: for He shall take of Mine, and shall declare it unto you" (John 16:13–14).

Here we learn the important lesson that we must not expect the Holy Spirit always to give us tokens of His Presence. He will ever seek to fix our attention upon Christ. The surest way to be filled with the Spirit is wholeheartedly to occupy ourselves by faith with Christ. We may rely upon the Holy Spirit to enable us to do this.

Begin every morning in God's Presence, and there commit yourself to Christ to accomplish His work in you. Thank the Father for the gift of the Holy Spirit, who enables you to abide in the love and the obedience of the Lord Jesus. Believe firmly that the Triune God works in your heart and has His hidden heaven there, which will be revealed to you as your heart is wholly given to His Son and Spirit. "Through Christ we have access to the Father through the Spirit."

Learn this important lesson. The stronger your faith in Christ the more freely will the Spirit flow from you. The more you believe in the ever-abiding Spirit, the more surely you will know that Christ dwells and works within.

Heavenly Father, strengthen my faith in Christ that Thy Holy Spirit will flow ever more freely from me. Amen.

The Spirit and Christ

"He shall glorify Me; for He shall take of Mine, and
shall declare it unto you" (John 16:14).

We have seen that Christ spoke of the gift of the Spirit as the fruit of faith in Christ. The Spirit would flow as a river from those who believed in Christ. Today we have the other side of the truth; the Spirit flows from Christ; the Spirit reveals Christ and imparts Him. This is a lesson of deep importance. Do you desire the Spirit? Have faith in Christ who bestows His Spirit. Do you desire Christ? Rely upon the Spirit to reveal Christ to you. The Spirit is sent from Christ glorified in heaven to impart Christ glorified to us upon earth, that Christ may be glorified in our hearts.

We have seen that the fullness of the Godhead dwelt in Christ in order that Christ as the life of God might dwell in us. All the life and love of God which the Spirit imparts to us is in Christ. Our whole life consists in Union with Christ. As the branch is in the vine, so are we in Christ and He in us. Our first requirement each new day is to know that Christ lives in us and that the Holy Spirit will make this an abiding reality. Count upon the quiet unseen working of the Holy Spirit in your heart.

Oh, Christian, this truth so deep and so divine is almost beyond our finite grasp. The Holy Spirit, who is God, will reveal it to us. Cling in childlike trust to Christ, confident that the Holy Spirit is working silently within you so that Christ may dwell in your heart by faith. Make it a matter of prayer every day that "the Father may grant you to be strengthened with might by His Spirit in the inner man, that Christ may dwell in your heart by faith." Fix your heart upon Christ on the Cross, upon Christ on the throne, in childlike trust that while you do so Christ will be revealed in your heart by the Holy Spirit, and you may confidently say: "Christ liveth in me—Christ is my life!"

Heavenly Father, as I fix my heart ypon Christ on the cross, upon
Christ on the throne, I pray: "Christ liveth in me—Christ is my life!"
Amen.

Carnal or Spiritual?

"And I, brethren, could not speak unto you as unto Spiritual,
but as unto carnal, as unto babes in Christ" (1 Cor. 3:1).

The difference St. Paul makes between the two kinds of Christians is of great importance. Man's natural life is altogether carnal. The Christian at his new birth receives the Holy Spirit, and immediately there begins a struggle between flesh and spirit. So long as the Christian allows the Spirit to conquer and is led by the Spirit, the power of the Spirit over him increases, and he becomes a spiritual man. The flesh is still there and in the flesh is no good thing, but he learns that it means that his flesh is crucified as something that deserves the accursed death, and he becomes the spiritual man of whom it may be said: "The spiritual man discerneth all things."

When, on the other hand, the Christian is ignorant about the Spirit or if informed, disobedient, then the flesh obtains the mastery, and the Christian remains weak; and as there is no spiritual growth, he remains a babe. He may try in his own strength to do better, and what was begun in the Spirit is continued in the flesh—a carnal attempt to become holy (cf. Gal. 3:3). By degrees the flesh triumphs, so that he has no power to resist the works of the flesh or the Spirit of the World.

This is the sad condition of the Church, that the majority of her members remain carnal. They constantly fall under the power of the flesh and, as a result, are overcome by envy and anger and uncharitableness. Such Christians have no insight into spiritual truth. If their life in Christ, daily fellowship with Him, and what God promises to do for His children is mentioned, they can hardly understand what is meant.

Heavenly Father, we earnestly pray that Thou wilt reveal to us what is carnal and what spiritual and enable us to yield ourselves completely to the guidance of Thy Spirit. Amen.

Go on to Perfection

"But solid food is for full-grown men. . . . Wherefore let us
cease to speak of the first principles of Christ, and press
on unto perfection" (Heb. 6:1).

In the Epistle from which this text is taken we read that the Hebrews
had long been Christians and now ought to be teaching others, but instead
they were still as babes needing to be fed on milk (Heb. 5:12–14). The
apostle seeks to rouse them "to cease to speak of the first principles of
Christ, not laying again a foundation of repentance." They were to go on
to perfection, to the status of full-grown adults and be prepared for deeper
truths which would be taught to them regarding Christ as the High Priest.
"But He, because He abideth forever, hath His priesthood unchangeable.
Wherefore He is able to save to the uttermost them that draw near unto
God through Him, seeing He ever liveth to make intercession for them"
(7:24–25). The truth of this ever-abiding unchangeable priesthood and complete salvation is the solid food of the believer who desires perfection. In
chapter 9 we are told of Christ appearing before the face of God for us
and later that we might enter into the holy place to live in communion with
God (10:19–20).

It is when he ceases to speak of the first principles of Christ, not laying
again a foundation of repentance, that the Christian will grow and be
strengthened in grace. He will then actually live in full fellowship with
Christ.

Oh, Christian, if hitherto you have been content to know that you have
repented and believe in God and so are sure of salvation, I beseech you,
do remember this is only the beginning of eternal life. Listen to the call to
press on to perfection. This is what God desires and what the Son Himself
will do for you. Learn to yield yourself fully to Christ and to find daily in
Him the hidden life, so that you may grow in grace and God use you as a
soul-winner. Nothing less than this conformity to Jesus Christ should satisfy you—a life wholly dedicated to God and to His dear Son.

Heavenly Father, may nothing less than conformity to Jesus Christ ever
satisfy me. Amen.

The Building and Its Foundation

"Let us press on to perfection, not laying again the foundation of repentance from dead works, and of faith toward God" (Heb. 6:1).

The parable of the difference between the foundations and the effect on the houses built on them will teach us important lessons about the two kinds of life. St. Paul lays the foundation of the house of God in the doctrine of Justification by faith in Jesus Christ. That is the one sure immovable ground upon which lost sinners find their eternal salvation (Rom. 5:2).

What is the house built upon this foundation? Read Romans 5:12–18. There the apostle points out that Justification and peace with God are not everything, they are only the beginning. Then he goes on to show that as in Adam we died, so in the second Adam, Christ, we receive the abundance of grace whereby we may live through Jesus Christ. That is the life built on the foundation. He points out in chapter 6 how in Christ we have died unto sin; we are baptized into His death; and as we are united to Him by the likeness of His death, we shall be united by the likeness of His resurrection. If we have died with Christ, we may be sure we really are dead to sin but alive unto God in Jesus our Lord.

It is union with the crucified and risen Christ that sets us free from the power of sin, and through the Spirit, Christ Jesus releases us wholly from the power of sin. This life in Christ is the edifice that must be built upon the foundation of Justification.

How little is Romans 6 grasped or appropriated. We are ever ready to lay the foundation and be content with that. Nay, Child of God, our experience must be deeper. We must experience that Christ is our life, that we are crucified with Him and in Him and in Him are dead and risen again. That only will enable us to live a holy, godly life in the joy of the Holy Spirit.

Heavenly Father, Christ is my life, I am crucified with Him and in Him, and in Him I am dead and risen again. Amen.

The Reformation

*"For other foundation can no man lay, than that which
is laid, which is Jesus Christ; but let each man take
heed how he buildeth thereon" (1 Cor. 3:10–11).*

"Not laying again the foundation"—these words to the Hebrews were certainly not applicable to the Reformation. In the course of centuries the Church of Rome in building had left the true foundation. Instead of justification by faith in Jesus Christ being the foundation of Christian life, the Church itself claimed power to forgive sin. Forgiveness could be obtained only through a priest; indeed it might be bought from a priest for money. The great work of Luther and Calvin was to lay anew the foundation of Jesus Christ, to the comfort of thousands of anxious souls. We can never thank God enough for the Reformation when Jesus was proclaimed anew our righteousness—our peace with God.

That great work of Reformation was not accomplished in a day or a year. It took fifty years to establish the Reformation and even after that time there were many priests whose conversion did not include the power of a holy life. Calvin himself said the Reformation was more in doctrine than in the lives of the people, and he felt deeply the need of the people to be taught and trained in the paths of righteousness. It was no wonder that so long as the foundation had to be relaid in the full truth of conversion and faith, there was delay in the building itself on the true foundation—a life of sanctification.

The Reformation is sometimes thought of as a return to Pentecost, but it was by no means that. Instead of brotherly love, separation from the world, and earnestness in preaching Christ by all who loved Him, there was much controversy among the Reformers. They trusted too much to the patronage of statesmen where these were kindly disposed toward them, and preaching was the work of ordained priests only, in contrast to the Pentecostal witnessing for Christ by all those who were constrained by His love.

Heavenly Father, may our lives reflect the return to Pentecost, showing brotherly love, separation from the world, and earnestness in preaching Christ because we love Him. Amen.

The Walk in Christ

*"As therefore ye received Christ Jesus the Lord, so walk in Him,
rooted and builded up in Him, and stablished in your faith, even as
ye were taught, abounding in thanksgiving" (Col. 2:6–7).*

Here again we have the two kinds of life. The first is described in the words, "Ye have received Christ Jesus." That includes conversion, forgiveness of sin through the blood of Jesus Christ, and acceptance as a child of God. Then comes the second, the walk in Christ, "rooted in Him," as a tree that must each moment receive its life from the earth in order to bear fruit. "Builded up in Him," who is the only foundation. "Stablished in your faith and abounding in it," by which each day the Christian by his walk and conversation proves that he abides and lives in Christ. As the roots of a tree receive life uninterruptedly from the soil, so the Christian receives his life and power moment by moment from abiding in Christ.

In the confessions of Faith drawn up by the Reformers, prominence is given to conversion, acceptance of Christ. "Justification" and "justified" are words in frequent use. But the word "sanctification" is rarely found. Emphasis is laid on the doctrine of forgiveness of sin, of faith in Christ as our righteousness before God, but we find little about Christ living in us and our life being rooted in Him. The Heidelberg Catechism gives the explanation of the Ten Commandments, but Christ's commands in Matthew 5 and John 13–16 are hardly mentioned.

Let us thank God for the Reformation as a time when the foundation truth of a crucified Savior was laid, but at the same time let us go on to perfection, to a daily uninterrupted walk in Christ wherein we may abound in faith, experiencing the abundance of grace from the fullness there is in Christ for us to enjoy daily. The earliest description of true godliness is in the words: "Enoch walked with God." So Christians must learn to walk in Christ daily, established in the faith and abounding in it.

Heavenly Father, may my life show that I walk with Thee. Amen.

"The Mediator of a New Covenant"

"Ye are come to Jesus the Mediator of a new covenant, and to the blood of sprinkling" (Heb. 12:24).

The Mediator is responsible that both sides shall faithfully fulfill the obligations as set forth in the Covenant. Jesus is our surety that God will fulfill His promise. He is surety to God for us that we on our part shall faithfully perform what God requires of us, and He will enable us to keep the Covenant.

It was as Mediator, in the night of the Last Supper, that He gave His disciples the great promise of a New Covenant, the gift of the Holy Spirit as prophesied by Ezekiel.

He also undertook to fulfill the promise, "I will cause you to walk in My statutes, and ye shall keep My judgments, and do them." It was in the fulfillment of this promise that He spoke so definitely to His disciples of the keeping of His commandments being the way by which God's designs would be accomplished. "If ye love Me, ye will keep My commandments, and I will pray the Father *and He shall give you another Comforter.*" "He that hath My commandments, and keepeth them, he it is that loveth Me, and he that loveth Me shall be loved of My Father, *and I will manifest myself unto Him.*" "If a man love me he will keep My word, and My Father will love him *and we will come unto him and make our abode with him.*" "If My words abide in you, ask whatsoever ye will, and it shall be done." "If ye keep My commandments, ye shall abide in My love." "Ye are My friends, if ye do the things which I command you."

Would the Lord definitely have said that all these blessings depend upon the keeping of His commandments, if it were impossible for His disciples to keep them? Assuredly not. He had given them a pledge that the Holy Spirit would enable them. Meditate on this until you have the assurance that Christ expects His disciples for love of Him, through the power of the Holy Spirit, to do all that He asks; and through His abiding in their hearts they will unceasingly keep His commands.

Heavenly Father, we thank Thee that Thy Holy Spirit enables us to keep Thy commandments. Amen.

Better Promises

*"He is the Mediator of a better Covenant, which hath
been enacted upon better promises" (Heb. 8:6).*

*"Ye are come to Jesus the Mediator of a New Covenant,
and to the blood of sprinkling" (Heb. 12:24).*

We have here some of the better promises of the New Covenant. Jeremiah 31:33: "This is the covenant: I will put My law in their inward parts, and in their hearts will I write it." Jeremiah 32:40: "I will put My fear in their hearts, and they will not depart from Me." Ezekiel 36:25, 27: "From all your filthiness will I cleanse you, and I will give you a new heart, and I will put My Spirit within you and cause you to walk in My statutes, and ye shall keep My judgments to do them." Ezekiel 36:36: *"I the Lord have spoken it, and I will do it.* For this moreover will I be inquired of by the house of Israel to do it for them."

Could there be better or more definite promises than these, that God Himself would put His fear into the hearts of His people *so absolutely that they would not depart from Him, and that He would cause them* to keep His judgments and do them?

This is the New Covenant of which Jesus is Mediator. Through the Holy Spirit He dwells in us and will keep us from sin, so that we shall have the desire and the power to do God's will in all things. Think of Zacharias's inspired words as he prophesied the deliverance Christ would bring. Luke 1:74: "That we being delivered out of the hands of our enemies should serve Him without fear in holiness and righteousness before Him all our days." These are the words of God and show what He will do for those who inquire of Him. The promises are sure. The Mediator gave first His blood and then His Spirit. He sees to it that the better promises are fulfilled to those who wholeheartedly and confidently desire and claim them from Him. Alas, how seldom is such a life either preached or experienced!

---

*Heavenly Father, we claim Thy indwelling Spirit to keep us from sin
and to give us the desire and the power to do Thy will. Amen.*

Fellowship with God

"That which we have seen and heard declare we unto you, that ye also may have fellowship with us: yea, and our fellowship is with the Father, and with His Son Jesus Christ" (1 John 1:3).

Fellowship with God is the unique blessing of the Gospel. Christ died for us "that He might bring us to God," that the prodigal son might return to the father's house and to a life in his father's love. By His blood He dedicated for us a new and living way into the holy place where we may walk in the light of God. The promise is, "They shall walk, O Lord, in the light of Thy countenance. In Thy name shall they rejoice all the day." Our walk with God may be as natural and as joyful as a walk in the sunshine. A life of unbroken fellowship with God—this is the Gospel.

Fellowship with God is the preacher's theme. If preachers are content to speak only of conversion, forgiveness of sin, and safety after death, they will fail grievously in their work. Christians must be educated to practice the Presence of God, to have fellowship with God, thereby ensuring holy living. This was the Apostle John's message: Fellowship with the Father and with His Son Jesus Christ.

Fellowship with God is the preacher's only source of power. If fellowship with God is the blessing of the Gospel and the burden of the minister's preaching, then it follows the preacher must show in his own life the possibility and blessing of such a walk with God. Experiencing it himself, he is able to tell others of it as most blessed and full of joy. A life of close fellowship with the Father and with the Son lived by the preacher, gives him the right to win others to the same joyous fellowship. What God can do for me He can do for you.

Heavenly Father, may fellowship with Thee and with Thy Son Jesus Christ be our daily life, first in the quiet hour, then in our daily duties, and finally in winning souls for Christ that they too may share this full salvation. Amen.

The Fullness of Christ

*"And the Word became flesh and dwelt among us (and we
beheld His glory, glory as of the only begotten from the
Father), full of grace and truth. For of His fullness we
all received, and grace for grace" (John 1:14, 16).*

Read these words again and again until you come under the impression
of the supreme fullness of Christ. Let the Holy Spirit teach you to worship this Christ as the One in whom dwells all the fullness of the Godhead.

I may receive a purse containing very little or nothing at all or the purse
may contain many golden pounds. There is a great difference between the
two! And so with us as Christians. Some receive Christ with the forgiveness of sin and the hope of heaven and know little of the fullness of Christ
and all the treasure there is in Him. Other Christians are not satisfied but
sacrifice all things until they can say, "Of His fullness have we received,
and grace for grace." St. Paul said: "I count all things loss for the excellency of the knowledge of Christ Jesus my Lord." Like the merchant seeking goodly pearls, when he had found the pearl of great price, sold all that
he had in order to buy it, so the Christian who grasps something of the
fullness of Christ, the fullness of love and joy, His holiness and obedience,
His utter devotion to the Father and to mankind, that Christian gives up
all, that he may be united to this Christ. Listen to our Lord's words: "These
things have I spoken unto you, that my joy might remain in you, and that
your joy might be full." "Your heart shall rejoice and your joy no man taketh away from you." "Ask, and ye shall receive, that your joy may be full."

Dear Reader, do you know this Christ in whom all fullness dwells? Or
do you live as a pauper, depending in a great measure upon the world for
joy? It is God's will that Christ should fill all things, even your heart and
its needs.

---

*Heavenly Father, let the Holy Spirit imprint deeply upon my heart the
words of our text in all its fullness. Amen.*

The Heavenly Life

"Ye died, and your life is hid with Christ in God.
Christ is our life" (Col. 3:3–4).

It is of the utmost importance for a Christian to know that the new life which he receives *actually is the life of Christ which He lives in the Father*. Our life, my life, is hid with Christ in God and must daily be received anew and preserved as a holy of holies.

It takes time and quiet thought and prayer in any measure to grasp this great marvel, that the life Christ lives in the Father is the same life He lives in me. Christ does not live one life in the Father and another in me. His words are: "I live and ye shall live." "In that day ye shall know that I am in My Father, and ye in Me, and I in you." As He is in the Father, so are we in Him, and He in us. One divine life in the Father and in Christ and in me.

How little have we grasped this! How little trouble do we take to experience it. Here is the secret of the necessity of taking quiet time and prayerful meditation each day, to become deeply impressed with the truth that the Lord Jesus whose life is hid in God has also His life hid in me. It is only by taking time to realize that the glorious heavenly Christ lives in my heart that I shall truly live as a child of my Father in heaven.

When we allow God's Holy Spirit daily to keep alive in us that heavenly life in Christ, we shall grasp what it means to say, "I died with Christ, and I die daily to sin and self and the world in order to make room for that glorious heavenly life that Christ actually lives in me." Then we shall experience, "our conversation is in heaven." Thus shall I have courage to believe that Christ lives in me and reigns and works that which is well pleasing to His Father.

Heavenly Father, make my life a humble and constant walk with Thee in the fellowship of Thy holiness and Thy love. Amen.

A Royal Priesthood

"Ye are an elect race, a royal priesthood" (1 Peter 2:9).

In the Old Testament the thought of the kingdom took the first place; in the New Testament prominence is given to that of Priesthood.

One of the chief reasons for the feeble life in the Church is the mistaken idea that man's happiness is the main object of God's grace. A fatal error! God's aim is far holier and far higher. He saves us on purpose that we in turn shall carry out His purpose in saving others. Each believer is appointed to be the means of imparting to others the new life received in Christ.

Those who are saved have the holy calling of being channels of God's grace to others. The feeble state of the Church is largely due to the fact that most Christians imagine that their chief concern is to desire and receive sufficient grace to reach heaven after death. The Church must so proclaim the Gospel that each saved soul shall apprehend its message, "Saved to serve," "saved to save others." "Ye are a royal priesthood."

A royal priesthood! The priestly heart is above all things a sympathetic heart in which the love of Christ constrains us to win souls for Him. And that by virtue of two compelling motives: love to Christ, whom I shall please and honor in winning others to love Him; and love for souls, which will constrain me to sacrifice everything that others may share this heavenly life.

A priestly heart! A heart that has access to God in prayer and intercession for those who are yet unconverted. A priestly heart that, having pleaded in prayer for souls, has courage to speak to them of Christ. A priestly heart—in which the life of Jesus, the Great High Priest who ever liveth to make intercession, is continued, and His power to save to the uttermost is manifested.

O Spirit of God, write upon my heart with indelible letters, "A royal priesthood." Amen.

"Apart from Me—Nothing"

"He that abideth in Me, and I in him, the same beareth much fruit, for apart from Me ye can do nothing" (John 15:5).

The Lord Jesus follows His great promise that those who abide in Him will bear much fruit, with the words, "apart from Me, ye can do nothing."

What a cause for humiliation! Because the nature we inherit from Adam is so corrupt that in us—that is, in our flesh—dwelleth no good thing. Nay, more, our flesh is at enmity against God. We are under the power of sin to such an extent that we are unable to do anything well-pleasing to God.

What a call to repentance! How often we as Christians have thought that we were able to do that which is good. How often we thought we were making ourselves better. Let us remember Christ's words, "apart from Me, ye can do nothing," and henceforth rely only upon Him.

What cause for thanksgiving! Christ has united us to Himself and so dwells within us. He may work in and through us each day and all day. This is the secret of the spiritual life: the Lord Jesus working in us, enabling us to do His work.

What cause for joy and encouragement! All that in the Christian life has appeared too high and unattainable for me, all that, Christ will work in me. I have to care for one thing only, that I remain utterly dependent upon Him to care for me and work through me all the day. Whenever I remember, "apart from Me, ye can do nothing," I remember too, "He that abideth in Me beareth much fruit."

He Himself will see to it that He abides in me and I in Him. This, praise God, is the great work of which the Eternal Spirit will make me capable. Thank God for the life of Christ in me. I in Him, He in me is the work of the Holy Spirit in each soul that humbly and believingly yields itself for such communion with God.

Heavenly Father, apart from Thee, I can do nothing. Amen.

The Thrice-Holy God

*"The God of peace Himself sanctify you wholly, and may
your spirit and soul and body be preserved entire, without
blame at the coming of our Lord Jesus Christ. Faithful is
He that calleth you, who will also do it" (1 Thess. 5:23–24).*

What inexhaustible words! The God of peace Himself. Yes, He Himself and none other can and will do the work. And what is this work? To sanctify you wholly. How is this work to be done? Your entire spirit and soul and even your body is to be preserved without blame at the coming of our Lord.

This promise is so great it appears incredible. The Apostle feels the difficulty and adds the words, "Faithful is He that calleth you, who will also do it." That leaves no room for doubt, but calls us to place our confidence in the faithfulness of God.

This work is accomplished by the Holy Trinity. God the Father says, "Be ye holy, for I am holy. I am the Lord that sanctifieth you." The Son prayed, "For their sakes, I sanctify myself that they also may be sanctified in the truth." And the Holy Spirit is the Spirit of sanctification through whom the Church of God consists of the sanctified ones in Christ Jesus.

How does the Thrice-holy God accomplish this great work of sanctifying us wholly? Through His continual indwelling and fellowship and breathing of His holy life into us. As upon a cold day a man may warm himself by standing in the rays of the sun until its warmth penetrates his body, so the soul who takes time for communion with God becomes permeated with the strength of the Triune Holiness.

Oh, my brothers and sisters, what a treasure there is in these words, what cause for adoration, what confidence that God who is faithful will do it. What encouragement to wait upon Him, to walk with Him as Abraham did, knowing God, being fully assured that what He had promised He was able to perform.

---

*Heavenly Father: Grant us a vision of this divine holiness and grace
and power, that we may confidently feel that Thou wilt sanctify us
wholly and preserve spirit, soul, and body without blame. Amen.*

"The Spirit of His Son"

"Because ye are sons, God sent forth the Spirit of His Son into our hearts, crying, Abba, Father" (Gal. 4:6).

The Spirit that dwells in you, O child of God, is none less than the same Spirit that was in Christ, the Spirit of God's holiness. In Gethsemane He taught Christ to cry, "Abba, Father, Thy Will be done." He teaches us to know God's father-love and to respond with childlike love and obedience. He will be in us even as He was in Christ, the Spirit of Sonship expressing itself in a life of prayer. I may most assuredly expect of Him that He will impart to me God's love and holiness.

I may also rely upon Him as the Spirit of God's Son to reveal Christ in my heart and always to keep alive in me Christ's life. All that Christ has said of His abiding in me and I in Him, the Spirit of Christ will work in me. Through the Spirit, Christ's indwelling becomes an actual experience, and as a result, the mind of Christ and His disposition may be formed in me and become manifest. I may with certainty expect this of the Holy Spirit.

And furthermore the Holy Spirit will fit me for God's service. As the Spirit that sanctifies, He will reveal Christ to me as my sanctification. *The Spirit will enable me to overcome the world and its entanglements and be a witness to what Christ's life in His child may be.* He will fill me with love to the brethren, with love to those who hate or ignore me, with love to all around me who are not yet saved, so that I shall pray for them and be ready to help them. He will give me love to all the world, so that I may labor with enthusiasm for missions that the Gospel may be brought to all people. Oh, my brothers and sisters, take time each day with the Lord for your heart to be filled with the confident expectation of what God's Spirit will do for you.

Blessed Father, my heart is full of confident expectation of what Thy Spirit is doing in me. Amen.

"Ye Are Bought with a Price"

"Know ye not that your body is a temple of the Holy Spirit which is in you, which ye have from God? and ye are not your own; for ye are bought with a price: glorify God, therefore, in your body" (1 Cor. 6:19–20).

Here you have the reply to the question: What does the Spirit expect of me? Your body is His temple. The temple of God is holy, devoted to His service. You are not your own, you have no right to please yourself. You have been dearly bought with the blood of Christ. The Spirit has absolute right to your whole life. Therefore you must glorify God in your body and your spirit, which are God's. The Holy Spirit is the Spirit of God's holiness, He comes to make me holy. He expects me to obey Him fully.

Let me dwell upon these words that I may comprehend clearly what the relationship must be between the Spirit and me, and what it is He has a right to expect of me. He asks that I, as one dearly bought with the blood of Christ and no longer my own, shall seek in all things to please Him and to follow His leading. All that I owe to God and to the Lord Jesus must be shown in my conduct toward the Holy Spirit. I must in all things be guided by Him, for as God He has absolute right to me. He expects me to say each morning, "Speak, Lord, Thy servant heareth, I yield myself to obey the prompting of Thy voice within me." He expects absolute obedience.

Furthermore He expects that I shall keep in close touch with Him by taking time each day to renew the bond between Him and me. My whole life must be yielded to Him, that He may bring to perfection in me all His glorious fruits.

He also expects that in His strength I shall witness for Jesus Christ and consider it my work to help to bring the souls around me to the Lord Jesus. The Spirit expects that my body, which has been dearly bought, shall be a temple of God from which adoration and praise to God the Father and His Son Jesus Christ shall continually arise.

Blessed Lord, may my body, dearly bought, be a temple of praise and adoration to Thee and Thy dear Son. Amen.

Revival

*"Turn us again, O Lord God of Hosts. Cause Thy
face to shine, and we shall be saved" (Ps. 80:19).*

Israel was in sore need. Their enemies scoffed at them as if God had forsaken them. Three times the Psalmist uses the words of our texts to reinforce his prayer, "Stir up Thy might, and come and save us."

In our day the enemy rejoices that in spite of our many churches, Christianity is so powerless in overcoming the sins of drunkenness, immorality, worldly-mindedness, and love of money. God's children are asking: "Can nothing be done? Is there no hope of Revival?" Is God not willing to lead His people into a fuller, deeper life of victory over sin and all that opposes Christ in Christian and heathen lands? Has not God in His great love promised to give us His Spirit in answer to prayer? Is God not waiting for our prayers to begin the work of revival? A revival is much needed, and it is possible. God is longing for us to claim His promise and exercise our right as members of the Royal Priesthood (1 Peter 2:9).

Where must the Revival begin? *With God's children*, who may offer themselves to God as instruments to be used by the Holy Spirit, separating themselves from sin, and devoting themselves to the work of saving souls. Christians must realize and prove that the object of their life is God's service and the saving of those for whom Christ shed His blood.

Revival has already begun wherever God's children offer up everything to live and work and suffer as Christ did.

Dear child of God, it avails little to desire a deeper or more abundant life unless this is the chief object: to be a witness for Jesus and to win others to His service and to intercede for them as a labor of love.

*Blessed Father, make me a witness for Jesus and one who brings others
into Thy service, and may I intercede for them as a labor of love. Amen.*

A Threefold Cord

"All things whatsoever ye pray and ask for, believe that ye have received them, and ye shall have them" (Mark 11:24).

To know, To feel, To will, these are the three chief activities of the soul. When a Christian realizes the fullness there is in Christ and the abundant life He gives, then these three words will show us the way to participate in this fullness.

To know—We must not be content with our own thoughts about growth in grace. We must see to it that we *know clearly what God promises to do in us, and what He requires of us.* God's Word teaches us that if we come honestly with all our sin and weakness and sincerely yield to Christ our Lord, He will do in us far above what we dare think. See to it that you know clearly what God says you may ask of Him.

To desire—We must be careful to desire with our whole heart that for which we pray and be willing to pay the price for it. It may be our desire is faint. God will create the desire in answer to prayer. It may cost us a struggle and much self-sacrifice to let go the world and self, but the Spirit will come to our aid. But without strong desire and self-sacrifice, progress will not be made.

To will—The will is the most important point; only by firmness will faith have courage to appropriate what God bestows. Often in the midst of fear and struggle and almost in despair, we *will* to grasp what God offers. Our confidence must be in God alone. Christ Jesus will give us the assurance that He is strengthening us to yield ourselves to the Spirit's guidance. When our desire has developed into a firm will, we shall have courage to believe all that God has promised.

Child of God, thousands have by these means come to experience such fullness in Christ as they never thought possible. The more you cast yourself upon the Word of God and the love and power of Christ, the sooner you will enter into the rest of faith that ceases from works and depends upon God to fulfill His purposes in you.

Heavenly Father, I cast myself upon the Word of God and the love and power of Christ, not looking to my own works, but depending upon Thee to fulfill Thy purposes in me. Amen.

The Vine and the Branches

*"He that abideth in Me, and I in him, the
same beareth much fruit" (John 15:5).*

In this parable we see what the new life is which the Lord promised His
disciples for the work of the Holy Spirit. It clearly mirrors the life of faith.

1. "Not fruit," "more fruit," "much fruit," "fruit that abides" (vv. 2, 8,
    16): The one object of the life of faith is to bear much fruit to the
    glory of God the Father.
2. Cleansing: (v. 2). The indispensable cleansing through the Word that
    is sharper than a two-cdgcd sword.
3. "Abide in Me": Intimate, continuous fellowship.
4. "I in you": Divine indwelling through the Spirit.
5. "Apart from Me ye can do nothing": Complete reliance, deep humil-
    ity, constant dependence.
6. "My words abide in you," "If ye keep My commandments ye shall
    abide in My love," "Ye are My friends, if ye do the things I com-
    mand you": Indispensable obedience.
7. "If My words abide in you, ye shall ask whatsoever ye will": Limit-
    less confidence of faith.
8. "It shall be done unto you": Powerful answer to prayer.
9. "Even as the Father hath loved Me, I also have loved you; abide ye
    in My love": Life through faith in Him that loved Me.
10. "These things have I spoken unto you that My joy may be in you
    and that your joy may be fulfilled": Joy full and abiding.
11. "This is My commandment, that ye love one another, even as I have
    loved you": The new commandment kept through the power of
    Christ's love in our hearts.
12. "I appointed you that your fruit should abide, that whatsoever ye shall
    ask of the Father in My name, He will give it you": The all-prevail-
    ing Name of Christ.

This is the life Christ makes possible for us and works in us through
the Holy Spirit. This is the life so sadly wanting in the Church and yet so
indispensable. This is the life assured to childlike faith and obedience.

---

*Heavenly Father, I thank Thee for the life Thou hast for me as I trust
Thee in childlike faith and obey Thy commandments. Amen.*

Give Time to God

*"To everything there is a season, and a time to
every purpose under the sun" (Eccl. 3:1).*

This is literally true, there is a time for everything. Can it be true, as so
many maintain, that there is no time for communion with God? Is not the
most important matter, for which we must find time, fellowship with God
in which we may experience His love and His power? Give God time, I
beseech you.

You need time to feed upon the Word of God and to draw from it life
for your soul. Through His Word, His thoughts and His grace enter our
hearts and lives. Take time each day to read the Bible, even if it is only a
few verses; meditate upon what you have read, and thus assimilate the
bread of life. If you do not take the trouble to let God speak to you through
His Word, how can you expect to be led by the Spirit? Meditate upon the
Word, and lay it before God in prayer as the pledge of what He will do
for you. The Word gives you matter *for* prayer and courage and power *in*
prayer. Our prayers are often futile because we speak our own thoughts
and have not taken time to hear what God has to say. *Let the Word of God
teach you what God promises, what you need, and in what manner God
wishes you to pray.* Thus by prayer and the Word your heart will be prepared to have fellowship with God through faith in Christ Jesus.

Dear child of God, it is of little use to speak of the deeper, more abundant life of Christ as our life if we do not daily, above all things, take time
for communion with our Father in heaven. The life and love and holiness
of God cannot be ours amid the distractions and temptations of the world,
unless we give God time to reveal Himself to us and to take possession of
our hearts.

---

*Blessed Lord: Here, midst the distractions and temptations of the world,
I take the time for Thee to take possession of my heart. Amen.*

Deeper Life

*"And others fell upon the rocky places, where they had not much
earth: and straightway they sprang up, because they had no
deepness of earth" (Matt. 13:5).*

The seed sown upon the rocky places where the soil was superficial
sprang up quickly, but it withered as quickly because there was no deepness of earth. We have here a striking picture of so much religion which
begins well but which does not endure. The Christian needs a deeper life.
Let your whole life be an entrance into that love which passeth knowledge. In Ephesians 3:17–19, St. Paul prays "that Christ may dwell in your
hearts through faith, that ye, being rooted and grounded in love, may be
strong to apprehend what is the depth, and to know the love of Christ which
passeth knowledge, that ye may he filled unto all the fullness of God." He
prays that Christians may stand rooted first in the love of Christ which
passeth knowledge, realizing and acknowledging that the depth of this love
passeth knowledge. He believes it possible for the souls of Christians to
be so rooted in this love that they may be filled with all the fullness of
God in such measure as may be granted to a saint upon earth.

And how may we attain to this? "I bow my knees unto the Father." The
way to remain rooted in love is in humble prayer upon your knees before
God. Furthermore, "That He would grant you according to the riches of
His glory"—great indeed, and wonderful—"that ye may be strengthened
with power through His Spirit in the inward man." Only in the life that
knows the powerful working of the spirit is such a life rooted in love possible. And yet more: "That Christ may dwell in your hearts by faith." The
most important is that Christ in His everlasting love shall dwell in you every
day, insuring a life ever more deeply rooted in the love of Him who gave
Himself for us.

I beseech you, dear child of God, take time to bow before the Lord in
prayer, and thus meditate upon and appropriate these words. Do not grudge
time or trouble. Commune with the Christ who loved you with the same
love with which the Father loved Him, that in so doing you may get an
insight into the greatness of the condescension of that love to you.

Heavenly Father, I bow my knees before Thee. Amen.

Soul-Winning

"He that abideth in Me, and I in him, beareth much fruit, for apart from Me ye can do nothing . . . Herein is My Father glorified, that ye bear much fruit" (John 15:5, 8).

Fruit is that which a tree or a vine yields for the benefit of its owner. Even so, all that the Lord Jesus has taught us about His abiding in us and we in Him is to make us understand that it is not for our benefit but for His good pleasure and the honor of the Father. We, as branches of the Heavenly Vine, receive and enjoy such astounding grace that we may win souls for Him.

May not this be the reason why you have not enjoyed unbroken fellowship with Christ? You have forgotten that the object of fellowship and communion is fruit-bearing in saving others. Have you not given too much thought to your own sanctification and joy, not remembering that as Christ sought His blessing and glory from the Father in the sacrifice of Himself for us, so we, too, are called to live solely to bring Christ to others? It is for this purpose that we become branches of the Heavenly Vine, in order to continue the work that He began and with the same whole-heartedness.

When Christ was on earth, He said, "I am the light of the world"; but speaking of the time when He should be taken from the earth He said, "Ye are the light of the world."

How often you have said to the Lord, "I yield myself to Thee for cleansing and keeping and to be made holy," but you have hesitated to add "to be used of Thee for the salvation of others." Let us acknowledge our failure here and humbly offer ourselves to the Lord for His work. Let us begin by praying for those around us, seeking opportunities of helping them, and not being satisfied until we bear fruit to the glory of the Father.

Christ said, "Apart from me ye can do nothing." He knows our utter weakness. He has promised, "He that abideth in Me beareth much fruit."

Heavenly Father, Let all that we learn of the more abundant life and abounding grace constrain us to live to win souls for Jesus. Amen.

Intercession

"If a man see his brother sinning, he shall ask,
and God will give him life" (1 John 5:16).

In the last night, when the Lord Jesus promised to send the Holy Spirit to His disciples, He said: "In that day ye shall know that I am in the Father, and ye in Me, and I in you." "Abide in Me, and I in you." "He that abideth in Me, and I in him, beareth much fruit." The things and the fruit thereof would be attained by prayer. They would pray and He would grant their desires.

He made a sevenfold promise: "Whatsoever ye shall ask in My name that will I do" (John 14:13). "If ye shall ask anything in My name, that will I do" (5:14). "If My words abide in you, ask whatsoever ye will, and it shall be done unto you" (15:7).

"I appointed you that whatsoever ye shall ask the Father in My Name He may give it you" (15:16). "If ye shall ask anything of the Father, He will give it you in My name" (16:23). "Ask and ye shall receive, that your joy may be full" (16:24). "In that day ye shall ask in My name" (16:26).

Read the above seven texts over and over until you are convinced that the believer who abides in Christ has the right to pray for souls and that Christ and the Father will answer that prayer.

Remember, too, that you are a branch of the Heavenly Vine not only for your own salvation, but that you may bear much fruit in the conversion of souls. It is as an intercessor that grace is granted you to pray for others, believing assuredly that God will answer you.

Think of the change that would come over a community if every believer in it would take time to pray for those who do not believe. How God would be glorified in our bearing much fruit!

Heavenly Father, Write these glorious promises upon my heart. Amen.

Christ Our Life

"Ye died, and your life is hid with Christ in God. . . .
Christ is our life" (Col. 3:3–4).

Let us now sum up what has been said about the new life we are to live in Christ. Let us see if we have grasped the lesson this book would teach us and whether we really intend to live this life.

St. Paul writes to the Colossians: "Ye died, and your life is hid with Christ in God." Only God's Spirit can enable the believer to grasp and appropriate the truth that he was actually crucified and died with Christ. The new life he receives in Christ through the Spirit is life out of death. In Christ as the Lamb in the midst of the throne, the power of that life is shown as a crucified life in each one who has received it. The Holy Spirit gives me the assurance that I died with Christ, and the power of His death works in me.

And of Christ's life: "Your life is hid with Christ in God." This is what Christ said in the last night: "Ye shall know that I am in the Father and ye in Me"—with Him in the Father. My life is safely hid with Christ in God, and from there I each day by faith receive it anew through the working of the Holy Spirit.

Is this not the reason why so many of God's children make so little progress? They do not know that the life of Christ who died on the cross and now lives in heaven is truly *their* life hid in God and must daily be received afresh from God in the quiet hour. What joy to know my spiritual life is not in my keeping but is hid in God. Christ and the Holy Spirit will grant to each humble believing child of God to receive this new life.

What joy to know that the new life of God's children around me is also hid with Christ in God! What a bond of union this will be. How sincerely we should love each other and pray for each other.

"Your life is hid with Christ in God . . . Christ is our life."

O Spirit of God, let me rely upon Thee to make this true in my life!
Amen.

The Throne of Grace

"Unto Him that sitteth on the Throne, and unto the Lamb,
be the blessing, and the honor, and the glory, and the
dominion, forever and ever" (Rev. 5:13).

In chapters 4 and 5 of The Revelation we are shown the difference between the Throne of God the Creator and the Throne of Grace. In chapter
4 John saw, "a Throne set in heaven, and One sitting upon the Throne;
and He that sat was to look upon like a jasper stone and a sardius." There
was no definite form but the shining light of precious stones. Round about
the Throne were four beasts, "and they rest not night and day, saying, Holy,
holy, holy, Lord God Almighty, which was, and is, and is to come." The
four-and-twenty elders fall down before Him, saying, "Worthy art Thou,
our Lord and our God, to receive the glory and the honor and the power:
*for Thou didst create all things, and because of Thy will they are, and were
created."* Here we have the Throne of God, the Almighty Creator!

In chapter 5 we read: "I saw in the midst of the Throne *a Lamb* standing, as though it had been slain, and the four living creatures and the four-
and-twenty elders fell down before the Lamb, and they sing a new song,
saying, Worthy art Thou, for Thou wast slain, and didst purchase unto God
with Thy blood men of every tribe, and tongue, and people." Then thousands and thousands of angels cried: "Worthy is the Lamb that hath been
slain to receive the power, and riches, and wisdom, and might, and honor,
and glory, and blessing. And every created thing, which is in the heaven
and on the earth, heard I saying, *Unto Him that sitteth on the Throne, and
unto the Lamb,* be the blessing, and the honor, and the glory, and the dominion, forever and ever."

There we have the Throne of Grace, the Throne of God and of the Lamb.
And the threefold song which we heard is the heavenly chorus which was
sung at the dedication of the Throne of Grace to the glory of God and of
the Lamb. O my soul, bow down and worship and adore. When you draw
near to the Throne of Grace, think of what it cost Christ to found that
Throne, and what assurance it gives that you will find grace to help in time
of need. I pray you take time this day to come under the deep conviction
that the Lamb as it had been slain is on the Throne and will make you and
your prayers acceptable to the Father.

---

*Heavenly Father, In deepest humility and with all my heart, I worship
the Lamb on the Throne of Grace. Amen.*

The Lamb in the Midst of the Throne

"Having then a great High Priest . . . Jesus the Son of God . . . One that hath been in all points tempted like as we are, yet without sin. Let us draw near with boldness unto the Throne of Grace" (Heb. 4:14–16).

Can you imagine, O child of God, any way by which the Father could have given us greater boldness of access than by giving His only Son as a Lamb upon earth with His godlike, gentle disposition to win our hearts to Him? After Jesus had given Himself on the Cross, a ransom for our sins, God placed Him in the midst of the Throne, that we as sinners might have perfect boldness through His blood to present our prayers through Him in full assurance that He as Intercessor will make them acceptable to the Father.

Truly the holy God has done His utmost to draw us to Himself and to grant us heavenly boldness to pray with the assurance that our defective prayers, through the Lamb on the Throne, the sympathizing High Priest, will be heard and find acceptance with God the Father.

O my brothers and sisters, take time with the vision of the Lamb on the Throne before you to give you boldness—take time in deepest humility and childlike faith and with all the love of which your heart is capable to worship Him as your Surety and Intercessor and great High Priest. When the Holy Spirit has given that vision of the Lamb on the Throne unto your heart, it will indeed be a Throne of Grace, and you can do nothing less than fall prostrate before Him in adoration and praise and give Him the glory to all eternity.

Your heart will then become a true temple of God where, day by day, yea, hour by hour, the song will arise: "Salvation be unto our God who sitteth upon the Throne, and to the Lamb."

When our hearts are filled with love for the Lamb upon the Throne who makes our prayers acceptable to God the Father, then we shall have the joy and the faith to expect a speedy answer.

Blessed Father, my song is: "Salvation be unto our God, who sitteth upon the Throne, and to the Lamb." Amen.

Abundant Grace

*"The grace of our Lord abounded exceedingly with faith
and love which is in Christ Jesus" (1 Tim. 1:14).*

If we would value and love the Throne of Grace aright, we must try to understand what it is that it provides for our use. Scripture uses great words to reveal this grace to us. It speaks of "the riches of grace," "the glory of grace," "the abundance of grace," "the exceeding riches of grace," "the manifold riches of grace." Let these words sink deep into your hearts as we point to them in God's Word.

"Much more *did the grace of God*, and the gift by the grace of the one man, Jesus Christ, abound unto the many" (Rom. 5:15). "Much more shall they that receive *the abundance of grace* and of the gift of righteousness reign in life through the one, even Jesus Christ" (v. 17). "Where sin abounded, *grace did abound ore exceedingly*" (v. 20).

"By the grace of God, I am what I am: and His grace which was bestowed upon me was not found vain [powerless]; but I labored more abundantly than they all: yet not I, but the grace of God which was with me" (1 Cor. 15:10). "God is able to make all grace abound unto you; that ye, always having all sufficiency in all things, may abound to every good work" (2 Cor. 9:8).

"To the praise of the glory of His grace, which He freely bestowed on us in the Beloved: according to the riches of His grace" (Eph. 1:6–7). "But God, being rich in mercy, for His great love wherewith He loved us, quickened us together with Christ; that He might show *the exceeding riches of His grace* in kindness toward us in Christ Jesus" (Eph. 2:4–7).

What treasures are contained in these words! Let the Holy Spirit write them in your heart, that you may receive the full impression of the "exceeding riches" and the abundance of the glory of the grace to be received at the Throne of Grace. Let the thought take possession of you that all day long the abundance of grace will be granted to the soul who approaches with boldness and is ready to receive from the sympathizing High Priest that which He has to bestow.

Blessed Father, impress upon my heart that abundance of grace is granted to the soul who approaches the Throne of Grace. Amen.

"With All Thy Heart"

*"Thou shalt love the Lord thy God with all thy heart, and
with all thy soul, and with all thy mind, and with
all thy strength" (Mark 12:30).*

In this great command the Lord our God has tried to teach us how greatly He needs us wholly for Himself. Our love, our prayers, our consecration, our trust, our obedience—in all these there must be an unreserved surrender to God's will and service.

"With all thy heart"—with its longings, with its affections, with its attachments, with all its desires. "With all thy soul"—with its vital powers and the will as a royal master in the soul. "With all thy mind—its faculties of thought, of knowledge, of reasoning, and its powers of memory and imagination. "With all thy strength"—this is nothing less than the sacrifice of everything and the putting forth of our utmost endeavors. All for God, for God alone, and our one desire must be to love and serve Him perfectly.

What a wonderful God it is who has such a right to expect so much from us! Is He not the Creator who has made us to show forth His glory and for this purpose must possess us wholly? Is He not the Perfect and Glorious One who is worthy that we should forsake all to follow Him? Is He not the Everlasting Love and Goodness and Mercy, ever desirous of pouring out blessings upon us? Is He not indeed worthy, ten thousand times worthy, that all that is within us shall love and honor Him with all our strength and all our heart?

Think what it would mean in your prayer-life if you were strengthened with all might to call upon God each day! Take this commandment into your heart and make it the rule of your life and try to realize that God must have all. It will make a great difference in your life, and you will go from strength to strength until you appear before God in Zion.

God will assuredly work in our hearts that which He has promised in this command. We are unable to keep it in our own strength. The Almighty One will, through His Spirit, pour out His love in our hearts.

Blessed Father, Our one desire is to give Thee our hearts, our desires, our very souls as we depend completely upon thee for strength. In thy strength we earnestly desire an answer to our prayers and approach with boldness the Throne of Grace. Amen.

The Lamb and Missionary Work

"Thou wast slain, and didst purchase unto God with Thy blood men of every tribe, and tongue, and people, and nation" (Rev. 5:9).

The Song of the Lamb tells us that the redeemed shall come from all the different tribes and nations of the whole earth. The many languages into which the Bible has been translated and the still greater number into which the New Testament or portions of the Bible have been translated gives us some idea of how strenuous work by missionaries in many lands is making known Christ and His Gospel.

Think for a little while of the extent of blessed work done by missionaries all over the earth! Christ came as a propitiation not for our sins alone, but for the sins of the whole world and to complete the great work of the redemption of mankind. When He had accomplished His share of the work, He entrusted the rest of the work to His people, trusting them to take the message of redemption to all parts of the world. As holy and divine as was Christ's part as an indispensable beginning, so equally holy is the second part of the work—to bring souls everywhere to know of and accept this great salvation.

In the Song of the Lamb we find this twofold truth—the Lamb upon the Throne has brought salvation to all the nations and tribes of the earth, and to the Church of the Lamb has been entrusted the distribution of the salvation by the power of the Holy Spirit. Unspeakably glorious is the task of the Missionary!

We shall only be able to understand this aright when we have seen the great multitude which no man can number, out of every nation and of all tribes and peoples and tongues, standing before the Throne and before the Lamb, arrayed in white robes with palms in their hands; and they cry, saying: "Salvation unto our God which sitteth upon the Throne and unto the Lamb."

May the Holy Spirit imprint deeply in our hearts the wonder of missionary work! Just as the Lamb of God gave Himself to die that He might send the glad tidings to all, let us so offer ourselves wholly and without reserve to live and to die that souls may be led to join in the Song of the Lamb before the Throne of God.

Blessed Father, we offer ourselves wholly and without reserve to live and to die that souls may be led to join in the Song of the Lamb before the Throne of God. Amen.

The Lamb and His Worshipers

"And hast made us unto our God kings and priests:
and we shall reign on the earth" (Rev. 5:10).

The four-and-twenty elders sang the new song that all those who are redeemed may now join in singing. If we take part with all our hearts in the Song of the Lamb, we shall realize that we are priests of the Throne of Grace. As priests we worship God and the Lamb and with hearts full of adoration may approach the Throne of the Lamb for ourselves and others. As kings we receive the abundance of grace that we may reign in life over sin and the power of the world, so that we may bring liberty to the captives. Such an overcoming life on earth will form and prepare us for sitting with Christ on His throne (Rev. 3:21).

Let all who read this take to heart the great thought: I come to the Throne of Grace, not only to receive the abundant grace for my own needs, but to be strengthened and fitted for taking that grace to others. How can God, how can the Lamb make known the glory of the Throne of Grace to those who sit in darkness? By means of those who know the Throne of Grace and will offer themselves wholly to the service of that Throne and are willing to share their experience with others. The Throne of Grace will become more precious to us as we understand that abundant grace will work within us in greater power when we give our lives to make this salvation known to others.

Then the Song of the Lamb will acquire a new meaning for us: "Unto Him that loved us, and washed us from our sins in His own blood, *and hath made us kings and priests unto God*; to Him be glory and dominion forever and ever" (Rev. 1:5–6). We shall realize that it is worthwhile living as Christians ready to fulfill a heavenly calling.

O my brothers and sisters, the Lamb on the Throne has chosen you to see Him upon the Throne and *to make Him and His love known to others*. Grace demands this of you; grace will strengthen you with heavenly power and joy.

Heavenly Father, may this grace for myself and others be sufficient
for my daily fellowship with the Lamb on the Throne. Amen.

The Lamb and the Spirit

*"I saw . . . a Lamb standing, as though it had been slain,
having seven horns, and seven eyes, which are the seven
Spirits of God, sent forth into all the earth" (Rev. 5:6).*

In the fourth chapter of The Revelation we read that John had seen "seven lamps of fire burning before the Throne, which are the seven Spirits of God." In our text we see that these Spirits have been taken up into the life of the Lamb; they are His eyes; and through them He works in all the earth. When the Lamb was upon earth, He was obedient to God's Spirit in all things—"Through the Eternal Spirit He offered Himself unto God." This is why His blood has such divine power, and why the Father gave Him unlimited power to pour out the Holy Spirit in full measure on whom He would.

Let us learn two great lessons. The first, that the Lamb on the Throne has power to fill us with the Holy Spirit and enable us to follow Him fully and so fit us to commune with God in the power of the blood and be more than conquerors. The second, that it is only through the Spirit that we shall understand the glory of the Lamb and be filled with His love and so stand firm in the faith of that which He can do in us and for us and through us.

Beloved Christian, let the Song of the Lamb ring in your ears continually. The Lamb who was slain is worthy to receive the power and the glory. God has exalted Him to the Throne and has put all things under His feet. Do you not long to give Him the place of honor in your heart and in fervent love submit all that you have to Him and His service? The glory of heaven is the worship of the Lamb and of Him that sitteth on the Throne. You, too, may experience the glory of redemption as you tarry at the Throne of Grace.

Blessed Father, I cannot rest until in silent adoration and deep humility the song of the Lamb arises as incense before Thee. "Unto Him that sitteth on the Throne and unto the Lamb, be the blessing and the honor, and the glory, and the dominion forever and ever." Amen.

The Lamb and Prayer

"The four-and-twenty elders fell down before the Lamb,
having each one a harp, and golden bowls full of incense,
which are the prayers of the saints" (Rev. 5:8).

We learn here that the prayers of the saints in the Old Testament concerning the promised redemption were preserved in heaven. Here, where
homage is paid to the Lamb on the Throne, these prayers are offered as
incense, that He may take them up and lay them before the Father.

The same thought is to be found in chapter 8 of The Revelation. John
saw an angel standing by the golden altar before the Throne and much incense was given to him, that he should offer it with the prayers of the saints
upon the golden altar: "And the smoke of the incense with the prayers of
the saints, went up before God out of the angel's hand" (Rev. 8:4).

What profound and heavenly thoughts do these words awaken within
us! The prayers of the saints are not answered at once. Just as men on earth
accumulate money and allow it to increase as capital for greater undertak-
ings, so the prayers of the saints are stored up in heaven until the measure
is full, and the answer can descend.

Remember this. You do not pray alone. All over the world God's children are praying. When with perseverance and faith they entrust their
prayers to the Lamb, then in His own time God will graciously send the
answer. Do not think your prayer is in vain because you do not at once
receive the answer. No, let your faith attach itself all the more firmly to
the wonderful truth that is here revealed, that *the Lamb on the Throne keeps
our prayers in safety* to lay them before the Father at the right time.

The Lamb is seated on the Throne of Grace with the purpose of drawing out your prayers and strengthening you through His Spirit for more
prayer. Pray for the Church of God all over the world, pray for preachers
and teachers; pray for all believers. Pray in love and fellowship with others who are also praying. Let your daily communion with God on the
Throne and with the Lamb be a means of receiving from that Throne the
rich abundant Grace for your every need and the need of those around you
in the Church and the world.

Blessed Father, I pray for the Church of God all over the world, for
preachers and teachers, and for all believers. Amen.

"The Blood of the Lamb"

"They have washed their robes, and made them white in the blood of the Lamb. Therefore are they before the Throne of God, and they serve Him day and night in His temple" (Rev. 7:14–15).

When I am to be presented to a king in his palace, my garments must be in accordance with the rules of the Court. What I wear helps to give me liberty to approach an earthly monarch. If I am to appear before God and serve Him day and night in His temple, I must wear "a robe made white in the blood of the Lamb."

What a close relationship to the Lord Jesus it gives me when I know that He has bought me with His blood—paid so great a price for me! It gives me the assurance that He places a great value upon me and will preserve me so that I may appear in His presence and serve Him day and night in His temple.

What new glory shines from the Throne of Grace as the Lamb of God lives each day to make me acceptable to the Father, and I receive the abundant grace that I need to abound in good works! How attractive the inner chamber becomes when we love and honor the Lamb on the Throne and ask to be fitted for His service!

O Christian, just as you are clothed in suitable garments to meet royalty, so you must each day put on the white robe which has been washed in the blood of the Lamb. You then become one of the royal priesthood who serve God and intercede for souls and for the whole world. The precious blood of Christ gives us access with boldness into God's presence. It links us closely to the Lord Jesus and gives us the needed power that we may be a blessing to others. Even here on earth the word may be fulfilled in us: "Therefore are they before the Throne of God, and serve Him day and night in His temple."

Blessed Lord, each day anew I put on the white robe, washed in the blood of the Lamb, to be one of the royal priesthood who serve Thee and intercede for souls and for the whole world. Amen.

Following the Lamb

*"These are they which follow the Lamb whithersoever
He goeth. These were purchased from among men, to be
the first-fruits unto God and unto the Lamb" (Rev. 14:4).*

The Lamb is the Leader of whom it was written: "For it became Him
. . . in bringing many sons unto glory, to make *the Captain of their salvation* perfect through sufferings" (Heb. 2:10). He was "the Author and Perfecter of our faith . . . who endured the Cross" (Heb. 12:2).

Let us consider:

The Lamb as our Leader and Example; and His redeemed ones, who
follow Him whithersoever He goeth.

The Lamb in His great humility, who says: "Learn of Me, for I am meek
and lowly of heart."

The Lamb in His perfect innocence and purity.

The Lamb in His patience and silence: "He was brought as a Lamb to
the slaughter."

The Lamb who offered Himself to God as a burnt offering and sweet-
smelling incense.

He is the Captain of our salvation whom the Father has given us to bring
many sons to glory and in whose footsteps we seek to walk.

The Lamb on the Throne is my Advocate with the Father, who liveth
to intercede for me. The Lamb on the Throne has power to lead me and
fashion me according to His own image. The Lamb on the throne of my
heart is willing and able to increase His own meekness and self-sacrifice
within me, and His love to the Father and His redeemed ones. "These are
they which have washed their robes and made them white in the blood of
the Lamb." *"The Lamb which is in the midst of the Throne shall be their
Shepherd, and shall guide them to fountains of waters of life"* (Rev. 7:17).

Follow the Lamb! Let this be our watchword and prayer each day! The
Lamb who was slain for us is now in the fullness of His grace in the midst
of the Throne, our chief Captain and the Perfecter of our faith.

---

*Blessed Father, I follow Thy precious Son, the Lamb of God, my Chief
Captain and the Perfecter of our faith. Amen.*

The Victory of the Lamb

"They overcame him [the old serpent, the devil], because of the
blood of the Lamb, and because of the word of their testimony; and
they loved not their life even unto death" (Rev. 12:11).

The Lamb is the Lord of lords and King of kings, and is the victor over every enemy; and those who are with Him, the called, the chosen and faithful, reign with Him. They conquered the foe through the blood of the Lamb. Faith in the power of Christ and His blood, in the assurance that every foe has been vanquished and that the blood now makes each one a conqueror in the power of God—this is the secret over sin and the world. The daily fellowship with Christ in the sprinkling of the blood makes us to triumph daily. Christian warrior—remember that there is victory through the blood of the Lamb.

Do not seek only your own salvation or blessedness. Note that, *They overcame because of the word of their testimony*. Here is that which Christ promised: "Ye shall receive power, when the Holy Spirit is come upon you: and ye shall he My witnesses" (Acts 1:8). As we make known the love of God and witness to the power of the blood and strive ever to bring souls to God, the enemy will be overcome, and souls will be rescued from his power.

And then again: *"They loved not their life even unto death."* This was the way the Chief Captain, the Lamb that was slain, gained the victory and won His place in the midst of the Throne. Those who follow the Lamb whithersoever He goeth, follow Him in this particular: they have dedicated themselves wholly to His service and "loved not their life even unto death." As the subjects of an earthly king offer themselves with enthusiasm to his service when needed, so they count nothing too great or too small in the service of the Lamb.

Dear children of God, if you would in the end be crowned as conquerors in life, be faithful followers of the Lamb. Live as He did. Let your trust in the wonderful life-giving power of the blood and the remembrance of all that He has done for you, be joined to the intense feeling that reckons even life not too precious to be offered up wholly for Him.

Blessed Father, not even life itself is too precious to be offered up wholly
for Thee. Amen.

The Marriage of the Lamb

"And He saith unto me, Write, Blessed are they which are bidden to the marriage supper of the Lamb" (Rev. 19:9).

All who rejoice in Salvation are called to the marriage of the Lamb, not merely as spectators, but unitedly they form the bride of the Lamb. We read that when one of the angels said, "Come, and I will show you the bride, the wife of the Lamb," he showed the Holy Jerusalem descending from heaven from God, and she had the glory of God, and the nations who shall be saved walk in her light. The time of the marriage feast of the Lamb will be when Christ presents His redeemed people as one body to the Father, and they are taken up to sit with Him on the Throne eternally.

When the prodigal son returned to his home, his father made a feast where all rejoiced together over the return of the son who had been dead and now was alive again. What joy there will be when the Everlasting Love that gave itself for us on the cross shall celebrate its triumph and the glory of God and the revelation of the love of God that passeth all understanding!

When we are invited to the wedding of a distinguished person, we take great care to be arrayed in suitable wedding garments. What concern then, mingled with joy, should there be in the hearts of those who are called to the marriage supper of the Lamb! O child of God, if you really cherish the joyful hope of sitting at the marriage feast of the Lamb, will you not each day make use of the unspeakable privilege of approaching the Throne of Grace? Will you not entrust yourself in loving surrender to Him and pray for grace that each day the way may be made more ready for the great heavenly marriage feast of the Lamb?

Heavenly Father, I not only prepare myself, but I seek for grace to win others and bring them as well to partake of the feast of Everlasting Love. Amen.

The Throne of God and of the Lamb

"He showed me a river of water of life, bright as crystal, proceeding out of the Throne of God and of the Lamb" (Rev. 22:1).

What does the river of water of life signify? Nothing less than the Holy Spirit which was not given until the Lamb was in the midst of the Throne.

Where does the river of the water of life flow? Through the whole earth. It gives us according to our faith and desire that which Christ has promised, a fountain springing up to eternal life. It gives streams of living water to each one who believes in Him fully. It surrounds us all, but through slowness and worldliness we are unable to grasp it and enjoy it.

This may be made clear to us by means of a parable. When Senator Marconi discovered the means for wireless telegraphy, he found that waves of ether were streaming through the whole world. He discovered that he could entrust a message to these waves, and it would be conveyed to distant places. When he sent his first message from England to Italy, it passed through France where there were millions of people who had no idea that any such message was passing. The message was heard and understood only when it reached the reception station which had been prepared for it in Italy.

Just so are we surrounded by the waves of the river of the water of eternal life without being aware of it. Yes, the waves of heavenly grace, of life and power, of love and joy surround us, and we know it not. Marconi spent years in trying to learn the secret of wireless telegraphy. It is only as we seek with an undivided heart that our eyes will be opened to see that the waves of the life-stream flowing from the throne of God and the Lamb really do surround us and are for our daily use.

O Christian, take time to worship God and the Lamb in the midst of the Throne and to be filled with their glory, and you will realize that the Holy Spirit as a stream of living water surrounds you each day and will be in you a fountain springing up to eternal life and as a stream flowing from you in blessing to others.

Heavenly Father, How wonderful it will be to see the Lamb in the midst of the Throne of God and the water of life that flows from beneath the Throne. Amen.

The Heavenly Life

"The Throne of God and of the Lamb shall be therein: and His servants shall do Him service; and they shall see His face; and His name shall be on their foreheads" (Rev. 22:3–4).

Many Christians seek the Throne of Grace that they may find grace sufficient for their need, but they do not tarry until the grace from the Throne of God and of the Lamb fills their entire life and enables them to walk night and day in its light and experience the full impress of its glory.

To those who have faith in the unseen life and know that they have come to the heavenly Jerusalem and the blood of sprinkling (Heb. 12:22–24)—to them the promises in our text are fulfilled. The earthly life becomes an actual experience of preparation for the heavenly life.

"His servants shall do Him service"; at first without the sight of His glory. The faithful soul finds a reward and goes a step farther, *"They shall see His face."* It becomes possible to walk in the light of His countenance and to rejoice in Him the whole day. The Omnipresent One is the Almighty One, and His presence abides with His servant.

There is a further promise—*"His Name shall be on their foreheads."* Obedience to God's commandments, the abiding in the light of His countenance, has an influence on the character and even the appearance of the children of God. As the fruit and reward of seeking to do all in the Name of Jesus (Col. 3:17), the likeness to His image is seen in them, and His Name is visible on their foreheads.

Dear Christian, it is a great thing to approach the Throne of Grace and to receive grace for each day. But there is a still greater blessing when the face of God and of the Lamb are revealed to our earnest gaze, and we walk each day in their light. When the Name of Christ is engraved upon our hearts and upon our foreheads, then we are changed into His image, from glory to glory as by the spirit of the Lord.

Blessed Father, Grant that we may all know the Throne of Grace in its holy and sanctifying influence! "His servants shall do Him service; and they shall see His face; and His Name shall be on their foreheads." Amen.

The Reign of Grace

*"They that receive the abundance of grace shall
reign in life through Jesus Christ" (Rom. 5:17).*

Let us once more think what the Throne of Grace can be to us. The grace that reigns through Jesus Christ enables us to gain the victory over sin in our life here below.

Salvation does not, as many think, mean a life of falling and rising again. No, it is God's will that His children should be conquerors in their life here upon earth. But on one condition—that they should day by day live in the abundance of grace that is to be obtained at the Throne of Grace. Let us read again the words in which the reign of grace is revealed to us. In the verses which follow on our text this point is made clear (Rom. 5:20–21). "The law came in beside, that the trespass might abound; but where sin abounded, grace did abound more exceedingly." Is it not wonderful, that although sin abounds, grace is always greater and more abundant than sin can ever be. I may, by reading God's Word, have an overpowering sense of the great power of sin, but I have also the assurance that grace, as the life-power of God within me, is far more abundant and powerful.

Then these words follow: "As sin reigned in death, even so might grace reign through righteousness unto eternal life through Jesus Christ our Lord." Whatever I may know or feel of the power of sin in the world or in myself, I know too that grace is stronger, grace always has the victory over sin—"We are more than conquerors through Him that loved us." This is a sure word. They that receive the abundance of grace reign already in this life through Jesus Christ.

Do you not see how everything depends on appearing daily before the Throne of Grace with a deep sense of need but fully assured that abundant grace, as the power to conquer sin, will be given us? Oh, that God's children would realize that the footstool of the Throne of Grace is the place where each one may experience that "God is able to make all grace abound unto us, that we, always having all sufficiency in everything, may abound unto every good work!"

Blessed Father, Every day may I appear before Thy Throne of Grace, assured that Thou wilt give abundant grace and the power to conquer sin. Amen.

Peniel: Face to Face

"I have seen God face to face, and my
life is preserved" (Gen. 32:30).

In these words of Jacob uttered after he had become Israel, a Prince with God, we find expression of that which prayer meant to him. The words show us what each child of God, through the grace of God and the power of the Holy Spirit, may experience each day. God will cause His face to shine upon us; *we shall see Him face to face* and be delivered.

How often Christians complain that they have so little experience of what it means to meet with God in prayer and to feel the light of His countenance upon them. They have done their best, but it seems of no avail. The thoughts of the inner chamber bring a feeling of self-reproach and shame; and yet they feel quite unable to overcome this disappointment.

Dear children of God, I bring you the message that your Father in heaven is not only willing but greatly desirous that the light of His countenance shall rest upon you. Perhaps the words of this book may be a help to you by giving you that assurance. If we can find out what the reason is that you cannot break through in your prayers that you may see God face to face, then we shall know what you need in order to make your inner chamber a true Peniel. Only there will you realize what it is to meet with God, to see His face, and to feel how certain and blessed it is that His love rests upon you.

Begin with the prayer: "Turn us again, O Lord God of hosts, cause Thy face to shine, and we shall be saved" (Ps. 80:19), and meditate on the words. Believe firmly that you may know the power and truth of this text— only then will you be able to say with Jacob: "I have seen God face to face, and my life is preserved." Remember how Jacob reached this point. He had learned to say: *"I will not let Thee go, except Thou bless me."* Persevering prayer is needed to bring the soul into the steadfast conviction that God will really make Himself known.

Heavenly Father, "I will not let Thee go, except Thou bless me." Amen.

"I Am the Lord, and There Is None Else"

"Jesus answered, The first (of all the commandments) is: Hear, O Israel! The Lord our God, the Lord is One" (Mark 12:29).

The law may command us to love, but it cannot make us love. It is powerless to force us to love God. Love can be called forth only by that which is worthy of love. Love to God can be born only of the knowledge of Him as the one true God in His excellent greatness and glory, His unspeakable love and compassion. When Moses said, "The Lord our God is one God," he was making known the supreme right that God has to our love. It is when the love of God expressed in these words enters our hearts, "The Lord God, full of compassion and gracious, slow to anger, and plenteous in mercy and truth," that we are willing to accept the truth and love Him whole-heartedly.

We have already referred to God's command that we should love Him with all the heart and all the soul and all the mind and all the strength. The soul that earnestly seeks will soon find the difficulty of continuance in this love unless it has a vision of how worthy God is to be loved with the whole heart. It is no wonder that Christians are afraid of the words "with all the heart and all the strength."

It is impossible for anyone, unless he has really confessed his sin, to understand how abundantly God forgives and how rich He is in mercy. The heart filled with a burning desire to serve God will say: "God is indeed worthy of my love; I will love Him with my whole heart."

Dear reader, here you have the secret of the prayer-life—to meet God each day, to live in the light of His love, to draw near in an absolute surrender to His will. We shall attain to this only as we daily approach the Throne of Grace with boldness. Let this be the great object of your life. You will find these two thoughts complete each other. God, the only Lord, in the glory of His unspeakable love, giving Himself wholly for us, and the soul in true worship and adoration giving itself to God with all the heart and all the strength.

Precious Father, Thou art indeed worthy of my love; I love Thee with my whole heart. Amen.

The Abiding Presence of God

"The Lord is nigh unto all them that call upon Him, to all that call upon Him in truth" (Ps. 145:18).

You long to experience continually the nearness of God. Here is the secret: Pray, pray without ceasing. Then you will have the assurance: "The Lord is nigh unto all who call upon Him." Prayer has a wonderful power of helping us to draw near to God and keeping us in His presence. God is everywhere and as the Almighty One is ever ready and able to grant us unbroken fellowship with Him.

Would you know the secret of always abiding in a state of prayerfulness? The answer is clear. Realize first that God is near you and within you, then you will feel how natural it is to talk with Him each moment about your needs and desires. This is the secret of the prayerful life of which Paul writes: "Night and day praying exceedingly" (1 Thess. 3:10). It is only when you live a life apart from God that you say: "I must take time, I must take trouble first of all to find God before I can pray." But to the true Christian, *life is a constant abiding with the Father. "In Thy Name do they rejoice all the day"* (Ps. 89:16). The communion between the Father and His child should be continuous. Even so prayer may become a daily life activity, like breathing or sleeping, instead of something that is brought into use only once a day. The principle of complete dependence on the unseen God and the holy habit of claiming His presence with us each moment of the day—this is the secret of a life of true godliness.

God always near, so that you may call upon Him at all times. According to the word of St. Paul, you will be "anxious for nothing, but in everything by prayer and supplication let your requests be made known unto God, and the peace of God will guard your hearts and minds." Remember these two things: A God always near with His infinite and abundant grace and His child in utter weakness, calling upon One who will surely hear and answer.

Blessed Father, in my utter weakness, I thank Thee that Thou art always near when I call, that my prayers are heard and answered. Amen.

Take Time with God

*"To everything there is a season, and a time to every purpose
under the heaven" (Eccl. 3:1).*

It should be the aim of every Christian to set aside a little time each
day for quiet communion with God. A time for everything—and shall there
be no time to spend in the presence of the Creator of all things? No time
to contemplate His will and purposes for us? The holy, loving God is indeed worthy of the best of our time—of all of our time. We should live in
constant fellowship with Him, but each day there should be a special time
of quiet when we are with Him alone.

We need a period daily for secret fellowship. Time to turn from daily
occupation and search our hearts in His presence. Time to study His Word
with reverence and godly fear. Time to seek His face and ask Him to make
Himself known to us. Time to wait until we know that He sees and hears
us so that we can make our wants known to Him in words that come from
the depth of our hearts. Time to let God deal with our special needs, to let
His light shine in our hearts, to let ourselves be filled with His Spirit!

What do you think? Will it be possible to give a quarter of an hour each
day for this purpose? If you are unwilling to make such an arrangement,
you must not be surprised if your spiritual life is enfeebled and becomes
ineffective. Fellowship with God should have a first claim on your time,
and if you will only arrange for this brief time with God, you will soon
learn to value it. It will not be long before you feel ashamed that there
was ever a time when you thought fifteen minutes would suffice.

Everything on earth needs time. Think of the hours per day for so many
years that a child spends at school gathering the rudiments of knowledge
that he may cope with this life. How much longer then should we spend
in learning from God for life everlasting?

O Christian, give the holy, gracious God all the time you can until His
light and life and love fill your whole life and you abide in Christ and His
love through His Word and through prayer.

---

*Heavenly Father, let me begin with just a quarter of an hour each day
to seek Thy face, to wait upon Thee, to let Thy light shine in my heart,
and to be filled with Thy Spirit. Amen.*

The Will

"All Judah rejoiced, for they had sought Him with their whole desire; and He was found of them" (2 Chron. 15:15).

The will is the royal faculty of the soul; it rules over the whole man. Many people become the slaves of sin because they do not decide with a firm will to listen to the voice of conscience. Many Christians make no advance in the prayer-life because they have not the courage to say with a strong purpose of will: "By God's help I will do all that God's Word and my own conscience bid me do. I will make time for prayer and quiet fellowship with Him."

In the practice of prayer it is quite indispensable to say in regard to wandering thoughts, or the brevity and haste of our prayers, or their formality and superficiality, *"I will not* give way to these things, *I will* call upon God with all my heart and strength."

This is not an easy task. One must face the position calmly and decide to go on praying without any real zeal or earnestness or else look to God to help them by His Holy Spirit to say: "In the few minutes that I spend with God and His Word I am determined to give the time *with an undivided heart.*" Keep on, even though you find it difficult. You will find it easier each time you say to God: "Lord, I can be satisfied with nothing less; *I will seek Thee with my whole heart.*"

All Judah sought the Lord with their whole desire (or will), and He was found of them. God is longing to bless you but is unable to do so as long as you are not willing to give yourself unreservedly and with all the strength of your will to let Him work out His will in you.

Heavenly Father: "Father, I will seek Thee with all my heart and will." Amen.

Christ's Love to Us

*"A new commandment I give unto you, That ye love
one another, even as I have loved you" (John 13:34).*

*"Even as the Father hath loved Me, I also have
loved you; abide ye in My love" (John 15:9).*

The Lord gave His disciples a perfectly new commandment, that *they
should love one another, as He had loved them.* To this end He wanted
them to know what the love was wherewith He had loved them. Nothing
less than *the love wherewith the Father had loved Him.* It is the everlasting, unchangeable, divine love wherewith the Father loved the Son, wherewith the Son loved us, and *wherewith we should love one another.*

The thought is so vast and so heavenly that it needs time to grasp it.
Pray about it and let God's Spirit make it a blessed reality: the love of God
to Christ, the love of Christ to me, my love to the brethren is one and the
same almighty, everlasting love.

God sent His Son to earth to manifest this love. The same love that God
had to His Son, He had in His heart for all mankind. This same love Jesus
exercised toward His disciples. This love was given them when the Holy
Spirit was poured out on the Day of Pentecost, that they might love one
another and more—even love those who were the enemies of Christ.

It is all one and the same love. Not merely a feeling or a blessed experience, but a living divine power, flowing from the Father to the Son and
working in the hearts of the disciples through the Son and so streaming
forth to the whole world.

We are ever ready to say: "We cannot love others as Christ has loved
us." It is not impossible. The Holy Spirit, as the power of this holy love,
sheds it abroad in our hearts. This is God's own Word. He who meditates
on it *until he believes it* will have courage to bring his petitions to the
Throne of Grace and to receive the love which passes all understanding.

---

*Heavenly Father, may I daily grasp this blessed reality: the love of God
to Christ, the love of Christ to me, my love to the brethren is one and
the same almighty, everlasting love. Amen.*

Our Love to Christ

"If ye love Me, ye will keep My commandments" (John 14:15).

In the Gospel of St. John, our Lord Jesus Christ speaks six times of our love to Him consisting in the doing of His will.

"If ye love Me, *ye will keep My commandments*" (14:15). "He that hath My commandments *and keepeth them*, he it is that loveth Me" (14:21). "If a man love Me, *he will keep My word*" (14:23). "*If ye keep My commandments*, ye shall abide in My love" (15:10). "If ye abide in Me, *and My words abide in you*" (15:7). "Ye are My friends *if ye do the things I command you*" (15:14).

It is not enough to read these words once. Take your Bible and go over them carefully and notice how in each verse there is a wonderful promise. Then you will realize the blessedness of the life of the one who loves Christ, keeps His commandments, and abides in His love.

Notice the striking promise in verse twenty-three of this chapter. "If a man love Me, he will keep My word: and My Father will love him, *and we will come unto him, and make our abode with him.*" The Father and the Son dwell in the hearts of those who love Jesus and keep His commandments. Such can say with St. Paul, "Christ lives in me," and will love the brethren and all around them with the love wherewith God loved His Son.

St. Paul says to all Christians: "Know ye not as to your own selves, *that Jesus Christ is in you?*" (2 Cor. 13:5). Many Christians do not realize this or the love Christ has for them. If we are strengthened through the Holy Spirit, Christ will dwell in our hearts by faith, and *we shall be rooted and grounded in love*. Then it will be quite natural for the love of God to work within in divine power, and we shall learn to love Him even as He loved us in the love of the Father.

Dear Christian, as Christ loved you and you abide in His love, you will be enabled to keep His commandments. The measure of His sacrifice for you will be the measure of your willing surrender to Him in all things.

Blessed Father, I long to do Thy will, to keep Thy commandments. I thank Thee that the power to love and obey comes from Thy Son living in my heart through the power of Thy Holy Spirit. Amen.

Our Love to the Brethren

"This is My commandment, that ye love one another,
even as I have loved you" (John 15:12).

So many people deem it quite impossible to keep this command, that they do not even attempt to keep it. But one who reads prayerfully and carefully the last two chapters of this book will see that the Lord has indeed made provision for the fulfillment of this command. The reader will learn that the great love wherewith the Father loved the Son is the love with which Christ loves us. Even as the love of the Father in the Son was His whole life and worked with a divine power in Him, so the relationship between the Lord Jesus and ourselves is the same. As He loves us, His love comes to abide in us because He Himself dwells within us.

Even the world agrees that if a man says, "I love God," and hates his brother, he is a liar; for he that loveth not his brother whom he hath seen, how can he love God whom he hath not seen? Hatred toward a brother is a sign that a man does not love God. Love toward a brother is an indication that he loves God.

Let us try to understand what the Lord really means by this command. He came to earth to make known God's love to us. He was returning to the Father. He had revealed the love of God the Father and would leave this love on earth in charge of His disciples. He said to them: "Love one another, as I have loved you. Remember that through the Holy Spirit, whom I will send, I am dwelling within you and will enable you to love the brethren with My own love. I dwell in each one of My disciples. As you love others in the power of My love, they will also grow strong to love. And this will be a powerful sign that My love is in you, when the world is convinced, that as in Me, so in you, the Father has shed abroad His love."

Child of God, bow at the feet of your blessed Lord and worship and adore Him for His wonderful grace, and He will take up His abode in your heart in the love of the Father and give you the love wherewith to love your brethren and so prove to the world that God is truly in our midst.

Heavenly Father, I bow at Thy feet, and I thank Thee for giving Thy Son to live in my heart through the power of Thy Holy Spirit so that I may love others and thus prove to the world that Thou art with me. Amen.

Love Demands All

"Hereby know we love, because He laid down His life for us; and we ought to lay down our lives for the brethren" (1 John 3:16).

It was not only on the Cross that Christ gave His life for us; that was the consummation of a life that from the beginning was surrendered to the service and healing of man. The debt that rests upon each one of us as a consequence is not discharged if we are called upon suddenly to lay down our life. The example of Christ bids us give our whole life in service to our brethren.

Try to grasp this truth. The strength of God's love in Christ enabled Him to give up His life wholly for us. The same strength is available for us, and as we yield ourselves wholly to it, we shall be able to make the welfare of souls the central object of our lives. One who gives himself wholly into the keeping of God's love will feel its power and all-sufficiency. This is the blessedness of the Christian life—*giving our lives wholly for others even as Christ did.*

One sometimes finds, even among unlearned people, that where the fire of love to Christ burns there is an unquenchable desire to pray and work for others. I read lately a story of a young girl only ten years of age, whose heart had been so touched by the love of Christ that she began at once to lead others to Him. A few years later, when she went to a boarding-school, it was her daily prayer and endeavor to bring others to know and love her Savior. This continued until her nineteenth year, when she became a regular worker among soldiers, giving all her time and energy to the work. The Lord gave her such a spirit of prayer and such love to souls that for many years she continued that work, a living example to all of how God could enable one to spend her life in the service of others and especially in winning them for Christ.

Dear reader, take this thought into your heart. Christ gave His life for you and you are a debtor who owes his life to the brethren. *The love of Christ constrains you and will supply all the power and strength needed.*

Heavenly Father, as Thy Holy Spirit lives in me, may I always and only look to Thee and Thy Son Jesus Christ for the power and strength to make the welfare of souls the central object of my life. Amen.

Topic Index

379

380

Scripture Index

384